Rendezvous:
A Cautionary Tale

"It is," Peter Coleman said, "really goddamned dark in here." He ran his fingers down the lapels of his suit out of nervous habit, checking to see that he was still immaculately groomed, even in pitch blackness. "I don't see why we have to wait in the dark."

He felt a soft finger on his lips in response. "Hush," came the voice of his associate from somewhere to his left. "You know exactly why we are here. If we do not stand in the dark, then we are visible to your little friend Kevin. If we are visible to your little friend Kevin, then Kevin may remember our faces and have that memory dragged out of him by any one of our rivals. I, for one, would prefer to minimize my risks."

Coleman rolled his eyes, he hoped invisibly. "As you say, Donata. I humbly beg your pardon, and I shall wait in silence until *our* little friend arrives." With that, Peter shut his eyes and began mentally fiddling with projections on a few IPOs that were scheduled for the next month and a half. He whistled tunelessly as he did so, feeling, rather than seeing, Donata bristle beside him.

"Must you do that?" she said, an edge of real irritation coloring her voice. Her words echoed hollowly in the space of the tunnel they stood in. "He'll hear you and get spooked, and then all this will be for naught."

Peter smiled and sat down on a projecting ledge. The concrete was surprisingly smooth and cool to the touch, and he found himself hoping that there wouldn't be too much dust on his suit when he got out of here. "Are you sure it isn't that I'm offending your delicate sensibilities? I'm sure that you've heard much finer whistling in Elysium."

Donata took a step to the left, gritting her teeth almost audibly. "Whatever you say, Peter. Don't make this more difficult than it has to be. We can go back to hating each other properly once all of this is finished, but in the meantime, I'll do my best to make this endurable if you will. Do we have an arrangement?"

"We have," Peter said, "several. But you are, as always, right." He checked his watch, which glowed a faint green. "Damn. The boy is late."

"His kind always is," said Donata, and sat in the darkness beside him. He glanced her way once, barely seeing her silhouette through the gloom, but made no move to acknowledge her presence.

Side by side, the two predators sat and waited. It was one of the things that they'd gotten very good at over the years.

✛   ✛   ✛   ✛

Kevin skulked up the storm drain tunnel, his boots making only the slightest of splashes as he trudged through the shallow stream that ran through the conduit. Every 15 steps or so, he paused to look behind him and make sure that he wasn't being followed, while he let the echoes of his footsteps fade away. He kept to the water because he'd been told that it made you harder to track, and he definitely didn't want anyone tracking him tonight.

("He's coming," Donata said, a quarter mile ahead. "I can hear him." Coleman frowned and said that he heard nothing. "That," she responded, "is your problem. To me he's clear as day. Now be quiet. He'll be here shortly.")

A full 20 minutes later, Kevin finally took the last cautious steps to the meet point. To outside eyes, the place was just another dank section of storm drain, but the instructions he'd received told Kevin that he would meet his contacts here. He looked around. The place was pitch black, and there was no sign of any other presence, human or otherwise. He stood for a minute, then muttered a curse under his breath and turned to go.

"That's far enough, Kevin," came a voice from the darkness. "Stop right there."

"What if I don't want to?" he blustered, making a big show of splashing back a few steps in the direction he'd come from.

"You really don't want to test me, Kevin," the voice said wearily. "I'm right behind you, and if you take another step, I'll rip your throat out and go looking for another runner. Kristof recommended you to me because he said you were smart. Be smart now, and stop."

Beside Coleman, Donata could barely swallow her laughter. Kristof the Nosferatu had recommended Kevin, yes — but because he was *expendable*. Intelligence was never part of the equation.

"Okay," Kevin said. "I'm stopping, but only because I want to." He turned around slowly. "So where are you? Show yourself. What's your name? Why the hell did we have to do this here?"

"Because," Donata said, "we know how important your friends are to you, Kevin. We know how they feel about us, too, and we know that if they found out you were talking to us, they'd turn on you in a minute. They'd abandon you, leave you to the streets on your own, maybe even try to hurt you." Her voice was full of loving mock concern. "We couldn't let that

happen to our favorite runner, now, could we? All this," and she paused breathily, "is for your protection."

Kevin snarled. "And you get nothing out of it? Bullshit. You don't want your high-and-mighty friends to know that you've been talking to someone like me, do you? Hell, you don't even want me to know who you are, because you're afraid I'll shoot my mouth off." There was silence for a moment, then he continued. "Well, we'll play it your way for now, but don't make the mistake of thinking I'm some kind of common idiot."

"Of course not," Coleman said soothingly. *You're a* unique *kind of idiot*, he thought instead.

"Yeah. Sure. Whatever. So, where's the package?"

"Taped to the underside of the manhole cover in the next chamber, and in a waterproof case. Directions on where to deliver it are attached. Deliver it to the drop point tomorrow at midnight, and your payment will be waiting for you at the address indicated on the papers inside." Truth be known, there was no such address at all. Coleman's plan was for Kevin to open the package — which contained important papers relating to the prince of the city's finances — at the drop point, then close it back without bothering to seal it properly. Coleman would, no doubt, get some blame for having chosen an unreliable courier, but the brunt of the prince's wrath would come down on Kevin and those like him. The prince was irrational that way, it seemed. And an irrational prince who was angry made mistakes — mistakes that meant that there might be opportunities for ambitious Kindred to move up in the city's hierarchy.

Peter Coleman was very, very ambitious. As for Donata del Este, she was not quite so driven, but she had a certain vested interest in seeing to it that Peter's star continued to rise higher than those of her rivals.

Kevin was simply belligerent. "And the money?"

Donata sighed. "Already waiting for you. Now, are you going to do it?"

"Yeah, I'll do it." He took a few steps toward the exit, smiling to himself, "but on one condition."

"What is that?" Peter said, his voice low and guarded. Unbidden, he got off the ledge and into a fighting stance.

"This!" Kevin took a camera out of his pocket, pointed it at the voices he'd heard and pressed the button.

Donata had heard the whine of the camera's flash charging up, but she had had no idea what it was. As a result, she was completely unprepared for the flood of white light. As she had been straining her vision to its utmost already, aided by her supernaturally acute perceptions, the tide of brilliance hit her like a sledgehammer. She screamed, staggered and fell.

Cursing, Coleman leapt down onto Kevin, who stood with his eyes half-shaded. The anarch saw him coming and tried to run, but he could only turn and take a single step before the Ventrue was on him. With a snarl, Coleman grabbed the back of Kevin's jacket and bodily slammed him into the concrete of the storm drain wall. There was a sharp crack, as several of Kevin's teeth shattered on impact. Coleman then pulled the dazed vampire back to glare at him.

"All right, little anarch, you've had your fun. What the hell was that about?" Behind him, Donata groped blindly in the water, weeping bloody tears of pain.

"It wasn't nothing, man! I just wanted a look at your faces! I wanted to know who I was dealing with!" Kevin was terrified, and he babbled the words out around the shards of his broken teeth.

"Not good enough," Coleman said, slamming Kevin's face into the wall again. "Who else are you working for? Who wanted to know about this meeting?" He spared a glance back at Donata, then turned his attention to Kevin again. "Tell me, and I may let you walk out of here. Don't, and all that's going to be left of you will be a bloodstain on this wall."

"No one, man! I swear, it was no one!"

"Wrong answer," Peter said grimly. He bashed Kevin into the concrete again. The impact would have pulped the skull of a human being, but both Peter and Kevin were a long way past human. "Now, are you ready to talk?"

"I'll talk, I'll talk," Kevin whimpered. "Just don't hurt me anymore."

"A much wiser choice." Coleman dropped the anarch. "So who was it?"

"Warburton. It was Warburton. He's moving up, so he wanted to find out who was 'consorting with anarchs' and turn them over to your prince. I was supposed to get your faces and then run, while his people picked up the package." Kevin was sobbing harder than Donata was. By now, she had pulled herself to her feet unsteadily and taken a few staggering steps toward the other two vampires.

"Well, Mr. Warburton is going to have to do without your services, Kevin. I'm sorry, but when you double-crossed us, you became a liability. And liabilities are only good for one thing: write-offs." Coleman's voice was surprisingly calm and controlled. "Say good night, Kevin."

"Wait." Donata spoke up. "I have a better idea."

"Oh?" Coleman turned to her. "Do tell."

"If you kill this piece of trash, we'll only look guilty in Warburton's eyes. Instead, I say we take little Kevin here," and there was no affection in her voice now, only cold rage, "and turn him."

"Hmm." Coleman rubbed his chin thoughtfully. "An interesting point. But how are we going to accomplish that, given the resources at hand?"

"Leave that to me," Donata said. "Leave that to me."

✚   ✚   ✚   ✚

Kevin loped west along High Street, smiling. His mouth was a bloody ruin, but Donata, lovely Donata, had assured him that his teeth would grow back soon enough. It was amazing to him that he'd ever thought of betraying her. He shook his head. How foolish he had been.

Now, though, he could repay her for that breach of trust. He could prove to her that he was worthy of being loved.

First, he thought, he would go to Warburton and bear false witness against two other Kindred who'd once said unkind things about his beloved. Then, he'd go hunting for a suitable gift for his lady. He didn't think either chore would take him very long.

"So what did you do to him?" Coleman's voice was only mildly curious, as if he were asking out of mere politeness.

Donata sipped at her goblet before replying. Both she and Coleman had been dreadfully late for the evening's gathering at Elysium because of the misadventure with Kevin, but she counted it as a blessing. The delay had allowed her to make a suitably attention-worthy entrance, and that sort of notice was worth more than gold to her.

"Oh, just a trifle," she said. "I made him love me."

Coleman's eyebrow shot up. "You can do that?"

She nodded, then leaned over and kissed him. Her mouth was cold, but so was his. He could taste blood on her lips; it was sweeter than he expected. "I can indeed. He's mine now. Think about that the next time you want to spend the evening in a sewer with someone." She smiled without mirth, and walked away.

Coleman stared after her, rubbing his mouth absently with the back of his hand. "I'll bear that in mind," he said softly. "Don't worry, I don't think I'll ever forget."

CREDITS

Written by: Jason Carl, Jess Heinig, Peter Woodworth

Additional writing by: Richard E. Dansky

Development by: Cynthia Summers

Editing by: Carl Bowen

Previously published material has appeared in: Vampire The Masquerade Revised, Laws of the Night

Art direction by: Rich Thomas

Art by: Pauline Benney, Louis Cahill

Front and back cover design: Pauline Benney

Layout and typesetting by: Pauline Benney

Mind's Eye Theatre Design: Mark Rein•Hagen, Ian Lemke and Mike Tinney

World of Darkness Created by: Mark Rein•Hagen

Playtesters: Kathryn Abromovich, Chris Arnold, David Blackwell, Michael Blank, Brian Clark, Shaun Crawford, Michael Dent, Julian Dillard, Jim Fillmore, David Flannery, Brian Gates, Misty Gates, Alyson Gaul, Jody Gerst Crystal Greenlee, Jason Hale, Brock Hall, James M. Hendricks, Geoff Hinkle, Matthew Kauffman, Tim Leber, Chris Loeffler, Tori Mauslein, Jeremiah McCoy, Glenys Ngaire McGhee, Sarah McIlvaine, Mike Metcalf, Laura Middleton, Joshua Patterson, Sarah Riggs, John Sargent, Matthew Skipper, Marc Spencer, Bill Terry, Golden Sky Tullis, Jim Vasquez, Peter Woodworth, W. Andrew Woodworth

SPECIAL THANKS TO:

Greg "Greener Pastures" Fountain, for finding them while he could.

Jess "Wax the Diablerist" Heinig, for putting the twinks to bed.

Earle and Kenndra "Tender Friends" Durboraw, for burdens lightened.

Sarah "Heavenward Path" Halter, to encourage her dreams.

Grande Masquerade II, for beginning the downward spiral.

…and you, the fans — it's all for you.

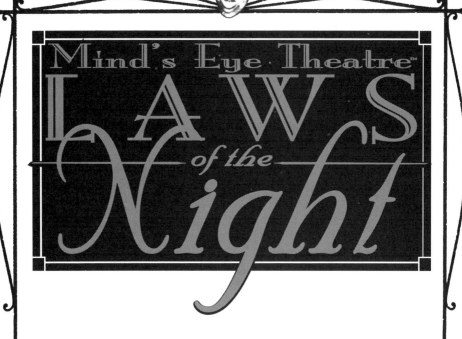

CONTENTS

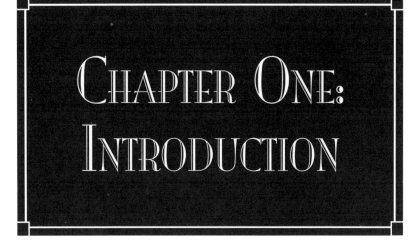

CHAPTER ONE: INTRODUCTION

STORIES AROUND THE FIRE

Once upon a time, long before television or computers or even books, people sat around the fire and told stories for entertainment. Whether it was a ballad of a hero's latest exploits or a cautionary tale about dealing with the hidden creatures of the world, storytellers were a valued part of the community as teachers and entertainers. And tale-telling was hardly a passive art — the storyteller relied on his audience for reaction to his tale as he spoke. How else would he know if they were enjoying the story, or if they were getting bored?

Time marched on, and technological developments began to change, if not interfere with, the storyteller's art. Books (and the development of greater literacy among people) meant that someone could simply read a story whenever he liked, instead of hunting down a storyteller to tell it. Radio and television remade the storyteller into an impassive creature that did not encourage audience participation. Stories were still told, and in great quantity, but they were largely sterile, unliving things.

Now we come to the 1970s, and the era of roleplaying. A group of players sits around a table, listening to their leader describe scenes of dank dungeons and dark cities, and they choose which path to take next. At one of these sessions, someone gets the idea to start standing up, moving and thinking as her character might. Over time, more players do the same, creating what will become known as live-action roleplaying (or LARP). In fact, this "new" entertainment is a return to the oldest — the leader was the storyteller, taking his listeners on a new journey, and the listeners were responding in kind, taking on the roles of the characters in the story, telling this new tale to the storyteller, the other player-listeners and to themselves.

WHAT IS Mind's Eye Theatre?

This game is probably unlike anything you have played before. In many ways, it's not really a game, because it doesn't have a lot of the trappings of games — such as cards, dice or a playing board. It's also far more concerned with the stories to be told along the way than "winning." It's far more like the make-believe of childhood than what most people typically think of when they imagine "games." This book contains all the information you'll need to start playing and telling your own stories. You create the action, you choose the path to follow, you decide what risks to accept. We call this style of game **Mind's Eye Theatre.**

Playing **Mind's Eye Theatre** is like being in a movie. You and your friends are the characters, but there is no script. There may be a framework or setting that determines the parameters of the world around you, but you and the others around you are creating the story as you play. The "director" of this movie is the Storyteller, assisted by Narrators. The Storyteller creates the stage and the minor characters that the players interact with to tell this story.

Most scenes in **Mind's Eye Theatre** are played out in real-time — an hour in the make-believe world is 60 minutes long, and it takes up 60 minutes in the real world — and always in character. Players always remain in character during the game unless there is a rules dispute.

CHARACTERS

When you play **Masquerade** (the game for which this book was developed), you take on another persona, most likely a vampire. Your character can be almost anything — from any walk of life, age, creed, race or sex. The only limit is your imagination. When you create this character, you decide what she says or does. You decide where she goes and what choices she makes. During the game, you speak as your character, unless you're resolving a rules dispute or talking to the Storyteller. Because most of what a **Mind's Eye Theatre** player perceives around him depends on the other players, all players must be vivid and expressive.

While the characters may direct the plot through their actions, the plot reacts in ways that direct the characters. For example, a character decides she wants to create a coffeehouse with space for people to perform, and she invites another vampire to sing for an evening — here, the characters are directing the plot through their actions. However, the plot reacts to this direction — the Storyteller tells the characters that the performance has aroused some suspicious attention. It seems that the performing character reminds someone of another famous human singer, who also just happened to die at the same time the character became a vampire. Thus is a story built in **Mind's Eye Theatre.**

Creating a character for **Masquerade** is easy, and it takes just a few minutes. Only a few things become necessary to define the basic capabilities of a character, and when they're done, you can start playing. There's another phase to creating a character, though. A character is, by and large, like a person, and people aren't just flat cardboard cutouts with a few numbers to represent what they can do. People have pasts, likes and dislikes, goals and dreams — all the intangible things that make a person into what other people see when he walks into a room or talks to them. It's not much different from all the care that an actor or author takes when creating a character. So as you're

---

VAMPIRE: THE MASQUERADE AND LAWS OF THE NIGHT

This book is based on the tabletop creation **Vampire: The Masquerade**. While it is not necessary to own or know **Vampire** to play this game, some players may find it helpful for more setting material. There are a number of **Vampire**-related books with material that can be adapted for live-action play.

This edition of **Laws of the Night** has been created to update the rules for **Vampire**'s live-action adaptation, **Masquerade**. Since the creation of the original rules, continuous play has seen a few bugs crop up, and this book is designed to correct some of the those problems. Those with older editions of **Laws of the Night** may find some significant differences between the two, and it is advised that a Storyteller rule which edition of **Laws of the Night** is canon for the game for the sake of clarity and consistency.

creating your character, think a little about where she comes from, what she wants out of her existence, what she'll do to get it, what she loves and hates. Does your character love thunderstorms and watch them from the window, or have they frightened her ever since she was a small child? Does your character want to build a business to replace one that was lost several years ago, and he'll bargain with the Devil himself to get it? While certain personality quirks and details will emerge as you play, it's a good idea to have the basics in place for the first time you walk into a room and meet the other characters.

Characters are the heart and soul of the story. Without them, all the efforts of the Storyteller would be for nothing, and there would be no stories to tell.

THE STORYTELLER

The Storyteller is the one who creates the world that the players move through. She creates a skeletal framework of setting and plot, then turns the characters loose to put flesh on its bones. More than that, she acts as an impartial judge when the rules are questioned, describes scenes that can't be staged and even plays the parts of antagonists or other people with whom the characters interact. The Storyteller is usually assisted by Narrators, who play their own characters but are ready to answer rules questions when necessary.

Storytelling is a demanding (and occasionally exhausting) task. A Storyteller must oversee the events to be certain that people have a good time, that the rules are being followed and that the story is running smoothly. Sometimes she must create plot elements on the spur of the moment or adjudicate between several quarreling players. In spite of all this responsibility, there is something immensely satisfying about watching the players create something remarkable with the plot elements given them. It really makes the headache all worthwhile.

More on the Storyteller's role can be found in Chapter Six.

ELEGANTLY SIMPLE

This game was designed to be easy to play and easier to start. Character creation takes only a few minutes. The basic rules are simple, and they cover most of the encounters a new player will enter. Even very new players who have never played **Masquerade** or LARP before will find that this game takes little effort to pick up.

HOW TO USE THIS BOOK

This book gives you all the basic rules that you'll need to start playing or Storytelling **Masquerade**.

Chapter One: Introduction — The introduction to both **Mind's Eye Theatre** and the World of Darkness.

Chapter Two: The Clans — A complete overview of the vampire clans and bloodlines available for play in the World of Darkness.

Chapter Three: Character Creation — Everything that you'll need to create a character to start playing.

Chapter Four: Disciplines — Descriptions of the mysterious powers granted on the Embrace.

Chapter Five: Rules, Systems and Drama — The chapter starts with the basic rules you'll need for play, followed with systems for combat, derangements, health, healing and more vampiric issues, such as the blood bond.

Chapter Six: Storytelling — This chapter speaks to Storytellers and Narrators, both old and new, containing all the ins and outs of how to craft stories and deal with players.

Chapter Seven: Allies and Antagonists — Vampires aren't the only creatures of the night. This chapter provides a basic overview of some of the other denizens of the World of Darkness, as well as ways to incorporate them into stories.

THE RULES THOU SHALT NEVER BREAK

These are the most important and immutable rules of **MET**, the ones that keep your game and your players safe from folks who either don't care that you're playing a game, or who take the game way too seriously. Always adhering to these rules will also keep your game amenable to law enforcement and other non-player folks.

NO TOUCHING. NO STUNTS.

That means none whatsoever. It's far too easy for things to get out hand in the heat of the moment. Save the stunts for your imagination. If you can imagine you're a centuries-old vampire, then you can sure imagine you're swinging on a chandelier or leaping across rooftops.

NO WEAPONS

No matter how careful you are. Whether it's to prevent some fool from skewering himself on your new dagger, or to make sure the police don't think you're a threat, weapons of any sort are forbidden. Even fake or toy weapons, trained attack gerbils or laser pens are not allowed. Use item cards instead.

NO DRUGS OR DRINKING

Well, duh. Drinking and drugs do not inspire peak performance, and players who are so impaired are a threat to other players and the game. It's one thing to *play* a character who is drunk or stoned, but another thing entirely to actually come to a game under the influence. At best it's tasteless; at worst it's illegal. Don't do it.

IT'S ONLY A GAME

If a character dies, if a plot falls apart, if a rival gets the upper hand, it's just a game. You and the rest of the players are doing this for fun. Taking things too seriously, or taking character issues into real life, will only spoil everyone's enjoyment, including yours. Remember, playing a game should be fun — if you're not having fun, it's time for a reassessment.

Remember to leave the game behind when the session's over. "Soft" roleplaying (conversing in character without challenges) can be fun, and there's nothing wrong with talking about the game afterward at the local diner. On the other hand, demanding weekly clan meetings or trying to rouse your primogen to talk business at three in the morning signifies the need for a change in perspective.

BE MINDFUL OF OTHERS

Not everyone around you is playing the game, and it's in extremely poor taste to try to feed off passers-by. You want to ensure that your game and your players are welcomed. Frightening people and getting the local law enforcement called on you is not the way to do it. This is especially true if you're playing in a public area, such as a park. It can be a very good idea to alert local merchants and police before you play so they're prepared. If you get curiosity-seekers, try to have some business cards on hand and offer to speak with them when you have more time.

DO WHAT WORKS FOR YOU

We at White Wolf often call this proviso "the golden rule." Your game may have special circumstances that require a few extra bells and whistles to the rules, or your troupe may find a way to handle something that works better for you. So long as people are having fun, go ahead and run with it — it's your game.

Likewise, if you see something that you want in your game that doesn't appear with an **MET** system, then sit down and cobble up something that will work for you. If **MET** is all about telling stories, then here's the part where the Storyteller improvises.

HAVE FUN

Not "Win." Not "Go out and conquer everyone else." Just have fun, because in **MET**, it's not about how the game ends, but what happens along the way.

THE WORLD OF DARKNESS

On the surface, the World of Darkness is not too much different from our own. People are born, grow up, work and die every day. Plants grow, as do skyscrapers. The same newspapers are sold on the street corner, and television is the same vast wasteland. Below the surface, however, is a much darker element, one that is fed by the violence and despair which the monsters need to fuel themselves. It is far less simple than throwing a coat of black paint over the veneer of our world. The monsters in the World of Darkness are far too real.

Gothic-Punk is the term used to describe the attitude of the World of Darkness. The "Gothic" aspect is that of the sinister, looming shadow that permeates life. Buildings here, encrusted with gargoyles, dwarf all below them. Despair is a common theme, and any banner that offers hope or power can be certain of many followers. The divisions between haves and have-nots are nearly insurmountable gulfs. The world is a place of mystery — the sort that is uncovered in old books and which is best left alone for safety's sake.

On the other side of the coin is "Punk" — what many citizens of the World of Darkness have done in order to give their lives meaning. They throw themselves against the walls of power in rebellion, often until they forget what they first despised. Crime is more prevalent and more violent. Speech is coarser, fashions are bolder, art seeks only to shock, and technology ensures that everyone gets it at the click of a button.

This is the world that the Cainites call home.

THE KINDRED

Vampires have been fixtures in myth and legend since time immemorial. Sometimes they've been monstrous creatures that swooped out of the darkness to ravish innocent virgins and steal babies from their cradles. Other times they've been predators of incredible beauty and sensuality, enchanting men and women alike, offering seductive death in return for a little nip. The vampires of the World of Darkness are all these things and more. There is enough about them that is similar to the vampires of myth and cinema, but more than enough that is different to cause some fatal errors for would-be hunters. The Kindred, as many call themselves, are sentient, with some faint similarities to their mortal selves, but as different from mortals and myth as night from day.

Some myths and suppositions about the undead (as well as the facts behind them) include:

• **Vampires are immortal.** While it is possible to kill a vampire, he will not age or die of natural causes. He does not need water, food or air. For all intents and purposes, he is a corpse.

• **Vampires require the blood of the living to survive.** While vampires are corpses, they still require nourishment to sustain themselves, and their preferred taste is for blood. Not only does it preserve their bodies, blood allows vampires to perform amazing supernatural feats of healing, strength or speed. A vampire need not kill her prey; some take only a little blood, then hide the evidence of their feeding. A vampire may close any wounds she makes with her fangs by simply licking the wounds. By and large, most vampires seek human blood, although some choose to drink animal blood. Some whisper fearfully that elder vampires must hunt their younger brethren for feeding, unable to gain sustenance from human blood any longer.

• **Anyone who dies from a vampire's bite will become a vampire.** The world would be overrun with vampires if this statement were true. Those bitten and drained by vampires in the course of feeding simply die. It takes a very special process, known as the Embrace, to create a vampire.

• **Vampires are burned by sunlight.** True. Vampires must avoid sunlight or risk death. Vampires are nocturnal creatures, and most find it difficult to stay awake during the day, even out of the sunlight.

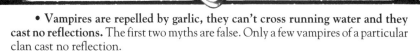

- **Vampires are repelled by garlic, they can't cross running water and they cast no reflections.** The first two myths are false. Only a few vampires of a particular clan cast no reflection.

- **A cross or other holy symbol can burn or repel a vampire.** Generally untrue. The symbol itself is of little power. It is the faith of the person who wields the symbol that the vampire must fear.

- **Vampires will die from a stake through the heart.** While they cannot die from such wounds, vampires *are* immobilized by wooden stakes, arrows, crossbow bolts and the like that pierce the heart, until the item is removed.

THE EMBRACE

The Embrace is the process by which a new vampire is sired, or created. It is almost never given lightly; after all, one more predator means more competition for resources. Some vampires Embrace to find companionship, others to have conspirators or dupes for schemes, others to "give back" something to Kindred society. Potential childer may be watched for weeks, months, even years, without ever realizing that they are being evaluated for immortality.

To Embrace a new vampire, the sire drains her chosen victim of blood, similar to a normal feeding. However, when the victim has been drained to the point of death, the sire places a small amount of her own vampiric blood in the victim's mouth. Even a drop or two can finish the process. The Embrace can even be given to a dead mortal, provided the body is still warm.

During the Embrace, the body reworks itself, sloughing off the imperfections present in every mortal form and becoming more beautiful, albeit with the grace of a predatory animal. The new childe reawakens, but his heart does not beat nor does his blood circulate. He is now one of the living dead. He wakes suffering a ravenous Hunger, his first acquaintance with the monster (or the Beast) that has also been awakened in him.

Over the next few weeks, the young vampire, usually under the tutelage of his sire, undergoes a series of subtle (and not-so-subtle) transformations. He learns to use the powers granted by his blood, such as speed or how to understand animals. He learns of the raging Hunger inside him and how to rein it in. He learns to hunt, often a difficult proposition, as need begins to force him to prey on his former species. He also learns that the Embrace truly makes vampires the living dead. Subtle, higher emotions are the province of mortals, and he may find that he can no longer bring to mind true pleasure or joy or love, except in memory. It is this last that many young Kindred cannot endure during their first weeks. Some choose to greet the morning sun, rather than look ahead to years of cold comfort.

For those vampires who survive their first nights, a much larger world awaits them.

THE CAMARILLA

The Camarilla dates back to the years of the Inquisition, as humanity turned its collective eye on vampires. The principle of the Masquerade took root and held sway, growing into the creation of today — a massive, global conspiracy of sorts, meant to deceive humanity about the monsters in its midst, and thus avert another purging. In these times of nuclear devices, powerful governments and enormous populations, the Masquerade has become both guiding principle and ironclad policy. Today, the Camarilla concerns itself with the Masquerade, maintaining harmonious relations between Kindred and kine, and thwarting the Sabbat.

The Camarilla claims all vampires to be under its aegis and proclaims itself the greatest sect of Kindred across the globe. Indeed, it claims that all Cainites are already under its banner, regardless of those vampires' wishes. In spite of the claims, only six clans hold full membership in the sect: Brujah, Malkavian, Nosferatu,

Toreador, Tremere and Ventrue. Vampires from the other clans may join, but they are often suspect, and without a voice in the Inner Circle, they are largely powerless.

The Inner Circle, considered the true hub of the sect, is said to consist of one representative for each clan, supposedly the very eldest of each. These elders plan out the business and direction of the Camarilla, or as much as a race of predators can be directed. It is also their business to select the justicars, those Kindred who become the walking will of the Inner Circle.

The six mighty vampires called justicars are appointed by the Inner Circle to be its eyes, ears and occasionally fists. It is they who are judge, jury and executioner of the entire sect, save the Inner Circle. They alone may adjudicate matters of the Traditions. They alone decide the punishment for those who have violated the Traditions on a wide scale, and none are above them in this respect. Those being judged by the justicars may not expect mercy. The power wielded by the justicars is immense and often resented by those who have been victims of it, but there is little that can be done about it beyond discontented grumbling. Every justicar is, without exception, several centuries old and extremely powerful.

Below the justicars are the archons, who are singly chosen by a justicar to act in her name as suits her purposes. Most archons are "young" elders and older ancillae, and such a prestigious appointment can make or break them in the halls of power. An archon typically serves for as long as a justicar wishes to retain her, or for the length of the justicar's tenure.

In the Camarilla, the conclave is the greatest political event that every Kindred can be privy to. Any Camarilla or friendly independent vampire who hears the call to

THE TRADITIONS

The Traditions are considered the inviolate rules of Kindred existence, and they have been the basis of all vampiric laws since the time of Caine. Most vampires follow them out of habit, whether because they are common sense suggestions or necessary for survival.

THE FIRST TRADITION: THE MASQUERADE

Thou shalt not reveal thy true nature to those not of the Blood. Doing so shall renounce thy claims of Blood.

THE SECOND TRADITION: THE DOMAIN

Thy domain is thy concern. All others owe thee respect while in it. None may challenge thy word in thy domain.

THE THIRD TRADITION: THE PROGENY

Thou shalt sire another one with permission of thine elder. If thou createst another without thine elder's leave, both thou and thy progeny shall be slain.

THE FOURTH TRADITION: THE ACCOUNTING

Those thou create are thine own childer. Until thy progeny shall be released, thou shalt command them in all things. Their sins are thine to endure.

THE FIFTH TRADITION: HOSPITALITY

Honor one another's domain. When thou comest to a foreign city, thou shalt present thyself to the one who ruleth there. Without the word of acceptance, thou art nothing.

THE SIXTH TRADITION: DESTRUCTION

Thou art forbidden to destroy another of thy kind. The right of destruction belongeth only to thine elder. Only the eldest among thee shall call the blood hunt.

conclave may come and participate, no matter her age. Justicars are the only ones with the power to call for a conclave, which is not done often owing to the immense concerns of security. Conclave business may cover any subject, from discussing matters that concern the sect as a whole to trials of very powerful Kindred (such as princes) to a docket of questions presented in an open forum. In these halls, quite literally anything can happen — a sire may introduce his newest childe to his great-grandsire, the youth may come to party and socialize and elders may meet in secret gatherings to whisper about new concerns. For the young, it is an opportunity to fraternize with clanmates from across the country and a chance to see the political machinery of the Camarilla in action, perhaps even to affect it. For the elders, it is both social opportunity and a time to take stock of the sect, not to mention a priceless opportunity to cement deals and accomplish business.

THE SABBAT

The Inquisition also spawned another movement of the vampires, but a far more brutal one. As the witch-fires raged, the elder vampires took threw their childer into harm's way in an effort to save their own hides. Finally, many of these abused childer rose up and rebelled against their sires. The resulting fight was called the Anarch Revolt. Fueled by youthful rage and strange secrets from Eastern Europe that allowed them to break the bonds of blood that held them to their sires, the anarchs wrought terror on the elders. But for all that they made the elders suffer, they also suffered losses to the Inquisition's fires.

The battle ground to a stalemate, and both sides called for parley. The Treaty of Thorns put an official end to hostilities, allowed those Kindred who wished to return to the Camarilla's fold to do so, and punished those who had been most instrumental in the fight. However, not everyone was so convinced of the Camarilla's promises, and these die-hard rebels turned their backs on the Camarilla entirely. Many of them joined to create their own force that would set itself opposite the Camarilla, called the Sabbat. Since those days, the Sabbat and the Camarilla have continued, diametrically opposed to one another, hounding and thwarting each other at any opportunity, up unto the modern nights.

The Sabbat claims two clans — the shadowy Lasombra and the monstrous Tzimisce — which make up the larger part of the membership. The rest are *antitribu* of the Camarilla and independent clans. These turncoats are like dark mirrors of their Camarilla brethren, reveling in their vampiric natures and often setting themselves fiercely opposite their former clanmates.

The Sabbat organizes itself in a parody of the Catholic Church, from which much of its ritual springs. At the lowest level is the pack, which is led by a leader and a priest. Above the pack are the bishop and archbishop, who oversee Sabbat activity in a city. Cardinals coordinate Sabbat activity in regions, while the regent in Mexico City oversees the entire sect, aided by the prisci. Paladins and templars serve as assassins and bodyguards for the regent, prisci and cardinals.

Freedom and loyalty are the guiding principles of the Sabbat. A vampire, as a superior being, is free to choose what she will, so long as she maintains her first loyalty to her sect. Above all, the sect looks ahead to the nights of Gehenna, fearing the prophecies of the Antediluvians, and it is determined to survive it by any means necessary. And the means of the Sabbat include merciless cunning, brutality and perversion — whatever it takes to both spite the enemy and thwart the future.

ALL THE REST

The other clans — including the Gangrel, Assamites, Giovanni, Followers of Set, Ravnos and the minor bloodlines (the Daughters of Cacophony, Salubri and Samedi) — do not claim membership in either sect. Those who choose to join the sects are a minor handful in comparison to their clanmates.

By and large, these clans have their own goals, which do not include playing sectarian politics. Though they follow the Traditions and may lean one way or another toward a particular sect out of convenience or personal philosophy, they follow their own paths. A few may choose to join with one sect or another, but they are exceptions to the rule, and they are distrusted by both their clanmates and sectmates.

The Gangrel were among the original founding members of the Camarilla, but they have chosen to leave the sect for their own reasons. The clan continues to lean toward many of the Camarilla's principles, but it does not include itself in politics or parley. While rumors of the circumstances behind the sudden departure abound, the Gangrel themselves do not talk of it. Many even become hostile when pressed about the matter.

Bloodlines are either Kindred who are some strange offshoot of a parent clan (which often does not acknowledge the relationship) or a former clan that has lost its founding Antediluvian (such as the Salubri). Bloodlines often walk perilous lines, as they make handy scapegoats, and many clans fear their strange abilities. Many are so rare that the average Kindred has never heard of them.

THE GENERATION SPREAD

As creatures who are (for all effects) immortal, age carries great weight among the Kindred. More importantly, a Kindred's generation can mark one as a youth or elder. Among some sects, age and generation can be one of the greatest barriers to advancement of any kind. This is a case where it can be truly said that less is more.

According to the most widely accepted history of the Kindred, vampires are descended from Caine, he of Biblical fame who murdered his brother Abel and was subsequently banished to the land of Nod by God. Caine's vampirism was said to be a curse from God in punishment for the crime. Caine sired three childer, who sired their own childer, and so on, down into the modern nights.

• **Second Generation** — Directly sired by Caine, little is known of these three. It is believed they died at the hands of their childer or during the Great Flood.

• **Third Generation** — These vampires are known as the Antediluvians, so called because they predate the Flood, and it is from them that the clans are said to descend. Every clan had an Antediluvian founder at one time, and most believe that they slumber the ages away in torpor. It is they who are the true players of the Jyhad, those who move their pawns in point and counterpoint, as they have for the past centuries. Antediluvians are considered almost divine in the scope of their abilities, and all vampires fear their touch upon the unlives of others, for none escape unscathed.

• **Fourth and Fifth Generations** — Called Methuselahs, these vampires are millennia old and almost as powerful as the Antediluvians. They involve themselves in the Jyhad behind screens of lesser Kindred, out of sight, as their potent blood makes them a favored target of diablerists. It is said that the most influential members of the Camarilla and the Sabbat's regent and prisci are Methuselahs.

• **Sixth, Seventh and Eighth Generations** — Members of these generations are typically considered elders. They are the most visible players of the Jyhad, and many princes, primogen and justicars tend to hail from their ranks. Most elders find it inconceivable that they could be manipulated in the Jyhad, although they often are, unknown to them.

• **Ninth and Tenth Generations** — The ancillae walk a dangerous line: While too old and experienced to be neonates, they are usually considered too inexperienced and weak to hold their own among the elders. Most prefer to meet the night on their own terms, and the elder generations are often pursuing other concerns to do much about it. Like mortal teenagers, ancillae are getting a taste for the power and influence that they may soon possess.

• **11th, 12th and 13th Generations** — Neonates and young ancillae hail from these generations. Most are relatively new to vampirism, and though more potent

than the mortals they hail from, they are as insects among the older generations. Inexperienced and often heady with their new power, some run rampant. Most **MET** characters will be of these generations.

• **14th and 15th Generations** — These Kindred are so far removed from Caine that their blood has become weak and the Curse does not manifest as strongly in them. Some are rumored to be able to bear the light of the sun or eat food, although they can rarely sire childer. Older Kindred fear these modern youth, as *The Book of Nod* makes claim that the thin-blooded ones will herald the coming of Gehenna.

Ghouls — Those Who Serve

Many vampires are served and assisted by mortal retainers. After all, it's quite useful to have someone who can go places a vampire cannot, such as outside (during the day) or into dangerous territory. Of these servants, there are those who have partaken of vampire blood without receiving the Embrace. These servants are known as ghouls.

Ghouls receive a number of benefits from their servitude — they often develop limited vampiric powers (such as speed, strength and accelerated healing), they cease to age as long as they have vampire blood in them and grateful masters may reward them with considerable wealth and influence. By and large, ghouls are still mortal and able to enjoy all the pleasures of mortal life. However, as in all things, there are drawbacks. Many ghouls become subject to the blood bond, developing a "devotion" to their masters that deepens into aberration or psychosis. Not every vampire is kindly to his servants, and abuses are common. And ultimately, no matter how prized, a ghoul is still a servant and disposable should the need arise.

The Sabbat scorns ghouls by and large, with two exceptions. Revenant families are comprised of hereditary ghouls who are born with vampire blood already in their veins. Many are seared with physical disability or psychoses, which suits the purposes of their Tzimisce masters. A few are occasionally rewarded with the Embrace for faithful service. The other exception are the fleshcrafted nightmares created by the Tzimisce known as *szlachta* and *vozhd*. These monstrosities are used as attack dogs, war-machines and tides of horror in the campaign against the Camarilla. Most have been so reshaped and molded by their masters that they are not even remotely human-looking.

Who Hunts the Hunters

It might be supposed from all this talk that the Kindred are powerful enough to run amuck, terrorizing humanity and using the world as their playground and abattoir. Centuries ago, certainly, vampires walked more openly among mortals, flaunting their immortality and supernatural powers, and stretching an iron hand over demenses of terrified mortals. Then the mortals finally rebelled, turning the collective might of the Church and humanity against their vampiric "lords." For over 200 years, the Inquisition held the Kindred in terror, and in these nights, no Kindred who recalls those times wishes to see them come again.

In these days, there are dedicated mortals who are aware of the vampiric threat and who hunt it with the fervor of their medieval predecessors. The most notable organization of hunters is the Inquisition, which bases itself in the Catholic Church but has opened itself to those of other denominations recently. Another, more scholarly group called the Arcanum has observed the Kindred for over a century, and it shares its knowledge occasionally with more "active" hunters. Individual hunters, men and women driven by their knowledge of the Kindred and often touched by experience, follow personal crusades against the Damned, although recent nights have seen these solitaries band together into organized cells. And of course, there will always be nosy reporters who find things that don't add up to their liking, or the detectives who insist on learning the truth behind a series of mysterious deaths.

Most Kindred youth scoff at the notion of witch-hunters being able to scratch them, still giddy with their own power. Elders, however, recollect the nights when humanity's basilisk eye fell on them, and they fear such a return in an era of automatic weapons, a mortal population in the billions and weapons that not even a Kindred could survive.

IN THESE NIGHTS...

The modern nights have seen a great deal of turmoil, and many Kindred fear that their world is about to turn over and reinvent itself, but none can say how that will happen or what will come of it.

One of the most disturbing developments has been the change in the Assamites. Somehow, the Children of Haqim have managed to release themselves from the Tremere curse that prohibited them from diablerie, and they have returned to their old cannibalistic ways. They kill without contracts or discretion to sect, and many claim that there is a marked change in the clan's general demeanor.

Cracks are appearing in the formerly monolithic Camarilla. The ranks of the anarchs swell with young vampires who see no future in a calcified society. The Gangrel's sudden departure from the fold sent ripples throughout the sect up to the Inner Circle. Even worse, the Camarilla has begun to lose ground in North America. Along the East Coast, a number of cities have either become contested territory or have fallen completely to the Sabbat. On the West Coast, incursions by the mysterious Asian vampires have caught the Camarilla in a very uncomfortable place. Some believe the Camarilla is a wounded animal in its death throes, but others know that a wounded animal is often the most dangerous.

The Sabbat has suffered its losses as well. In 1997, a mysterious incident wiped out the entire faction of Tremere *antitribu*, depriving the sect of its arcane resources. Just as mysteriously, the Malkavian *antitribu* communicated their Discipline of *Dementation* to their Camarilla brethren, and the Sabbat have lost another powerful tool. The Camarilla has not let go of its cities as easily as imagined, and many of the contested cities have become nightly struggles. The Sabbat majority likes to believe it has the upper hand, but much of its leadership fears that some of their oldest prophecies and worries are finally showing themselves.

LEXICON

A new existence calls for new words. Many young vampires often invent slang, while elders favor older forms; either usage dates a vampire's age with fair accuracy.

Ancilla — A Kindred "adolescent", usually at least a century old.

Anarch — A rebel among the Kindred, one who disdains elders and their highly structured society.

Antediluvian — A vampire of the Third Generation, so called because she predates the Great Flood.

Archon — An agent of a justicar.

Barrens, the — Areas of a city unfit for living, such as cemeteries, abandoned buildings, industrial wastelands and areas of urban blight.

Book of Nod, The — A collection of Kindred legends and history, which some Kindred equate with the Bible.

Beast, The — The personification of the vampire's predatory nature, to which is attributed animal instincts and bloodlust.

Blood — A vampire's heritage; that which makes a vampire a vampire.

Bloodline — A group of vampires that is an offshoot of its parent clan, often displaying particular characteristics or even strange powers.

Blood Bond — A mystical power over another individual (mortal, Kindred or ghoul) created by drinking a vampire's blood three times.

Boon — A favor owed between vampires.

Cainite — Any vampire; an older term.

Caitiff — A vampire without an identifiable clan or bloodline, usually of thin blood and very high generation; such vampires are scorned by others.

Camarilla, the — A sect of vampires concerned primarily with maintaining the Traditions, particularly the Masquerade.

Cathayan — One of the mysterious vampires of Asia; very little is known about these vampires, but many believe they are unrelated to Kindred.

Childe — A vampire created through the Embrace; the progeny of her sire.

Clan — A group of vampires who share common characteristics passed on by the Blood

Coterie — A group of Kindred who protect and support one another.

Damned, The — A collective name for vampires.

Diablerie — The act of murdering another vampire by drinking both her blood and her spirit; considered the worst crime among vampires.

Disciplines — The powers of a vampire, such as strength, speed or supernatural senses, which come with the Embrace.

Domain — An area of a particular vampire's influence; her "turf."

Elder — A vampire of at least three centuries or more.

Elysium — A place where vampires may meet without threat of violence to conduct business or discuss art; often held in places of art or culture.

Embrace, the — The act of turning a mortal into a vampire.

Final Death — Destruction of a vampire.

Frenzy — An emotional state where the Beast rises to the forefront, and the vampire reacts as an enraged animal would.

Generation — The number of steps that a vampire is removed from Caine.

Gehenna — The time when the Antediluvians will rise and devour their descendants before beginning a reign of darkness and terror; equated with the mortal Judgment Day.

Ghoul — A mortal who has drunk vampire blood, but has not been Embraced.

Golconda — A fabled state of being to which many vampires aspire, wherein the predatory instincts of the Beast and the higher thoughts of the Man come to balance.

Haven — A vampire's home or where he sleeps during the day.

Inconnu — A little-known sect composed entirely of elders.

Inquisition — A mortal organization based in the Catholic Church dedicated to hunting vampires and other supernatural creatures.

Justicar — A traveling judge of the Kindred who ensures that the Traditions are enforced.

Jyhad, the — The secret, centuries-long war waged among the Antediluvian Kindred, using younger vampires as pawns.

Kindred — Any Camarilla vampire; their name for themselves.

Lick — A vampire; considered vulgar by many.

Lupine — A werewolf; used by vampires.

Masquerade, the — The collective effort made after the advent of the Inquisition to hide the Kindred from mortal notice.

Methuselah — An elder vampire who no longer lives among other Kindred. Many Methuselahs are Inconnu.

Neonate — A young, newly created vampire, often recently released from her sire's care.

Numina — Special powers possessed by certain, gifted mortals.

Pack — The basic social unit of the Sabbat.

Prestation — The system of owing and granting favors; used as a bartering tool among Kindred.

Primogen — A city's ruling council of elders.

Prince — A vampire (male or female) who has established a claim of rulership over a city, and is able to support that claim.

Progeny — The collective offspring of a single vampire sire.

Regnant — A vampire who holds a blood bond over another Kindred.

Retainers — Humans who serve a vampire master

Rites — Special Sabbat rituals performed for religious or other reasons.

Sabbat, the — A sect of vampires that believes the Masquerade to be useless and that vampires should revel in their darker natures. They are violent and often bestial, using horror and cruelty as their tools.

Sect — General name for one of the major groups among the Kindred, such as the Camarilla or the Sabbat.

Sire — The parent-creator of a vampire.

Thrall — A vampire who is blood bound to another.

Vaulderie — A Sabbat ritual involving the communal sharing of blood.

Vessel — A source of blood (past or potential); usually a human.

Vinculum — The communal blood bond within a pack, forged through Vaulderie.

Vitae — Blood.

Mind's Eye Theatre **Terms**

Attribute — The raw potential of an individual, from social acumen to intellect to physical prowess.

Ability — The things that a character knows or can do.

Challenge — Any time that two opponents face off and throw Rock-Paper-Scissors to determine the outcome.

Extended Challenge — A challenge that continues until the tester loses.

Health Level — A measure of how injured a character is.

Static Test — A challenge that requires someone to risk a certain number of Traits to complete a task.

Simple Test — Any time two opponents throw Rock-Paper-Scissors without risking Traits.

Scene — A location where action is taking place.

Trait — An adjective used to describe a character's Attributes, such as *Quick*, *Gorgeous* or *Knowledgeable*.

Turn — A unit of time in **Mind's Eye Theatre** play, usually considered to be the equivalent of about three seconds.

Elysium had closed without difficulty — a few words played into the right ears, and suddenly all of the movers and shakers knew that Warburton had chosen to square off politically against Donata. Subtle whispers and hurried deals had rippled through the room, especially in light of Warburton's hurried exit midway through the evening.

Now, though, it was back to business. That meant bringing Kevin back to heel, and finding out exactly what sorts of sweet little lies he'd told to flavor the equation.

"Why can't we simply send someone else to scrape up the fool?" Peter had grumbled as Donata had directed him to drive into the bowels of the city's decaying downtown projects.

Donata had scowled in response to Peter's complaints. "The 'fool' only responds to my commands and my power. I must question him directly."

Peter simply shook his head as he passed the burned-out wreckage of abandoned businesses. He could very well tear the information from the anarch's weak mind with the strength of his commanding will, but best not to let Donata know the full extent of his capabilities. In the back of his mind, he calculated expenses and possibilities involved in restoring business to the projects, tabulating any angle for profit out of habit.

"Wait here." Donata directed Peter to pull up to the curb, and he did so smoothly, setting the alarm on his car as they exited, as if it would do some good. A small gathering of youths loitered on the corner, and Kevin chatted in hushed tones among them.

Donata slid up the street, resplendently out of place in her debonair gown, approaching the group as Peter stayed a step or two behind. A few of the gang gave out hoots or whistles, and Kevin turned slightly to regard the approaching pair. With a quick slash of his hand, Kevin silenced the gang, breaking away in a swaggering gait to meet Peter and Donata. His various head wounds had healed — probably from a little blood judiciously taken from the gangers — and he grinned at Donata.

Gently touching Kevin's arm, Donata brought the full spark of her potent charisma to the fore. "How delightful to see you again, my dear. I presume that our assignments have proceeded well?"

Kevin nodded amicably. "Of course," he murmured, shooting a jealous look at Peter. "Warburton will look like an idiot, and a treacherous one at that. His cronies just *happened* to let Kristof get his hands on the package, and everyone knows how the Nosferatu like to sell out secrets." Kevin grinned. Even if the prince forbade the Nosferatu from selling the financial information, he'd never be able to be *sure* that the Nosferatu hadn't copied and distributed it somehow — and Warburton would bear the brunt of that wrath.

"Excellent," Peter said crisply, as Donata smiled. It appeared that the alliance would bear some fruit, after all.

CHAPTER TWO: THE CLANS

Tracing their lineage through millennia back to legendary founders, the families of vampires organize themselves along their lines as clans — vampires who share common heritage, abilities and weaknesses. Each clan claims descent from one of the near-mythical Antediluvians, the grandchilder of Caine and progenitors of the vampiric race. The predilections and curses of these Antediluvians, it is said, mark each member of the clans. As a result, the members of given clans often share similar tastes and potentials.

Further removed from the clans and Antediluvians are the bloodlines. While technically any lineage of vampires may be considered a bloodline, the term (in common parlance) refers specifically to members of a peculiar sub-clan, a grouping of vampires with common powers and interests like a clan but lacking an Antediluvian founder. These bloodlines are small and rare; indeed, few neonates are even aware of their existence. However, any clan can be humbled and brought to the level of mere bloodline should its Antediluvian be devoured and his power stolen by a claimant to a new clan — a process that has happened more than once in times past.

In nights of old, clans would only Embrace new members along fairly strict lines; only those with enough aptitudes and tastes corresponding to their prospective clans' predilections would be considered as candidates for unlife. The cosmopolitan modern age has changed this exclusivity, though, as it does to all things. Now vampires are Embraced along broader lines, and knowledge of a particular vampire's clan does not necessarily bring a corresponding knowledge of the individual's strengths, weaknesses and interests. Many young neonates, Embraced for some potential outside of the clan's normal interests, rebel against the stultifying influence of the elders, taking up habits and alliances against all expectations of clan.

Occasionally, some new fledglings are abandoned by their sires, knowing little of the clans or the ways of vampiric society. These clanless, referred to as Caitiff, are often a threat to the Masquerade, and they rarely survive without instruction. Some vampires claim that such weak-blooded mules lack identifying clan characteristics and upbringing, and thus, they herald the coming End Times. These paranoid vampires hunt the clanless ones whenever they can.

Bloodrights

Carrying the strengths of the founders, each clan holds certain particular strengths and weaknesses. These characteristics pass from sire to childe; in some rare instances, these characteristics do not manifest fully, but most often, a childe holds the same potential as the sire (limited, of course, by weaker generation).

Bound together by blood, each member of a clan shares certain predilections. A vampire's clan dictates the Disciplines that come most naturally. Though the Curse of Caine bestows a wide range of capabilities, the specialized powers of vampires manifest in different propensities among the clans. Thus, each clan or bloodline has three signature Disciplines, powers that are most common among members of that line and that come more easily than others.

Conversely, each clan also passes on certain weaknesses and frailties to its childer. This effect may manifest as faults in personality, temperament or disposition; in others, more mystical traits or even physical alterations appear. These weaknesses often tie to some apocryphal story of the clan's founder, usually of some failing or curse on that luminary.

Because clan members tend to be Embraced due to similarities in disposition and interest to the clan's areas of expertise, most vampires of a given clan share certain abilities or benefits. As a result, a vampire's clan also offers particular advantages that are common to all members. Even those individuals who are Embraced outside of a clan's normal range are instructed or assisted quickly in developing these benefits. It is always the choice of the individual whether or not to follow such direction.

Allegiances

The Camarilla and Sabbat claim the nearly exclusive membership of certain lineages. Among the Camarilla, the six clans of the Brujah, Malkavians, Nosferatu, Toreador, Tremere and Ventrue predominate. In the Sabbat, leadership and the bulk of membership is claimed by the Lasombra and the Tzimisce, though a good portion of the sect is made up of *antitribu* members of the other clans. The Assamites, Followers of Set, Gangrel, Giovanni and Ravnos are largely independent, with the majority of their individuals holding membership in neither sect.

Among the bloodlines, individual vampires are so scattered and rare as to make any sort of sectarian classification pointless, and allegiances break down to an individual basis. The elusive Cathayan vampires of Asia are not known to conform to any clan, either, and indeed, they do not even claim any relationship to Caine. What this disavowal bodes is unknown to western Kindred.

The Camarilla

Founded in the late Dark Ages to resist the fires of the Inquisition, the Camarilla relies on the Masquerade to hide vampires from humanity. As the largest global sect of vampires, the Camarilla offers prestige to the elders and security to the youth. In theory, all vampires are invited to join the Camarilla, but aside from a few expatriates and loners of other clans, only six clans have real membership. Among the member clans of the Camarilla, representation comes through a member of the Inner Circle and the appointment of a justicar. Other clans or bloodlines of vampires may nominally have members, even officers such as princes or primogen, but without an Inner Circle member and justicar, their true clout in the upper halls of the organization is limited.

The Sabbat

For centuries, the elders of Cainite society maintained a rigid status quo over their childer. The elders retained positions of power and influence, keeping the younger Cainites trapped in relative impotence and servitude. The formation of the Camarilla only exacerbated this relationship, as the elders banded together to support their own authority. Obviously, the existence of hordes of neonates, itching for advancement and giddy with their own vampiric power, created incredible friction between the generations. As the Dark Ages closed with the Renaissance and the newer, larger cities and populations of Europe, the number of younger, dissatisfied and educated vampires increased. Finally, matters came to a head in the Anarch Revolt, where hordes of the younger Cainites, fired by their mistreatment at the hands of their elders, rose up and destroyed the institutions of their society in wholesale rebellion.

Eventually, the Camarilla crushed the Anarch Revolt, the Convention of Thorns forming an uneasy truce between anarchs and Camarilla vampires. Still, many Cainites remained outcast due to their heinous crimes against the Camarilla, or retained a desire to overthrow the organization. Bolstered by early successes and the discovery of ancient Tzimisce rituals that bonded them together into unified packs, these vampires formed their own organization, the Sabbat. Though a thorn in the side of the Camarilla at first, the vampires of the Sabbat recruited dissatisfied younger Cainites in their war and overtook more territory and control.

In the modern age, the Sabbat stands in direct opposition to the Camarilla. Though only one-third the size of the Camarilla, the Sabbat makes great strides in taking territory, partly because it flouts the Traditions and partly because its fanatically motivated and loyal packs destroy the disorganized Camarilla individuals. Members of the Sabbat seek to overthrow the hold of the elders and, ultimately, the Antediluvians. The two pre-eminent clans of the Sabbat, the Lasombra and the Tzimisce, are held in great esteem among their sect for their successful destruction of their own Antediluvians. However, many vampires of other clans also ally with the Sabbat, becoming *antitribu* or "anti-tribes" in opposition to their original blood heritage. The Lasombra and Tzimisce are the most common clan members of the Sabbat, but a fair number of *antitribu* claim allegiance in the never-ending war to overthrow the elders, establish the rule of vampires over the kine and shatter the illusions of Cainites who hold on to their lost humanity.

The Independents

The Camarilla claims the allegiance of six great clans, the Sabbat's core comes from two — but what of the other five? These other clans call no sect master, instead charting their own courses. For them, their own key philosophies, often intertwined with the mortal beliefs of their homelands, are the only guiding principles necessary.

For several hundred years, the Assamites, Followers of Set, Giovanni and Ravnos were the only four independent clans. Recently, though, the Gangrel left the Camarilla *en masse*, taking up a neutral position once more. Whether the Camarilla's shaky foundations will further erode, or whether a new clan will take the Gangrel's place, remains to be seen.

BRUJAH

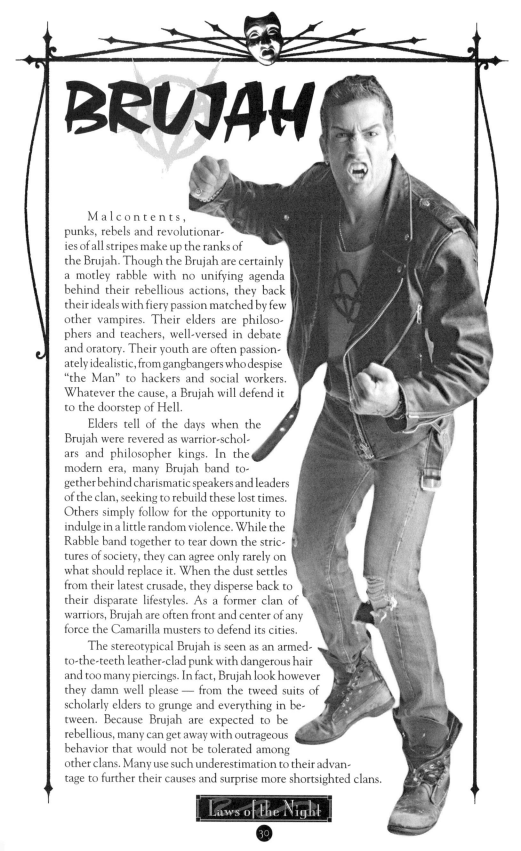

Malcontents, punks, rebels and revolutionaries of all stripes make up the ranks of the Brujah. Though the Brujah are certainly a motley rabble with no unifying agenda behind their rebellious actions, they back their ideals with fiery passion matched by few other vampires. Their elders are philosophers and teachers, well-versed in debate and oratory. Their youth are often passionately idealistic, from gangbangers who despise "the Man" to hackers and social workers. Whatever the cause, a Brujah will defend it to the doorstep of Hell.

Elders tell of the days when the Brujah were revered as warrior-scholars and philosopher kings. In the modern era, many Brujah band together behind charismatic speakers and leaders of the clan, seeking to rebuild these lost times. Others simply follow for the opportunity to indulge in a little random violence. While the Rabble band together to tear down the strictures of society, they can agree only rarely on what should replace it. When the dust settles from their latest crusade, they disperse back to their disparate lifestyles. As a former clan of warriors, Brujah are often front and center of any force the Camarilla musters to defend its cities.

The stereotypical Brujah is seen as an armed-to-the-teeth leather-clad punk with dangerous hair and too many piercings. In fact, Brujah look however they damn well please — from the tweed suits of scholarly elders to grunge and everything in between. Because Brujah are expected to be rebellious, many can get away with outrageous behavior that would not be tolerated among other clans. Many use such underestimation to their advantage to further their causes and surprise more shortsighted clans.

Roleplaying Hints: Revolution is your cause, passion your strength. You throw your heart and soul into anything that could help tear down the old, dead ways and make room for the new. Although you may just like chaos or tearing things down, chances are, you have some ideal that you want to see come to fruit, and this drive pushes you to engage in revolt. You use the skills available to you, whether you are a subtle creature manipulating courts and Kindred socially or a gangbanger punk who beats the opposition down mercilessly. When you join with your clan to change the status quo, other concerns drop aside. Once the revolution's over, though, you fight for your idea with the same ferocity, which may put you at odds with others who have different goals. It's about changing the world for something that you think is better — whether just for yourself, or for everyone.

Disciplines: *Celerity, Potence, Presence*

Advantage: As free-thinkers and rebels, all Brujah have some sort of contacts from their field of revolution, be it gang warfare or socio-political theory. Thus, all Brujah characters gain one free Trait in *Political, University* or *Street* Influence, and an associated Ability Trait of *Politics, Academics* or *Streetwise*.

As an aside, Brujah tend to stick together tightly when trouble erupts, and indeed, a "call to arms" draws Brujah together for common cause even in spite of personal differences. Failure to respond to such a call causes the offender to lose standing within the clan, and to be unable to gain help from other Brujah. However, if there are only three Brujah in a given city, this solidarity is obviously not such an obvious advantage.

Disadvantage: The Brujah clan bears the scars of many insults and oppressions from the past. Thus, its members are easily prone to violence and frenzy. Indeed, among modern Brujah, even debate and discourse can become heated enough to incite rage. All Brujah suffer a one-Trait penalty on Virtue Tests of *Self-Control/Instinct*.

Bloodlines: Brujah of any allegiance are functionally similar; there are no particularly special bloodlines of Brujah in any sect. Far and away, the largest amount of anarchs tend to be Brujah. Rare rumors of a secretive group calling themselves the "True Brujah" rise on occasion, but whether they are actually a separate bloodline or simply a group of deluded dissidents is unknown by the Cainite population at large.

MALKAVIAN

Dismissed as madmen and kooks, the clan of seers is alternately derided and feared. Every last member of the Malkavian clan is twisted in some fashion, rendered incurably insane by the power of the clan's blood. For some, this madness takes the form of hideous homicidal displays or outrageous chaotic behavior; in others, a quiet, insidious bent makes its way through the vampire's thoughts. In all cases, the blood makes Malkavians unpredictable, potentially dangerous and absolutely free from the confines and expectations of normalcy.

No unifying purpose or goal binds the Malkavian clan, only a bond of shared madness. Some revel in their insanity, others deny it, but they are all inevitably drawn together by their insight into a world altered by twisted perceptions. None can guess what Malkavians *really* see or think. Indeed, to do so is to invite the Lunatics to share their madness. Unbidden, the Malkavians seek to open the perceptions of others, using pranks, misdirection and chaos to force others into new viewpoints and to shatter accepted norms. Some vampires whisper that the Malkavians control the Jyhad subtly, that the war of ages is simply a great joke of their founder… and a few fear that the Malkavians are already laughing at the coming end.

The Lunatics Embrace seemingly at whim. Many members of the clan are insightful, some even brilliant. Any other categorizations, aside from their common insanity, fail. A Malkavian usually Embraces someone on the edge of insanity or one already driven mad, but none can really say what might motivate a Lunatic to bring another into the fold. Some new childer are not insane when they are Embraced, but their sires seek to rectify this "shortcoming" as quickly as possible. A few are physically brutal, and some can be quite socially charming when not visibly afflicted, but these outlyers serve only to point up the commonality of the clan: Madness — and enlightenment — can infect anyone.

Most Malkavians seem to have little care for sect politics, although those who do so are terrifying in their dogged pursuit of their aim. The true loyalties of the Malkavians likely lie with whatever greater goal drives their shared insight, though. Even the most chaotic Lunatics occasionally find themselves working in tandem at the most unusual of tasks.

Roleplaying Hints: You see and understand things that nobody else comprehends. Maybe they're right when they say you're mad, but maybe it's just that they can't handle the *truth*! You're not feeble, helpless or stupidly comical. You have a vision, and though it sometimes makes unlife difficult, you can look at things from directions that nobody else contemplates. You can sometimes get others to see brief moments of your vision by tricking their minds into thinking in strange ways, so you create plans designed to interrupt the "normalcy" of other peoples' existences, so that they are forced to examine their motives and places more carefully. You may have a lot of trouble with unlife, or you may be only subtly touched and pretty much functional in normal society — but you are *always* aware of the invisible pulse of currents underlying everything.

Disciplines: *Auspex, Dementation, Obfuscate*

Advantage: The Lunatics seem "blessed" with a special insight into the workings of the hidden world. Whether they discern small bits of knowledge from watching leaves fall or they work divination with human entrails, all of Malkavs's brood seem to follow hidden patterns that few others are even aware of. Because of this bizarre insight, all Malkavians gain a free level of *Awareness*.

Some Malkavians possess a strange link to others of their kind. Indeed, the Lunatics seem to be able to recognize one another on sight, and they even pass along bits of knowledge from time to time. This "madness network" may be the result of a true sharing of minds, or simply ranting — none outside the clan really know, and few wish to explore the matter too deeply.

Disadvantage: The members of the Malkavian clan are universally insane. All Malkavian characters suffer from a derangement of some sort. These sorts of personality disorders are not humorous — they are cracks in the workings of the mind, turning the Malkavian into something beyond the comprehension of even vampires. A Malkavian is unlikely to regress to a childlike or clownish state, collecting teddy bears and silly clothing. A Malkavian who wears blood-stained pajamas and babbles in a room full of teddy bears covered in entrails, seeking wisdom from the charnel pit — *that's* the sort of insanity that infects the Lunatics.

A Malkavian's initial derangement can be temporarily suppressed with Willpower Traits like any other derangement, but it can never be removed or cured permanently.

Bloodlines: Most Malkavians claim nominal membership in the Camarilla, though *antitribu* are found in the Sabbat — the Freaks are usually the most deranged and homicidal of their kind. Some Malkavians of the Camarilla still possess the Discipline of *Dominate* (instead of *Dementation*), but most of the Lunatics were "converted" to the ways of *Dementation* in a wash of madness that swept through the clan in recent years.

NOSFERATU

Hideous deformities and misshapen features are the hallmarks of the Nosferatu, vampires reshaped by the Curse of Caine. Though they (usually) remain aware and intelligent, all Nosferatu are physically altered in some way by the blood of the clan. Boils, growths, altered features, hairy spots, warts, odd skin colors, animalistic features and even scales sprout on the faces and bodies of these wretches. Little wonder, then, that the Nosferatu prefer to congregate in sewers and caverns, away from the judgmental eyes of others.

Whether the deformities of the Nosferatu hail from a curse placed on the line by Caine himself or from some other unwholesome source, the results are the same. As the Nosferatu cannot hope to interact with the rest of society, they must survive on their own, which they do with incredible skill. Shunned by everyone else, the Nosferatu gather in their own groups or avoid contact altogether. The outskirts of civilization and the refuse of society become their homes and sustenance.

As the Nosferatu scurry through the secret byways and catacombs in which they lair, they unearth lost secrets and find hidden caches of knowledge. Indeed, with the incredible stealth engendered as a necessity of their condition, they find it easy to spy on Kindred and kine alike in search of valuable bits of information. Spies and rumormongers of the first order, the Nosferatu parlay such information in exchange for favors, trading with clanmates freely and treating with outsiders for services and boons. Some Nosferatu develop their powers of concealment well enough to eavesdrop unnoticed in the middle of meetings of other Kindred, selling their secrets to the highest bidders. Woe unto the outsider who seeks to turn a Nosferatu against his clan, though — in their communal misery, the Nosferatu have forged strong ranks of loyalty. When the only ones to keep company with a monster are other monsters, they develop powerful bonds indeed.

As outcasts, the Nosferatu often Embrace among those like themselves — derelicts, vagrants, the antisocial, the wayward and unstable individuals — in a commonality of social pariahs. Other victims include the beautiful and vain, or sociopaths and criminals, to whom the Nosferatu wish to teach a permanent and disfiguring lesson. Whatever the case, the Embrace often has a surprising effect. Aside from inflicting the deformities characteristic of the clan over the next few weeks, the abrupt and extreme changes often force the fledgling into an utterly new existence, one in which his clan is his only anchor. It's unsurprising, then, that recruits find themselves with friends and allies among those they would otherwise scorn.

The Nosferatu remain on the fringes of vampire society. The clan lacks any sort of overarching organization as a whole, but among themselves, the Nosferatu are unfailingly polite and well-versed in the pecking order. Outsiders may see nothing but a ragged band of deformed and pitiable creatures, but among their unearthed secrets and hidden tunnels, the Nosferatu hide far more influence and knowledge than the other clans would care to know....

Roleplaying Hints: Though you may appear hideous to others, you are no less a person for it. You may shun the trappings of your humanity like the visage you sloughed off during your Embrace, or you may seek to regain the feelings of mortality; either way, you are cursed with this form. Outsiders treat you with contempt, fear or hostility. Among others of your kind, though, you can be civil; after all, you are brothers in arms. Outsiders expect you to act like a crude, bestial monster, so you play up that stereotype for what it's worth, and you use your sophistication to learn the secrets that can be sold or put to good use. You have to take care of yourself since nobody else will now.

Disciplines: *Animalism, Obfuscate, Potence*

Advantage: All Nosferatu learn the ways of skulking and hiding, simply to avoid unwanted attention. With their signature command of a city's hidden byways, they discover lost hideaways and secrets. As a result, all Nosferatu have at least one Trait of *Stealth* at no cost and they also gain one Ability Trait of *Survival* at no cost.

Disadvantage: The hideous countenance of the Nosferatu precludes ever holding normal social relationships without the use of concealment or misdirection. No Nosferatu may possess the Social Traits *Alluring, Gorgeous* or *Seductive* without calling on special powers (such as the *Obfuscate* Discipline) to gain those Traits. Furthermore, all Nosferatu suffer from the Negative Social Traits *Repugnant* x 3 whenever their true forms are apparent. These Traits may never be removed with Experience Traits or Free Traits. A Nosferatu in his "normal" visage cannot initiate any Social Challenges except for the purposes of intimidation, although he may defend against Social Challenges normally.

Bloodlines: There are no distinctive bloodlines of Nosferatu; indeed, the Nosferatu *antitribu* of the Sabbat actually retain cordial (if distant) relations with their Camarilla counterparts. Some inside the clan maintain that there exists a line of monsters, Embraced by an ancient, which hunts the rest of the Nosferatu clan. These beasts, called the Nictuku, are considered mythical by most Nosferatu, but whenever a warren goes silent or a clanmate vanishes mysteriously, the fears return.

TOREADOR

Artists, dilettantes and degenerates make up the ranks of the Toreador clan, a lineage ensconced in sensuality and experience. Whether patronizing the arts or creating works of their own, these vampires are rarely far from the pleasures of expression and beauty. Ultimately, though, whether for aesthetics or indulgence, it is beauty that carries the members of this clan.

Works of beauty and history are found among the holdings of the Toreador, and pieces of physical art are not the sole treasures of the clan. Toreador are as likely to work with music, song, literature, poetry, physical beauty or aesthetics as any other form of expression. Bitter infighting divides much of the clan regarding what constitutes "art," but all are united in their zeal to defend the ideals of art and beauty — and sensuality — though artistic expression. Some members of the clan do not possess any notable artistic ability, but they support their clan's interests through their patronage and social graces. When a party, ball or showing is arranged in Cainite society, it is most likely a Toreador organizing the event, and it is certain that the clan will bring out its most glittering members in force. In cramped artists' studios or opulent manors, the Toreador surround themselves with the trappings with art in all forms, and carry that elegance wherever they travel and meet. The common desire to indulge in the elevation of art draws the clan together. Even when sniping over matters of status and prestige, these vampires re-

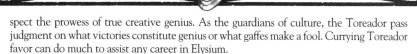

spect the prowess of true creative genius. As the guardians of culture, the Toreador pass judgment on what victories constitute genius or what gaffes make a fool. Currying Toreador favor can do much to assist any career in Elysium.

Obviously, the Toreador are quick to Embrace those mortals with great artistic talents, the better to preserve those talents for all eternity. In some cases, members of the clan also Embrace from passion, and they are the most likely to Embrace for companionship. Though the Toreador are not uniformly beautiful, a disproportionate number are good-looking — works of physical art to some thinking.

Time, however, is often unkind to the Toreador. Many become jaded with the passing years, seeing works fall to ruins or mortal beauty crumble with age. Consequently, they seek greater thrills and experiences to whet their palates, often falling into hedonism and decadence. Most Kindred agree that few things are more disturbing than a Toreador needing a new hobby. Even worse is the Toreador who has become bored. Like decadent, pleasure-loving nobility, they snipe and disparage those who do not meet their exacting standards. For every hostess with the mostest or inspired artist, there is a catty preener whose only interest is destroying others.

Roleplaying Hints: You are a creature of eternal magnificence. You may have an artistic talent (or talents), or you may yourself *be* a work of art. Either way, it is your duty and your pleasure to raise awareness and culture through the spread of art, both its creation and its patronage. You want people to strive for higher ideals and to experience new heights of feeling due to art, so you encourage others to indulge in works of passion. After all, a great artist must be immersed in art.

Disciplines: *Auspex, Celerity, Presence*

Advantage: With their predilection for artistic skills, the Toreador all have some sort of unique talents. Even those Toreador who have no real artistic ability learn to become patrons of the arts, to engage in social sniping and to buy what they can't create. Every Toreador vampire begins with *Academics, Crafts, Performance* or *Subterfuge* Abilities (one Trait each of any two, or two Traits of one).

A Toreador can also call on artistic talents to hunt and feed. Though she may have a stable *Herd* like any other Cainite, a Toreador can also find willing mortal victims by use of artistic ability or patronage ("Would you like to come upstairs and see my etchings?"). A Toreador can gain one Blood Trait for each level possessed in the aforementioned Abilities; each Blood Trait gained in this fashion requires 15 minutes out of play. Gaining Blood Traits in this fashion *does* use up the Abilities in question, so the Toreador may be limited in her feeding if she has already used some of her Abilities.

Disadvantage: The Toreador are easily entranced by beauty. Every work of art is a key to insight, whether in the form of sculpture, poetry, a lovely face, even a clear sky spangled with stars. As such, beauty draws the attention of Toreador, often to the exclusion of all else. When presented with a work of great art (generally, one executed with the equivalent of three levels of *Crafts* or *Performance* Traits, though some special cases may require more or less), a Toreador becomes absorbed in the task of examining and understanding the work, lost in a fugue state. The Toreador can only break from this state willingly by expending a Mental Trait, although injury or other distractions (such as attack or being elbowed by a neighbor) can break this enthrallment.

Bloodlines: The Toreador clan has no offshoot bloodlines; the *antitribu* of the Sabbat share the predilections and capabilities of their Camarilla brethren, although they find their pleasure and artistic expression in horror as much as beauty. These *antitribu*, instead of becoming paralyzed with fascination, instead have a disturbing tendency to act out their sociopathic tendencies on whomever is at hand through socially cutting remarks, intellectual dominance or physical torture. A Toreador *antitribu* given a chance to act out such tendencies must expend a Mental Trait if the player wishes to resist the urge, though such an expenditure need only be made once in any given scene.

TREMERE

Once a cabal of mortal wizards, the Tremere supposedly wrested the secrets of vampirism through their own arcane studies in a covert war during the Dark Ages. With their stolen birthright, they carved a place for themselves in vampiric society, hunting down and extinguishing an ancient of another lost bloodline in order to gain legitimacy while refining their own potent magics with their new unliving powers. Tightly bound by common studies of the arcane and the mistrust of other clans, the Warlocks are mysterious, distrusted and feared — and that's just how they like it.

Though not all Tremere had mystical leanings in life, the ritualistic structure of the clan brings all recruits into a rigid hierarchy in death. Occult practices from the Dark Ages shape many of the clan's ways, while secret orders of initiation mark rites of passage in the clan's ranks. The clan itself is divided into circles of ranking, moving from apprentices (who carry out the day-to-day tasks of the clan) to regents (who oversee clan affairs in a city) to lords (who exercise dominion over a particular region) to pontifexes (whose rule extends to all Tremere activities within a large geographic area) to, ultimately, the fabled Council of Seven (whose members each oversee a continent). Initiates strive diligently to outperform their peers in order to rise in rank, yet maintain a rigid code of loyalty to clan and Camarilla (in that order). This chain of command promotes ambition while making the Tremere more insular and structured than any other Camarilla clan.

Among the ranks of the Tremere are Freemasons, mystics, witches, New Agers and antiquarians. The clan does not draw from practitioners of the arcane exclusively, though. Politicians, financiers, scientists and soldiers can all be found among the ranks of the clan. Self-discipline, a keen mind and a will to power are qualities inherent to the prospective neonate. Loyalty to the clan and knowledge of the occult can be instilled later.

Because of their stolen blood and their hidden secrets of magic (so secretive that other vampires whisper rumors of Tremere assassins who hunt and slay vampires learning *Thaumaturgy* outside the auspices of the clan), the Tremere occupy an uncertain place within the Camarilla. Their prowess grants them grudging respect, but it is no secret that any Tremere advances the clan's agenda first and foremost. As a result, most Tremere are superlative manipulators. Vampires of this clan barter their impressive magical skills for favors, calling in debts later to consolidate the clan's claims to specific political goals and mystical treasures. Their magical powers allow them to counter the actions of the Camarilla's many enemies, yet they grant an unpredictable edge over their allies at the same time. The Tremere exert an insidious influence over vampire society from their chantries (part stronghold, part academy), directing crusades and research to their own occult ends.

Roleplaying Hints: You have taken an oath to uphold the goals of clan and Camarilla. You hail from a distinguished house of wizards, and in return for your dutiful service, you can expect instruction in the mystic arts. You obey the laws of Kindred society unswervingly, but you always work to advance the interests of your clan first. Since unknown abilities cannot be opposed, you conceal the true measure of your own power and your clan's knowledge, acting when appropriate and before others can fathom your plans. You possess a strong will, capable of undertaking difficult tasks in order to succeed. Other vampires may not understand or trust you, and that's just fine — you have other plans.

Disciplines: *Auspex, Dominate, Thaumaturgy*

Advantage: As a result of their training in the mystical arts, all Tremere gain one *Occult* Ability and one *Occult* Influence automatically. This bonus represents their basic knowledge of magical practices and their clan's contacts within arcane circles.

Because of the tightly knit structure of the clan, Tremere can expect assistance and instruction from higher-ranking members of the clan. However, members must still perform their duties. Tremere cannot simply expect all of their problems to be solved by their superiors — the clan does not tolerate laggards. Tremere vampires can expect that any *Mentor* they may have will always offer assistance (if the Storyteller rules that doing so is within the *Mentor's* capabilities), but conversely, they will always be required to fulfill a specific duty afterward.

Disadvantage: On receiving the Embrace, all new Tremere are forced to drink from a chalice containing the blood of seven elders of the clan. From this mixture of blood, the neonate comes one step toward a blood bond to the elders and, through them, to the clan as a whole. Tremere who fail in their duties or who disobey orders may be forced to drink again of such a mixture, stepping closer to total obedience to the clan.

Tremere who fail to report to their superiors, or who do not successfully carry out their duties, can also expect their superiors to deal with them harshly. Members of the clan who do not pull their own weight quickly find that they are expendable.

Bloodlines: At one time, a small faction of *antitribu* claimed membership within the Sabbat. However, a recent turn of the Jyhad has seen to the extermination of all of those expatriates, with no survivors whatsoever. Also, during the Dark Ages, a small group of Lithuanian pagans formed several cults. These Telyavelic Tremere possessed the Discipline of *Presence* instead of *Dominate*, but they suffered mightily from displays of Christian faith. These pagans were finally exterminated before the 17th century. With the rigid structure of the Tremere clan, there is no room for the deviance of any other bloodlines.

Ventrue

While the other clans play at games of status or rebellion, the Ventrue take up the mantle of leadership and guide Cainite society itself. Nobility, sophistication and duty are the hallmarks of this clan. Rulership is a difficult burden indeed, but the Ventrue know themselves equal to the task. Alternately derided and respected, the Ventrue are the framework on which the Camarilla rests.

The responsibilities and privileges of authority are assumed by vampires of the Ventrue clan. Power belongs to those who can wield it, and so the Ventrue accumulate prestige, influence and wealth. In order to defend against the plots of subtle foes, the vampires of this clan call on their associates to form staunch allegiances.

The responsibilities and privileges of authority are assumed by vampires of the Ventrue clan. Power belongs to those who can wield it, and so the Ventrue accumulate prestige, influence and wealth. In order to defend against the plots of subtle foes, the vampires of this clan call on their associates to form staunch allegiances.

When seeking mortal allies and compatriots, the Ventrue look to the cream of the crop. Those who rise to heights of prowess through talent, hard work and noble character are the foremost recruits among the Ventrue. Of course, among the older members of the clan, blood will tell; scions of wealthy and noble families are often inducted, with the expectation that their rarefied lineage provides insight and potential beyond that of commoners.

As the rulers of the Camarilla, the Venture hold a *noblesse oblige*, a duty and responsibility to lead and protect. Members of the clan use their political savvy and influential powers to sway Kindred and mortal politics alike, bringing prosperity to vampires and protecting the society of the undead from discovery. Thus, Ventrue naturally gravitate toward positions of power and authority, or attempt to do so. Even those Ventrue who join the Sabbat take their duties as protectors of Cainite society very seriously, serving as dark crusaders of a holy cause. Of course, since the Ventrue cannot let other clans know the hidden secrets and burdens that they carry in the war to defend all vampires, they must assume the burdens of leadership alone. However, they are certain to drop hints about the burdensome task.

Roleplaying Hints: You are among the elite nobility of Kindred society. Above mortal or even petty Cainite concerns, you bear the right and responsibility of leadership. You have a firm respect for tradition, for the ways that have worked for hundreds of years; even the most rebellious youth understands the power of tradition. No other vampires have the necessary talents or capabilities to take on the burden of guiding Cainite society. Thus, it is up to you to take up that mantle. You lead not necessarily out of desire or habit (though such factors may figure in), but because your clan has gifted you with the duty to assume responsibility. All that is done must advance the sect, for the sect will protect the weaker ones. Your conviction is your armor, your honor a shield, your birthright your weapon. Honed to perfection, you uphold all that is noble, ordered, ancient and wise in the children of Caine.

Disciplines: *Dominate, Fortitude, Presence*

Advantage: Because of their keen financial acumen and savvy, all Ventrue characters begin play with an extra Trait of the *Resources* Background that can never be lost permanently. All Ventrue additionally gain one Trait of *Finance, High Society* or *Political* Influence (player's choice) due to their connections to society and social manipulation. Even those Ventrue without such ties themselves may call on their clanmates for the appropriate aid, effectively granting them the same capabilities.

Ventrue tend to keep detailed records of lineage and heritage. As a result, the Ventrue clan, though not as hierarchical as the Tremere, can prove difficult to infiltrate; nearly every Ventrue is recorded somewhere in the clan's family trees. Though it may take several months to track down a particular lineage, a Ventrue can usually contact others of his clan and discover the sire, grandsire and so on of a particular Ventrue claimant, thus establishing "credentials" of a sort.

Disadvantage: All Ventrue have rarefied tastes, to the point of excluding all other prey except their chosen taste. Ventrue may only feed from mortal blood meeting with their particular dietary restriction. A given Ventrue might be able to feed only from young women or from businessmen or perhaps only from those experiencing terror. A Ventrue reflexively regurgitates any blood taken from any other source, gaining no nourishment. This restriction does not apply to vampiric vitae, though, and it may be suppressed long enough for a Ventrue to Embrace a new childe.

Because of their restrictions on feeding, Ventrue typically come into play each game session with one Blood Trait less than other vampires (though this shortage can be ameliorated with the *Herd* Background, as usual).

Bloodlines: The Ventrue *antitribu* are crusaders who lead in the holy war of the sect, feeling that the others of their blood have failed in their mission to protect Cainites from the machinations of the Antediluvians. Despite differences of philosophy, though, Ventrue of the Camarilla and the Sabbat are functionally similar; *antitribu* are the true dark knights of their kind. There are no distinctive bloodlines of Ventrue, though some family lines do form "dynasties" within the clan.

LASOMBRA

Master manipulators, influence brokers and scions of hidden power — the Lasombra, as their moniker implies, ply the Jyhad as a vicious game from the comfortable obscurity of darkness and misdirection. Raised from the Spanish and Italian upper class, the Lasombra exercised their influence over the Church and nobility of the Dark Ages, turning mortal rulers to their whims and bending entire societies to their service. This practice continues unabated as the Lasombra bow to no other clan, instead leading the Sabbat with keen, cultured sensibilities and ruthless efficiency.

In elder days, the Lasombra were considered an honorable and impressive clan, possessed of strong character. None underestimated their skill at diplomacy or intrigue, of course, but as a whole, they exerted a powerful hierarchy from elder courts to younger students. During the Anarch Revolt, though, many young Lasombra rebelled against their controlling sires, seeking to lead their own unlives instead of existing in eternal servitude as pawns. After decades of warfare, a Methuselah of the clan betrayed their Antediluvian, and that ancient was supposedly slain. Now, the Lasombra are free of their Antediluvian's control, free to exercise their whims as they see fit and free to rule the Sabbat in its quest to liberate all other Cainites from the thrall of the elders. Naturally, their superior knowledge in this matter grants them the right to lead the other clans in this war.

Among the clans of the Sabbat, the Lasombra are treated with respect and reverence; many positions of authority and influence are held by the Keepers. For destroying their Antediluvian, the Lasombra are accorded honor second only to the Tzimisce. For serving the Sabbat loyally, they are granted service in turn. Though suspicion follows many Lasombra motives, the Lasombra deal with the other clans through strength and cunning. Even in the Camarilla, the Lasombra are considered urbane and dangerous. A Cainite dealing with a Lasombra shows the utmost consideration, despite any thoughts of spite or treason — an attitude that the Keepers return in kind. After all, one can never tell who dances on the puppeteers' strings.

As befits their heritage, the Lasombra choose their potential childer from strong-willed mortals, selecting those with courage, cleverness and a talent for manipulation. Artistic skill, specialized knowledge and physical prowess are all secondary considerations compared to the *will to power* necessary to be a true Lasombra. The Lasombra recruit must have the confidence and authority to master himself and others. Naturally, these conflicting inner drives lead to friction between sire and childe as the fledglings refuse to bow to the potent wills of their sires, but the Lasombra wouldn't have it any other way — through conflict comes strength, and to the victor go the spoils.

Roleplaying Hints: You shape the world to your desire. By leading those around you and influencing the keys of power, you can achieve your own goals, whatever they are. When social acumen is required, you can be silver-tongued or threatening; your insight into motives allows you to discern what others want and how to use them. If force is necessary, though, you don't hesitate to use it (though the necessity of force generally means that something went wrong along the way). Sophistication, confidence and knowledge are the means to power, but power in and of itself is not your end. Power is simply the means to achieve your true desires, the ends that you set for yourself.

Disciplines: *Dominate, Obtenebration, Potence*

Advantage: A long heritage of influence and manipulation makes the Lasombra puppeteers *par excellence*. During the Dark Ages, the Lasombra exercised subtle authority within the Church and over secular rulers; in the modern age, these old habits die hard, even among the more rebellious elements of the clan. All Lasombra gain one Trait of *Church, Political* or *Underworld* Influence.

As founders of the Sabbat, the Lasombra are respected for their destruction of their Antediluvian, and they hold positions of leadership and power. All Lasombra automatically gain one free Status Trait.

Disadvantage: Mirrors and reflective surfaces do not show any trace of the Lasombra. Some say that this oddity occurs because the Lasombra have no souls; others claim that it is part and parcel of their *Obtenebration* Discipline. Whatever the cause, Lasombra (and their clothes and carried possessions) do not show up in any sort of reflective surface, such as mirrors, pools of water, reflective windows, polished metals, photographs and black-and-white film (which uses a reflecting silver emulsifier).

Also, because of the Lasombra clan's ties to darkness, all Lasombra suffer an additional level of damage from exposure to sunlight.

Bloodlines: A small number of Lasombra — about a hundred — claim allegiance with the Camarilla, calling themselves Lasombra *antitribu*. Most of these Lasombra are old and potent, from days before the formation of either sect. The few modern ones still have the backing of their powerful sires. These Lasombra are all accorded respect within the Camarilla, so they keep their usual clan advantages but within their sect. The Sabbat Lasombra denounce the existence of their wayward brethren, and they hunt the traitors mercilessly whenever the opportunity presents itself.

Tzimisce

Potent sorceries, crumbling castles, forbidding mountains, villages of huddled and fearful peasants these images play through the history of the Tzimisce. The scholarly Fiends trace their roots to the demesnes of Eastern Europe, where they ruled as feudal lords over a superstitious populace (and, in some places, they still do, it is whispered). Even in the modern day, anachronistic behavior and uncommon occult insight are hallmarks of the Tzimisce. Once the pre-eminent sorcerers of Cainite society, they now serve the Sabbat as terrifying, alien creatures that epitomize the traditional characteristics of vampires. The great Vlad Dracul himself is said to be one of the Tzimisce, though in the Sabbat, he is counted a traitor to the clan.

The Tzimisce have existed since time immemorial, ruling for generations in the fiefs and provinces of Eastern Europe. There, they extended their taloned hands over the mortal villages and authorities, brooking no resistance. Their broods of blood-bound childer exacted fearsome tribute, while the *koldun* sorcerers performed hideous rites, calling on the black-stained power of the twisted lands. With the coming of the Anarch Revolt, legions of childer broke away from their domineering masters, putting castles and elders to the torch. The mystical ritual of the Vaulderie, corrupted from *koldun* rites, broke the blood bonds and sent childer screaming as bands of terror ravaging the landscape. At last, the anarchs destroyed the Tzimisce Antediluvian, and together with the Lasombra, the remaining Fiends formed the core of the Sabbat. The few surviving *voivodes* and *koldun* shut themselves away in their castles, avoiding the strife and closeting themselves in an earlier age. Now, the Fiends' influence in the Sabbat is second only to the Lasombra clan's, and many believe that the Tzimisce manipulate the Lasombra as well.

Few can understand the motives of the Tzimisce. Many are insane or simply alien to human or vampiric minds. Uninterested in secular power yet wrathful and deadly when balked, incredibly intelligent but unwilling to grasp the modern age, by turns courtly and torturous, the Tzimisce are a study in contrasts — yet the Fiends themselves admit to no dichotomy. Other vampires treat the Tzimisce with a guarded sort of respect. The Fiends take the greatest insult when their domains are trespassed, yet they hoard insights that the other clans have long since lost. Once angered, a Tzimisce never fails to exact retribution. To their allies, they seem erratic, yet their knowledge is useful and their minions are potent in battle. Suffice to say that few would want Tzimisce "friends," and none would want Tzimisce enemies.

In keeping with their bizarre predilections, the Tzimisce Embrace from an eclectic selection of mortals. The insane are sometimes chosen, but most often the Fiends choose those whose minds were broken by some terrible insight. More often, the Tzimisce Embrace those strong wills who were twisted but unbowed by unusual knowledge, whether scientists, magicians or philosophers. In some cases, the Tzimisce will Embrace their revenant relatives or mortal minions as a gift or reward for devoted service. Though the Embrace does not alter the fledgling Tzimisce physically, it exacts its price on the mind; few Tzimisce have the capacity to empathize with their former mortal days, while more than a few pick up disturbing new habits, sharper tempers and more territorial natures.

Roleplaying Hints: Existence is a process of learning and evolution. You have evolved beyond simple humanity, and through further work and study, you can evolve past the vampire condition, too. However, all of your work is still built fundamentally on the blocks that you have already laid. The ways of the past, those which have stood for centuries, have withstood the test of time and shown themselves correct. Therefore you mix anachronistic tradition with bizarre speculation and thought. If other Cainites do not understand you, that is their own problem; they have not reached your level of insight. You act with the elegance and politeness of a higher creature, but by the same token, you do not brook failure — you are a superior being, after all.

Disciplines: *Animalism, Auspex, Vicissitude*

Advantage: Because of their feudal heritage and ancient ways, the Fiends keep secrets long since thought lost by the other clans. All Tzimisce start with one free Ability Trait of *Occult*, and they can also purchase *Lore* Abilities with greater ease than most vampires — at Storyteller discretion, the Fiends may learn the first two levels of any *Lore* Ability without the need for extensive work or specialized resources, since the clan's libraries and holdings usually include such knowledge.

Tzimisce may have revenants as *Retainers*. A revenant *Retainer* can be treated like a ghoul, except that the revenant does not require regular upkeep with vitae. More detailed descriptions of revenants and their unusual families and powers can be found in other books, such as **Ghouls: Fatal Addiction** and **Liber des Goules.**

Disadvantage: The warped Carpathian Fiends exhibit some inexplicable tie to the lands of their birth. Whether this tie is a result of the ancient demonic pacts levied there in the Dark Ages, or a result of their bodies' craving for stability in response to their mutable Discipline of *Vicissitude*, the results are the same. A Tzimisce must sleep within at least two handfuls of soil from his grave or his native homeland. Each day that a Tzimisce fails to get such rest, he suffers a one-Trait penalty on all challenges. These penalty Traits are removed on a one-for-one basis as the Tzimisce regains rest in a safe haven with the appropriate earth. For this reason, many Tzimisce keep multiple havens, and they are loath to travel. A Tzimisce whose haven is compromised is in dire straits indeed.

Bloodlines: Many Tzimisce come from the revenant families, ancient lines of mortals transformed into ghoulish creatures through centuries of ingestion of vampiric vitae. The Bratovich Tzimisce hail from a family known for its brutality and animalistic tendencies; they learn *Potence* instead of *Auspex*, but they suffer a one-Trait penalty on their *Self-Control/ Instinct* tests against frenzy. Also, the Tzimisce claimed a heritage as sorcerers unparalleled among vampires until the eminence of the Tremere clan. These ancient sorcerers called themselves *koldun*, and some young Tzimisce take this title while studying the more modern magics of *Thaumaturgy* instead of *Vicissitude*. The modern *koldun* endure a one-Trait penalty when defending against opposing magic, though, since they must attune themselves to magical energies in order to learn *Thaumaturgy*.

Almost no Tzimisce are found in the Camarilla — the Fiends' distaste for the humanistic trappings of that organization is tremendous. Any Tzimisce who works with the Camarilla does so merely to further a particular personal agenda. More often, a Tzimisce without Sabbat leanings simply remains a cloistered independent.

Assamite

From hidden fortresses in the Middle East, the Assamites emerge as the silent stalkers of other Cainites. Secretive, insular and fanatically loyal to the precepts of their clan, the Assamites claim to be descendants of Haqim (Assam), who is said to fight against Khayyin (Caine) and his curse. As a result, the Assamites seek to convert or slay other Cainites, attempting to purge the foul curse of Khayyin and bring honor to Haqim's cause of justice. Needless to say, such pursuits — including hunting other Cainites for blood, and engaging in diablerie in attempts to strengthen their clan and their closeness to Haqim — are not popular with the other clans.

Due to their attacks on elders of the other clans in the Dark Ages and their assistance of the rebels during the Anarch Revolt, the Assamites were fought by the Camarilla and forced into capitulation. With their home fortress of Alamut compromised and peace enforced on them, they were subjected to a great curse by the Tremere. Through this curse, the Assamites were rendered unable to drink Kindred vitae, making it impossible for them to commit diablerie. Recently, though, the curse was broken (speculations have been rampant and none confirmed), and every Assamite across the globe awakened to discover a renewed thirst for the potent vitae of other Kindred. Though this development is not known publicly (because some Assamites, all *antitribu*, refused to submit to the curse and thus retained this ability), the Assamites are hoarding their secret, striking where they can to eliminate threats and draw on their returned strength.

The Assamite clan has undergone much upheaval recently, and not only due to the overturning of the Tremere curse. While previously young Assamites would take out contracts for the assassination of other Kindred and collect blood tithes as fees, now the Assamites hunt and kill without any sort of contracts, codes or strictures. In addition, the clan has moved away from its former Islamic ties, instead looking to more ancient gods. With these changes have come the awakenings of lost powers and the resurgence of the clan's physical and political clout. Where once the Assamites were seen as honorable and contract-bound (and thus useful tools), they are now silent terrors that plague elders of every clan and sect.

In older times, Assamites Embraced primarily males, those of Middle Eastern descent and strong faith. In modern days, women also fill the ranks and even a few Westerners have been brought in. Skill now plays more of a role in selection than heritage; prospective clan members are Embraced from those with a penchant for the hunt or kill—assassins, mercenaries, terrorists and gang warriors of any descent. Recruits are expected to undertake rigorous training, and they are indoctrinated in many of the clan's precepts and history. These *fida'i* (apprentices) are watched closely, but they are allowed to progress based on their own worth and skill. Many *fida'i* run in small packs called *falaqi*, hunting other Cainites for blood and practice.

Roleplaying Hints: You are a predator who preys on others of your kind. The cursed Get of Khayyin must be swayed from their path of bickering madness or be destroyed before they destroy all else. Your cause is just, and though you may not enjoy your tasks, you do your duty. You may be humorous, angry or withdrawn, but you go about your work professionally. Only by drawing on the strength of Haqim can the corrupted Kindred be fought, so you must steal their power and make sure that the clan is ready when Gehenna arrives. Khayyin was debased and had neither honor nor soul. His children share the same flaws, so they must be saved or destroyed, so that the powers of the blood are used only by the dutiful. The elders of the clan direct how to fight so that Gehenna may be survived. By following their commands and working within the strictures of the clan, you may hope to achieve some small piece of that battle.

Disciplines: *Celerity, Obfuscate, Quietus*

Advantage: Assamites are trained killers, and they are all subjected to a lengthy process of apprenticeship before the Embrace. Even those hurriedly Embraced for some reason have at least a modicum of training or skill. As a result, all Assamite characters gain one *Melee* Ability and one *Brawl* Ability at no cost during character generation.

At the Storyteller's option, Assamites may be able to access weapons and equipment through their clan. Players of Assamites should not use this benefit as a replacement for the proper *Mentor* and Influence Backgrounds — the clan doesn't reward those who rest on their laurels at the clan's expense — but a competent assassin who needs a little specialized help may be able to garner some additional tools from the clan's stores.

Disadvantage: With the lifting of the Tremere curse comes a renewed thirst for blood. All Assamites suffer from a hunger for vampiric vitae, one that cannot be easily controlled. Once an Assamite has tasted the blood of a particular vampire, she may become addicted to it — the player must make a *Self-Control/ Instinct* Virtue Test with a difficulty of four Traits, or the Assamite acquires a taste for the Kindred's blood. When encountering the same Kindred later, the character's player must succeed on a *Self-Control/ Instinct* Test or fly into a frenzy, attempting to devour the other Cainite. Even if the Assamite retains control, the lust for blood is immediate and evident, and it should be roleplayed accordingly.

Bloodlines: Assamites generally hold allegiance only to their own clan. A few exist in the Camarilla, as loners who broke from the clan; the Sabbat also claims *antitribu*, who differ from the rest of the clan only in that they never allowed themselves to be subjected to the (now-defunct) Tremere curse. In the Assamite homelands and fortresses exists a line of viziers who research blood magic and the nature of vampirism. Assamite vizier researchers gain *Thaumaturgy* as a Discipline instead of *Celerity*, but they must expend an additional Blood Trait on all uses of *Thaumaturgy* (in addition to their weakness for Kindred vitae), as their control of blood magic is not as refined as the Tremere's. This flaw comes in the viziers' magical practices; should another Cainite somehow learn *Thaumaturgy* from a vizier, all effects of the Discipline would be similarly difficult to cast, with the increased blood cost. Viziers also gain one *Occult* Ability Trait in place of either the free *Melee* or *Brawl* Trait (player's choice as to which).

ASSAMITES of EARLIER DAYS

After the Treaty of Tyre but before the breaking of the Tremere curse, the Assamites suffered from a different set of problems. The Assamites were unable to consume Kindred blood — indeed, each Trait of Cainite vitae (other than the Assamite's own blood) ingested or otherwise introduced into the Assamite's system inflicted one health level of damage. Furthermore, since the only means of lowering generation was through certain alchemical blood potions (diablerie having been rendered impossible by the curse), Assamites would hire themselves out on contracts to assassinate other Cainites, accepting blood as payment (and sending a tenth of all such blood earned to their elders as a tithe). Should the target manage to escape the Assamite, he would never be targeted again — until now, when the clan's members cast aside their former strictures of honor and obligation in favor of their former bloodthirst.

Followers of Set

The desert sands of Africa hold many secrets long buried, some best left undisturbed. Claiming literal descent from the dark Egyptian god Set, the Setites hoard the secrets of their lost civilizations. According to the Setites, Set himself will rise — soon — and he will reward his faithful while plunging the world into eternal night. Organized more like a cult than a clan, the Followers eagerly search for the mystic means to rouse Set, while they simultaneously spin webs of deceit and fixation to sway others to their service. Needless to say, the Setites are regarded with wariness at best and horror at worst.

Vague and contradictory rumors surround the Serpents' origin. Most Cainites hold that the Serpents are simply another branch of Caine's tree, from the far-wandering days of the Antediluvians and their mythical sires. For their part, the Followers of Set often insist that Set himself was no mere Cainite, but a true god of darkness. Such wild stories are discounted by most vampires, though the Serpents seem to hold bits of lore and wisdom from lost days that would legitimize their claims....

With respect to the other clans, the Setites are carefully neutral. During the formation of the Camarilla, it is said, the Setites were invited to join, but few deigned to do so — much to the secret relief of that sect's elders. As far as the Serpents are concerned, the Jyhad is just a petty struggle between the upstart children of Set's inferiors. The Setites thus broker their influence carefully, trading in commodities and vices that make them valuable, if covert, suppliers for many Kindred. Where a particular vampire has a weakness or desire, the Setites quickly move in to fill the vacuum, indebting the buyer to them and sometimes exacting favors through blackmail and addiction. Such tactics naturally don't endear the Setites to the other clans, so most Serpents make a great show of dissembling and an outward display of friendship. Of all the clans, the Setites reserve their greatest hate for their own kind: The Serpents of the Light, a small cult of Haitian Setites who broke away from the clan to join the Sabbat, are viewed as heretics and wiped out ruthlessly.

Setites tend to Embrace from among people who share an understanding of dark appetites and forbidden desire. Scholarship is highly prized in the clan, for only with the ancient lore of the earliest days can Set be found and awakened. Secrets of all manner are their stock in trade, and the vices that humiliate others are their best weapon. Those who partake of desire are naturally inclined to understand it, and so they form the basis of the clan's recruits. With time and education, Setites learn to weave webs of subtle deceit, drawing in ever more unwitting servants while plucking out the dirty secrets and lies that others try so carefully to bury.

Roleplaying Hints: You are a disciple of a dark god, and you must do your best to uphold that faith. None outside your clan will serve Set willingly, so it is your duty to ensnare them with their own weaknesses. By plying the illicit trades to support the hungers of others, you can gather their support and force them to pay for their needs — in deeds, in secrets or simply in "a few favors later." With such secrets and assistance, you can gather the knowledge necessary to raise Set, to enshroud the world in the darkness of your clan's grip and to cause all others, vampire or mortal, to bow before you.

Disciplines: *Obfuscate, Presence, Serpentis*

Advantage: The Followers of Set choose recruits with connections in the underworld, crime and politics. By preying on the weaknesses of influential and important individuals, the Setites turn them into allies, willing or otherwise. Every Setite thus has one bonus *Streetwise* Ability Trait and a level of *Political, Street* or *Underworld* Influence. The rare Followers who eschew such connections can still gather a modicum of aid from their clanmates, equivalent to the same Traits. The Setite philosophy, though Darwinian, stresses the need for the clan to cooperate in raising Set, so resources are shared (albeit begrudgingly).

Disadvantage: Just as Set was banished from Egypt into the darkness, so too do his followers hide in the shadows and the night. Setites are particularly sensitive to light, especially sunlight. Exposure to sunlight always inflicts an extra health level of damage on Setites. Even bright spotlights, flares or floodlights are uncomfortable, causing the Setite to suffer a one-Trait penalty on all challenges.

Bloodlines: Among the Followers, different philosophies divide the clan into sects that practice disparate methods of serving Set. Most Setites espouse the Path of Typhon, seeking occult knowledge to raise Set from his age-long sleep. A few work as martial students in Set's army; these "Serpent Warriors" study *Potence* instead of *Obfuscate*. Some Ecstatics indulge themselves in the pleasures of debauchery, and a small, heretical splinter sect affiliated more with *voudoun* than Egyptology, called the Serpents of the Light, claims allegiance with the Sabbat.

Gangrel

From the frozen northlands, the thick forests and icy mountains, the lands of vicious beasts and monsters come the Gangrel. By turns animalistic and insightful, they embody the most fearsome predators among vampires. From their kind come the tales of such horrors as Grendel and the Norse berserkers. The undisputed masters of the wild ways, the Gangrel are feared and respected for their unmatched prowess in survival. Some, it is whispered, even hunt or deal with the dread Lupines; certainly, their clan's shape-shifting powers and animal features bring to mind legends of dire wolves.

The history of the Gangrel is disputed. Some claim that they are descended from the same line as the Ravnos, while others insist that they are a separate clan (and, indeed, animosity between Gangrel and Ravnos is often quite fierce). For their part, the Gangrel put little stock in rumors. They trade stories when they meet, test their strength in combat and evade the machinations of politics. To the Gangrel, simple survival is more than enough.

Once a part of the Camarilla, the Gangrel seceded abruptly. Theories as to the reasons behind this departure abound; in their usual detachment, the Gangrel do not discuss the matter, however. This is not to say that all Gangrel are without affiliations — some remained in the Camarilla out of loyalty or friendship, while antitribu still claim allegiance in the Sabbat — it's simply that the clan as a whole no longer bothers with politics, after several centuries of Camarilla support. Naturally, this withdrawal makes Gangrel suspect in Camarilla courts, and without the support of a justicar or Inner Circle member, they can be subjected to political persecution — but few Gangrel really care.

Survivors, woodsmen and animal-lovers make up the ranks of the Gangrel clan, so it's no wonder that they have little use for political infighting or social maneuvering. Typically, a Gangrel watches a potential recruit for some time, judging the individual's ruggedness, determination and wanderlust. Those who fail the selection process are either ignored, or they become an evening meal. Those few who are chosen are Embraced and then left to fend for themselves. The Gangrel sire typically watches from afar, only intervening in dire situations and waiting until the new childe has proven her merit before introducing himself and undertaking the process of instruction.

Roleplaying Hints: You come from a long line of hardy explorers, both living and undead. In the Dark Ages, the Gangrel were Norsemen and warriors; in the modern age, you are still explorers, and you maintain the warrior spirit. You don't care about politics, or the Jyhad or sects, because they just don't matter to you. With all of eternity, who wants to waste immortality on foolish social maneuvering? There are new horizons to see and realms to conquer. The animals are your kind and your kingdom, and you give fealty only to those worthy of the warrior's heart.

Disciplines: *Animalism, Fortitude, Protean*

Advantage: While most vampires are uncomfortable outside of the cities, the Gangrel are hardy nomads, capable of survival in any territory. Although Lupines make travel dangerous for any Kindred, the Gangrel are better equipped than most to take to the open road or hide in the wilds outside of humanity's civilization. This wandering nature means that Gangrel hold to the requirements of any societies to which they may claim allegiance only rarely. Camarilla and Sabbat alike tend to give free rein to Gangrel wanderlust, and the sects rarely demand any sort of presentation or recognition. Few princes or bishops could really enforce a ban on the movements of the Gangrel in any case, so they rarely try.

The Gangrel are known to deal with the Lupines from time to time. Though any individual Gangrel probably risks much in confronting Lupines, most Gangrel at least know how to stay out of Lupine territory and what to do to avoid antagonizing the shapechanging killing machines. Gangrel who spend time in the wilds can learn *Lupine Lore* by observing (and hopefully evading) the Lupines. This fact doesn't grant that Lupines are any more favorably disposed toward Gangrel, but a Gangrel is more likely to know how to encounter a werewolf and survive.

All Gangrel gain a free level of Ability in each of *Animal Ken* and *Survival*.

Disadvantage: The marks of the Beast make themselves known on a Gangrel's visage. Whenever a Gangrel frenzies, she gains an animalistic feature. Further frenzies cause such features to become more pronounced, or introduce new features. Elder Gangrel often barely resemble humans, with cat- or doglike ears, sharp nails, tufts of fur, slitted eyes or stranger features. Each time the Gangrel frenzies, the character gains a new Negative Social Trait of *Bestial, Feral* or *Repugnant*. These Traits can never be bought off or removed without some sort of magical assistance (such as *Vicissitude* or *Obfuscate*). No more than five Negative Traits can be gained with this Disadvantage.

Bloodlines: Within the Sabbat exists a small urban group of predators known as the City Gangrel. These Gangrel trace their heritage to one of the two original Gangrel to join the sect, and they Embrace from among those who survive in the cities — criminals, street people, lower-class laborers and the like. The City Gangrel possess the Disciplines of *Celerity, Obfuscate* and *Protean*. Although they manifest the same weakness as the rest of the clan, they tend to feature animalistic traits from urban beasts, such as rats' whiskers, cat tails and the like.

Giovanni

The upstart Giovanni clan maintains a genteel exterior, dealing in matters of finance and internal family business. Of course, as with all vampires, their outward facade merely hides much worse. Rumored to have wrested their position from some clan now lost to antiquity, the Giovanni keep their small and secretive ties within their own family. Where there's money to be made, it's said, there's probably a Giovanni. However, the business dealings of the Necromancers hide their debauched dealings in the magics of the dead. The Giovanni traffic in mortal crime and politics more as a way to fulfill expected stereotypes. Underneath, they study hideous necromancy, indulge in debauched rituals and wallow in the wealth of an incestuous immortal family.

Elders whisper that the Giovanni were nothing more than an Italian merchant family of great ambition and perversity in the early Renaissance. Boredom with earthly pleasures led them to delve into necromancy. This study attracted the interest of an obscure branch of Cainites, who watched and guided the family's dabbling. In a surprising turnover, though, the head of the family managed to secure the Embrace from a now-forgotten Methuselah, and he finally stole the power of that ancient's blood. The foundling Necromancers banded together, Embracing only the most loyal members of their own family in order to protect themselves against the newly forming Camarilla and Sabbat, neither of which looked kindly on their usurpation. At length, they signed extensive treaties forbidding Giovanni involvement in Cainite politics, leaving them to their own devices in the practice of necromancy and the financial markets that they influenced.

Because of their ostensible neutrality, the Giovanni are sometimes called on to engage in business dealings that cut across sect lines. However, they are never trusted, and they are always watched carefully. After all, they have had centuries to perfect the art of the deal, and their ghostly spies are said to be everywhere. The Necromancers' patricidal origins hardly endear them to the other clans, so for the most part, they are left alone, treated as one might treat a dangerous and unpredictable beast. This wariness on the part of the other clans suits them just fine — the Giovanni have great plans, and the involvement of the other clans isn't among them. Like the brokers that they are, the Giovanni are willing to play either side, but ultimately their loyalty always lies within the family. Who'd betray a family that has as much use for you dead as undead?

Since their inception as a clan, the Giovanni have always been particular to Embrace from within their own family. Most commonly, this nepotism involves the Giovanni of Italian descent, but intermarriages over the years have brought different families into the fold. Only very rarely is someone of a minor family or side marriage ever inducted into the undead ranks. Undeath is a reward; the best businessmen and most studious scholars are granted eternity to work their skills on behalf of the family. Others may remain ghouls for eternity, or they may even stay mortals. The Giovanni are no strangers to power-brokering, infighting and influence-mongering — but, ultimately, it's one's value to the family and clan as a whole that determines suitability for eternity.

Roleplaying Hints: You're twice-related to a family of murderous, incestuous, nihilistic undead. What more could anyone want? You have the opportunity to earn massive wealth, exercise your will over the very souls of the dead and to exist forever. All you have to do is follow instructions when someone older in the family talks and avoid causing a political scene with those dumb-ass "Kindred" of the various sects. You're smooth, you're urbane, you're educated and you're in charge.

Disciplines: *Dominate, Necromancy, Potence*

Advantage: The insular Giovanni family lends its experience and financial control to all of its members. Those who manage the family's assets well are rewarded; those who fail serve in a more "spiritual" capacity. Giovanni characters start with an automatic Influence level in *Finance* or *Health*, and they can either take a further additional level in one of those Influences or else gain an automatic one Trait *Retainer* — a wraith. A ghostly *Retainer* cannot help with Influence or perform other functions in the physical world, but it is capable of spying and exerting some ghostly powers on behalf of its master (see **Oblivion**).

Disadvantage: The bite of a Giovanni holds no Kiss, only pain and terror. When a Giovanni uses the bite to feed, mortal victims are rendered insensible with pain (instead of ecstasy). Furthermore, blood drained with a bite inflicts an extra level of damage for each Blood Trait stolen. Note that this extra damage applies only to mortal victims, and only if the Giovanni bites to feed — a tearing, mauling attack bite used for battle inflicts no additional damage.

Bloodlines: Several prominent financial and occult families have found their way into the Giovanni fold. The sorcerous Pisanob hold sway over South and Central America, the "respectable" Milliners work in New England, the cannibalistic Dunsirn maintain banks in Scotland and England and the della Passaglia trade in the Far East. These families do not have different powers, but they indicate that the Giovanni family is more widespread than many Cainites believe. All Giovanni are loyal to the family alone — there are no *antitribu*, and those who attempt to rebel or flee are hunted down in short order.

Ravnos

Once a great clan like the other 12, the Ravnos have, in modern nights, been reduced to a shell of their former selves. The treacherous tricksters once walked randomly among the other Cainites, untrusted and beholden to no one. In a recent storm of madness and death, though, they have been slain and lost until they are but a shadow of their former ranks. No more than a few hundred now claim Ravnos lineage and the strange illusions and philosophies that come with it.

The Ravnos came originally from India, predating the exodus of the Gypsy peoples by a few centuries. At first misunderstood, they wandered from place to place, ignoring the strictures of Cainite society and bringing chaos with them. Many vampires wondered if the Ravnos were Cainites at all, due to their strange behavior, foreign beliefs and unusual Disciplines. As the Dark Ages passed and the Camarilla and Sabbat arose, the Ravnos changed little; they cared not for the beliefs of the Westerners. Instead, the Ravnos continued to spread their unique brand of illusions and mind-twisting treachery across Europe. By the modern age, they had become known well enough that any court would dread the arrival of a Ravnos, but they would never be barred from a city for fear of bringing down a horde of vengeful Deceivers.

Obviously, the charlatanry of the Ravnos grates on the other clans, yet none have bothered to move against the Deceivers. Perhaps it's because Ravnos solidarity ensures that any aggressor would suffer an excruciatingly annoying demise, or maybe it's just because the Ravnos aren't worth the time. For their part, the Ravnos seem to espouse a philosophy that places most Cainites somewhere below invertebrates on the karmic scale — to the Ravnos, the undead are without purpose in the greater scheme of things, and they must be taught properly (by tearing the veils of illusion from their eyes through lies, subterfuge and thievery) or destroyed. It is for this reason that the Ravnos spread discord in their wake: They hope that an enlightened few will awaken to their true purpose as heralds of change, while others may be slain and reincarnated into new roles.

During their heyday, the Ravnos most often brought in new recruits from the Gypsy families, mostly male. The diluting blood and customs of the modern age brought in a few more worldly recruits, and now that the Ravnos are scattered and few, they take potential childer where they can get them. Just about anyone with a keen wit can qualify for entry into the clan. Once regarded as buffoons, the Ravnos are now deadly serious. It seems that they may be the first casualties of an impending Gehenna.

Roleplaying Hints: It's not only the power of the illusions that you craft, but the voices that bubble in your blood. You are one of the few survivors of a world gone mad. *Svadharma* has taken hold of the Ravnos as a whole and spun them about, slaying many and leaving only a few to balance the wheel of karma. The world continues on a terrifying course to destruction, and there is no time left to save it. Perhaps all you can do now is survive, playing off greater forces while you hide and see what madness strikes next.

Disciplines: *Animalism, Chimerstry, Fortitude*

Advantage: The Ravnos tricksters, even those not of Romani blood, are expected to be chaotic whirlwinds of deception. Those who fall into their labyrinthine plots often blame themselves for their stupidity, and they would be too embarrassed to admit to their foolishness in any case. Thus, Ravnos can often get away with cons and deceptions that would land other Cainites in a great deal of trouble.

Since they all tend to practice various vices and move from city to city, all Ravnos gain one level of *Streetwise* Ability for free. They also have a level of *Street* Influence or *Transportation* Influence.

Disadvantage: Perhaps trickery runs in the blood, or maybe the Ravnos truly are harbingers of some greater chaos. Whatever the cause, all Ravnos suffer from a particular weakness for their own favored con games, scams and crimes. Each Ravnos has a particular "signature crime"; once each game session, the Ravnos must make an attempt to indulge in the particular vice, unless a test of *Self-Control/ Instinct* (difficulty of three Traits) can be made, with the usual risks for failed Virtue Tests.

Bloodlines: The Ravnos hail from several families of Gypsy stock. Different sorts of Ravnos thus have different capabilities. A Phuri Dae Ravnos learns *Auspex* instead of *Fortitude*; the Urmen learn *Chimerstry* more than any other Discipline, and the Vritra and Kalderash remain in India and the East, where they supposedly deal with the Cathayans. A few younger Ravnos — mostly *gorgio* — are found as *antitribu* in the Sabbat, but they are functionally similar to their independent cousins.

DEATH of AN ANTEDILUVIAN

One of the first signs of Gehenna, the Ravnos Antediluvian is rumored to have actually awakened from torpor. Supposedly, so the tale goes, the creature tore itself free from the lands of Pakistan, roaring its hunger as it sought to sate the thirst of ages on the blood of its kin. Ravnos across the world experienced spells of delusion, madness and uncontrollable *Chimerstry* as the terror fought its way through waiting opponents. At last, it was felled by the combined might of many assailants, though no two stories agree on the nature of its slayers.

On the one hand, it would appear that the Sabbat is right — the Antediluvians are indeed awakening, hungry to devour their childer. On the other hand, the Camarilla's Masquerade may be the only way to avoid the notice of forces powerful enough to slay an Antediluvian. A World of Darkness, indeed....

BLOODLINES

Outside the strictures of the 13 great clans and the two sects lie a small set of independent bloodlines. A bloodline is a minor lineage, tracing its distinctiveness to a founder of generation weaker than an Antediluvian, or whose birthright has long since been stolen. Found only in tiny numbers, the bloodlines pursue specialized interests that rarely come into confluence with either sect. Some can and do join sects — the Camarilla and Sabbat alike boast some members of the bloodlines — but in general, members of the bloodlines are rare enough to be unknown to most neonates and objects of curiosity to elders.

Without any formal protection of a sect or clan heritage, vampires of bloodlines often find themselves persecuted by the more "established" lines. Still, they rarely come into direct conflict, since their interests are usually esoteric enough to preclude interacting much with other Cainites. Most cities do not even boast a member of a bloodline; these vampires are rare, often reclusive and usually possessed of highly specialized agendas. Furthermore, the full extent of their powers and capabilities is usually unknown to other Cainites, so established Kindred are loath to risk themselves by antagonizing unknown quantities.

Ultimately, with the exceptions of a few individuals, the bloodlines are footnotes in the Jyhad.

DAUGHTERS OF CACOPHONY

The Daughters of Cacophony are a distinctly modern phenomenon, with none described in records before 1700. The Cainites of this talented bloodline espouse music and the voice as tools for the soul. Through their enchanting arts, they perform arias of exquisite beauty, sing verses of ethereal consistency and fire emotions in even undead hearts.

None can say where the Daughters of Cacophony began, and no one knows the name of their elusive founder. The Toreador and the Malkavian have been suggested as parent clans from time to time, with little substantive proof. Some scientifically minded Kindred claim that the Daughters diverged from their parent clan in antiquity due to their focused studies into song, while others speak of myths in which the bloodline's progenitor dealt with faeries or mermaids. The latter seems probable occasionally, as there is more than a hint of fey madness in the Daughters.

The Daughters of Cacophony seem to find the events of the Jyhad singularly uninteresting. These vampires spend their nights in practice and performance, trying to reach new pinnacles in their art. A few take the opportunity to perform for other Cainites, and their services are in great demand — though it is whispered that their arts can easily create terror and madness along with their inspiration. Most claim nominal membership in the Camarilla — finding the best patrons among that sect's ranks, and circumstances largely ideal for pursuing unlives in music — but sectarian considerations generally fall by the wayside. The music is all that matters.

Naturally, the Sirens Embrace only those females with musical and oratory talent. Every type of music and musician is represented in the ranks, from rotund opera divas to waiflike guitar-players to piano ingenues and even frontwomen of punk or jazz bands. However, they all share an inspired touch, a spark that strives for expression, even before the Embrace, and many are snatched away from the

mortal world and turned before they can achieve true mortal fame beyond their little-known careers. It is said that in the past, the Sirens allowed men in their ranks, in an even smaller bloodline called the Sons of Discord, but a recent vicious purge saw the destruction of all males (including castrati) in their ranks.

Roleplaying Hints: At the edge of your consciousness is a haunting song, the very music of the spheres. You can sense a spiritual state, the energy of creativity, that pushes itself through you and pulses in your otherwise still blood. Though your words and songs can strike listeners deaf, mad or dead, you care not — your Muse compels you. In short, you sing because you must. The music is all — blood, life and lover.

Disciplines: *Fortitude, Melpominee, Presence*

Advantage: At least one level of *Performance: Singing* is a requisite for Daughters, thus they get one for free at character creation. The Sirens often Embrace from talented or up-and-coming performers, so new inductees also have at least one level of *High Society* Influence or an additional level of the *Performance* Ability, as well.

Disadvantage: The constant throb of the Sirens' music plays through the minds of all Daughters of Cacophony, and a Siren is often deaf to all but her own music. As a result, in any test of perception, the Daughter suffers a two-Trait penalty on challenge resolution. No Daughter of Cacophony can ever have more than two perception-related Mental Traits.

SALUBRI

Of all Cainites, the Salubri are perhaps the most misunderstood. Billed as soul-eaters and infernalists, they are hunted wherever they go, cast out from vampiric society and reviled as monsters among monsters. Few Salubri remain in this age, for time and witch-hunts have conspired to destroy their past, their elders and their hopes.

Long ago, it is said, the Salubri were a true clan, led by an enigmatic Antediluvian. Somewhere in the past, their Antediluvian was destroyed and diablerized, his power stolen; with his death came the breaking of the Salubri. Once they were proud warriors and scholars in the Dark Ages, but with their leader's destruction they were forced to go underground, fleeing the persecution of the other clans, who perceived them as dangerous. Even today, those vampires who know of the Salubri consider them threats of the highest order, and only a rare few will knowingly give a Salubri aid or shelter. The Tremere in particular hold a special hatred for the Salubri, and they hunt them down at the merest rumor.

In truth, the Salubri are a line of healers and pacifists. Their founder, before his diablerie, disseminated the knowledge of special studies that he learned in the mystical East. Through these practices, the Salubri discovered ways to mend both flesh and spirit. The development of such insights is believed to lead to the development of a third eye in each Salubri's forehead, which most take pains to hide. Despite their persecution, the Salubri often remain gentle beings, concerned with the search for Golconda and the salvation of Kindred souls. They are still vampires, though, and predators. Woe betide the errant Tremere or unsuspecting mortal who takes a Salubri for a fool or weakling.

Salubri share a peculiar form of Embrace: Once the deed is done, the sire calls on the childe to diablerize her. None are certain where this practice came from; even the few Salubri asked aren't entirely certain, although some believe it may

have roots in an earlier time. Whatever the reason, the Tremere have been quick to add it to their arsenal of propaganda against the Salubri as infernalists.

Roleplaying Hints: Within your veins is the blood that heals; within your mind is the wisdom of centuries; within your spirit is the door to salvation. Vampires may be damned by their state, but you — and anyone with strength of character — can rise above that curse, learning to moderate man and beast in an understanding of your true nature. Through your arts, you learn to sense the wounds of flesh and spirit, to close the rifts that people set in their hearts and to bring about the end to suffering.

Disciplines: *Auspex, Fortitude, Obeah*

Advantage: Salubri are almost all of powerful generation; only a few elders survived the purge of their clan from the Dark Ages, and since each childe diablerizes her sire, there has been little thinning of the lineage. A Salubri receives two bonus Traits that she may put toward decreasing her generation. If the Salubri does not wish to decrease her generation, however the bonus Traits may not be used for anything else.

Disadvantage: The pacifistic nature of the Salubri precludes feeding on unwilling victims. A Salubri who takes blood from an unwilling or resisting victim automatically loses one temporary Willpower Trait immediately, and he must make a *Conscience/Conviction* Virtue Test with a difficulty of three Traits. Failing this test results in the usual loss of Humanity/Path Traits.

The Salubri are also a hunted clan, marked for death. Few neonates have heard of them, but those who hear about or actually meet a Salubri soon hear a litany of infernal crimes and accused misdeeds. The most dedicated enemies of the Salubri are the Tremere, who go out of their way to hunt and slay these vampires and who spread propaganda about the bloodline's supposed misdeeds.

SAMEDI

The Samedi are universally reviled as the most disgusting of Cainites, for all of them share a singular curse: Upon the Embrace, a Samedi becomes immortal like other vampires but he has only an imperfect preservation of the flesh. Some appear leathery and emaciated, like unwrapped mummies, while others look like corpses in various arrested stages of decay with a variety of noisome features — foul fluids oozing from tattered skin, rotted noses, death-rictus grins and sunken eyes.

The Samedi are a recent phenomenon, with none recorded as older than 250 years. The eldest, known only as the Baron, is said to lair in the Caribbean, where the line is said to have first appeared. The Giovanni are most often believed to be the parent clan of the bloodline, and indeed, enmity over some old wrong runs deep between the two groups. Occasionally rumors of Nosferatu involvement circulate, but neither group seems to give it great credence. For the most part, the Stiffs have little interest in sect politics beyond the good pay that princes or bishops fork out for Samedi skills as mercenaries or assassins.

The Stiffs Embrace rarely and then only from a small selection of candidates. Generally, the Samedi include those who find a fascination in the study of death and its physical processes. Morticians, existentialists, *houngans* and death cultists have all been inducted into their ranks. Candidates come from a wide range of races and social groups; the only real requirement seems to be an appreciation for death in all its forms.

Roleplaying Hints: Death comes to all things in time; it simply came to you in an unusual way. Life itself is defined by the fact that it ends. Such beginnings and endings are your passion: the animating moments of life, the pains that it endures and the moment that it succumbs. This quest is not so much a spiritual one as a drive to know *how* the process of creation and cessation works. By extension, you learn about the vampiric condition, the means by which life is extinguished and true death held at bay. You will see death in many forms, whether you are a simple witness or a delivering demon.

Disciplines: *Fortitude, Obfuscate, Thanatosis*

Advantage: With their strong connections to the process of death, combined with a tradition of dark spiritualism and insight, the Samedi have a significant knowledge of the shadowy Underworld and its ghostly denizens. Although they must pay the additional Experience Trait costs usual for non-clan Disciplines, Samedi can learn the *Necromancy* Discipline and its paths without need for a Giovanni instructor — a great number of the clan's members are necromancers *par excellence* without any traceable instruction. Samedi necromancers start with the *Sepulchre Path*, as usual, and most extend their insight rapidly to the *Bone Path*.

Disadvantage: Like the Nosferatu, the Samedi are physically repulsive in the extreme. When a Samedi's true form is apparent, the creature cannot initiate any Social Challenges except ones involving intimidation. No Samedi can possess the Social Traits of *Alluring*, *Gorgeous* or *Seductive*, and they all have the Negative Social Traits of *Repugnant* x 3 which can never be removed.

With Donata's influence, it was a simple matter to convince Kevin to return with her and Peter to the old loft where the next part of the plan could proceed. The uncomfortable union made its way out of the projects and closer to the uptown areas, near art galleries and museums. Peter finally parked in a nearby structure. Donata guided Peter and Kevin across the street and up a flight of stairs to studios in a historical building, above a busy restaurant.

Once in the studio, Donata shut and locked the door. Peter noted that most of the artistic furnishings were somewhat substandard. Doubtless, this tiny studio served only as a meeting ground, and not as a true haven. He made a mental note to check up on the ownership of the building anyway, while he removed a small vial and a lighter from his pocket.

Kevin turned to regard Peter as the lighter was flicked into operation. Donata remained an impassive mask, but Kevin flinched at the sudden glow of flame. With a tiny smirk, Peter applied the fire to the tips of candles on a large candelabrum. Donata waited, impatient, as Peter unscrewed the lid of the vial, daubing tiny amounts of the bloody contents on his fingers.

"This will settle matters. Nobody will be able to confirm anything out of Kristof, and that simply leaves Warburton to take all of the blame," Peter said in a reverential whisper. *And*, he thought to himself, *when the sheriff finds the paraphernalia in Donata's property, she'll take the fall for Kristof's death.*

Now simultaneously entranced and repulsed by the flame, Kevin watched the unfamiliar proceedings, eyes flicking occasionally to regard the impassive Donata.

Peter closed his eyes and traced a slow circle in the air, then steeled himself as he passed his fingers through the flame. Tiny wisps of smoke rose from the fire, and the blood on his fingers vaporized, but he held his hand steady, his dry, dead flesh resisting the hungry heat. Peter knew better than to push his luck, though, and withdrew his hand as quickly as possible, opening his eyes.

The flame danced a merry yellow on the candles.

Donata snarled with disgust. "You idiot! You fouled it up!" she spat at Peter, who tried to puzzle out his failure.

"I did it just as the Warlock instructed. He said to make that symbol, to burn the blood, and that all of the enchantments he'd placed on it would be released, that it would consume Kristof!" Peter shouted in retort.

Kevin bared his fangs, hissing angrily at Peter. "That was your plan? Leave the damn spells to the Warlocks!"

Peter shook his head slowly. "No, I studied this... it should have worked."

"Unless that Tremere double-crossed us!" growled Donata.

"Or unless he were killed before his magic were released," Peter mused. "I'd better check on him. If he betrayed us, I'll take care of him myself. If he's dead, then someone's ahead of us. Either way, this business is now personal."

Donata and Kevin watched Peter, frowning, as he left in a hurry.

CHAPTER THREE: CHARACTER CREATION AND TRAITS

Without characters, there can be no game. Each player takes on the role of a character, a persona within the context of the game. To guarantee that all players use the same potentials and capabilities for their characters, the rules of **Mind's Eye Theatre** provide a single simple set of guidelines for character creation.

QUICK CHARACTER CREATION PROCESS

- Step One: Inspiration — Who are you?
- — Choose a concept
- — Choose a clan
- — Choose a Nature and a Demeanor
- — Choose a Morality Path
- Step Two: Attributes — What are your basic capabilities?
- — Prioritize Attributes (seven primary, five secondary and three tertiary)
- — Choose Traits
- Step Three: Advantages — What do you know?
- — Choose five Abilities
- — Choose three Basic Disciplines (four for Sabbat)
- — Choose five Backgrounds (none for Sabbat)
- Step Four: Last Touches — Fill in the details.
- — Assign Blood Traits
- — Assign Willpower Traits
- — Assign Virtue Traits
- — Choose Negative Traits and Flaws (if any)
- — Choose a Derangement (if desired)
- — Spend five (or more) Free Traits and choose Merits (if any)
- Step Five: Spark of Life — Narrative descriptions

STEP ONE: INSPIRATION

Arguably the most important step in character creation is the formation of the basic concept. Every vampire was once a normal human, after all, with hopes, fears, dreams and ambitions. Once Embraced, the character brings her particular views to her new unlife. These strengths and weaknesses shape the character's Traits, capabilities and limitations.

The first step in creating a character is to come up with a basic idea of the person. This initial concept can usually be summed up in a single word — scholar, drifter, dilettante, laborer, whatever. Don't worry about details now; think more in terms of broad brushstrokes. Create the *person*, before you create the vampire.

CLAN

With a base concept in mind, determine your character's clan. An artistically inclined mortal, for instance, is likely to be Embraced as a Toreador; a businessman from European stock could be a Ventrue. It's fine to break stereotypes, of course, but the initial concept, even if it does not determine clan, will shape a character's outlook to her own clan (and others).

The choice of clan influences a character's development heavily. The clan determines the sorts of goals and accomplishments for which the character will be lauded in Cainite society, and the expectations to which she will be held. The clan also determines the sorts of Disciplines, strengths and weaknesses innate to the character. Note that some clans or bloodlines are more rare than others, and the Storyteller may very well restrict access to some — not every city will have a population of Lasombra *antitribu* or Daughters of Cacophony, after all.

If no clan strikes a particular chord, a character can always be Caitiff — bereft of any known clan and possessed of an eclectic assortment of Disciplines — but these vampires are almost uniformly weak of blood, higher in generation and limited in Cainite standing.

NATURE AND DEMEANOR

To define a character's personality, choose a particular Archetype. Each Archetype lists an underlying motivation, a reason for a character to behave in specific ways. The Archetypes described here are, by no means, the final list of personalities; Storytellers can suggest and approve any further numbers of Archetypes.

A character's Nature is her inner-most persona, the true basis of her motives. Though many people bury their desires behind facades, the drives of the Nature often shine through.

THE CLANS

• Assamites — (Independent) Dreaded Assassins from the Middle East, the Assamites hunt other Cainites for vitae and study powers of silent death.

Disciplines: *Celerity, Obfuscate, Quietus*

• Brujah — (Camarilla) Ideological revolutionaries and rebels, the Rabble serve their causes with passion.

Disciplines: *Celerity, Potence, Presence*

• Followers of Set — (Independent) Distrust and suspicion follow the Serpents in their quest for forbidden knowledge and service to a sleeping god.

Disciplines: *Obfuscate, Presence, Serpentis*

• Gangrel — (Independent) No city holds sway over the Outlanders, who wander the wilderness and survive as vampiric predators among animals.

Disciplines: *Animalism, Fortitude, Protean*

• Giovanni — (Independent) The Necromancers keep a veneer of businesslike respectability over their family's dark practices.

Disciplines: *Dominate, Necromancy, Potence*

• Lasombra — (Sabbat) The majestic and terrible Keepers control spiritual darkness itself in seeking to manipulate mortal and undead societies.

Disciplines: *Dominate, Obtenebration, Potence*

• Malkavians — (Camarilla) The deranged Lunatics claim a fractured insight into the workings of reality.

Disciplines: *Auspex, Dementation, Obfuscate*

• Nosferatu — (Camarilla) The hideous curse of blood warps the physical visage of each of the Sewer Rats, but others respect and fear their mastery of hidden byways and secret-gathering.

Disciplines: *Animalism, Obfuscate, Potence*

• Ravnos — (Independent) Claiming kinship to Gypsies, the wandering Deceivers hail from India with power over illusions.

Disciplines: *Animalism, Chimerstry, Fortitude*

• Toreador — (Camarilla) Protectors of culture and promoters of art make up the Degenerates, but they also include sycophants and pleasure-seekers in their ranks.

Disciplines: *Auspex, Celerity, Presence*

• Tremere — (Camarilla) Ruthless and insular, the Warlocks and their potent blood magic are untrusted, but grudgingly respected.

Disciplines: *Auspex, Dominate, Thaumaturgy*

• Tzimisce — (Sabbat) Hailing from Eastern Europe, the inhuman Fiends study mortal and vampire alike with clinical coldness and utter ruthlessness.

Disciplines: *Animalism, Auspex, Vicissitude*

• Ventrue — (Camarilla) Rulers of board room and battlefield, the Blue Bloods lead other Kindred as their right and responsibility.

Disciplines: *Dominate, Fortitude, Presence*

Since the character's Nature is a result of her upbringing and life experiences, Nature changes rarely. It takes extraordinary events to cause someone to change Natures.

By contrast, the Demeanor is the public face, the one a character shows to everyone else. Even if radically at odds with the character's Nature, the Demeanor provides a convenient mask against intrusion. Demeanors are subject to change at whim; some characters may change Demeanors like some people change socks, while others may choose a single face to present to the world. On occasion, Nature and Demeanor may be the same, but few individuals are so open, especially in Kindred society.

ARCHETYPES

Architect, Autocrat, Bon Vivant, Bravo, Caregiver, Celebrant, Child, Competitor, Conformist, Conniver, Curmudgeon, Deviant, Director, Fanatic, Gallant, Judge, Loner, Martyr, Masochist, Monster, Pedagogue, Penitent, Perfectionist, Rebel, Rogue, Survivor, Thrill-Seeker, Traditionalist, Trickster, Visionary

MORALITY PATHS

Every vampire struggles with the Beast Within, the predatorial drive of hunger that pushes Cainites to acts of fury, desperation and horror. Only by clinging to a moral compass — a philosophical ground to stand against the ravages of amorality — can a vampire resist the slide into total depravity.

Most vampires cling to a semblance of their human morality, repressing their monstrous urges. The vicious politics of Cainite society take an inevitable toll, though. Similarly, the ravages of uncontrollable frenzy, combined with the vampire's alienation from humanity, push many to terrible deeds. Only through strong will and determined control can a vampire resist losing the last shreds of humanity as centuries of ennui erode the vestiges of mortal feeling. A few even take to inhuman codes, seeking balance through constructed vampire ethics. Regardless, many fail to hold to their ethics *well*, instead sliding into amorality driven by their hungers.

The majority of new vampire characters choose Humanity for their morality. Neonates cling to the memories of their human existences, seeking to reconcile their consciences with their new bloodthirst. Often, many of them are unaware of any other choices. Only a vampire of extreme determination takes to one of the Paths of Enlightenment, a created code of vampire behavior.

At this step in character creation, decide on a form of morality for the character: Humanity or a Path of Enlightenment. Traits will be assigned later. The important step is to determine how the character holds onto sanity against the relentless Beast. Most vampires default to Humanity.

This chart lists the Paths of Enlightenment common to vampires of many sects or independent loyalty, and it also shows the Virtues espoused by each Path.

• Humanity — The default morals of mortal life include: Avoid killing, stealing or hurting; try to help others, or at least live without impacting others overmuch. Most vampires follow Humanity, even though many fail to uphold very much Humanity after a few decades or centuries. (*Conscience, Self-Control*)

• The Path of Blood — (Assamite) A means to redemption through the teachings of Haqim, founder of the Assamites. Vampires on the Path of Blood hunt and kill in the holy quest to ascend to the level of Haqim. (*Conviction, Self-Control*)

• The Path of Bones — (Giovanni, Samedi) This Path espouses the study of physical death and the transformation of the body from life to death or undeath. A follower of this Path seeks an understanding of death and what lies beyond it, whether Cainite existence or that of a ghost. (*Conviction, Self-Control*)

• The Path of Metamorphosis — (Tzimisce) The science of the Slavic Fiends in their search for a higher form of existence expresses itself through this Path. As vampires are above mortals, the followers of this Path believe that a higher consciousness awaits beyond vampirism. (*Conviction, Instinct*)

• The Path of Night — (Lasombra) This hideous Path delves into the vampire's existence as a tool for showcasing evil and serving the needs of the darkness that created him. (*Conviction, Instinct*)

• The Path of Paradox — (Ravnos) This Path teaches that the material world is illusion, and that each individual must find his own place in the cycle of existence. Followers of this Path delve into riddles and puzzles to seek the underlying fates of all beings. (*Conviction, Self-Control*)

• The Path of Typhon — (Followers of Set) The Setites hope to raise their dark god, and they use hidden knowledge and forbidden wisdom as their tools in binding others to this end. (*Conviction, Self-Control*)

The Sabbat also teaches certain other Paths, but such Paths are reserved for their savage children and not for vampires of the Camarilla or independent clans.

Paths of Enlightenment are advanced moral codes. They espouse an utterly alien viewpoint, with little grounding in anything resembling human morality. These are best played by experienced players. Consult a Storyteller before choosing a Path.

STEP TWO: ATTRIBUTES

Natural capabilities use Attributes for descriptions. Every character has certain innate qualities. Attributes describe these qualities, marking a character's particular areas of intrinsic talent.

CHOOSING ATTRIBUTES

Each character has areas of modest skill and other areas of excellence. You determine your character's natural talents, selecting whether your character is to be physically adroit, mentally agile or socially adept. The character's concept should guide these choices, so a mountaineer is likely to be physically exceptional while a bookish historian probably has more mental development than social.

• Physical Attributes measure your character's general health, stamina, agility and power. A character with modest Physical Attributes is probably not very athletic, while a character with high Physical Attributes is exceptionally strong, dexterous or tough.

• Social Attributes determine the force of a character's personality and ability to interact well with others. If your character has few Social Traits, she may be awkward, shy or just plain-looking. A socially potent character is attractive, compelling or smooth.

• Mental Attributes help in problem-solving, learning, deduction and general alertness. With limited Mental attributes, a character is not particularly well-educated, quick-thinking or perceptive. A strongly Mental character is conversely attentive, logical or intuitive.

Choose the priority of your character's attributes. Each character is stronger in some areas than in others, at least at first. Obviously, clan and concept shape these attributes to some degree, but only a broad outline is needed in this step.

Choosing Traits

Once you've decided on your character's inherent strengths, you should describe exactly the sorts of exceptional characteristics he possesses. In your primary area of attribute development, choose seven Traits; in your secondary, choose five; in your tertiary area, select three Traits. Traits are adjectives describing the character, just like the descriptions in a novel or play. Thus, a Mentally focused character might be more *Intuitive* than *Rational*, or a strong Physical character could be *Brawny* and *Tough* but not very *Quick* or *Nimble*.

A complete list of Traits starts on p. 80. Pick Traits that describe your character as if you wanted to write down the particular qualities of the individual. You can pick a particular Trait multiple times, if you like, to denote spectacular depth in an area.

Step Three: Advantages

No character begins play unformed and without education. The skills and training picked up in the course of life, and the friends made among various fields of work, all gift a character with special resources. Furthermore, vampiric powers, called Disciplines, flow from the blood of all Cainites, granting them superhuman capabilities. Collectively, these advantages are learned or developed benefits not inherent to one's raw potential.

Advantages are divided into several categories. Abilities represent skills or training, allowing characters to perform tasks. Backgrounds are connections among the mortal and immortal communities, representing such diverse facets as friends, social standing or Cainite sponsors. Disciplines are the powers of the blood, the finely honed endowments that come with the Curse. Lastly, Virtues represent a character's strength of moral behavior, defining how well a particular vampire comports himself and holds to his ethics in the face of the Beast.

Choosing Abilities

Select five Abilities that represent your character's education and training. Whether learned in mortal days or honed after death, Abilities set apart your character by letting her attempt tasks that less skilled compatriots cannot understand or complete. You can choose

---

Attributes

• **Physical Traits:** *Agile, Brawny, Brutal, Dexterous, Enduring, Energetic, Ferocious, Graceful, Lithe, Nimble, Quick, Resilient, Robust, Rugged, Stalwart, Steady, Tenacious, Tireless, Tough, Vigorous, Wiry*

• **Social Traits:** *Alluring, Beguiling, Charismatic, Charming, Commanding, Dignified, Diplomatic, Elegant, Eloquent, Empathetic, Expressive, Friendly, Genial, Gorgeous, Ingratiating, Intimidating, Magnetic, Persuasive, Seductive, Witty*

• **Mental Traits:** *Astute, Attentive, Clever, Creative, Cunning, Dedicated, Determined, Discerning, Disciplined, Insightful, Intuitive, Knowledgeable, Observant, Patient, Rational, Reflective, Shrewd, Vigilant, Wily, Wise*

ABILITIES

Academics, Alertness, Animal Ken, Athletics, Brawl, Computer, Crafts, Dodge, Drive, Empathy, Etiquette, Expression, Finance, Firearms, Hobby/ Professional/ Expert Ability, Intimidation, Investigation, Law, Leadership, Linguistics, Medicine, Melee, Occult, Performance, Politics, Repair, Science, Security, Stealth, Streetwise, Subterfuge, Survival

an Ability multiple times, if desired, to show greater expertise. A complete list of Abilities starts on p. 85. Note that some Abilities may be restricted by your Storyteller.

CHOOSING DISCIPLINES

Select three Basic Disciplines for your vampire character. You must select them in the order listed (that is, you must take the first Basic level before taking the second Basic level in any given Discipline), and you can only take the Basic levels at this time. These Disciplines must come from your clan's specialty Disciplines. If you are Caitiff, you may simply choose any three Basic Disciplines desired, but your Storyteller may restrict you to the eight most common Disciplines — *Animalism, Auspex, Celerity, Dominate, Fortitude, Obfuscate, Potence* or *Presence* — unless you have an exceptional reason for learning a more specialized power.

A complete list of Disciplines starts on p. 132. See the previous table for a quick list of your clan's specialty Disciplines.

Sabbat characters begin play with four Basic Disciplines.

CHOOSING BACKGROUNDS

You may take five Background Traits for your vampire. Each Background represents a tie to a particular agency, organization or resource, whether mortal or Cainite. You can have up to five Traits in any Background, though your Storyteller may prohibit certain Backgrounds based on your concept, and most Storytellers will scrutinize any Background above three Traits heavily.

Background descriptions start on p. 93.

Sabbat characters do not begin play with any Backgrounds — they must expend Free Traits to take Backgrounds.

STEP FOUR: LAST TOUCHES

The final character Traits come together once concept, clan, Attributes and advantages are chosen. Your last touches include Blood Traits, Willpower Traits, Morality Traits and Virtue Traits.

BLOOD TRAITS

Each vampire has a certain number of Blood Traits, or vitae. This blood can be used for a variety of different tasks, from temporarily improving one's physical prowess to healing wounds to powering Disciplines. You can hold a number of Blood Traits determined by your generation, as shown on p. 95. This number is modified by any clan disadvantages or Flaws that you may have relating to feeding, and it can be improved by the *Herd* Background (see p. 96).

WILLPOWER TRAITS

When all other avenues are exhausted, your Willpower measures your innate drive for self-preservation, your sense of mental fortitude and your ability to resist temptation and defeat. You can use Willpower Traits for a variety of tasks, like redoubling your efforts in a task or resisting supernatural coercion.

You come into play with a number of Willpower Traits dependent on your generation. The generation table on p. 95 shows your starting permanent Will-

QUICK DISCIPLINES

- *Animalism* — Communion with and control over natural animals, through the Beast.
- *Auspex* — Incredible sensory acuity, even extending to psychic sensitivity.
- *Celerity* — Superhuman speed granted by the power of blood.
- *Chimerstry* — The Ravnos gift of crafting illusions and hallucinations.
- *Dementation* — The Malkavian ability to catalyze madness and spread the gift of insanity.
- *Dominate* — Control of minds through piercing gaze and strong will.
- *Fortitude* — Resilience against even the forces that normally injure vampires.
- *Melpominee* — The Daughters of Cacophony manipulate their voices to madden or inspire their listeners with this power.
- *Necromancy*—Commerce with and power over the spirits of the dead. The *Sepulchre Path* communicates with ghosts; the *Bone Path* deals with corpses; the *Ash Path* sees across the barriers of death and manipulates the lands of the dead.
- *Obeah*— This little-understood power of the Salubri allows them to shelter and heal the injured, whether in body or mind.
- *Obfuscate* — Concealment through tricking the minds of onlookers.
- *Obtenebration* — Manipulation of tangible, soul-smothering darkness is the province of the Lasombra.
- *Potence* — Incredible strength, beyond even the unfaltering might of dead limbs.
- *Presence* — Unnatural charisma and ability to sway emotions.
- *Protean* — Shapeshifting and wilderness survival in primal forms, specific to the Gangrel.
- *Quietus* — The Assamites have learned to manipulate blood to bring silent, poisonous death.
- *Serpentis* — The Setites' Discipline of reptilian transformation from Egyptian legend.
- *Thanatosis* — The Samedi's control of the processes of death and decay.
- *Thaumaturgy* — Tremere blood magic exercised through the will over vitae. The *Path of Blood* controls Cainite vitae; *The Lure of Flames* summons unnatural fire; *Movement of the Mind* controls objects telekinetically; the *Path of Conjuring* allows a caster to pull objects from thin air.
- *Vicissitude* — This art and craft of shaping flesh and bone like clay is known to the Tzimisce.

power, indicating how many Willpower Traits you have. The maximum Willpower listing shows the highest rating that your Willpower can reach. You may choose to have a card for each Trait of Willpower you possess, and you must turn the card over to a Narrator or Storyteller when you expend Willpower.

VIRTUE TRAITS

Every vampire must resist the temptation to "sin" in some fashion. Virtue Traits are the spiritual endurance with which a character fights against the talons of the Beast.

Virtue Traits come in three categories: *Conscience/ Conviction* Traits, *Self-Control/ Instinct* Traits and *Courage* Traits. You get seven Traits to split among these categories. Each category must range from one to five total Traits.

Your *Conscience/Conviction* is your degree of adherence to your chosen morality. If you have many Traits here, you feel remorse for your evil deeds (or you refuse to be bowed by concern for such), thus preventing the Beast from eroding your morality.

Self-Control/ Instinct Traits represent the ability to guide or resist frenzy. High Traits in this category help to fight off berserk rage or hunger.

Courage Traits battle against Rötschreck, the Red Fear. With many *Courage* Traits, you can withstand the terror of fire or sunlight.

The Virtue Traits that you possess depend on your chosen morality. You always start with one free Trait in *Courage*, and if you have *Conscience* or *Self-Control*, you start with one free Trait in each of those. Characters with *Conviction* or *Instinct* have thrown away their more human drives in favor of vampire ethics, but this effort means that you get no free Traits in the appropriate Virtue (so you must assign at least one of your seven Virtue Traits there). See the quick listing of morality for a summation of the Virtues prized by each Path. More complete descriptions of the Virtues and Virtue Tests appear on p. 108.

MORALITY TRAITS

While your Virtue Traits represent your ability to hold off against the Beast, your Morality Traits show how closely you adhere to your chosen codes of ethics. A high rating in your Morality Traits indicates that you set high standards for yourself, but you risk losing ground to the Beast even with relatively trivial violations of your chosen morals. Low Morality Traits indicate that you are close to losing control to the Beast forever.

Your starting Morality Trait total equals the average of your *Conscience/ Conviction* and *Self-Control/ Instinct* Traits, rounded up. Thus, you have a Morality rating from one to five Traits. Your number of Morality Traits determines how well you avoid some of the problems associated with the bestial nature of vampires (such as staying awake during the day, rising from torpor and dealing with mortals), but it also indicates what circumstances call for a test of Virtue.

During character creation, you may choose to lose one Morality Trait in exchange for gaining two Free Traits. You may do so only once — losing a Morality Trait counts as taking two Negative Traits. Be warned though, that doing so is a dangerous course; a low Morality Trait total practically guarantees eventual disintegration into the Wassail, the final frenzy.

NEGATIVE TRAITS

Some characters have particular weaknesses or shortcomings. Others just never developed in some fashion, or suffered injuries that set back otherwise strong attributes.

BACKGROUNDS

- *Allies* — Mortal confederates and aides.
- *Contacts* — Sources of reliable information.
- *Fame* — Outstanding reputation in mortal society.
- *Generation* — Potency of one's blood and closeness to the power of Caine, the first vampire. Available only with Storyteller approval.
- *Herd* — Mortal followers or thralls who provide easy access to blood.
- *Influence* — Sway over the institutions of mortal society in any number of areas: *Bureaucracy, Church, Finance, Health, High Society, Industry, Legal, Media, Occult, Police, Political, Street, Transportation, Underworld* or *University*.
- *Mentor* — An older or more experienced Cainite instructor and patron.
- *Resources* — Material wealth and access to ready cash.
- *Retainers* — Loyal servants who oversee projects and property.

Such hindrances are represented with Negative Traits. Though Negative Traits are not required, they can represent a deficiency or injury in your character.

Since few people actually want to play a character with handicaps and problems, Negative Traits grant bonuses in other areas of character creation. Each Negative Trait taken is good for one Free Trait later. You may take up to five Negative Traits, though you should not take more than three Negative Traits in any one attribute category.

Unlike other Attributes, you should only take Negative Traits from the list here. Although there are certainly other adjectives that would appropriately describe a character's drawbacks, nobody can be expected to guess a Trait that isn't covered in the rules.

Remember to take Negative Traits that you can roleplay accurately and well. The Storyteller may force you to "buy off" Negative Traits that you ignore consistently.

A complete listing of Negative Traits, and how they affect play, begins on p. 81.

DERANGEMENTS

In addition to Negative Traits, you can choose derangements for your character. A derangement represents some sort of mental instability or neurotic behavior. Taking a derangement counts as two Negative Traits and thus grants you two Free Traits, but you can only take one derangement at character creation (or one extra, in the case of Malkavians, who all start with one). Be warned, derangements cause unpredictable and uncontrollable behavior at times, and a Storyteller is justified in asking you to "buy off" any derangement that you do not roleplay accurately.

Remember that playing a derangement is an exercise in advanced roleplaying. Insanity is neither humorous nor light. You should always consult your Storyteller before deciding to take a derangement.

CHOOSING FLAWS

Representing specific deficiencies or drawbacks aside from inherent weaknesses common to many people, Flaws showcase particular problems. As with Negative Traits, Flaws grant additional Traits to the user. Each Flaw is rated in terms of its value, ranging from one to seven Traits. The higher the value, the more debilitating the Flaw. A character may total up to seven Traits of Flaws. Elder vampires may have more Flaws; after all, age takes its toll.

Flaws begin on p. 112, with the listings for Merits and Flaws.

FREE TRAITS

Because no two Cainites are alike, each character gets an allotment of Free Traits to spend on any area of development desired. If you want your character to be socially adept but also intelligent, for instance, you can use Free Traits to improve your Attributes so that you have a high number of Traits in both categories. You could decide to use Free Traits for extra Backgrounds if your character has strong mortal connections, or for Disciplines if she has studied her vampiric powers especially well.

Each character gets five Free Traits at this stage. Additional Free Traits are earned from Negative Traits, Flaws or Derangements taken earlier, or by removing Morality Traits. One Negative Trait grants a single Free Trait. A derangement or Morality Trait is worth two Bonus Traits, and Flaws have variable values listed individually.

• One Free Trait can be spent to take an additional Attribute Trait.

• One Free Trait allows for an additional Ability Trait.

• A single Free Trait allows you to declare a specialization in one Ability Trait. Remember that each Ability can only have one specialization.

• One Free Trait converts to an additional Background Trait, though subject to normal Storyteller approval.

- Two Free Traits can be used for an extra Virtue Trait. Raising Virtues in this fashion does affect total Morality Traits.
- Three Free Traits can be spent for a Morality Trait.
- Three Free Traits allow for an extra Willpower Trait, subject to generational limits.
- Three Free Traits can be used to purchase the Basic level of *any* one Discipline, in the usual progression, subject to Storyteller approval.
- Merits have a variable Free Trait cost, dependent on the individual Merit.

CHOOSING MERITS

The antithesis of Flaws, Merits represent special bonuses and capabilities beyond the norm. Each Merit is rated in terms of its Trait value. To take a Merit, you must expend Free Traits equal to the Merit's value. You can take no more than seven Traits of Merits, total (though some older vampires may have more).

Merits start on p. 112, with the Merits and Flaws section.

STEP FIVE: SPARK OF LIFE

Your character is more than a summation of Traits and adjectives. At this stage, take the concepts that you've emphasized and develop a story for your character. Look for explanations to why the character learned certain things, failed in others and developed as she did. Think about the sort of person that you're playing and the motives of the individual.

- Background — Think about the mortal life from which your character came. Where and when were you born? How were you raised? What sort of education did you have, if any? Did you have any particularly spectacular successes, failures, romances or businesses?
- Secrets — Secrets are one of the major commodities of Cainite society. Do you have any secret regrets? Hopes? Ambitions? Do you know something that you shouldn't?
- Motivations — Figure out why your character interacts with other Cainites and deals with vampire society. Do you seek personal gain? Are you hunting someone or running from persecution? Perhaps you want to impress your sire or find a companion. If you have trouble figuring out why your character would show up in the game, ask a Narrator or Storyteller for a couple of possible motives.
- Appearance — The Embrace often wreaks changes on the body, whether to imbue it with the grace and beauty of a predator or to twist into some strange visage. How he stands, walks, holds a cigarette or dresses will be one of the things that other characters will remember him by.

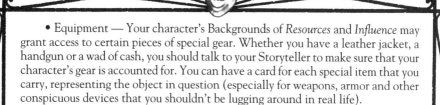

- Equipment — Your character's Backgrounds of *Resources* and *Influence* may grant access to certain pieces of special gear. Whether you have a leather jacket, a handgun or a wad of cash, you should talk to your Storyteller to make sure that your character's gear is accounted for. You can have a card for each special item that you carry, representing the object in question (especially for weapons, armor and other conspicuous devices that you shouldn't be lugging around in real life).

- Quirks — Everybody has distinctive behaviors. Anything from a habit of saying "Great Caine!" to playing with a ponytail — such mannerisms show off your character's uniqueness. A quirk can even be used to distinguish you when in disguise or using Disciplines to possess another body — or you could copy someone else's quirks.

ARCHETYPES

Each Archetype describes an essential form of personality. Though a character is more than a simple set of drives, an Archetype provides a basic springboard from which the character's motives and behaviors can develop. An archetypal Nature shows the underlying elements making up a personality, while archetypal Demeanor is the face the character shows to the world around him.

In game play, a character's Nature Archetype serves to provide concrete goals and codes of behavior, which means that a character can call for a retest on a Virtue Test automatically if a frenzy would violate the character's Nature. However, if someone discovers your character's Nature, it can be used against you in the same way a Negative Trait might be, forcing you into a challenge.

Example: *Ian, a Malkavian with a Fanatic Nature and a fervent hatred of the Sabbat, is leading five other Kindred against a marauding pack. One of the pack brandishes a Molotov cocktail at Ian, who tests for frenzy and fails. However, Ian's player calls for a retest based on Ian's Nature — he's too driven to let some shovelhead punk fresh out of the ground try to scare him with a cheap tactic. The player makes a second test and wins. Ian pauses only for a moment at the sight of the Molotov before launching himself at the startled pack member.*

Later, Ian is wounded and winded, and the prince asks him to lead another charge. Ian is in no shape to do so, and he refuses. The prince commands him angrily: "I am your prince and too Commanding for you to refuse." The prince then adds, "You're too much of a Fanatic, Ian, to let these rabble run unchecked through the city." The prince's player calls for a Social Challenge, and because he guessed Ian's Nature correctly, Ian's player must advance two Traits. The challenge is made, and Ian loses. Wearily, the Lunatic rises to his feet and prepares for the next assault.

- Architect — You hope to leave a lasting legacy, to build something for the future.

- Autocrat — You want to take charge, since nobody else can do the job right.

- Bon Vivant — Only a good time can assuage your otherwise empty existence.

- Bravo — Other people only get in your way of doing things, and you do not hesitate to bully them into line.

- Caregiver — You protect and comfort others.

- Celebrant — You find that joy springs from your overriding passion.

- Child — You need others to nurture and help you.

- Competitor — Everything is a contest, and you plan to win.

- Conformist — You take the lead and the cues from someone else, letting others handle the responsibility.

- Conniver — There's no point to doing it yourself when you can get someone else to put in the effort.

- Curmudgeon — Nothing's perfect, everything sucks and you're going to make sure that everybody knows it.

- Deviant — Normal? What's that? You have no use for social norms and mores.
- Director — You feel an overriding need to impose order.
- Fanatic — One cause, one truth, one purpose — you serve and proselytize with absolute conviction.
- Gallant — Everything you do is geared toward flamboyance and excess, since you need the attentions of those around you.
- Judge — You have a deep sense of right and wrong, and you seek justice measured by your principles.
- Loner —You just don't belong, either by choice or by nature.
- Martyr —Everyone benefits when you shoulder the burdens of your ideals.
- Masochist — You test yourself through suffering, and find meaning in enduring pain.
- Monster — Build your purpose from a malignant drive to showcase evil through your actions.
- Pedagogue — Everyone can learn from your example and experiences; you were born to teach others.
- Penitent — You have sinned, and you cannot rest until you atone for it.
- Perfectionist — You do everything with wholehearted zeal aimed at immaculate completion. There's no excuse for flawed efforts.
- Rebel — Whether from habit or drive, you lash out at the system and try to break it down.
- Rogue — First and foremost, you look out for number one.
- Survivor — Nothing stops you, for your drive to pull through is indomitable.
- Thrill-Seeker — You're always after the next high, by pushing danger to the edge.
- Traditionalist — The old ways are the best ways, so you preserve and protect them.
- Trickster — Existence is absurd, so you fill it with humor and irreverence to avoid looking too deeply at the pain.
- Visionary — A goal fills your mind, and your dreams bring faith to others.

Morality Paths

The Embrace strips a fledgling vampire of all ties to life and humanity. Turned into an animated mockery of life that subsists on the blood of others, the new vampire can only hope to hang onto some memory of mortal morality. The feelings of compassion, the ineffable tie to life, trust and love are all cast aside by a curse that separates the vampire from the rest of humanity. With all human drives and desires twisted into a raging Beast that demands survival at any cost, only a code of morality stands between the Cainite and utter animalistic insanity.

Most vampires, thrust suddenly into undead society, cling to the trappings of their mortal lives. This Humanity guides vampires to control their urges and to hang on to the shadows of their former consciences. Indeed, many vampires, suddenly terrified by the Hunger, hold themselves to higher standards in death than in life. However, as the ages pass, emotions fade and Cainites become jaded, their Humanity flickering like a dying candle. The Humanity of the most ancient of elders hangs only by a thread, and many lose their Humanity entirely, falling into a final grand dance of frenzy and slaughter until they are put down like rabid dogs by their fellow Kindred. As a vampire loses her Humanity, she comes to resemble a pallid, desiccated corpse and is driven more by her vampire habits: sleeping deeply during the day, giving in to the lassitude of age and finding it difficult to interact with mortals as anything other than prey.

A rare few vampires have the presence of mind to set for themselves moral standards alien to humanity. As long as the Cainite holds to a rigid code of conduct, the Beast can be kept at bay. Such a restructuring of one's lifetime of morals requires incredible will and many years of dedicated study. Over the centuries, vampires have developed several such alternate moralities, called Paths of Enlightenment. These Paths cast aside all that is humane in favor of a specialized code more appropriate to the undead. Needless to say, despite their stabilizing affect, these Paths are sociopathic — indeed, their practitioners are unquestionably divorced from anything resembling mortal thought or belief. A follower of a Path may channel his vampire urges, but such channels cause instinctive fear and revulsion in mortals.

When you create a vampire character, you default to the morality of Humanity. Your Morality Traits can range from zero to five, with zero Traits indicating that the character has fallen completely to the clutches of the Beast (and is thus no longer suitable for play) and five indicating a character with a highly developed sense of morality. With the permission of a Storyteller, you can start with a Path of Enlightenment, but keep in mind that Paths are difficult and demanding to roleplay. To study a Path, your character must have at least three Willpower Traits, and he must have spent several years abandoning Humanity in favor of a new set of morals (with instruction). Paths also sometimes use different Virtues, and you may not start with as many Virtue Traits if you have *Conviction* or *Instinct* (since it takes work to strip away your human virtues in favor of these inhuman ones).

Each Path (including Humanity) has a Hierarchy of Sins. This Hierarchy elaborates on what constitutes a moral failing for its particular set of ethics. The higher the rating, the stricter the standards. Everything below that rating is automatically considered a failing if performed. Thus, a rare vampire with a Humanity of 5 doesn't *need* to grapple with his conscience over the notion that killing someone is wrong — he already knows that. He does, however, have qualms about putting himself first too often.

A character with several Morality Traits is distanced from the Beast, but conversely, he must hold himself to high standards of behavior, as shown by the many possible sins. With few Morality Traits, a character risks succumbing to the Beast, but trivial moral concerns are too minor to erode his morals further. The details of Morality Traits and Virtue Tests appear on p. 108-111.

The Paths of Enlightenment in this book are often found among non-aligned vampires, or among a few vampires of any sectarian allegiance. Camarilla vampires usually uphold Humanity, though a rare few elders follow different beliefs. Vampires of the Sabbat have their own inhuman Paths of Enlightenment, which are a subject for another book.

HUMANITY

The majority of vampires default to Humanity. Even the depraved vampires of the Sabbat and the jaded elders of the Camarilla cling to some vestige of Humanity, though such monsters usually have very few Humanity Traits.

The ethics of Humanity uphold what constitutes humane behavior: Humanity warns against stealing, killing, harming others or behaving selfishly.

Humanity Five — Kindred with a score this high can be, ironically, more human than other humans. Many fledgling vampires cling to their moral codes more strictly as a reaction against the new predator roiling in them. Though not necessarily treacly sweet or passive, these Kindred have excruciatingly high standards for themselves and often hold clearly defined concepts of right and wrong.

Humanity Four — Theft is wrong. Murder or harming others is wrong. But sometimes the speed limit is just too damn slow. Vampires at this level are approximate to "normal" social morals, and are on par with most of mortal society. The vampire is concerned with the natural rights of others, but there's some natural selfishness mixed in.

HUMANITY HIERARCHY of SINS	
Traits	Violations
Five	Selfish thoughts and actions
Four	Theft; causing injury
Three	Accidentally killing; intentionally causing property damage
Two	Killing with premeditation
One	Casual killing or acts of great evil (as your culture defines "evil")

Humanity Three — People die. Stuff breaks. This vampire has little difficulty with the fact that she is a predator. While she won't always go out of her way to vandalize or kill, she accepts that sometimes fate has it in for some people. She does what needs doing with little griping or effort on her part to avoid it. Something of the vampire's inner monster starts to shine through at this stage, causing mortals to feel uncomfortable around her or manifesting some physical eeriness.

Humanity Two — Hey, some people ought to die. Killing is very acceptable to this Kindred, provided the victim deserves to die (and only the vampire knows who's deserving). Theft, injury, torture and destruction are tools to be used to accomplish one's goals, and one's goals are always paramount. Such a state reflects many vampire elders. The vampire begins to acquire a corpselike aspect, and may find it difficult to interact with mortals (who often find him more than a little disturbing).

Humanity One — The lives and property of others mean nothing to a Kindred this far gone. Such a vampire more than likely indulges in twisted pleasures, which can be all manner of atrocity. Perversion, cold-blooded murder, mutilation, wickedness for its own sake are all signs of a Kindred who has not long to continue. The next frenzy may well be the last. Such a vampire may be physically mistaken for human, but only under certain conditions (such as dim lighting and plenty of distractions).

THE PATH of BLOOD

Studied by the Assamites, this Path espouses a connection to Haqim, founder of the clan, through the power of blood. Vampires on this Path hunt down other Cainites, drinking their blood in order to improve their own potency. Those few who evidence distaste for their condition or hatred for the "Get of Khayyin" (descendants of Caine) may be offered the opportunity to convert, to serve the will of Haqim in his battle

PATH of BLOOD HIERARCHY of SINS	
Traits	Violations
Five	Killing a mortal for blood; breaking your word to a clanmate
Four	Refusing to allow an outsider to convert; failing to destroy an outsider who refuses conversion
Three	Succumbing to frenzy; refusing to pursue lore of Khayyin
Two	Failing to pursue lesser blood for your clanmates; refusal to aid a more enlightened follower of the Path
One	Failing to take a chance to lower your generation; acting against another Assamite

PATH OF BONES HIERARCHY OF SINS	
Traits	Violations
Five	Showing fear of death; failing to study death
Four	Accidentally killing; failing to feed when hungry
Three	Succumbing to frenzy; refusing to kill
Two	Heeding emotion; showing compassion
One	Preventing the occurrence of death

against Khayyin's evil childer. By diablerizing their enemies and holding aloof from other Cainites, the students of the Path of Blood seek to overcome the blot of Khayyin's curse and redeem themselves in a transcendence awash in stolen vitae.

The so-called Dervishes hunt for lore and ancient vitae, so that they may understand their enemies and take their power. Even Cainites of weak blood are not immune to the hunts; the Dervishes are said to have ways of mystically preserving the vitae so that other members of their clan can use it. By stealing away the power of other vampires, the Dervishes hope to concentrate it in the hands of the faithful, who purify it through their honor.

Only old and faithful Assamites, and a few converts, study the Path of Blood. Most outsiders and neonates are completely ignorant of this Path. Instruction begins only when the supplicant proves his worth and his desire to be shed of Khayyin's curse in the light of Haqim's glory.

Students of the Path of Blood practice *Conviction* and *Self-Control*.

THE PATH OF BONES

As walking corpses, vampires truly exist on the cusp of mortality. Death comes to all things sooner or later, so the Gravediggers study the process of physical death, the decay of the body and the extinguishing of the spirit. Practiced largely by Giovanni and some Samedi, these scholarly Cainites strive to unlock the mysteries of death, to understand why death occurs and how vampires cheat the natural cycle. Though they are neither murderers nor cavalier about death, they do occasionally "assist" if death seems to be unnaturally delayed.

Necromantic curiosity drives followers of the Path of Bones to seek out experiments and hidden lore about death. Many consort with ghosts, trying to discern the very motives of the soul. To a Gravedigger, the vampire cheats eternity. The answers to how and why this happens hold the keys to understanding all of mortality, and thus, to all existence. While the Gravediggers may be quite erudite about ghosts and thanatology, many are completely divorced from society, mortal or Cainite.

The Path of Bones upholds *Conviction* and *Self-Control*.

THE PATH OF METAMORPHOSIS

Long have the Carpathian Fiends studied the ways of the flesh. Through *Vicissitude*, they twist themselves into new visages until they do not have a recognizable gender or even

PATH OF METAMORPHOSIS HIERARCHY OF SINS	
Traits	Violations
Five	Postponing feeding; indulging in vices
Four	Asking for or sharing knowledge with another
Three	Refusing to kill for knowledge; failing to guide a frenzy
Two	Considering others; failing to experiment
One	Neglecting to practice alteration and evolution; showing compassion

PATH OF NIGHT HIERARCHY OF SINS	
Traits	Violations
Five	Killing a mortal for food; acting altruistically
Four	Failing to devise new and shocking forms of evil; asking for assistance
Three	Accidentally killing; following another Cainite's will
Two	Intentionally killing rather than prolonging suffering; showing compassion
One	Accepting another's authority; repenting of your evil

look remotely human. True Metamorphosists, though, aim not to shock but to evolve. Just as vampires are superior to humans, they claim, there is another state superior to vampirism. By controlling the physical flesh and learning the ways of the body, they hope to cause spirit and mind to follow suit, turning into something beyond vampire.

In keeping with their practices, the Metamorphosists are solitary and cold. Reason, experimentation and self-discipline are the keystones to improvement. Each individual must find the secret keys to her own existence. As such, the students of the Path of Metamorphosis individually chart disparate paths leading to that state above and beyond vampirism.

The Path of Metamorphosis teaches *Conviction* and *Instinct*.

THE PATH OF NIGHT

Vampires are monsters, claim the Nihilists, and as such, they embody all of the terrible sins of the world. Since vampires serve a place in the greater scheme of existence, the evil of vampirism must be preordained. Thus, instead of simply giving in to the Beast, adherents of the Path of Night seek to spread their evil in cultivated ways, tempting people to damnation and terrifying the faithless. By acting as an agent of evil, the vampire fulfills his role to higher powers.

A vampire on the Path of Night is not a ravening, insane beast. He seeks to show the true depth of evil to others, luring them into vice and highlighting virtue by its opposite. These vampires plague humanity with all manner of terrors and temptations, seeking not only mortal fears but their own escalation as dark angels. By spreading the taint, the vampire hopes to fulfill a preordained destiny, and thus to eventually move on.

The Path of Night teaches *Conviction* and *Instinct*.

THE PATH OF PARADOX

Espousing riddles that delve into the illusory nature of existence, the Ravnos followers of the Path of Paradox seek to fulfill the demands of karma. By testing others (often with traps or riddles), the Shilmulo determine each person's place in the wheel of ages. Once the veils of the transitory material world are cast aside, the philosopher can lead the subject to his proper place in destiny — even death.

Kindred are believed to be locked outside of *maya* (the cycle of the universe). While most individuals are reincarnated through *samsara*, the way of rebirth, vampires have dodged this cycle. Therefore, they have also lost their *svadharma*, or individual purpose. Thus, it remains to the Shilmulo to determine each vampire's *svadharma* and get him back on that path, thus advancing *maya*, by whatever means necessary. If other Kindred fail to understand their *svadharma*, then it's up to the Ravnos to push them back into *samsara*. The state of undeath is considered a curse, but Ravnos believe this *shruti* (what has been learned from the gods) to be due to their failure to understand *maya*. Only by weaving illusions themselves can they hope to tear away the veils that hide the Ultimate Truths.

The Path of Paradox upholds *Conviction* and *Self-Control*.

PATH OF PARADOX HIERARCHY OF SINS	
Traits	Violations
Five	Embracing a woman or someone outside the *jati* (family)
Four	Destroying another Shilmulo; killing a mortal for sustenance
Three	Failing to destroy a vampire outside this Path; killing a mortal needlessly
Two	Failure to aid another's *svadharma*; allowing other concerns to override *dharma*
One	Becoming blood bound; Embracing needlessly

THE PATH OF TYPHON

Set himself is said to lie in wait in the sands of Egypt. His followers, the Setites, work diligently to spread his influence through vice, favors and chains of ecstasy. Using the desires of others for control, the Theophidians gather information about their sleeping god, prepare agents for his return and seek the means to resurrect their deity.

The Corrupters are mistrusted by other Cainites, and with good reason. All Setites keep their motives carefully hidden so that they might draw on the resources of their hapless slaves without hindrance. After all, an ally (unwitting or otherwise) who does not know one's plans cannot effectively counter them. To this end, the Corrupters weave subtle webs of control, holding themselves aloof from petty indulgences while pandering the innermost desires of others. With their religious rites in hidden temples, they offer service and obedience to Set; through their carefully built chains of dependents, they gather the occult secrets and services necessary to strengthen their clan and god.

The Path of Typhon teaches *Conviction* and *Self-Control*.

PATH OF TYPHON HIERARCHY OF SINS	
Traits	Violations
Five	Pursuing your own vices or failing to aid another Theophidian
Four	Failing to destroy a vampire in Golconda; failure to observe a Setite ritual
Three	Failing to undermine the social order in favor of the Setites; failing to do what is necessary to bring another to ruin
Two	Failing to pursue occult knowledge; hindering another Setite
One	Failing to take advantage of another; refusing to aid in raising Set

ATTRIBUTES (BIDDING TRAITS)

The Traits that describe your character's innate capabilities are called Attributes. These Attributes are used in the game to perform actions and overcome obstacles. While certain situations may also require Abilities, such matters are a function of training. Even with the appropriate training, you must call on your own strengths to finish the tasks set before you.

When you enter a situation with a questionable outcome, you bid a Trait appropriate to the challenge. If you are trying to knock someone over, for instance, you might bid the Physical Trait *Brawny* as you use your strength. The nature of the challenge determines the Trait used — Physical, Social or Mental.

You should try to bid a Trait appropriate to the nature of each given challenge. That is, using your strength may call on the *Brawny* Trait but not the *Dexterous* Trait. If you and your opponent agree, you can use other Traits, but in general, choose Traits fitting the challenge.

Remember, when you bid a Trait for a challenge, you risk that particular Trait. If you fail the challenge, you may temporarily lose the use of the Trait, as you exhaust your resources and lose your confidence. Some situations may require the use of an additional Trait or more — any time that you are considered "bids down," you must risk additional Traits. Conversely, if you are listed as "Traits up" or "Traits down," you modify your current number of Traits when comparing for overbids or ties.

For the purposes of determining what kinds of Traits are appropriate to specific challenges or Disciplines, the Trait listings include a run-down of what sorts of Traits fit into what specialized categories. For example, the Physical Trait *Tough* is appropriate for the Discipline of *Potence* because it is a strength-related Trait. Of course, you can ignore these categories if you wish, in favor of speeding the game. Remember, unique situations may allow Traits to be used in unusual ways.

New players may find it easier to bid a generic Trait from the appropriate pool instead of picking a specific one. Doing so allows them time to get the hang of the system. When they're more comfortable with bidding, then start having them choose Traits.

PHYSICAL TRAITS

Strength-related: *Brawny, Ferocious, Stalwart, Tough, Wiry*

Dexterity-related: *Dexterous, Graceful, Lithe, Nimble, Quick*

Stamina-related: *Enduring, Resilient, Robust, Rugged, Tireless*

Miscellaneous Physical: *Agile, Energetic, Steady, Tenacious, Vigorous*

Agile: You have a well-honed and flexible body. You can bend, twist, run and jump with ease.

Uses: Acrobatics. *Athletics*. Competitive events. Dodging.

Brawny: Bulky muscular strength.

Uses: Punching, kicking or grappling in combat when your goal is to inflict damage. Power-lifting. All feats of strength. *Potence*.

Brutal: You are capable of taking nearly any action in order to survive.

Uses: Fighting an obviously superior enemy.

Dexterous: General adroitness and skill involving the use of one's hands.

Uses: Weapon-oriented combat (*Melee* or *Firearms*). Pickpocketing. Punching. *Celerity*.

Enduring: A persistent sturdiness against physical opposition.

Uses: When your survival is at stake, this Trait is a good one to risk as a second, or successive, bid. *Fortitude*.

Energetic: A powerful force of spirit. A strong internal drive propels you and, in physical situations, you can draw on a deep reservoir of enthusiasm and zeal.

Uses: Combat.

Ferocious: Possession of brutal intensity and extreme physical determination.

Uses: Any time that you intend to do serious harm. When in frenzy. *Potence*.

Graceful: Control and balance in the motion and use of the entire body.

Uses: Combat defense. Whenever you might lose your balance. *Celerity*.

Lithe: Characterized by flexibility and suppleness.

Uses: Acrobatics, gymnastics, dodging, dancing and *Celerity*.

Nimble: Light and skillful; able to make agile movements.

Uses: Dodging, jumping, rolling, acrobatics. Hand-to-hand combat. *Celerity*.

Quick: Speedy, with a fast reaction time.

Uses: Defending against a surprise attack. Running, dodging, attacking. *Celerity*.

Resilient: Characterized by strength of health; able to recover quickly from bodily harm. *Fortitude*.

Uses: Resisting adverse environments. Defending against damage in an attack.

Robust: Resistant to physical harm and damage.

Uses: Defending against damage in an attack. Endurance-related actions that could take place over a period of time. *Fortitude*.

Rugged: Hardy, rough and brutally healthy. Able to shrug off wounds and pain to continue struggling.

Uses: When resisting damage, any challenge that you enter while injured. Earth Melding. *Fortitude*.

Stalwart: Physically strong and uncompromising against opposition.

Uses: Resisting damage, or when standing your ground against overwhelming odds or a superior foe. *Potence*.

Steady: More than simply physically dependable — controlled, unfaltering and balanced. You have firm mastery over your efforts.

Uses: Weapon attacks. Fighting in exotic locations.

Tenacious: Physically determined through force of will.

Uses: Second or subsequent Physical Challenge.

Tireless: You have a runner's stamina — you are less taxed by physical efforts than ordinary people.

Uses: Any endurance-related challenge, second or subsequent Physical Challenge with the same foe or foes. *Fortitude*.

Tough: A harsh, aggressive attitude and a reluctance to submit.

Uses: Whenever you're wounded. *Potence*.

Vigorous: A combination of energy, power, intensity and resistance to harm.

Uses: Combat and athletic challenges when you're on the defensive.

Wiry: Tight, streamlined, muscular strength.

Uses: Punching, kicking or grappling on combat. Acrobatic movements. Endurance lifting. *Potence*.

NEGATIVE PHYSICAL TRAITS

Clumsy: Lacking physical coordination, balance and grace. You are prone to stumbling and dropping objects.

Cowardly: In threatening situations, saving your own neck is all that is important. You might even flee when you have the upper hand, just out of habit.

Decrepit: You move and act as if you are old and infirm. You recover from physical damage slowly, you are unable to apply full muscular strength and you tire easily.

Delicate: Frail and weak in structure; you are damaged easily by physical harm.

Docile: The opposite of the *Ferocious* and *Tenacious* Traits. You lack physical persistence, and you tend to submit rather than fighting long battles.

Flabby: Your muscles are underdeveloped. You cannot apply your strength well against resistance.

Lame: You are disabled in one or more limbs. The handicap can be as obvious as a missing leg or as subtle as a dysfunctional arm.

Lethargic: Slow and drowsy. You suffer from a serious lack of energy or motivation.

Puny: You are weak and inferior in strength. This Trait could refer to diminutive size.

Sickly: Weak and feeble. Your body responds to physical stress as if it were in the throes of a debilitating illness.

SOCIAL TRAITS

Charisma-related: *Charismatic, Charming, Dignified, Eloquent, Expressive, Genial*

Manipulation-related: *Beguiling, Commanding, Ingratiating, Persuasive*

Appearance-related: *Alluring, Elegant, Gorgeous, Magnetic, Seductive*

Miscellaneous Social: *Diplomatic, Empathetic, Intimidating, Friendly, Witty*

Alluring: An attractive and appealing presence that inspires desire in others.

Uses: Seduction. Convincing others.

Beguiling: The skill of deception and illusion. You can twist the perceptions of others and lead them to believe what suits you.

Uses: Tricking others. Lying under duress.

Charismatic: The talent of inspiration and motivation, the sign of a strong leader.

Uses: In a situation involving leadership or the achievement of leadership. *Presence.*

Charming: Your speech and actions make you attractive and appealing to others.

Uses: Convincing. Persuading. *Presence.*

Commanding: Impressive delivery of orders and suggestions. This Trait implies skill in the control and direction of others.

Uses: When you are seen as a leader.

Dignified: Something about your posture and body carriage appears honorable and aesthetically pleasing. You carry yourself well.

Uses: *Presence.* Defending against Social Challenges.

Diplomatic: Tactful, careful and thoughtful in speech and deed. Few are displeased with what you say or do.

Uses: Very important in intrigue. Leadership situations.

Elegant: Refined tastefulness. Even though you don't need money to be elegant, you exude an air of richness and high society.

Uses: High society or Toreador parties. Might be important in some clans for advancement. Defending against Social Challenges.

Eloquent: The ability to speak in an interesting and convincing manner.

Uses: Convincing others. Swaying emotions. Public speaking. *Presence.*

Empathetic: Able to identify and understand the emotions and moods of people with whom you come in contact.

Uses: Gauging the feelings of others.

Expressive: Able to articulate your thoughts in interesting, meaningful ways.

Uses: Producing art of any kind. Acting. Performing. Any social situation in which you want someone to understand your meaning.

Friendly: Able to fit in with everyone you meet. Even after a short conversation, most find it difficult to dislike you.

Uses: Convincing others.

Genial: Cordial, kindly, warm and pleasant. You are pleasing to be around.

Uses: Mingling at parties. *Presence.* Generally used in a second or later Social Challenge with someone.

Gorgeous: Beautiful or handsome. You were born with a face and body that is good-looking to most people you meet.

Uses: Modeling, posing.

Ingratiating: Able to gain the favor of people who know you.

Uses: Dealing with elders in a social situation. Defending against Social Challenges.

Intimidating: A frightening or awesome presence that causes others to feel timid. This Trait is particularly useful when attempting to cow opponents.

Uses: Inspiring common fear. Ordering others.

Magnetic: People feel drawn to you; those around you are interested in your speech and actions.

Uses: Seduction. First impressions.

Persuasive: Able to propose believable, convincing and correct arguments and requests. Very useful when someone else is undecided on an issue.

Uses: Persuading or convincing others.

Seductive: Able to entice and tempt. You can use your good looks and your body to get what you want from others.

Uses: Subterfuge, seduction.

Witty: Cleverly humorous. Jokes and jests come easily to you, and you are perceived as a funny person when you want to be.

Uses: At parties. Entertaining someone. Goading or insulting someone.

NEGATIVE SOCIAL TRAITS

Bestial: You have started to resemble the Beast of your vampiric nature. Maybe you have clawlike fingernails, heavy body hair or a feral glint in your eyes; however your Beast manifests, you definitely seem inhuman.

Callous: You are unfeeling, uncaring and insensitive to the suffering of others.

Condescending: You just can't help it; your contempt for others is impossible to hide.

Dull: Those with whom you speak usually find you boring and uninteresting. Conversing with you is a chore. You do not present yourself well to others.

Feral: The animalistic predator in you is evident in your actions. You scratch yourself, sniff at people or otherwise behave in a primitive fashion.

Naive: You lack the air of worldliness, sophistication or maturity that most carry.

Obnoxious: You are annoying or unappealing in speech, action or appearance.

Repugnant: Your appearance disgusts everyone around you. Needless to say, you make a terrible first impression with strangers.

Shy: You are timid, bashful, reserved and socially hesitant.

Tactless: You are unable to do or say things that others find appropriate to the social situation.

Untrustworthy: You are rumored or perceived to be unreliable, whether or not you really are.

MENTAL TRAITS

Perception-related: *Attentive, Discerning, Insightful, Observant, Vigilant*

Intelligence-related: *Cunning, Disciplined, Knowledgeable, Rational, Reflective*

Wits-related: *Alert, Clever, Intuitive, Shrewd, Wily*

Miscellaneous Mental: *Creative, Dedicated, Determined, Patient, Wise*

Alert: Mentally prepared for danger and able to react quickly when it occurs.

Uses: Preventing surprise attacks. Defending against *Dominate*.

Attentive: You pay attention to everyday occurrences around you. When something extraordinary happens, you are usually ready for it.

Uses: Preventing surprise attacks. Seeing through *Obfuscate* when you don't expect it. Preventing *Dominate*.

Clever: Quick-witted resourcefulness. You think well on your feet.

Uses: Using a Mental Challenge against another.

Creative: Your ideas are original and imaginative, which implies an ability to produce unusual solutions to your difficulties. You can create artistic pieces. A requirement for any true artist.

Uses: Defending against *Auspex*. Creating anything.

Cunning: Crafty and sly, possessing a great deal of ingenuity.

Uses: Tricking others.

Dedicated: You give yourself over totally to your beliefs. When one of your causes is at stake, you stop at nothing to succeed.

Uses: Useful in any Mental Challenge when your beliefs are at stake.

Determined: When it comes to mental endeavors, you are fully committed. Nothing can divert your intentions to succeed once you have made up your mind.

Uses: Staredowns. Useful in a normal Mental Challenge.

Discerning: Discriminating, able to pick out details, subtleties and idiosyncrasies. You have clarity of vision.

Uses: *Auspex*. Investigation and tracking.

Disciplined: Your mind is structured and controlled. This rigidity gives you an edge in battles of will.

Uses: *Thaumaturgy*. Staredowns. Useful in a Mental Challenge.

Insightful: The power of looking at a situation and gaining an understanding of it.

Uses: Investigation (but not defense against it). *Auspex*.

Intuitive: Knowledge and understanding somehow come to you without conscious reasoning, as if by instinct.

Uses: Spontaneous deduction.

Knowledgeable: You know copious and detailed information about a wide variety of topics. This Trait represents "book-learning."

Uses: *Forgetful Mind* tests. Remembering information your character might know. Employing *Thaumaturgy*.

Observant: Depth of vision, the power to look at something and notice the important aspects of it.

Uses: *Auspex*. Picking up on subtleties that others might overlook.

Patient: Tolerant, persevering and steadfast. You can wait out extended delays with composure.

Uses: Staredowns or other mental battles after another Trait has been bid.

Rational: You believe in logic, reason, sanity and sobriety. Your ability to reduce concepts to a mathematical level helps you analyze the world.

Uses: Defending against emotion-oriented mental attacks. Defending against an aura-reading. Not used as an initial bid.

Reflective: Meditative self-recollection and deep thought. The Trait of the serious thinker, *Reflective* enables you to consider all aspects of a conundrum.

Uses: Meditation. Remembering information. Defending against most Mental Challenges.

Shrewd: Astute and artful, able to keep your wits about you and accomplish mental feats with efficiency and finesse.

Uses: Defending against a Mental Discipline.

Vigilant: Watchful. You have the disposition of a guard dog; your attention misses little.

Uses: Defending against investigation or *Forgetful Mind*. Seeing through *Obfuscate*. *Auspex*. More appropriate for mental defense than for attack.

Wily: Sly and full of guile. Because you are wily, you can trick and deceive easily.

Uses: Tricking others. Lying under duress. Confusing mental situations.

Wise: An overall understanding of the workings of the world.

Uses: Giving advice. Dispensing snippets of Zen.

NEGATIVE MENTAL TRAITS

Forgetful: You have trouble remembering even important things.

Gullible: Easily deceived, duped or fooled.

Ignorant: Uneducated or misinformed, never seeming to know anything.

Impatient: Restless, anxious and generally intolerant of delays. You want everything to go your way — immediately.

Oblivious: Unaware and unmindful. You'd be lucky if you noticed an airplane flying through your living room.

Predictable: Because you lack originality or intelligence, even strangers can figure out what you intend to do next.

Shortsighted: Lacking foresight. You rarely look beyond the superficial; details of perception are usually lost on you.

Submissive: No backbone; you relent and surrender at any cost rather than stand up for yourself.

Violent: An extreme lack of self-control. You fly into rages at the slightest provocation, and frenzy is always close to the surface. This Trait is a Mental one because it represents mental instability.

Witless: Lacking the ability to process information quickly. Foolish and slow to act when threatened.

ABILITIES

The particular bits of knowledge learned over the years, the tricks of the trade and the hard-won secrets of crafts are all Abilities. A character's Ability Traits represent special training or talent, and as such, they often allow performance of tasks that would be otherwise impossible. Even with more mundane situations, Abilities allow for a much improved chance of success.

When a character performs a risky or uncertain action, Abilities aid the outcome. If you try a task and fail, you can temporarily expend one of your appropriate Abilities, to gain an immediate retest. You lose the Ability used and the initial Trait(s) bid for the task (if any) because you lost the initial test, but you can still overcome the challenge. Abilities used like this are recovered at the next game session.

A character with multiple levels in a given Ability is certainly more experienced and proficient than an individual with just one. Most characters will fall into one to three levels of Ability; greater amounts are very rare, and anything beyond five levels is almost certainly superhuman (and limited to elder vampires and their ilk). The total level of Ability in a given field corresponds roughly to the character's professional capabilities:

Competent (Able to earn a living)

Professional (Licensed, capable of supervision)

Journeyman (Bachelor's degree or instructor)

Expert (Master's degree or researcher)

Master (Doctorate or true innovator)

Some tasks are simply too difficult, or they require too much skill, to be attempted by a character without the requisite Abilities. The Storyteller may occasionally require the possession or use of an Ability Trait to perform a specific task. In this case, characters without the Ability, or who have already used all of their levels of the Ability, cannot attempt the task at all.

When an Ability is used against a set scenario or object (such as using *Security* to pick a lock), the feat usually has a difficulty assigned by the Storyteller. In such a Static Challenge, you may be required to risk a Trait for a trivial task, or even be asked to bid two or more Traits for a difficult, risky or frustrating undertaking.

Some Abilities can be used against an opponent instead of facilitating a regular task. In this case, the Ability is expended to gain a retest in a challenge with the opponent. See the rules for challenges and retests on p. 195 for complete details.

Focusing Abilities

A few Abilities specifically require a concentrated area of study. One cannot simply study all *Crafts* at once, after all. These Abilities are specifically noted in the descriptions. When you take such an Ability, you must choose an area of study, a specific topic that you have concentrated on. Each area is considered a separate Ability, so *Science: Biology* counts completely separately from *Science: Metallurgy*, for instance.

Ability Specializations

Within a given area of expertise, some practitioners further hone their knowledge to a razor's edge. By choosing a specialization in an Ability, you hone your skills with a particular facet of that talent.

Ability specializations are a wholly optional rule. Remember to ask your Storyteller before taking a specialization.

Taking a specialization requires that you spend one Experience Trait or Free Trait on an Ability that you already have. Whenever you perform a task with that specialization — even if you do not expend the Ability — you gain a one-Trait bonus on resolution of challenges, as long as you have at least one level of the Ability left. You may only have one specialization in any given Ability; you cannot take *Firearms: Pistols* and *Firearms: Rifles* together, for instance. You also can never gain more than one Bonus Trait at a time from specializations, even if more than one would be appropriate to a given challenge. That is, even if you have *Medicine: Physiology* and *Science: Biology Research*, you only get a one-Trait bonus on a test of biochemistry, despite your multiple specializations.

A specialization is a fairly narrow area of research or practice. You cannot, for instance, take a *Firearms* specialization in "guns," nor could you have an *Occult* specialization of "writing." An appropriate specialization refers to one small class of items or to one type of practice within the Ability, such as *Firearms: Antique Pistols* or *Occult: Superstitions*.

You may take a specialization in an Ability with an area of study. In such a case, you concentrate your research in one particular facet of that sub-Ability, or in one application of it. Thus, you could have *Crafts: Woodworking* with a specialization in *Hidden Panels*, or *Science: Botany* with a specialization in *Exotic Flora*.

Note that the Bonus Trait from a specialization does not have an adjective, and it is not bid or used like other Traits. You simply are "one Trait up" on challenges within the specialization.

Example: *Marcus von Schlagenhanz is an experienced Brujah fighter, but he is especially good with fencing weapons. He has the Ability: Melee x 3 with the specialization: Fencing. When Marcus*

engages a foe in combat, he normally uses his 11 Physical Traits. With a fencing blade, however, he has 12 Physical Traits because of his intense training. Of course, if he gets tired out or wounded (loses several challenges), he may not have as many Traits, but as long as he has at least one level of his Melee Ability left, he gets to add the one Bonus Trait to his remaining Physical Trait total.

Academics

You possess a level of education and general knowledge beyond rudimentary schooling. With *Academics*, you can express artistic criticism, debate the classics, consider philosophy and indulge in studies of culture. This broad Ability covers all sorts of humanities in learning.

Academics allows you to recognize historical, art and cultural references. You can use *Academics* when working in such fields, when developing a critique or researching. Calling on *Academics* Ability may require a Mental or Social Challenge to determine your exact level of competence.

You may further direct your studies by choosing a specific field, such as *Art Criticism, Classical Studies, History, Journalism, Theology* or anything else that could be studied with higher education.

Animal Ken

Most animals find Kindred frightening. With *Animal Ken*, you have learned to understand animals, and you can sometimes deal with them more equitably. Though they may retain a healthy fear of the predator lurking within you, you know what drives them and how to assuage their fears.

Animal Ken is often used with the *Animalism* Discipline. With *Animal Ken*, you can train an animal (especially a ghoul) into particular behaviors (stay, fetch, attack), or attempt to deduce an animal's state of being (injured, angry, frightened, etc.) with a Mental Challenge. If you work with an animal over a long period of time (generally a month or so), you may be able to teach it a simple trick, up to a limit of one trick for each Mental Trait that the animal has.

Athletics

Whether due to a background in sports or just personal talent, you are skilled in all manner of athletic endeavors. You can throw a ball, sprint, climb, jump and swim. This last can be especially useful to vampires, who do not naturally float.

Your *Athletics* Ability is used for retests on most forms of raw physical activity: acrobatics, swimming, jumping, throwing, climbing and running. You may choose to focus on something you do especially well.

Awareness

You have a talent for knowing when things are not as they should be, whether by that strange feeling in the pit of your gut or through tested observation. This is particularly useful for sensing when other supernatural creatures about, detecting evidence of Numina or other strange phenomena, or just getting that weird feeling when the laws of nature are about to take a hard left.

Awareness requires a Mental Challenge to use, and retests are made with the *Occult* Ability.

Brawl

Back-alleys, martial arts schools and rough bars are your stomping ground. You might have military training, or maybe you just grew up with a passel of rough-and-tumble siblings. Whatever the case, you know how to dish out damage with your fists and feet.

Use the *Brawl* Ability for retests in combat when you are using your natural weapons (teeth, claws or fists). This Ability is also the province of the martial arts, although you should specify which art when taking this Ability.

Computer

Most Cainites have difficulty adapting to modern inventions. As a result, an understanding of cutting-edge technology makes for dangerous knowledge. With the *Computer* Ability, you understand how to use, program and access computers of all sorts.

Use *Computer* with a Mental Challenge (difficulty determined by the Storyteller) to break into systems, alter data, write programs or figure out unfamiliar operations.

Crafts

You can build things. Depending on your area of expertise, you know how to manufacture items and make handy tools or decorations. You must choose a focus for *Crafts*, specifying your form of creation: *Carpentry, Clockworks, Blacksmithing, Leatherworking* and the like are all possibilities. You can fashion works of art, studying *Painting, Drawing* or similar physical media. *Crafts* also covers more technical skills done with labor, such as *Mechanics* and *Electronics*.

Making or repairing an item with *Crafts* usually involves a Physical Challenge of your dexterity, with difficulty set by the Storyteller based on the type of job (making a concealed spring-loaded trap is far more difficult than planing a board, for instance). Artistic works designed with *Crafts* x 3 or better may entrance Toreador, at the discretion of the Storyteller.

The Tzimisce practice a focus of *Body Crafts* when using *Vicissitude*. This Ability covers tattooing, piercing, flaying and all other applications thereof regarding the alteration of the body.

Dodge

When trouble rears its ugly head, you know how to get out of its way. Unhesitating reactions let you evade blows and shots, getting out of the way of injury. You can use *Dodge* against any attack that you're aware of: diving for cover as someone fires a gun or twisting away from a sword, for instance. *Dodge* may be used as a retest when defending against an attack that you can see or sense coming.

Drive

Though most people can drive in the modern age, you can drive well. You're equally at home with a stick shift or an automatic, rush hour is no concern and you can get the most performance out of a car. In dangerous situations, you can evade traffic and even use your vehicle as a weapon. Bear in mind that just because you can drive a station wagon doesn't mean you can drive a semi with equal ease. A Mental Challenge may be required to allow you to figure out where everything is in an unfamiliar vehicle.

Drive tests most often involve a Physical Challenge of your reflexes.

Empathy

You are sensitive to the moods and emotions of people around you. When you listen to someone, you understand her feelings. You can identify with others and tell when people are lying or holding back while talking to you.

With a Social Challenge and the expenditure of an *Empathy* Ability, you can determine if the last thing that someone said was a lie (although *Subterfuge* can defend against this expenditure). Alternately, you can attempt to determine the subject's current Demeanor.

Etiquette

Even though knowing which fork to use isn't as important to Kindred society, you do know the proper way to greet someone, when to rise and how to make introductions. You can hold a toast with the best of them, and you keep your cool in any social scenario, from high tea to a gang's rally.

The *Etiquette* Ability can be used with Social Tests to impress or blend in at parties. If you make a social *faux pas*, you may expend an *Etiquette* Ability immediately to negate the gaffe — your character knew better than to make the mistake.

Expression

Words and feelings flow freely from you. When the muse strikes, you put pen to paper (or fingers to instrument) and pour out a torrent of emotion and stirring imagery. You can convey message and meaning in your art, from symphonies to poetry, and whatever you write is both clear and moving.

When writing or composing, you can sink true *Expression* into the work. Works created with *Expression* x 3 or more have the potential to entrance Toreador, as per their clan weakness.

Finance

The world of money and business awaits your whim. You understand interest, CDs, stock market transactions, currency exchanges and GNPs. A little *Finance* lets you make quite a bit of money. You can also use your *Finance* to balance books or run a business of your own.

Typically, you can run a business, follow a money trail, perform an audit or clean up an accounting mess with a Mental Challenge (difficulty dependent on the task, as determined by the Storyteller). Alternately, you can expend a level of *Finance* Ability to raise $250 in cash between games. Not every use of *Finance* is so benign — money laundering operations have to come from somewhere.

Firearms

A little time at the gun range goes a long way. You know how to hold, fire and clean a gun. You can unjam one, too, and you can tell different models apart. You know how to stand to get the best aim, how to handle recoil and how to take care of problems in the field.

If you possess the *Firearms* Ability, you may use your Mental Traits for gun combat instead of using Physical Traits, at no cost. You can expend *Firearms* for a retest in ranged-fire combat.

Hobby/Professional/Expert Ability

In a certain area of expertise not covered by another Ability, you have achieved some level of skill. You may have a small grasp of a trade due to some work on the side, or perhaps you've specifically studied a topic.

Hobby/ Professional/ Expert Ability is a catch-all category for highly unusual Abilities like *Cainite Lore, Thanatology, Demolitions* and so on. Any Ability of this type must be specifically approved by the Storyteller, and it has its capabilities defined by the Storyteller.

Intimidation

Intimidation represents any of a broad variety of techniques for terrifying people into compliance. This could be anything from physical size, to a particularly frightening grin, to knowing which emotional buttons to push.

You can use *Intimidation* when trying to scare someone with a Social Challenge, or with certain Disciplines.

Investigation

You know how to pick up clues and put together disparate pieces of information. By habit and training, you can set a jumbled mass of data into order, discovering identities, motives and patterns in an otherwise chaotic scene. You can use *Investigation* with a Mental Challenge when trying to puzzle out meaning to a random scene, or with most *Auspex* Discipline powers.

Law

Nobody is above the law, except those who know how to use it to their own advantage. You're one of the latter. Perhaps you uphold the law, or maybe you twist it to your own ends. Your knowledge of *Law* allows you to understand legal processes, courts and lawyers, and to use them effectively.

Use the *Law* Ability in court situations or with Social Challenges involving legal matters. Because the legal body is so vast, your Storyteller may require you to select a particular area of study (Criminal, Civil, Tax, etc.). Alternately, you may choose to study Kindred law in depth.

Leadership

When you speak, people listen. A good speaking voice and self-confidence lend a powerful presence to a leader. The *Leadership* Ability represents your ability to motivate people and to get them to follow your guidance. Even among those who do not know or respect you, you can demand attention.

You can use *Leadership* with a Social Challenge to try to get a minor favor or task from a character. *Leadership* is also used with many *Presence* powers.

Linguistics

You've studied a language — or languages — other than your native tongue. Whether you're an older vampire whose childhood language is no longer spoken, you frequent the global community, or it is necessary for other studies, you can speak, write and read other languages.

You must choose one language for each level of *Linguistics* you possess. Thus, you could have *Linguistics: Cantonese* and *Linguistics: German*. Alternately, you can focus on the underlying study of *Linguistics* itself, granting some understanding of the principles behind the structure of language. Languages need not be spoken; American Sign Language or Egyptian hieroglyphics would also be considered fields for study. Those who wish to converse in another language (but cannot actually do so) should hold up one hand with the first finger and thumb making an L-shape to indicate to other players the characters are not speaking English. Those who wish to listen in must also possess the language.

Medicine

You know how the human (and, to a lesser extent, Cainite) body functions. You can speed the recovery and healing of an injured mortal, or you can use your knowledge to inflict injury. Many Cainites learn just enough to know where to bite their victims or how to punish their ghouls.

You can use the *Medicine* Ability to speed a mortal's healing by one category: a *Wounded* mortal would heal as if *Bruised*, for instance. *Medicine* may be used for other sorts of research and lab work with a Mental Challenge. As *Medicine* represents such a vast field, your Storyteller may require you to specify what you know (*Pharmaceuticals*, *Internal Medicine*, *General Practice*).

Melee

If you've got something in your hands, you're a deadly fighter. Be it a sword, a stick or a set of nunchaku, you can use it to damaging effect. Expend *Melee* for retests in hand-to-hand combat when you are using a close combat weapon like a knife or a chair. Certain weapons function best when wielded by a character with *Melee*.

Occult

The hidden world teems with mysterious secrets. By unlocking universal keys and studying the basics of spirituality, you can learn the shadowy paths of the cosmos. Your *Occult* Ability serves as a general knowledge of the supernatural, alerting you to the existence of many varied sorts of inhuman creatures and paranormal events.

Some Disciplines, most notably *Thaumaturgy*, rely on the *Occult* Ability. *Occult* grants some basic (and sometimes erroneous) knowledge of the various denizens of the supernatural world; for more detailed information, study *Expert Ability: Lore* in your particular subject of interest.

Performance

You are a true virtuoso. Whatever your chosen medium, you have a gift for artistic endeavors. Whether playing an instrument, singing, dancing or acting, your skills allow you to entertain and even earn money.

Your *Performance* Ability can be used to earn a modest income, just like other artistic trade skills. If you execute a work with *Performance* x 3 or better, you may transfix Toreador in the area with the beauty and grace of your style.

You must choose a specific art form when you take *Performance*, such as playing an instrument, singing, acting or dramatic readings. Note that *Performance* is generally anything done before an audience, while *Expression* most often focuses on literary works, and *Crafts* concentrates on the creation of physical objects (such as paintings or sculptures).

Politics

The world of influence-trading and favors is extensive enough among mortals. In vampire society, where one's prowess is measured in standing with one's peers, the game of *Politics* is all-consuming. Through observation, intrigue and a bit of spin-doctoring, you've learned how to handle appearances, what a speech *really* means, and where the deal-making is going on. In short, it's *Politics* as usual.

The *Politics* Ability is useful primarily in dealings with mortal society or Influence. You may be able to manipulate the outcome of local political actions, with the proper Influence and some well-placed Social Challenges; *Politics* Ability ensures that matters proceed in the direction that you desire. *Politics* is also used to discern hidden motives and broker deals, and as such, it is almost a requirement of any harpy. With *Politics*, you can usually set an appropriate level of debt for a prestation boon. The hierarchies of power are often obvious to you, granting you insight into whether the prince is really in charge, or is simply a puppet of the primogen, for example. *Politics* also makes you aware of who's in favor and who's out, and you can determine how much Status a particular vampire possesses once introduced. (If you know your quarry's name, expend a *Politics* Ability to determine the subject's Status Traits.)

A knowledge of *Politics* includes, by extension, an understanding of the bureaucratic levels of power. You know how to cut through red tape, or how to obstruct others with it. By determining who's important in a given strata, you can usually avoid wasting time and simply go straight to the person with the power to do what you want.

Repair

You possess a working understanding of what makes things tick. With times, tools and parts, you can fix or slightly alter most of the trappings of modern society. This knowledge also allows you to excel at sabotage. The *Repair* Ability is widespread among inventors, mechanics and handymen. Using this Ability usually calls for a Mental Challenge, the difficulty of which depends on such factors as the item's complexity, tools and parts available, extent of damage and time spent on the repairs.

Science

The modern Information Age sees the explosion of all manner of studies. Categorizing and breaking down the world into many different forms, the methods of logic and reason give sentient beings the means to understand the universe, or at least small pieces of it. Education in *Science* covers techniques of inquiry, modern studies and a broad range of underpinning work in a diverse range of fields.

Science Ability requires an area of particular study: *Biology, Chemistry, Physics, Metallurgy, Electrical Engineering, Mathematics, Geology* and *Botany* are all possibilities, though such a list is far from comprehensive. Combining a *Science* with different fields may give a wide variety results. For example, *Science: Metallurgy* with *Academics* may

give results regarding historical research and theory, while the same *Science* with *Occult* may center around ancient alchemy or parapsychology. Actually constructing objects or devices theorized with *Science* may require use of the *Crafts* Ability.

Using a particular branch of *Science* usually requires a Mental Challenge of some sort to determine the success of research or the viability of theoretical work.

Security

Whichever side of the law you've worked on has granted you experience in *Security* techniques. You know about police operations and guard work, how they make their schedules and how they undertake their business — and how to disrupt such operations. Locks, traps, security systems and alarms are all within your purview. With a little time, you can put together *Security* measures for a location; you can also defeat such measures.

Use the *Security* Ability with Mental Traits to set up a secure area or network, or to formulate a plan for breaching such a network. *Security* Ability is also used to disarm traps, alarms and other devices, and to defeat locks. At the discretion of a Narrator, you may be required to use a Physical Trait related to dexterity when attempting to bypass a physical lock or alarm.

Scrounge

You're exceptionally good at finding *stuff*. Whether it's a crucial part for a 1890s' gramaphone, invitations to the most exclusive gallery opening in town, or just haven space in the downtown, you're a wiz at knowing where to go, who to talk to and how to get what you need. Granted, the things you get are rarely brand-new or exactly right and do take time and favors to acquire. Still such an ability is useful when your finances are less than sparkling or theft is out of the question.

Scrounge is typically used in conjunction with Mental Traits (although the Storyteller may occasionally require a Social Challenge for haggling), and can be useful when looking for particular items or searching a place that is in shambles.

Stealth

By blending into cover, blurring your lines and moving carefully and quietly, you can evade notice or sneak past people. You know how best to take advantage of surrounding cover and how to use light and shadow. Opportunities for unnoticed movement are not lost on you, as you understand the uses of timing and diversion.

With an appropriate Physical Challenge, you can sometimes sneak past the notice of guards and searchers (who contest your Ability with their Mental Traits and *Investigation* Ability). You also use *Stealth* to augment the *Obfuscate* Discipline.

Streetwise

Word on the street is known to you. Even if you don't have any particular friends or contacts in the area, you know about the different communities and gangs that hang out in town. You recognize tagging and other territorial markers, and you know some of the signs, colors and clothes that denote street people, homeless, gangbangers, hoodlums, criminals and social workers.

Using the *Streetwise* Ability, with your Mental Traits, lets you recognize the influence of various gangs or street communities. You also know about criminal organizations and activities, and you could perform a little larceny yourself. An appropriate Social Challenge can help smooth dealings with a hostile gang (though you may need *Etiquette* to make a really good impression).

Subterfuge

There are many ways to talk about subjects, and equally many ways to uncover the truth of the matter. Even in idle conversation, people use little white lies, slip hints about their true motives, try to guide the course of discussion and give away their secrets indirectly. The art of *Subterfuge* is the art of reading these tricks and using them effortlessly.

When someone confronts you with one of your lies, you can use the *Subterfuge* Ability in your own defense (if someone uses the *Empathy* Ability, for instance). By guiding a conversation, you can also unearth someone's Negative Traits; if you manage to steer conversation to a particular topic in play, you can expend a *Subterfuge* Ability and make a Social Challenge to determine one of the subject's Negative Traits related to the topic. Furthermore, because it deals in deceit and subversion, *Subterfuge* is used for retests with the *Chimerstry* Discipline.

Survival

Survival Ability represents a knowledge of terrain, how to find shelter, where to find water, techniques in hunting, edible and poisonous plants and fungi and so on. Though a vampire needs only blood to live, use of *Survival* makes hunting of animals much easier, and it provides some assurances of a safer existence for those who travel outside the cities.

Hunting and avoiding danger in the wilderness usually relies on a Physical Challenge. With *Survival*, you can substitute your Mental Traits if you so desire. *Survival* is also a measure of the character's ruggedness and ability to overcome obstacles and injury, so it can be used in retests of the *Fortitude* and *Protean* Disciplines.

BACKGROUNDS

Your character's Backgrounds help to flesh out ties with mortal agencies, role in vampire society and beneficial resources available. Each Background is used differently. In general, having multiple Traits in a given Background allows for better or more common use of that benefit. Some Background directly affect your character's creation and development; others are called into play later during the game.

ALLIES

A few friends, either kept from your mortal days or made after the Embrace, help you out in your endeavors. You can make a few calls and cut a few deals to get assistance in a wide range of activities. Your Storyteller will probably require you to define how you keep your allies and their relations to you.

Each *Allies* Trait possessed represents one person that you can call on for aid. Unlike Influence, your *Allies* have special talents that make them better than the average person on the street. Though your allies may not be aware of your vampire nature, they can be quite useful if directed properly.

In general, your allies do not show up in play directly. Instead, you can use them for certain services between play sessions, by notifying your Storyteller:

• An ally can be directed to follow up on research or activities that you have started. If you undertook a specific task previously, like tailing someone, researching a project or building a device, your allies can continue the work, doing so with one Ability Trait's worth of expertise. As long as they work on the project, your *Allies* Trait for the individual is tied up.

• If you need a particularly competent ally, you can expend multiple Traits to gain access to a mortal with multiple levels of an Ability or Influence. Each *Allies* Trait that you spend after the first gives an extra level of expertise to your allies. They may use this expertise on your behalf, though rarely with your own skill, and they only help as long as you tie up your *Allies* Background Traits in this manner.

• An ally can help you to hunt, though obviously, it's not a good idea to rely on your allies as blood sources, or to even tell them exactly what they're doing when they bring people to you. Each Trait of *Allies* that you use for hunting lets you make a Simple Test. A win or tie grants you one additional Blood Trait. Doing so counts as a project that lasts for the entire time between game sessions.

Be wary of calling on your allies too often. An ally may call on you for mutual aid or refuse to help if pressed into dangerous or illegal activities.

Contacts

With the right contacts in all walks of life, you can get a line on all sorts of useful information. Although having an "ear to the wall" doesn't necessarily provide you with good help or loyal servants, it does mean that you know who to ask when looking for the movers and shakers behind the scenes.

In game terms, your rating in *Contacts* allows you to discern rumors and information. When you call on your contacts, you make a few phone calls, check with likely snitches and grease a few palms. In return, you get rumors and information as if possessed of a certain amount of Influence. Doing so lets you find out exactly what's going on in the city within a particular area. You can get information of a level equal to however many contacts you use. If you use *Contacts* x 3 on *Industry*, for instance, you get information as if digging up dirt with *Industry* x 3 Influence. The advantage of the *Contacts* Background is that contacts can be switched from place to place each game, getting information in different areas at your demand.

Using *Contacts* for especially dangerous or secret information may require you to spend some money or perform a few favors, at the discretion of a Storyteller. On occasion, accidents can cause contacts in one area to dry up, such as a strike that affects your *Industry* contacts, or a particularly unlucky astronomical conjunction sends your *Occult* contacts running for the hills. Your contacts will not generally function as aides or lackeys; that is the purview of the *Allies* and *Retainers* Backgrounds.

Example: *Langley, a Nosferatu, has* Contacts x 5. *This month, his player, Robert, decides that Langley is going to engage in a little corporate espionage. Robert allocates* Contacts x 4 *to* Industry, *learning about local projects and where they're bound for; he leaves one level of* Contacts *in reserve, for life's little emergencies. Next month, he plans to use his contacts to find an* Underworld *buyer for his secrets.*

Fame

Some vampires are Embraced from among the ranks of the wealthy or talented elite. As a result, many Cainites can make a claim to some distinction in their breathing days. Though such notoriety often fades with the years, your *Fame* lingers on to influence mortal society.

Fame allows you to exercise your connections over a longer distance than usual. Certainly, if you've got the right Influence, you can push things around on an interstate or even national scale, but with *Fame*, you can just make a few calls and get your *Contacts*, Influence or *Resources* exerted over a greater range without any impediment. This is not to say you must have *Fame* to get anything done, only that it may help. Your total *Fame* determines your maximum range for unimpeded use of your *Contacts*, Influence and *Resources*.

When you make an effort to exert your *Contacts*, Influence or *Resources* over a long range, you lean on your popularity and image, thus expending your *Fame* Traits until the next game session. *Fame* is most often used in the downtime between sessions to facilitate long-range plans.

Fame Ranges	
Fame Traits	Maximum Range for Backgrounds
Fame x 1	Local scene
Fame x 2	City
Fame x 3	State
Fame x 4	Adjoining states
Fame x 5	Entire country

In a less mechanical fashion, your *Fame* also dictates how recognizable you are to mortals, for one reason or another. The Storyteller will certainly make the effects of your *Fame* apparent, and mortals may take notice of you at bothersome times. Being profiled on "America's Most Wanted" or spotted at the Academy Awards does things to one's reputation, after all.

Fame does have its limitations. It makes little sense for you to have this Background if you're known to be dead in the mortal world. Also, *Fame* does not always indicate widespread instant name recognition; you may only be known to a subset of a particular group, or a recognized expert in a field who's unknown to those outside.

GENERATION				
Generation	Max. Traits	Max. Abilities	Blood	Willpower
Thirteen	10	5	10/1	2/6
Twelve	10	5	11/1	2/8
Eleven	11	5	12/1	4/8
Ten	12	5	13/1	4/10
Nine	13	5	14/2	6/10
Eight	14	5	15/3	6/12
Seven	16	6	20/5	7/14
Six	18	7	30/6	8/16
Five	20	8	40/8	9/18
Four	25	9	50/10	10/20
Three	30	?	?	?

Max. Traits shows your maximum number of total Traits in your primary area of development. As an *optional* rule, your Storyteller may lower this quantity by one in your secondary Attribute and by two in your tertiary Attribute, meaning that you will always have your best potential in your strongest original Attribute area. This limit does not count against Bonus Traits, but you can never claim more than twice your maximum Traits even with bonuses.

Max. Abilities is the maximum levels you can take in any one Ability. With a maximum of five, for instance, you cannot advance beyond *Melee* x 5, though you may take multiple focused Abilities (*Crafts: Woodworking* x 5 and *Crafts: Leatherworking* x 5). Optionally, your Storyteller may allow you to exceed this limit by one in one Ability in which you have a particular area of study.

Blood is your maximum number of Blood Traits. You can hold that amount of blood in your system. The number after the slash is how many Blood Traits you can spend in any given turn. Optionally, your Storyteller may choose to use a "compressed pool" for ease of play. Under such a system, characters have *half* the Blood Traits listed here, rounded up, but all other functions remain the same (exception: the *Thaumaturgy Path of Conjuring* Blood Trait costs are also halved, rounding up; characters come into play with two Traits of blood if they lose a Blood Test at the beginning of a game). This system makes for faster combat resolution and less bookkeeping, but it also makes vampires less powerful. All vampires in a system should use the same Blood Trait scale.

Willpower lists your starting Willpower Traits before the slash, and your maximum Willpower Traits after the slash. Should the Storyteller choose to use the compressed Blood Pool, characters have half the Willpower listed (rounded up).

GENERATION

Generation is the measure of one's fundamental closeness to Caine. Each vampire is Embraced from a long chain of sire to childe, and the blood weakens with each passing. Those Embraced by a sire closer in the chain to Caine and the Antediluvians find that their blood is strengthened by that proximity. The less scrupulous among the younger generations steal this power through the foul process of diablerie. Since a vampire's sheer power and eventual potential are limited by *Generation*, much of vampire society is ordered by those of low *Generation* (close to Caine) while the neonates of weak, thin blood and high *Generation* (many steps removed) champ at a bit that cannot be removed.

You must spend one Background or Free Trait for each *Generation* purchased. Thus, if your character is of the 10th generation, you must spend three Background or Free Traits for this privilege. The Storyteller may place a limit on how low the generation spread may go.

The total number of Traits placed in this Background determines your exact generation. You start at the 13th generation, and drop one generation for each Trait spent — thus, with five Traits of *Generation*, you are of the eighth generation removed from Caine. (You could theoretically have a "negative generation" by taking the Flaw *Fourteenth Generation* — see p. 114.)

Your generation affords great power, for it determines your ultimate potential and raw potency of blood. However, being of low generation also makes you a tempting target for would-be diablerists, who seek to steal your vitae to enrich their own.

HERD

Whether surrounding yourself with mortal cultists, or just making sure that you have regular access to a blood bank, your herd gives you a guaranteed volume of blood for feeding. You don't have to go very far to hunt; your herd, when available to you, offers you a safe and easy way to sustain your powers.

You should work with your Storyteller to describe the exact nature of your herd, since these Traits can be lost through hazards or deliberate sabotage. You could have mortals who are conditioned to enjoy the Kiss, access to medical blood supplies outside of the normal channels or a religious cult that gives you blood freely. Each Trait of *Herd* can be used to gain one extra Blood Trait once per session. You can do this immediately on entering the game to represent that you have previously fed, thus improving your blood from your starting Traits for the evening (based on your Blood Test, as described on p. 106). You can also take 15 minutes out of play to call on a herd and gain a Blood Trait. You can split up *Herd* Traits if you wish, so you may use some Traits to start with extra blood, then use more later to replace spent vitae.

Members of your herd (assuming it is composed of people and not plastic bags) are not necessarily particularly competent or loyal — they simply let you feed from them. You must take *Allies* or *Retainers* if you want them to do other tasks for you.

Example: *Xavier, a 10th-generation Tremere, has Herd x 3. The player, Paul, ties on his Blood Test as he enters play. He starts with half his blood pool (rounded up), or seven Blood Traits. Paul decides to expend Herd x 1 to gain one additional Trait before play, placing him at eight Blood Traits. Later, after a particularly strenuous Thaumaturgical battle, he is in desperate need of sustenance, so the player marks off another Herd x 2 and spends 30 minutes out of play. Xavier returns with two extra Blood Traits.*

INFLUENCE

Mortal society builds on institutions. As humans raise their cities, they form gatherings of expertise that are manipulated by the Cainites hiding in their midst. If you

have Influence, you can sway the direction of some areas of mortal society, pushing cities to grow as you direct. Your Influence can be used to strike indirectly at your foes while protecting your own assets, or to gain information and special resources.

Influence comes in many different areas. You must allocate Traits separately to each Influence; thus, if you have *Legal* x 4, you could still have *Police* x3 independently but you would have to spend the Traits for each.

You cannot manage more Influence than the sum of your permanent Physical, Social and Mental Traits combined. This limit counts against all of your total Influence — your combined levels cannot exceed this total. After all, there are only so many things you can do in a night.

When you exercise Influence, you expend temporary Influence Traits. The tables for various Influence areas detail what you can do with a specific number of Traits. Performing an action requires a number of Traits equal to the level of the action; you must use three Traits to perform an action listed at the third level of an Influence chart, for instance. Thus, with high levels of Influence, you can perform many small actions, or a few significant ones.

Certain levels of Influence gift you with items, money or aides. Unlike the *Resources* Background, money and equipment garnered with Influence does not come automatically each month. If you want a steady income from Influence, you must direct your Influence in that direction continually, and this income does not come with any associated trappings of wealth (you'd have to buy a house and car separately, for instance). Aides garnered with Influence generally help only for one specific task, and they usually only have the equivalent of one level of Ability in their area of skill — for more competent and readily available help, take *Allies*.

Most cities have only a set amount of Influence in various areas. For instance, Atlanta has a great deal of *Transportation* Influence, because it is a hub of travel, while Hollywood would have a lot of *High Society* and *Media* Influence. A Rust-Belt city where manufacturing and heavy industry has all but disappeared would have very little to no *Industry* Influence.

Storytellers should map out the total amount of each type of Influence to be had in the city. Once all of the Influence of a given type is used up, the only way to get more is to use Influence to grow that area of society (making new projects or sponsoring investment), to destroy someone else's Influence and thus free up those resources, or to acquire an adversary's Influence in an area. Also, each city may have different reflections of the Influences listed here. A city with a thriving independent film community is going to have a different picture of *Media* or *High Society* than a city where the arts are being literally starved out due to budget cuts.

Each area of Influence has its own description. Elder vampires may possess truly far-reaching Influence, giving them the power to exert control beyond the levels included here.

BUREAUCRACY

You can manage various government agencies and bureaus. By dealing with social programs and public servants, you can spin red tape, bypass rules and regulations or twist bureaucratic regimentation to your advantage. *Bureaucracy* is useful in operating or shutting down businesses, faking or acquiring permits and identification papers and manipulating public utilities and facilities. Government clerks at the city and county level, utility workers, road crews, surveyors and other civil servants are potential contacts or allies.

Cost	Effect
1	Trace utility bills
2	Fake a birth certificate or driver's license
	Disconnect a single small residence's utilities

	Close a small road or park
	Get public aid ($250)
3	Fake a death certificate, passport or green card
	Close a public school for a single day
	Shut down a minor business on a violation
4	Initiate a phone tap
	Fake land deeds
	Initiate a department-wide investigation
5	Start, stop or alter a city-wide program or policy
	Shut down a big business on a violation
	Rezone areas
	Obliterate records of a person on a city or county level

CHURCH

Though the modern church has arguably less control over temporal society than it did in the Middle Ages, its policies still exert considerable influence over the direction of politics and communities. Knowing the appropriate people allows insight into many mainstream religions, such as Christianity, Judaism, Islam, Hinduism, Shinto or Buddhism (fringe or alternative groups, such as Scientology, are considered *Occult*). When you exercise *Church* Influence, you can change religious policy, affect the assignment of clergy and access a variety of lore and resources. Contacts and allies affected by *Church* Influence would include ministers, priests, bishops, Church-sponsored witch-hunters, holy orders and various attendees and assistants.

Cost	Effect
1	Identify most secular members of a given faith in the local area
	Pass as a member of the clergy
	Peruse general church records (baptism, marriage, burial, etc.)
2	Identify higher church members
	Track regular church members
	Suspend lay members
3	Open or close a single church
	Find the average church-associated hunter
	Dip into the collection plate ($250)
	Access private information and archives of a church
4	Discredit or suspend high-level church members
	Manipulate regional branches of the church
5	Organize major protests
	Access ancient church lore and knowledge

FINANCE

Manipulating markets, stock reports and investments is a hobby of many Cainites, especially those who use their knowledge to keep hidden wealth. Though your actual available money is a function of your *Resources*, you can use *Finance* Influence to start or smother businesses, crush or support banking institutions and alter credit records. Clearly, such power over money is not to be trifled with — fortunes are made and destroyed with this sort of pull. CEOs, bankers, stockbrokers, bank tellers, yes-men, financiers and loan agents are found among such work.

Cost	Effect
1	Learn about major transactions and financial events
	Raise capital ($1,000)
	Learn about general economic trends
	Learn real motivations for many financial actions of others

2	Trace an unsecured small account
	Raise capital to purchase a small business (single, small store)
3	Purchase a large business (a few small branches or a single large store or service)
4	Manipulate local banking (delay deposits, some credit rating alterations)
	Ruin a small business
5	Control an aspect of city-wide banking (shut off ATMs, arrange a bank "holiday")
	Ruin a large business
	Purchase a major company

HEALTH

Some vampires rely on connections in the medical community to acquire blood. Necromancers and practitioners of arcane arts may also require body parts or medical data to further their studies. Furthermore, maintaining the Masquerade often calls for alteration of medical records or faking of particular diseases; some Cainites even specialize in the study of blood-borne ailments. All of these sorts of research and development fall under the purview of *Health* Influence. Coroners, doctors, lab workers, therapists, pharmacists and specialists are just a few of the folks found in this field.

Cost	Effect
1	Access a person's health records
	Fake vaccination records and the like
	Use public functions of health centers at your leisure
	Get a single Blood Trait of mortal blood
2	Access some medical research records
	Have minor lab work done
	Get a copy of a coroner's report
	Instigate minor quarantines
3	Corrupt results of tests or inspections
	Alter medical records
4	Acquire a body
	Completely rewrite medical records
	Abuse grants for personal use ($250)
	Have minor medical research performed on a subject
	Institute large-scale quarantines
	Shut down businesses for "health code violations"
5	Have special research projects performed
	Have people institutionalized or released

HIGH SOCIETY

The glitterati at the top of society move in circles of wealth and elegance. Many Kindred find such positions alluring, and they indulge in the passions of the famous and wealthy. Access to famous actors, celebrities and the idle rich grants a certain sway over fashion trends. Combined with *Fame*, a modicum of *High Society* Influence turns a vampire into a debonair darling of the most exclusive social circles. Among these circles, one finds dilettantes, artists of almost any stripe, old money families, models, rock stars, sports figures and jetsetters.

Cost	Effect
1	Learn what is trendy
	Obtain hard-to-get tickets for shows
	Learn about concerts, shows or plays well before they are made public

2	Track most celebrities and luminaries
	Be a local voice in the entertainment field
	"Borrow" idle cash from rich friends ($1,000)
3	Crush promising careers
	Hobnob well above your station
4	Minor celebrity status
5	Get a brief appearance on a talk show that's not
	about to be canceled
	Ruin a new club, gallery, festival or other posh gathering

INDUSTRY

The grinding wheels of labor fuel the economies and markets of the world. Machines, factories and blue-collar workers line up in endless drudgery, churning out the staples of everyday living. Control over *Industry* Influence sways the formation of unions, the movements of work projects, locations for factories and the product of manufacturing concerns. Union workers, foremen, engineers, construction workers, manual laborers and all manner of blue-collar workers exist among these ranks.

Cost	Effect
1	Learn about industrial projects and movements
2	Have minor projects performed
	Dip into union funds or embezzle petty cash ($500)
	Arrange small accidents or sabotage
3	Organize minor strikes
	Appropriate machinery for a short time
4	Close down a small plant
	Revitalize a small plant
5	Manipulate large local industry

LEGAL

Since many of the operations that Cainites undertake are at least marginally illegal, a good amount of sway over judges and lawyers is indispensable. Those Kindred who dabble in law often pull strings in the courts to make sure that the questionable practices of Cainite society go unnoticed and unpunished. Of course, a little *Legal* Influence is also excellent for harassing an enemy's assets, too. Such Influence ranges from law schools and firms, to lawyers, judges, DAs, clerks and public defenders.

Cost	Effect
1	Get free representation for minor cases
2	Avoid bail for some charge
	Have minor charges dropped
3	Manipulate legal procedures
	(minor wills and contracts, court dates)
	Access public or court funds ($250)
	Get representation in most court cases
4	Issue subpoenas
	Tie up court cases
	Have most legal charges dropped
	Cancel or arrange parole
5	Close down all but the most serious investigations
	Have deportation proceedings held against someone

MEDIA

Directing media attention away from vampire activities is a key component of the Masquerade. Putting specific emphasis on certain events can place an enemy in an uncomfortable spotlight or discredit a rival. With *Media*, you can crush or alter news stories, control the operations of news stations and reporters and sway public

opinion, with DJs, editors of all varieties, reporters, cameramen, photographers and broadcasters at your disposal. At Storyteller discretion, *Media* Influence may also allow access to the more technical areas of television, radio or movies.

Cost	Effect
1	Learn about breaking stories early
	Submit small articles (within reason)
2	Suppress (but not stop) small articles or reports
	Get hold of investigative reporting information
3	Initiate news investigations and reports
	Get project funding and waste it ($250)
	Ground stories and projects
5	Broadcast fake stories (local only)
	Kill small local articles or reports completely

OCCULT

The hidden world of the supernatural teems with secrets, conspiracies and unusual factions. Obviously, a vampire is aware that there are strange things out there by dint of his very existence (after all, if vampires exist…), but hard knowledge of such things is a function of Abilities. By using *Occult* Influence, you can dig up information to improve your knowledge, get inside the occult community and find rare components for magical rituals. Even parts of the elusive *Book of Nod* are available to those with the right connections. Cult leaders, alternative religious groups, charlatans, occultists, New Agers and a few more dangerous elements can be found here.

Cost	Effect
1	Contact and make use of common occult groups and their practices
	Know some of the more visible occult figures
2	Know and contact some of the more obscure occult figures
	Access resources for most rituals and rites
3	Know the general vicinity of certain supernatural entities and (possibly) contact them
	Access vital or rare material components
	Milk impressionable wannabes for bucks ($250)
	Access occult tomes and writings
	Research a Basic ritual from your sect
4	Research an Intermediate ritual from your sect
5	Access minor magic items
	Unearth an Advanced ritual from your sect

POLICE

"To protect and serve" is the motto of the police, but these days, Kindred and kine alike may have cause to wonder who is being protected and served. That said, *Police* Influence can be very handy to assist with the Masquerade, to protect one's holdings or to raid the assets of another. After all, attitude won't save the anarchs whose haven is the target of a daylight raid. Police of all ranks, detectives, clerical staff, dispatchers, prison guards, special divisions (such as SWAT or homicide) and local highway patrol make up these ranks.

Cost	Effect
1	Learn police procedures
	Hear police information and rumors
	Avoid traffic tickets
2	Have license plates checked
	Avoid minor violations (first conviction)
	Get "inside information"
3	Get copies of an investigation report

	Have police hassle, detain or harass someone
	Find bureau secrets
4	Access confiscated weapons or contraband
	Have some serious charges dropped
	Start an investigation
	Get money, either from the evidence room or as an appropriation ($1,000)
5	Institute major investigations
	Arrange setups
	Instigate bureau investigations
	Have officers fired

POLITICAL

Deal-making is second nature to most vampires, so they can get along very well with other bloodsuckers — that is, politicians. Altering party platforms, controlling local elections, changing appointed offices and calling in favors all falls under the purview of *Political* Influence. Well-timed blackmail, bribery, spin doctoring or any sundry tricks are stock in trade on both sides of this fence. Some of the likely contacts and allies include pollsters, lobbyists, activists, party members, spin doctors and politicians from rural zoning committees to the mayors of major cities or Congressional representatives.

Cost	Effect
1	Minor lobbying
	Identify real platforms of politicians and parties
	Be in the know
2	Meet small-time politicians
	Garner inside information on processes, laws and the like
	Use a slush fund or fund-raiser ($1,000)
3	Sway or alter political projects (local parks, renovations, small construction)
4	Enact minor legislation
	Dash careers of minor politicians
5	Get your candidate in a minor office
	Enact encompassing legislature

STREET

Ignored and often spat on by their "betters," those in the dark alleys and slums have created their own culture to deal with life and any outsiders who might come calling. When calling on *Street* Influence, you use your connections on the underside of the city to find the homeless, gang members of all sorts, street buskers, petty criminals, prostitutes, residents of the slums or barrios, and fringe elements of so-called "deviant" cultures.

Cost	Effect
1	Open an ear for the word on the street
	Identify most gangs and know their turfs and habits
2	Live mostly without fear on the underside of society
	Keep a contact or two in most aspects of street life
	Access small-time contraband
3	Get insight into other areas of Influence
	Arrange some services from street people or gangs
	Get pistols or uncommon melee weapons
4	Mobilize groups of homeless
	Panhandle or hold a "collection" ($250)
	Get hold of a shotgun, rifle or SMG
	Have a word in almost all aspects of gang operations
5	Control a single medium-sized gang
	Arrange impressive protests by street people

TRANSPORTATION

Most Cainites make their havens in defensible parts of cities. Traveling across the wilderness is difficult, with the problems of daylight and marauding Lupines. Without this Influence, the vampiric world shrinks into islands of "civilization" with dangerous wastelands in between. Getting access to special supplies and services can also take a measure of *Transportation*. All these things can be controlled with a bit of sway over truckers, harbors, railroads, airports, taxis, border guards, pilots and untold hundreds, as well as more mundane aspects like shipping and travel arrangements.

Cost	Effect
1	Know what goes where, when and why
	Travel locally quickly and freely
2	Track an unwary target if he uses public transportation
	Arrange passage safe (or at least concealed)
	from mundane threats (robbery, terrorism, sunlight, etc.)
3	Seriously hamper an individual's ability to travel
	Avoid most supernatural dangers when traveling
	(such as Lupines)
4	Shut down one form of transportation
	(bus lines, ships, planes, trains, etc.) temporarily
	Route money your way ($500)
5	Reroute major modes of travel
	Smuggle with impunity

UNDERWORLD

The world of crime offers lucrative possibilities to strong-willed or subtle leaders. Guns, money, drugs and vice — such delicious pastimes can be led by anyone talented or simply vicious enough to take them. *Underworld* Influence lets you call on such favors for all manner of illegal dealings, and its ranks are filled by the Mafia, La Cosa Nostra, drug dealers, bookies, Yakuza, tongs, hitmen, fences and criminal gangs.

Cost	Effect
1	Locate minor contraband (knives, small-time drugs,
	petty gambling, scalped tickets)
2	Obtain pistols, serious drugs, stolen cars
	Hire muscle to rough someone up
	Fence stolen loot
	Prove that crime pays (and score $1,000)
3	Obtain a rifle, shotgun or SMG
	Arrange a minor "hit"
	Meet someone in "the Family"
4	Make white-collar crime connections
5	Arrange gangland assassinations
	Hire a demolition man or firebug
	Supply local drug needs

UNIVERSITY

Institutions of learning and research are the purview of the *University* Influence. Access to the halls of learning can help you with any number of resources, from ancient languages to research assistance to many impressionable young minds. School boards, students from kindergarten through college, graduate students, professors, teachers, deans, Greek orders and a variety of staff fill the ivy-covered halls.

Cost	Effect
1	Know layout and policy of local schools
	Have access to low-level university resources
	Get records up to the high school level

2	Know a contact or two with useful knowledge or Abilities
	Have minor access to facilities
	Fake high school records
	Obtain college records
3	Call in faculty favors
	Cancel a class
	Fix grades
	Discredit a student
4	Organize student protests and rallies
	Discredit faculty members
5	Falsify an undergraduate degree

MENTOR

An older or more experienced Cainite looks after you and comes to your aid occasionally. Whatever the case, you can get assistance from your mentor, though his favor may be fickle.

When you call on your mentor, you risk a certain number of Traits to achieve a given effect. A lowly one-Trait mentor probably knows only little more than you, while a five-Trait mentor may well have luminous standing within your sect and a wide range of potent powers. Regardless, taking up your mentor's valuable time is costly. You must engage in a Simple Test when you call on your mentor. If you succeed, your mentor deigns to aid you. If you tie, your mentor grants you assistance, but then requires something in return. If you fail, your mentor demands the favor first before helping. In any case, your mentor can be called on only once in any given game session, and only if you have an appropriate way to contact him or her.

The level of aid that your mentor can give depends on the number of Traits in this Background (and Storyteller approval, of course):

• For one Trait, your mentor is privy to a single piece of specialized information at a level above your own. If you have *Cainite Lore* x 2, for instance, your mentor can be called on to gift you with one piece of information from *Cainite Lore* x 3.

• For two Traits, you can borrow one level of *Contacts*, Influence, *Resources* or Status from your mentor for the duration of the game. If your mentor is very powerful (four or five Traits), you can borrow two levels.

• Two Traits allow your mentor to instruct you in a Basic Discipline that you do not know.

• For three Traits, your mentor can instruct you in an Intermediate Discipline that you do not know.

• Also at a cost of three Traits, your mentor can train you in the ways of a special *Hobby/ Professional/ Expert Ability* that is outside your normal ken, such as *Wraith Lore*.

• For four Traits, your mentor can train you in an Advanced Discipline beyond your grasp.

• For five Traits, your mentor can train you in the phenomenal powers of the elders, if your blood is potent enough to learn such secrets.

Since *Mentors* can prove unbalancing by providing too many different powers over the course of a long game, the Storyteller may lower your total *Mentor* Traits as you call on his knowledge. This decrease represents the fact that as your character learns the mentor's secrets, the mentor has less left to teach.

RESOURCES

You have access to liquid capital and spending money. You also have some solid resources that you can use when times are tight. Unlike the use of *Finance*, these resources are always readily available, and they come to you automatically due to your investments, jobs and holdings.

Resource Allocation	
No Traits:	Poverty. Income $200. Get roommates. Bus pass.
One Trait:	Small savings and holdings; income $500. Have apartment, cheap means of transportation.
Two Traits:	Modest savings and holdings; income $1,000. Have condo and motorcycle or modest car.
Three Traits:	Significant savings and holdings; income $3,000. Own house, car.
Four Traits:	Large savings and holdings. Income $10,000. Own large house or some small properties, two vehicles, some luxuries and unusual items.
Five Traits:	Rich. Income $30,000. Own estate and grounds, multiple small properties, several vehicles, arts and treasures, luxury items.

Your number of *Resources* Traits determines the amount of money and capital that you can secure. By expending temporary *Resources* Traits (which return at the next game session), you can draw on your regular income, as shown in the accompanying table. If you expend permanent *Resources*, you can divest yourself of holdings, allowing access to 10 times the amount shown on the table. However, the limits of what you can buy are always adjudicated by the Storyteller. Truly powerful uses of *Resources* are best left to downtimes and moderation between game sessions.

RETAINERS

Whether out of personal loyalty, love, *Conditioning*, the blood bond or some other power, you have managed to secure the fellowship of a mortal (or several mortals) who obeys your every whim. Unlike the *Allies* Background, your retainers are nearly always around, overseeing your personal effects, defending your property and furthering your goals. They may not have the specialized knowledge of allies, but they are mostly loyal to your cause, and they serve your needs first.

You should work with your Storyteller to determine how you managed to secure a loyal retainer. Your retainer's exact capabilities are up to the Storyteller; a retainer may be skillful but unmotivated, or loyal but inept. No retainer is ever perfect, but they all can be a great help.

• A retainer can be assigned to watch over a particular location. Generally, if someone attempts to break into your house, the retainers there will attempt to stop the intruder. In this case, they are treated as normal humans, run by Narrators.

• A retainer can be used to manage your assets and perform tasks. Retainers tied up in this fashion allow you to manage more Influence than normal; they add to the number of Attribute Traits that you possess for purposes of counting your total Influences. Each retainer directed in this fashion adds one to your maximum Influence Traits. If retainers are later lost, killed or reassigned, the excess Influence Traits are lost, starting with the highest levels of Influence held.

• A retainer can perform other menial functions, as allowed by the Storyteller. You can get someone else to pick up your character's dry-cleaning.

You may choose to declare that any one of your retainers is a ghoul, if you so desire. However, for each ghoul that you have in your holdings, you begin each session's play one Blood Trait down from usual, as you must feed and maintain the servant. Ghouls have the usual benefits of Disciplines and an improved understanding of vampire society, so they make useful guards, but too many can be troublesome. Jealous ghouls (especially when many are blood bound to the same domitor) can cause no end of troubles.

For more about ghouls, see **Liber des Goules**.

BLOOD

Blood is the power that fuels all vampires. Unable to enjoy the pleasures of mortal flesh or the comfort of more mundane gratification, only blood offers sustenance to Cainites. Vampires must consume blood to survive, and it is with the life contained in blood that a vampire draws on the strengths of the undead condition.

Blood Traits do not have adjectives. Rather, each Trait simply represents a quantity of blood. In general, a vampire is assumed to have 10 pints of vitae in her system when full. Elder vampires, however, concentrate their blood more efficiently, and thus they have more than 10 Traits.

Blood Traits can be represented with cards. When a character gains Blood Traits by feeding, take the cards from the victim. When Blood Traits are spent, give the cards to a Narrator or Storyteller.

Your starting Blood Trait total is determined by your generation. When you come into play for an evening's game, make a test with a Narrator as you pick up your character sheet. If you win, you come into play with all of your Blood Traits, as determined by generation. If you tie, you have half your generational limit of Blood Traits, rounded up. If you lose, you come into play with only four Blood Traits. Certain Merits, Flaws, clan disadvantages or other circumstances may alter your number of Blood Traits at the beginning of play, and possession of the *Herd* Background allows you to come into play with more Blood Traits, up to your generation limit (see the appropriate Background descriptions on p. 96 for *Generation* and *Herd*).

When you have expended a great deal of blood, you become hungry. A hungry vampire is susceptible to the Beast and to frenzy due to the ravenous lust for vitae. You are considered hungry if at five or fewer Blood Traits; you may be susceptible to frenzy at the sight, smell or taste of blood (see *Self-Control/Instinct*, on p. 109). If you have two or fewer Blood Traits, you are ravenous, and your difficulty to resist frenzy due to hunger goes up by one Trait, making it very likely that you enter frenzy at the first opportunity to feed.

Feeding is the only way to replenish blood. You can take Blood Traits from mortals, other vampires or other creatures with blood, such as animals or Lupines. When you bite someone to drain blood, you invoke the Kiss; your bite causes a rapturous helplessness in normal mortals, and it is pleasurable even to other creatures. However, each Blood Trait drained inflicts a level of lethal damage on the victim. Up to three Blood Traits may be drained each turn. You can close the wound by licking it to seal up traces of your feeding. You may only heal such wounds that were made by your fangs.

You can expend Blood Traits for a variety of functions:

- You must spend a Blood Trait each night at sunset, for simple sustenance.
- One Blood Trait can heal one health level of bashing or two levels of lethal damage. You are still limited to your generation limits of blood expenditure (so most young vampires cannot heal more than one health level of damage in a turn). Healing in this fashion requires your concentration and a full turn.
- One Blood Trait can be spent to gain an extra Physical Trait for the duration of a conflict. You can bid this Trait like any other ("by the power of my blood,"), and you can count this Trait in ties and overbids. You can spend blood like this as a reflexive action at any time, not counting as your action, though of course you still obey the limits of blood expenditure according to generation. You can raise your Physical Traits up to the limit of your generation for one conflict; any additional Traits added with blood beyond that remain only for the duration of a single challenge.

Example: *Romero de la Salle, Lasombra antitribu scourge, wants to augment his already-mighty Potence by increasing his Physical Traits over his usual 14. As he is of the Seventh*

Generation, he can normally have up to 16 Traits in a category. Shane marks off three Blood Traits; Romero goes up to 17 Traits for the turn, and even after the turn ends, he has 16 Traits for the rest of the conflict (assuming that he doesn't lose any challenges). Even if he loses some Physical Traits, he can spend more blood to bring his total back up to 16.

• One Blood Trait — generally measured as a full pint— is sufficient to turn a mortal into a ghoul. This state lasts for a month; after that time, the ghoul must be fed more blood, lest he revert back to mortality.

• One Blood Trait enables a vampire to take on a semblance of humanity for a scene. The vampire flushes and becomes capable of mimicking human activity (such blinking, sneezing or having cool skin rather than cold)Doing so is difficult for vampires with low Humanity; a vampire must spend an extra Blood Trait for each Trait that her Humanity is below five — a vampire with four Humanity Traits must spend two Blood Traits to appear mortal, a vampire with three Humanity Traits spends three Blood Traits to masquerade and so on. Vampires following Paths of Enlightenment cannot do this trick at all. You can take on a mortal visage while performing other tasks. If you must spend multiple Traits to perform this feat but your generation prohibits spending enough blood at once, you must spend the Blood Traits over successive turns. That is, a 13th-generation vampire with a Humanity of three Traits would have to spend three turns, spending one Blood Trait per turn, although he would still be able to perform other actions.

• Three Blood Traits can be spent to heal one level of aggravated damage. This damage heals over the day, as the vampire sleeps. Blood Traits spent this way can be accumulated; that is, you need not spend the three Traits all at once, or even all in the same day. You should note Traits expended in this fashion with marks next to your level of aggravated damage; once you have spent three Blood Traits on the injury, it heals the next time the sun sets. You can only heal one level of aggravated damage per day in this fashion, though, unless you also spend a Willpower Trait for each extra wound healed in the same rest period.

• Many Disciplines require the expenditure of Blood Traits, as listed in their individual descriptions. If a particular Discipline costs multiple Blood Traits but your generation prohibits you from spending all of the blood at once, you must spend the blood on successive turns. Spending blood in this fashion is usually reflexive, though the Discipline itself may require an action. For instance, activating *Celerity* is reflexive; you spend a Blood Trait and still get your normal action, plus extra actions from *Celerity*. Casting a *Thaumaturgy* effect, on the other hand, requires your full turn in addition to the blood expenditure.

You can acquire blood from any creature that has blood, including other supernatural creatures, but doing so can cause certain side effects. See pages 202-203 for information about the effects of drinking such "special" blood.

WILLPOWER

Willpower Traits measure the strength of your character's resolve and sense of self. By exerting your Willpower, you can withstand otherwise untenable conditions, renew your commitment to a course of action and empower certain difficult Disciplines.

Willpower Traits are not described with adjectives. You simply have permanent Willpower — your normal limit of Willpower Traits — and temporary Willpower, your expendable Traits. Your starting permanent and temporary Willpower are determined by your generation; your generation also determines the maximum level to which you can improve your permanent Willpower. When you expend temporary Willpower Traits or raise your permanent Willpower, you regain temporary Traits at a rate of one per game session (though your Storyteller may vary this pace to suit the needs of her game or to simplify bookkeeping).

Expending a Willpower Trait allows for one of any number of effects. Generally, Willpower Traits allow you to keep self-determination and to empower extremely difficult or complex actions. Using Willpower is almost always a reflexive action, and does not count as your turn.

• A Willpower Trait can be spent to refresh all of your lost Traits in one Attribute category—Physical, Social or Mental. You may do so once per category per game session.

• Expenditure of a Willpower Trait allows you to gain a retest when defending against a Mental or Social Challenge. Trait loss works as normal for such retests. Note that certain Disciplines or powers may override this stipulation—for instance, you can not use Willpower to see through *Obfuscate*.

• Spending one Willpower Trait enables you to enter a challenge for which you lack an appropriate Ability. Thus, you can make a test even if you would normally require a specific Ability that you don't have or have used up.

• You can spend a Willpower Trait to try to control yourself briefly while in frenzy. You are able to act normally for one turn when you spend Willpower in this fashion, though you otherwise keep all the other stipulations of frenzy—ignoring wound penalties and so on. You do not actually regain control so much as you fight mightily to direct yourself for a few moments in the face of overwhelming rage or terror; roleplay your actions appropriately.

• You can expend a Willpower Trait to ignore all wound penalties, up to and including Incapacitated, for the duration of one full turn.

• Spending a Willpower Trait lets you suppress a derangement temporarily. If you spend enough Willpower Traits on suppressing a derangement, you may overcome it eventually. Malkavians cannot overcome their primary derangement this way. (See "Derangements" on p. 212-214.)

• Certain Disciplines or powers require the expenditure of Willpower.

VIRTUE TRAITS

When pressed by overwhelming stresses or destructive forces, vampires may find themselves lost in the fury of their predatory instincts. The Beast in every vampire strives to survive, forcing you to hunt for blood, to kill others who threaten you and to flee the power of fire and sunlight.

You have three categories of Virtue Traits. Each type of Trait is used for a specific sort of Virtue Test. *Conscience/ Conviction* is used to hold to your moral path, even if you have a lapse of behavior. *Self-Control/ Instinct* allows you to deny or direct the terrible urges of your hungry and destructive Beast. *Courage* stands against the primal fear of the forces that can destroy you. Your Morality Path determines the sort of Virtues that you have; you cannot have both *Conscience* and *Conviction* or *Self-Control* and *Instinct* — you have only one from each category. Each Virtue Trait rating goes from zero to five Traits, though you do not use adjectives to describe the Traits.

VIRTUE TESTS

When you suffer from an ethical dilemma, overpowering rage or incredible fear, you may use a Virtue Test to resist succumbing to the Beast. Such a test is a Static Challenge. The difficulty varies with the stimulus, as described for each sort of Virtue. Note that you are never required to make a Virtue Test; you may relent and automatically lose, if desired.

If you win a Virtue Test, your morals overcome the Beast and you hold fast against the predator. When you lose a Virtue Test, you suffer a lapse of virtue. You suffer from a debilitating Negative Trait or problem, as described under the appropriate Virtue.

You may make one retest on a failed Virtue Test by risking an appropriate Virtue Trait; if you succeed in the retest, you only lose a Virtue Trait temporarily (for the

rest of the session, making you more likely to succumb to further failings if you are not careful). If you lose the retest, you gain a temporary derangement related to your failure in addition to suffering the normal results of a Virtue Test loss. Note specifically that you may not overbid on a Virtue Test.

Regaining Virtue Traits requires the expenditure of Experience, as well as consistent roleplaying for the particular strength that you wish to cultivate.

See the specific Virtue descriptions for examples of Virtue Tests.

Conscience/Conviction

Conscience represents your tie to feelings of remorse and guilt. If you have a high *Conscience*, you suffer whenever you do something that you find morally wrong. As a result, your tie to your feelings keeps you from losing Morality Traits.

Conviction, on the other hand, is the strength to resolve yourself against future failings. If you suffer a lapse of Morality but have a high *Conviction*, you chastise yourself and steel yourself against ever making the same mistake. This strength of character also keeps you from losing Morality Traits.

A Virtue Test of *Conscience/Conviction* is appropriate whenever you violate your Morality Path, as described on the Hierarchies of Sin. Whenever you commit a violation that is at or below your current Morality Trait total on the Hierarchy of Sin, you must make a *Conscience/Conviction* Virtue Test. If you have only two Morality Traits, breaches of higher Morality are too trivial to cost you any further ground, but if you have four or five Morality Traits, you must be careful to uphold your ethics with every action. The difficulty of the challenge is the level of the sin on the Hierarchy table; if you commit a sin at level four on the Hierarchy of Sins table, you have a four-Trait difficulty to your *Conscience/Conviction* challenge.

Losing a *Conscience/Conviction* Virtue Test causes you to immediately lose a Morality Trait.

Example: *Adian Gray, a rather cold Ventrue with a Humanity of three Traits, winds up killing a mortal in the course of his investigations. Outright murder is a two-Trait sin, so Adian's player makes a Conscience test with a difficulty of two Traits. If he wins or ties, Adian feels remorse for his actions and does not lose Humanity; if he loses, he suffers the loss of a Humanity Trait, dropping to two. Adian's player makes the test and wins — Adian realizes that he could have avoided killing the mortal and feels shame and remorse for the deed.*

Later, Adian steals some documents while sneaking about the local police building. Since that is a four-Trait sin and he only has three Humanity Traits, it is too minor a crime to cause him further risk of Humanity. The player need not make a test of Conscience for that action.

Self-Control/Instinct

When you are overcome with murderous rage or hunger, you can use your *Self-Control* to stand against the Beast, to fortify your will and to keep control over yourself. When you would normally enter frenzy, you can make a Virtue Test of *Self-Control* (though you are not required to do so); the difficulty varies as shown on the accompanying table. If you succeed, you manage to push aside your feral urges for the time being. You then need not make any further *Self-Control* challenges against the same stimulus for the rest of that conflict.

Similarly, *Instinct* allows you to guide your frenzy, keeping some modicum of direction over your actions. If you have *Instinct*, you *always* enter frenzy, unless you have more *Instinct* than double the rating of the frenzy shown on the table, in which case, you may choose whether or not to enter frenzy. Once in frenzy, you can make an *Instinct* Virtue Test, if desired, to control your actions for one turn. If you win the test, you manage to direct your frenzy for the turn, though of course you still suffer all the usual conditions of frenzy — resistance to injury, inability to use your Mental or Social powers and so on. If you lose, your frenzy proceeds as normal; in the event

of a tie, compare your current *Instinct* Traits to the provocation rating to determine whether you manage to direct your frenzy.

You can never use more *Self-Control/ Instinct* Traits on Virtue Test resolution than your current number of Blood Traits. If you are hungry, it is hard to resist the call of frenzy. Note that you do not frenzy automatically if you run out of blood; however, you are very likely to frenzy if you are exposed to a stimulus, since you won't be able to use any *Self-Control/ Instinct* Traits in the event of a tie.

If you attempt to make a test of *Self-Control/ Instinct* and fail, you automatically gain the permanent Negative Social Trait: *Callous* or *Condescending* (your choice), though it can be bought off normally.

Example: *Starved, stumbling down a side alley, Arithon catches sight of a mortal meal. Although he is out of blood, he does not frenzy immediately, since he is not yet agitated and has not scented blood. As he closes in, the punk belligerently turns to face him, and gives him a rude gesture. Now that he's been harassed, Arithon must make a Self-Control Virtue Test, with a difficulty of two Traits. Since he is out of blood, he effectively has no Self-Control; he tests against another player (since it's just a Static Challenge) and ties. With his lack of blood leaving him with no Self-Control Traits, Arithon enters a frenzy, attempting to drain the mortal. He also gains a new permanent Negative Trait. Realizing that he can't win on ties and that the mortal is unlikely to pose a problem, Arithon's player decides not to risk any further Traits on a retest.*

Later, full of blood, Arithon is at a local club when he is accosted by an Assamite. The Assamite attacks him from surprise — a three-Trait provocation. Arithon's player makes a Static Challenge. If he wins, he manages to control himself, and does not frenzy as the Assamite attacks him. If he ties, his Self-Control of two Traits is insufficient to best the frenzy stimulus; if he loses, he frenzies automatically.

COURAGE

The eternal life promised by the curse of Caine can be ended by varied means, the most painful of which are probably fire and sunlight. The searing wounds inflicted by these banes galvanize Cainites to extremes of self-preservation. Few can remain calm in the face of this destruction.

Courage Traits measure self-possession and the ability to resist the terror inflicted by fire, sunlight and True Faith. You must make a *Courage* challenge when confronted with such attacks. If you succeed, you manage to resist the urge to flee for the duration of the conflict (or for 10 minutes). If you fail, though, you enter Rötschreck, a form of terrified frenzy in which you attempt to escape by any means possible. Losing a *Courage* Test also causes you to suffer from the Negative Physical Trait: *Cowardly* or the Negative Mental Trait: *Submissive*, permanently, although such Traits can be removed later with Experience.

Note that you generally do not need to make a *Courage* Virtue Test against fire under your control. If you are lighting your own cigarette, for instance, or using the *Thaumaturgy* path *The Lure of Flames*, you are in control of the fire and thus

SELF- CONTROL/ INSTINCT DIFFICULTIES	
Traits	Stimulus
One	Smell of blood when hungry
Two	Sight of blood when hungry; harassed; life-threatening situation
Three	Physical provocation or attacks; taste of blood when hungry
Four	Loved one in danger; humiliated
Five	Outright humiliation; mortal insults

unaffected by fear of it. However, if someone uses fire against you as a weapon (a hunter threatening to touch a lighter to your hair, facing someone brandishing a torch), you may need to make a *Courage* Test.

Example: *Due to some rather rash actions, the haven of Marcus the Brujah is engulfed in flames. Marcus, Cassandra and John Slime are all surprised by the fire that bursts up from the floor. The Storyteller calls for a Virtue Test of Courage with all the vampires present, to see who succumbs to Rötschreck. The Storyteller throws Scissors. Marcus' player throws Rock, and thus Marcus remains unaffected. John Slime and Cassandra's players both throw Paper, so they're in trouble. Both of the players risk a Courage Trait for a retest, and test against the Storyteller again. This time, Kurt wins, so John Slime manages to control himself, but he loses a Courage Trait for the evening — he's shaken by the experience and more likely to flee from later threats. Katherine, on the other hand, ties on her retest, but Cassandra only has two Courage Traits. She loses the test, gains a Negative Trait, gains a temporary derangement and goes into Rötschreck.*

MORALITY TRAITS

As described previously, your Morality Path shows the particular code that you try to uphold. Your Morality Traits measure your distance from the Beast and your success in adhering to that moral code. Ranging from zero to five Traits, these Traits simply serve as an indicator of your ethical strength. You do not expend or use Morality Traits in any fashion. However, your total Morality Traits do affect your condition; a vampire close to being overtaken by the Beast is more likely to succumb to vampiric instincts like slumber during the day or the long torpor of ages.

Morality Traits are lost when you suffer a lapse in *Conscience* or *Conviction*. See the Morality tables on p. 75-79 for the Hierarchies of Sin, which determine what constitutes a moral violation for your beliefs. You can only gain Morality Traits through consistent adherence to your ethics, good roleplaying and the expenditure of Experience with your Storyteller's approval.

• When sleeping during the day, your total Morality Traits determine how deeply you slumber. You can never bid more than triple your Morality Traits for any action during the day (so even a mighty elder is susceptible to mortals due to such sluggishness).

• The length of time that you spend in torpor varies with the strength of your Morality. Normally, you spend six game sessions in torpor and out of play; lower this number by one session for each Morality Trait that you possess. Note that certain circumstances can rescue you from torpor prematurely: magical healing or imbibing a Trait of blood from a vampire three generations lower than you, for instance. This imposed length of time applies only if you are sent to torpor involuntarily — if you choose to take the long sleep, you can rise at any time that you desire.

• If you have Humanity, you appear more like a normal mortal. Vampires with low Humanity Traits, or on alternate paths of morality, have trouble dealing with normal humans. Such monstrous creatures acquire pallid, corpselike visages and

COURAGE DIFFICULTIES	
Traits	Stimulus
One	Being bullied; lighter; sunrise
Two	Torch; obscured sunlight
Three	Bonfire; uncovered window during daylight
Four	House fire; being burned
Five	Trapped in a burning building; direct sunlight

sociopathic demeanors that repel humans subconsciously. For every Trait of Humanity below four, you suffer a one-Trait penalty in resolution of Social Challenges with mortals, except for intimidation. If you follow a Path, you suffer the full three-Trait penalty automatically. This penalty applies only in dealings with normal humans; your bestial countenance terrifies them and they sense your predatory nature, but other vampires and supernatural creatures are not so easily frightened.

• If you ever run completely out of Morality Traits, your character falls to the Wassail, the final frenzy. Your character enters a totally uncontrolled state of berserk rage and instinctive survival. Such a character cannot be coaxed from frenzy, cannot control himself and is no longer suitable for play. Other Cainites generally put down such unfortunates very quickly.

DERANGEMENTS

Mental instability and insanity plague many vampires, who are gripped by their guilt, remorse and inability to deal with the changing world. Derangements represent specific mental problems that sometimes crop up in situations of stress.

Derangements are tools of advanced roleplaying, and they should only be taken with the consultation of the Storyteller. As a result, they are listed in the Storytelling section of this book, on pp. 212-214.

NEGATIVE TRAITS

As listed previously under Attributes, you can take Negative Traits to specify particular weaknesses inherent to your character. The listings of Negative Traits are included with the other Traits on pp. 80-85.

When someone guesses your Negative Trait successfully in a challenge, you are forced to risk an additional Trait to continue with the challenge. Thus, if you enter a Mental Challenge but your opponent successfully guesses one of your Negative Mental Traits, you must bid and risk an additional Trait to continue with the challenge. If you do not have any more Traits to risk, you automatically lose the challenge.

MERITS AND FLAWS

As optional Traits to flesh out your character, Merits and Flaws allow you to specify particular advantages or disadvantages that are not covered by Attributes, Abilities or Backgrounds. All Merits and Flaws are organized into specific categories, according to their type. To purchase a Merit, you must expend Free Traits equal to the cost of the Merit; taking a Flaw, conversely, hinders you with a handicap of some sort, but it offers additional Free Traits. You can take up to seven Traits each of Merits and Flaws. Some elder characters may have more; certainly, very old vampires may develop potential capabilities and resources outstripping their younger childer, or they may succumb to more terrible illnesses of body and mind.

Normally, you must purchase Merits and Flaws during character creation. However, with an appropriate story, you may be able to buy a new Merit (with Experience equal to double its value) or overcome a Flaw (again, with Experience equal to double its value).

PHYSICAL MERITS AND FLAWS
ACUTE SENSE (1 TRAIT MERIT)

You have a particularly sharp sense (specify which one). In all tests with that sense, you are two Traits up on challenge-resolution. Combined with the *Auspex* power of *Heightened Senses*, this Merit can gift you with truly superhuman acuity. You may have multiple *Acute Senses*, but you may only take this Merit once for each sense.

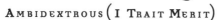

AMBIDEXTROUS (I TRAIT MERIT)

You have a high degree of coordination, and you can use both of your hands equally well. Normally, you suffer a two-Trait penalty for performing tasks with your "off" hand. With this Merit, you have no penalty for using either hand. Of course, if you use both hands, you still suffer the coordination penalty for both (see "Two-Weapon Combat" on p. 207).

CATLIKE BALANCE (I TRAIT MERIT)

You almost never slip, stumble, fall or even get dizzy. Your sense of balance is so well-developed that you can walk with ease even on a narrow ledge or wire. You are two Traits up on resolution of challenges where your balance is a deciding factor.

EAT FOOD (I TRAIT MERIT)

Perhaps you developed this capacity after your Embrace, or maybe you never lost the ability to eat food. Whatever the case, your atrophied organs can still stomach solids. You do not digest such food, however, and you gain no sustenance from it; you must regurgitate the food at a later time. Having this Merit can be invaluable in maintaining the Masquerade.

BLUSH OF HEALTH (2 TRAIT MERIT)

Unlike other vampires who become pallid and gaunt, you retain a flush of life to your skin. Your appearance is still healthy, and you only feel slightly cool. This Merit is a great boon in blending in with mortals, though you still suffer Negative Traits from low Humanity or Path ratings (as those are more a result of your innate monstrousness than your appearance).

ENCHANTING VOICE (2 TRAIT MERIT)

Your voice is naturally resonant and commanding. All uses of your voice grant you two Bonus Traits; you can seduce, intimidate and cajole with just a few well-chosen words. This gift is most effective in combination with *Presence* or *Melpominee*.

DAREDEVIL (3 TRAIT MERIT)

Not only do you take outrageous risks, you survive them. Whenever you take a risky (some would say foolhardy) course of action — one with a Static difficulty of at least eight Traits or a potentially harmful outcome — you get one Bonus Trait on the attempt. This bonus applies only to combats where you are outnumbered or sorely outclassed (Narrator's discretion).

EFFICIENT DIGESTION (3 TRAIT MERIT)

You manage to draw extra nourishment out of blood while feeding. You gain three Blood Traits for every two that you drain from a mortal (rounding fractions down). This efficiency applies only to mortal blood, and you cannot take more than your normal Blood Trait maximum.

HUGE SIZE (4 TRAIT MERIT)

Nearly seven feet tall and hundreds of pounds in weight, you tower over most adversaries (and allies). You have one extra Bruised health level. You should represent your incredible mass appropriately — wearing bulky clothing is a good start.

HARD OF HEARING (I TRAIT FLAW)

You have some difficulty hearing. You suffer a two-Trait penalty on all tests of hearing. Obviously, you cannot have this Flaw and the Merit: *Acute Sense: Hearing*.

SHORT (I TRAIT FLAW)

You have trouble seeing over things, interacting with tall people and escaping notice due to your proportions. You can only take two steps in an action instead of three, due to your small size. You also have trouble reaching countertops and manipulating objects designed for normal people (like cars). You should wear a tag to note your condition if you are not actually that short.

Smell of the Grave (1 Trait Flaw)

You exude the unconcealable stench of wet earth, which puts you one Trait down on social interactions with mortals automatically. Your loamy scent is quite distinctive to those familiar with you.

Bad Sight (1 to 3 Trait Flaw)

Defective sight causes you no end of trouble. Any time you are called on to perform a challenge that involves careful eyesight, you suffer a two-Trait penalty. If your vision problem is correctable with glasses or contact lenses, it is only worth one Trait; if it is uncorrectable, it is worth three Traits. Obviously, you cannot have the Merit: *Acute Vision: Sight* with this Flaw.

Fourteenth Generation (2 Trait Flaw)

Embraced in the modern age, your blood is thin beyond even that of most Caitiff. You are no more than five years as a vampire, created by one of the 13th generation. You have 10 Blood Traits, but you can only use eight of them; the other two are inert, treated like mortal blood. You must take the Flaw: *Thin Blood* (although you do get Free Traits for it), and you are most likely Caitiff, for your blood is too weak to pass the distinguishing characteristics of clan. You may not take the Backgrounds of *Generation* with this Flaw.

Disfigured (2 Trait Flaw)

A hideous disfigurement afflicts you, twisting your countenance in a memorable fashion. You cannot take any Appearance-related Social Traits. Furthermore, you suffer a two-Trait penalty on all Social Challenges except intimidation.

One Eye (2 Trait Flaw)

Whether by injury or defect, you are missing an eye or one of your eyes does not function. You are two Traits down on tests of depth perception, including ranged combat. Depending on the nature of your eye damage, you may choose to wear an eyepatch, or you may simply have one blind eye.

Addiction (3 Trait Flaw)

Some chemical or biological substance hooked you, and now you crave it in the blood. You try to feed from people whose blood will satiate your cravings. This substance generally has negative effects on you — alcohol or depressants may give you the Negative Trait: *Lethargic* for the rest of the evening after feeding, or amphetamines may cause you to suffer from the Negative Trait *Impatient*. You can only draw nourishment from blood with your "fix" in it; you vomit up any other blood.

Child (3 Trait Flaw)

You were embraced as a child, between five and 10 years of age. Your age causes some decided problems: you cannot have more than six Physical Traits normally, and you suffer a two-Trait penalty on tests of authority with adults. Since you never age or grow up, this Flaw will probably be with you forever. You must additionally take the Flaw: *Short* (though you do get Free Traits for it).

Deformity (3 Trait Flaw)

A physical deformity of some sort not only mars your appearance, but it makes physical activity difficult for you. You have a one-Trait penalty on challenge resolution for Physical tests, and two for Social tests. You should work with the Storyteller to define the nature of your deformity (be it a hunchback, club foot, withered limb etc.).

Infectious Bite (3 Trait Flaw)

Due to enzymes, a disease or just some unknown mystical factor, you cannot heal your bite simply by licking the wound. In fact, mortals can be infected with a serious disease if you feed on them — if you fail a Simple Test after leaving a mortal alive but bitten, the mortal contracts a serious disease (see **Laws of the Hunt** for information about mortals and infection).

LAME (3 TRAIT FLAW)

More than simply suffering from a twitchy limb like the *Lame* Negative Physical Trait, you have severe damage to your legs. You can only take one step per action, you cannot run and you should take the Negative Trait *Lame* as well. You should roleplay this Flaw with a cane or a set of leg braces.

MONSTROUS (3 TRAIT FLAW)

Something about you became wholly monstrous when you were Embraced. Your outward form twists to reflect your inner Beast. You cannot initiate Social Challenges, except ones concerning intimidation, when your true form is apparent, and you may not take Appearance-related Traits, such as *Alluring* or *Gorgeous*. Nosferatu and Samedi may not take this Flaw.

PERMANENT WOUND (3 TRAIT FLAW)

Before your Embrace, you suffered some sort of wound which your transformation failed to repair. As a result, you rise each night with the same affliction. You wake up each evening at your first *Wounded* health level with lethal damage, although this damage may be healed normally.

SLOW HEALING (3 TRAIT FLAW)

Your blood is not very efficient in healing your wounds, or maybe you just never really learned to direct your vitae for regeneration. Repairing one level of damage costs you two Blood Traits, and you can only restore one aggravated level of damage per week (though you can bank your blood for healing, as described under "Blood Traits", p. 106).

DEAF (4 TRAIT FLAW)

You are completely deaf. You must use sign language or some other form of communication. You cannot hear *Dominate* commands, and so you are usually immune to them (unless they are implanted telepathically or otherwise without voice), but you suffer a three-Trait penalty on tests of perception and alertness. You cannot have *Acute Sense: Hearing*, and you are surprised automatically by anyone who approaches you from outside your line of sight.

DISEASE CARRIER (4 TRAIT FLAW)

You suffer from a fatal disease, and you spread it readily to anyone who drinks your blood. Though it has little effect on Cainites, it does require you to spend an extra Blood Trait when awakening in the evening if you wish to avoid suffering its debilitating symptoms. Furthermore, other vampires who feed on you must make two Simple Tests — if both tests are lost, the vampire contracts your disease as well.

MUTE (4 TRAIT FLAW)

You cannot speak at all. To communicate, you may need to sign or write out your thoughts. You can explain actions to a Storyteller, but that is the limit of your speaking. Without *Linguistics*, you may not even be able to sign. This Flaw can be difficult to roleplay, so choose carefully.

THIN BLOOD (4 TRAIT FLAW)

The curse of Caine is weak in your vitae. As a result, your blood sustains you only poorly. All costs for Blood Traits are doubled, and may require you to spend multiple turns when powering Disciplines or healing. You cannot create a blood bond, and you can only Embrace someone if you win (not tie) a Simple Test — otherwise, the victim simply dies.

FLESH OF THE CORPSE (5 TRAIT FLAW)

When you suffer injury, your flesh knits with terrible scars and puckering seams. Every time you take a wound, you suffer from the Negative Trait *Repugnant*, and it persists even after you heal the injury. After a day's sleep, your skin finally restores itself, but the marks are still a difficulty when dealing with the Masquerade before you have slept.

BLIND (6 TRAIT FLAW)

The world of sight is lost to you. You automatically lose all ties where sight would be a factor (tests of manual dexterity, for instance). You fail any challenge requiring sight automatically. You cannot be affected by *Dominate* because you cannot see the opponent's gaze, but that is about the limit of the benefits. If you have this Flaw, you should wear a special tag or glasses to indicate its nature. Interestingly, you can still use the *Auspex* Discipline power of *Aura Perception*, though you perceive the aura through other senses (smell, sound, etc.).

MENTAL MERITS AND FLAWS

COMMON SENSE (1 TRAIT MERIT)

You still have a lot of gut insight and everyday practicality. Whenever you're about to do something that runs counter to common sense, the Storyteller or Narrator can make suggestions about the action. This Merit is excellent for new players who are not familiar with the intricacies of the game.

CONCENTRATION (1 TRAIT MERIT)

You can shut out distractions and annoyances that would hinder others. Whenever penalty Traits are assigned for some outside phenomenon (harsh lighting, rain, loud noise, etc.), you suffer none of the penalty.

TIME SENSE (1 TRAIT MERIT)

You can estimate time accurately to the nearest one or two minutes without the use of a watch or clock. This Merit is obviously very useful in getting back to safety before sunrise.

CODE OF HONOR (2 TRAIT MERIT)

A specific code of behavior and ethics, separate from your Path of Enlightenment, guides your actions. This code is very personal, shaped by your own experiences. You should work with your Storyteller to build an appropriate code (which should include some hindrances and prohibited activity in addition to beliefs and passions). You gain one free retest whenever facing a Mental or Social situation that might cause you to violate your code, be it supernatural persuasion or possible frenzy.

EIDETIC MEMORY (2 TRAIT MERIT)

Your memory is nearly perfect, and you recall almost everything you experience with incredible clarity. A single turn of attention is sufficient to commit a page, picture or short conversation to memory. If you are involved in combat or otherwise distracted, you must make a Static Mental Challenge, difficulty of six Traits, to successfully memorize the contents of your subject of scrutiny. You should keep a "cheat sheet" of your memories to aid you and the Storyteller in "recollection."

LIGHT SLEEPER (2 TRAIT MERIT)

While most vampires sleep soundly during the day, you are still sensitive to your surroundings. You wake easily and instantly at any sign of disturbance. You also suffer no limit to your Traits due to sleepiness during the day, regardless of your Morality Trait total.

NATURAL LINGUIST (2 TRAIT MERIT)

You have a remarkable grasp with any languages that you speak or write (as per your *Linguistics* Ability). You gain three Bonus Traits on all challenges related to language.

CALM HEART (3 TRAIT MERIT)

Though the Beast moves in you, it is more subdued than in other vampires. You control your passions better than most, or you are just naturally more temperate. You are one Trait up on resolution of *Self-Control/ Instinct* and *Courage* Virtue Tests. Brujah may not take this Merit.

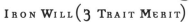

Iron Will (3 Trait Merit)

When your mind is set, your will is not broken easily. If you are affected with the *Dominate* Discipline, you may expend a Willpower Trait to retest the effect. If you win, the effect is negated and you receive a five-minute immunity to further *Dominate*. If mind-altering magic or *Thaumaturgy* with a Mental Challenge affects you, you get three Bonus Traits in defense. Note that this Merit does not defend against *Presence* or other social manipulations.

Deep Sleeper (1 Trait Flaw)

You are even more sluggish than the normal vampire during the day. You have great difficulty awakening, even at signs of danger. During the day, waking up is a Static Mental Challenge versus 10 Traits.

Nightmares (1 Trait Flaw)

Hideous nightmares (daymares?) flit through your mind whenever you slumber. At a Narrator's discretion, you may suffer nightmares so bad that you are unable to sleep restfully, causing you to lose one Trait on all challenges for the evening. A crafty Storyteller is usually quick to take advantage of this Flaw.

Prey Exclusion (1 Trait Flaw)

For some reason, you refuse to hunt a certain class of prey, such as children, clergy or police. If you accidentally feed on your excluded subject, you immediately enter frenzy and must make a four-Trait *Conscience/ Conviction* Challenge or lose a Morality Trait. Furthermore, if you witness someone else feeding on your excluded type, you must make a *Self-Control/ Instinct* Virtue Test as if provoked. Ventrue cannot take this Flaw, due to their more restrictive clan diet.

Shy (1 Trait Flaw)

Unlike the Negative Trait *Shy*, which indicates difficulty dealing with other individuals, you have a specific problem with large groups of people. You take a two-Trait penalty on all Social Challenges with three or more people, three Traits for groups of 10 or more.

Soft-Hearted (1 Trait Flaw)

You cannot abide suffering, because of the emotional disturbance or pain that it causes you. You must avoid causing pain or suffering to anyone; only by spending a Willpower Trait can you overcome this limitation for a scene (one hour). You must have at least four Morality Traits of Humanity to take this Flaw.

Speech Impediment (1 Trait Flaw)

A stammer, Tourette's Syndrome or other speech deficiency makes communication difficult for you. Roleplay your deficiency, and suffer a two-Trait penalty on all verbal communication. You cannot have this Flaw with the Merit: *Enchanting Voice*.

Amnesia (2 Trait Flaw)

The past is a blank slate. You know nothing of your history, family, friends or foes. Your Storyteller makes up your character's history, including the reasons for your *Amnesia*. The Storyteller may even keep your character record partially hidden, only revealing your Abilities, Disciplines, Merits and Flaws when you try to use them. In general, the only things obvious to you are the things you can see in the mirror.

Lunacy (2 Trait Flaw)

The cycles of the moon shift your moods, making you unpredictable and wild. Under a crescent, half or gibbous moon, you suffer a one-Trait penalty to all *Self-Control/ Instinct* Virtue Tests; under a full moon, this penalty increases to two Traits.

Phobia (2 Trait Flaw)

Some object, creature or circumstance fills you with dread. This fear goes far beyond the normal level of phobias: Your vampiric Beast instinctively flees the

thing, treating it as a dire threat. When confronted by the object of your fear, you must make a *Courage* Virtue Test with a difficulty of at least three Traits (more if the Narrator decides that the circumstances are particularly severe). Should you fail, you suffer the usual penalties of failed *Courage* and R^tschreck.

SHORT FUSE (2 TRAIT FLAW)

Even for a vampire, your temper is ferocious. You suffer a one-Trait penalty on all Virtue Tests of *Self-Control/ Instinct*. Brujah cannot take this Flaw.

TERRITORIAL (2 TRAIT FLAW)

You stake out a particular area and claim it as your hunting grounds. You do not tolerate trespassers, especially other predators (vampires and Lupines). If you catch another vampire entering your turf uninvited, you must make a *Self-Control/ Instinct* Virtue Test as if provoked, or fly into a frenzy and attack. You generally dislike leaving your home for extended periods; roleplay this reticence.

VENGEFUL (2 TRAIT FLAW)

You want to even a score, either from your mortal days or with some group or individual thereafter. You plan ways to get your revenge constantly, and if presented with an opportunity for vengeance, you must spend a Willpower Trait to take some other action for the scene.

WEAK-WILLED (3 TRAIT FLAW)

Mind-altering powers like *Dominate* or even simple threats can break you easily. You get no test against the *Dominate* Discipline (although you are still immune to uses of *Dominate* from Cainites of weaker generation). You also suffer a two-Trait penalty on all Mental and Social Challenges. You cannot exceed a total of three Willpower Traits, regardless of your generation, unless you overcome this Flaw.

CONSPICUOUS CONSUMPTION (4 TRAIT FLAW)

The organs and blood-bearing tissue of your victims are staples of your diet. You believe that you must consume the liver, kidneys, heart and other pieces in order to sustain yourself. You must purchase the *Eat Food* Merit so that you can devour the meaty bits. You can only absorb Blood Traits by eating these organs; blood drunk from other sources is vomited back up. This hunger will necessitate the deaths of your victims, and it could lead to interesting problems with the Masquerade and maintaining Morality.

SOCIAL MERITS AND FLAWS

NATURAL LEADER (1 TRAIT MERIT)

Natural magnetism and leadership capabilities spring from your actions and words. Others want to follow you, and you easily take charge. You gain two Bonus Traits on tests of leadership (including most *Presence* tests). You must have at least six Social Traits to take this Merit.

PRESTIGIOUS SIRE (1 TRAIT MERIT)

Your sire is well-known in Cainite society, and he is held in some esteem. You gain a small measure of prestige due to your sire's fame, even if you no longer have any contact with her. Many other vampires treat you with at least a modicum of respect, as they fear or revere your sire. You are generally treated as if you possess one Status Trait more than you really have, although this Trait is not actually used — it shows that people accord you slightly greater standing.

DEBT OF GRATITUDE (1 TO 3 TRAIT MERIT)

An elder owes you prestation due to a favor performed by you or your sire. In keeping with the strictures of Cainite society, there is no easy way for the vampire to get out of this debt without repaying you. One Trait indicates a minor boon; two

Traits indicate a major boon; three Traits indicate a blood boon. Work with your Storyteller to create the circumstances of the debt.

ENEMY (1 TO 5 TRAIT FLAW)

A particular enemy is out to ruin you, or worse, to kill you. You may even have a group of powerful enemies hounding your steps. The value of this Flaw depends on the power of the enemy: A single vampire of power similar to your own is worth one Trait, while a cabal of mages or an entire organization of hunters would be worth five Traits. The Storyteller will ensure that your enemy figures into plots. He may not appear every game, but his machinations will be there.

DARK SECRET (1 TRAIT FLAW)

You have some sort of secret that, if exposed, would cause you great embarrassment or hardship. The Storyteller will work to make sure that your secret *could* be exposed in the course of play. If the secret gets out, you may either buy off the Flaw immediately by taking a Negative Trait (*Untrustworthy* is a good one), or by the loss of a Status Trait, depending on the circumstances.

INFAMOUS SIRE (1 TRAIT FLAW)

Your sire is well-known and well-hated among vampires of your sect. You are treated as if you have one less Status Trait than you actually possess. This penalty does not affect your true amount of Status; it simply means that others treat you with scorn for your lineage.

MISTAKEN IDENTITY (1 TRAIT FLAW)

Another Cainite happens to bear a striking resemblance to you. Worse, others in your area have heard descriptions of this person or even met your lookalike, causing no end of confusion. You should wear a tag that indicates your *Mistaken Identity*. This Flaw can be especially problematic if your look-alike is particularly powerful or notorious in Cainite society.

SIRE'S RESENTMENT (1 TRAIT FLAW)

For whatever reason, your sire has decided that your Embrace was a mistake, and she wishes you ill. You are unlikely to have a *Mentor* or any allies of note among Cainites, and your sire will attempt to hinder your plans at any opportunity.

HUNTED (4 TRAIT FLAW)

A powerful and dangerous mortal hunter has decided you are a danger to the world, and he seeks to snuff out your existence. The mortal has the contacts and skills necessary to make your unlife dangerous and unpleasant (and very short, if you aren't careful). Your friends, allies and other associates may all be at risk if the hunter decides to turn his eye on them.

PROBATIONARY SECT MEMBER (4 TRAIT FLAW)

You turned your back on your former organization, and now you stand with another. You may be a Camarilla turncoat, a Sabbat refugee or an independent who joined with one of the greater sects. As long as you have this Flaw, you are suspect within your new organization. You can have Status normally, but elders are likely to cast a suspicious eye over you regardless of your actual standing (treating you as if you had only one Status Trait). Even those with whom you associate may be judged tainted.

SUPERNATURAL MERITS AND FLAWS

MAGIC RESISTANCE (2 TRAIT MERIT)

The magical forms and rituals of *Thaumaturgy* and other magic seem to have difficulty affecting you. You gain two Bonus Traits when testing against any form of magic, though this bonus applies to both benevolent and harmful effects. You can never learn *Thaumaturgy* if you have this Merit.

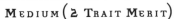

MEDIUM (2 TRAIT MERIT)

The voices of the dead sometimes come across the Shroud to haunt you. Ghosts flock to give you messages for the living world, and you can sense their presence in a room without using any special powers. Although you cannot normally see wraiths, you can always hear them, and you can communicate with them for favors or information. Of course, the Restless Dead always want *something* in return.

LUCKY (3 TRAIT MERIT)

You were born lucky — or the Devil looks after his own. Either way, you get three retests per story (for which you bid a *Lucky* Trait: "I got *Lucky* — you missed me last time."), though you may not use more than one retest on any challenge.

ORACULAR ABILITY (3 TRAIT MERIT)

The signs and portents of everyday life are clear to you, offering up the course of the future. Once per session, you may attempt to read a particular omen by making a Static Mental Challenge with a difficulty of eight or more Traits (Narrator's discretion). If you succeed, you receive some insight into the current situation, allowing you to claim one retest at some point during the night as you draw on the visions that you interpreted.

SPIRIT MENTOR (3 TRAIT MERIT)

A ghostly companion and guide follows you about, exercising its powers on your behalf. Maybe it's a deceased lover or friend, or maybe it's just curious about you. Its exact powers are up to the Storyteller (it's recommended that you build a basic wraith with the **Oblivion** rulebook to represent this character). If it really exerts itself, it can sometimes affect the material world. More often, it provides advice and company.

UNBONDABLE (3 TRAIT MERIT)

The blood bond cannot take hold on you. No matter how much blood you drink, you will never be bound, even partially.

TRUE LOVE (4 TRAIT MERIT)

You have found (and perhaps lost) a *True Love*, a piece of comfort and companionship in an otherwise despairing world. When confronted by adversity, the thought of your *True Love* provides strength and peace of mind. You effectively gain one extra Willpower Trait each session, spent as a *True Love* Trait. (These Traits are not cumulative; you cannot save them up.) However, your *True Love* may require rescuing or assistance from time to time.

NINE LIVES (6 TRAIT MERIT)

You have nine chances to cheat death. Your Storyteller should keep a tally of your lives (you can also mark them on your character sheet). Any time that a lost challenge would result in your death, you get a retest. You can keep retesting, even on the same challenge, until you survive or until you use up all of your *Nine Lives*.

TRUE FAITH (7 TRAIT MERIT)

The light of God, Allah, Buddha or whatever name you use for the Almighty shines from your soul. You have one Trait of True Faith, which can be used in a variety of ways. You can use your Faith Trait as a Willpower Trait. You can also repel other vampires with a Social Challenge, saying, "In the name of ____" and brandishing a holy symbol. If you win the Social Challenge, the other vampire flees, and even if you lose, the opponent cannot approach closer than 10 feet of you unless he overbids you in a test of Willpower against Willpower. You must maintain a Morality of five Humanity Traits to keep this Merit. This Merit is exceedingly rare among the Damned, and the Storyteller will demand a *very* good explanation from you. See **Laws of the Hunt** for more ideas about *True Faith*.

CURSED (1 TO 5 TRAIT FLAW)

A powerful curse — other than vampirism — afflicts you. The number of Traits in this Flaw determines the power and tenacity of the curse. A one-Trait curse might

cause you to stumble whenever you cross a doorstep; a three-Trait curse could cause any weapon you use to break after one strike; a five-Trait curse may result in all your best efforts being eventually turned against you. The exact particulars of the curse, as well as any way to overcome it, are up to the Storyteller.

Cast No Reflection (1 Trait Flaw)

Like the Lasombra, you cast no reflection in mirrors or silvered surfaces. Obviously, this Flaw constitutes a breach of the Masquerade, and it can draw a great deal of attention in certain circumstances. Lasombra cannot take this Flaw for free Traits.

Repulsed by Garlic (1 Trait Flaw)

Even the smallest whiff of garlic is sufficient to send you from the room. When you are confronted with a bit of garlic, you must expend a Willpower Trait or else be forced at least 10 feet away. If you spend the Willpower, you are able to abide the stench for one scene.

Touch of Frost (1 Trait Flaw)

Your chilling caress pulls away heat and kills plants. This Flaw is mostly an eerie effect, though you should certainly mention your ice-cold touch to anyone who has physical contact with you.

Eerie Presence (2 Trait Flaw)

You radiate an otherworldly air that causes nervousness and unease in everyone around you. You suffer a two-Trait penalty in all Social Challenges with mortals. Furthermore, your unusual nature is apparent to anyone who interacts with you; you should wear a tag or armband to indicate your *Eerie Presence*.

Can't Cross Running Water (3 Trait Flaw)

As per the old folk tales, you believe that you cannot cross running water, and indeed, something prevents you from doing so. You must be at least 50 feet above a body of water to cross it. Running water is considered to be any body of water at least two feet wide in any direction and not completely stagnant and enclosed (thus, sewer lines under the street don't count).

Haunted (3 Trait Flaw)

A malicious ghost, possibly of one of your victims, has decided to torment you from beyond the grave. Though it usually limits itself to phantasmal moaning, eerie manifestations and the occasional push, it does its best to make your unlife difficult. The Storyteller should make up the spirit, and possibly assign a Narrator to follow you and make sure that you pay for the Flaw. (Use of **Oblivion** is highly recommended.)

Repelled by Crosses (3 Trait Flaw)

You may have some residual religious guilt, or perhaps you take vampire legends too seriously. Whatever the reason, the sight of the cross causes you to flee unless you expend a Willpower Trait (in which case you can resist it for the rest of the scene). If you are struck by a cross on your bare skin, you take one level of aggravated damage for each blow, and you cannot reduce this damage with *Fortitude*. (This Flaw pertains to the actual religious symbol, not two crossed popsicle sticks or whatever else.)

Grip of the Damned (4 Trait Flaw)

There is no ecstasy in your Embrace — only terror and pain. When you bite to feed, you do not cause the Kiss, so your victims scream and struggle. This Flaw necessitates some method of restraining your prey. The torture that you inflict on your victims can be considered a form of suffering, and it may be inimical to vampires with high Humanity Traits.

Dark Fate (5 Trait Flaw)

Some horrible end awaits you, and you cannot avert it. Worse still, you have glimpses or some foreknowledge of your demise or eternal torment. The Storyteller will determine a particular fate, which will invariably strike you, removing your

character from play. Furthermore, in any particular session where the Storyteller deems appropriate, you may receive a vision of your impending misery. You must spend a Willpower Trait to shake off the experience, or you are a Trait down on all challenges for the rest of the session. This Flaw can be difficult to roleplay, and players are advised to think carefully before choosing it. Some may believe that this Flaw removes free will, but foreknowledge of one's demise can be quite liberating.

Light- Sensitive (5 Trait Flaw)

You are even more vulnerable to light than most vampires. Sunlight inflicts double damage, and even moonlight hurts — direct moonlight causes one level of lethal damage per turn. You must use sunglasses to shield your eyes, and you tend to stick to dark places out of habit and safety.

Experience

As sentient beings, we collate the information that is presented to us in our daily lives and hopefully become better people for our experiences. During our life, we learn from the mistakes of yesterday and prepare for the challenges of tomorrow.

Experience in **Laws of the Night** is represented by giving each character one to three Experience Traits at the end of each session. The number of Traits awarded is based on how well a character performed during the course of the story and how active a player was in the game. The Narrator decides how many Traits each player receives on completion of the session. All players receive one Trait — this is standard. Exceptional roleplayers, those who played an exceptionally memorable part, should receive two. Three Traits should be awarded to those characters who performed acts of incredible insight and courage, making the game truly memorable for everyone involved. On a normal night, each player will receive one Experience Trait.

If you are a Narrator, you should be consistent and fair in awarding Experience. Do it in the open, and be prepared to explain the rationale for your decisions in accordance with the rules. If the players disagree, hear them out and make sure you know the whole story, then award Experience to those who have earned it.

Be careful, as awarding too many Experience Traits can make characters too powerful too quickly and give players lax attitudes toward working for their goals. On the other hand, awarding too few disheartens the players and damages their sense of achievement.

Awarding Experience Traits, therefore, requires a delicate balance between satisfying players and maintaining the integrity of the game. If you follow the guidelines listed here, you probably won't get into too much trouble.

- **Automatic** — Each character receives one Experience Trait per game, representing the acquisition of common, everyday knowledge.
- **Roleplaying** — Narrators should encourage roleplaying. The best way to do so is to reward it tangibly with Experience.
- **Leadership** — You should award one Trait to each of those few players who had starring parts in a story. Someone who got involved, and by her efforts propelled the plot, deserves a third Trait. It should be noted that if more than one of the players were integral to the progression of the story, each of the players who showed such leadership should be awarded a Trait.

Using Experience

Experience Traits may be spent to purchase new Abilities, Traits and Disciplines, improving a character and giving the player a sense of satisfaction as he watches his character grow more potent. The on p.124 chart lists the costs for improving Traits, Abilities and Disciplines.

CONVERTING CHARACTERS FROM PREVIOUS EDITIONS

Players of the previous version of **Laws of the Night** can easily convert characters built on those rules to the updated rules of the Final Nights. Simply follow the character creation outline, using the conversions listed here.

CONVERTING CONCEPT, CLAN, MORALITY, NATURE AND DEMEANOR

Your character's concept probably remains unchanged as a result of the rules — your background story is not affected by the vagaries of Traits.

Similarly, clans remain largely unchanged. The Gangrel may have left the Camarilla en masse, but individuals still choose their own allegiances. Some bloodlines have changed their Disciplines — most notably, the Samedi now have *Fortitude* instead of *Necromancy*. Samedi characters should simply be charged extra Experience for their levels of *Necromancy*, appropriate to the difference in cost; they can then purchase *Fortitude* as desired. Older characters are considered to be "typical" of their clans, and thus, they may not swap out to become one of a bloodline. Malkavians can swap their *Dominate* for *Dementation*, as explained under the *Dementation* Discipline on p. 145.

A character's Morality is still the same Humanity or Path of Enlightenment, but Beast/Path Traits are no longer used. Instead, the character has five Morality Traits, minus one Trait for each Beast/Path Trait. Thus, a character with two Beast Traits now has a Humanity of three Traits.

Natures and Demeanors follow the Archetypes listed here, though there is certainly nothing to prevent the use of previously published Archetypes.

UPDATING CLAN

Note specifically that the clan advantages and disadvantages for this edition of **Laws of the Night** differ from the predecessors, which may grant certain characters extra Traits or penalties.

CONVERTING ATTRIBUTES

For the most part, Attributes remain unchanged. The number of Traits possessed by a character stays the same, and most of the adjectives are the same, too. The sole exception is the Physical Trait *Athletic*, which was replaced with *Agile* to prevent confusion with the *Athletics* Ability. The *Calm* Mental Trait was removed, as that is a function of *Self-Control*; substitute *Patient*, *Disciplined* or *Determined* instead.

CONVERTING ADVANTAGES

CHANGING ABILITIES

Abilities remain largely unchanged — converted characters may choose specializations, as described for Abilities. Certain highly particular Abilities can be converted to *Hobby/ Professional/ Expert* Abilities at the discretion of the Storyteller: *Demolitions* or *Cainite Lore*, for instance.

CHANGING DISCIPLINES

Disciplines are perhaps the most difficult area to convert. Since many Disciplines now have different levels or additional levels, it can be hard to see exactly how a character can come across to the new system.

Characters keep their existing levels of Disciplines, if there are any correspondences. Thus, a character with Intermediate *Presence* still has the powers of *Dread Gaze*, *Entrancement* and *Summon*, though using the new rules. Under this conversion system, the character must buy any missed levels of Disciplines before improving to higher levels of the Discipline. Therefore, the aforementioned character would have to buy *Awe* before learning *Majesty*. Charge the difference in Traits for missed levels — even though

- **New Attribute Trait** — One Experience per Attribute Trait.
- **New Ability Trait** — One Experience per Ability Trait up to 5. Two Experience per Ability Trait 6-10 (as you learn more, it becomes harder to find things you *don't* know).
- **New Background Trait** — One Experience per Trait with Storyteller approval. Backgrounds may also rise or fall based on roleplaying.
- **New Discipline** — Three Experience Traits for Basic Disciplines, six for Intermediate Disciplines and nine for Advanced Disciplines. Remember to add one Trait to the cost if the Discipline is considered "out of clan" for a character.
- **New Humanity/Path Trait** — Two Experience per Trait (and Storyteller approval).
- **New Merit** — Double the listed cost of the Merit, with Narrator approval. This acquisition should not happen instantaneously; it should be worked into a character's ongoing story. The addition of a Merit should not be treated lightly.
- **New Necromancy or Thaumaturgy Ritual** — Two Experience for a Basic ritual, four for an Intermediate ritual and six for an Advanced ritual.
- **New Specialization** — One Experience Trait in an Ability already known.
- **New Virtue** — Three Experience per Trait, plus the change must be an important part of a character's ongoing story-line somehow.
- **New Willpower** — Three Experience per Trait.
- **Buy off Negative Trait** — Two Experience per Trait.
- **Buy off Flaw** — Double the cost of the Flaw, with Storyteller approval, and worked into the character's ongoing story.

Awe is a Basic power, the previous character spent Traits for two Basic and one Intermediate Discipline levels, and thus would have to spend the Traits for another Intermediate power (to gain the otherwise Basic *Awe*) before moving on to *Majesty*.

For powers without an easily convertible correspondence like *Animalism*, a Storyteller may choose to award the character the equivalent levels. A character with the Intermediate level of *Animalism* (*Song of Serenity*) would now have *Quell the Beast* and would keep *Beckoning*, but would exchange *Beast Within* for *Feral Whispers*. Conversely, the Storyteller may set a "wholesale price" of Experience to acquire these new Disciplines, such as requiring the player above to pay a set price of six Experience Traits before making the exchange.

Characters with Advanced Disciplines won't be forced to buy new power levels since they won't be improving (unless they reach elder levels). However, the utility of many of the lower-level powers means that they will often be bought in any case. There's no real need to require players to do so; a character with Advanced *Presence* should not be forced to spend six Traits for *Awe* unless the player wants the power.

Characters with *Necromancy* get the *Sepulchre Path* in exchange for their former levels of power. Similarly, *Thaumaturgy* users take their highest path as their primary path; if any other paths equal this rating, they should be kept but not allowed to improve until the primary path advances.

Changing Backgrounds

Influence Backgrounds remain unchanged. The same categories of Influence still exist, with the same levels, so they are no trouble for converted characters.

The various other Backgrounds were not previously used in **Laws of the Night**, but converting characters now get two Traits to choose among those Backgrounds (except Sabbat, who get none). Characters who lowered generation with Negative Traits get back some of those Traits: since generation used to cost two Negative Traits per step, the character gets a refund of one Trait per step, usable as Bonus Traits. The character's generation should not change as a result, though.

Converting the Last Touches

Changing Blood Traits

Generation determines a character's total Blood Traits. Don't worry about existing Traits; simply test for blood, as described previously, the next time that the character comes into play. Since all characters now use the adjusted Blood Pools, this conversion should not prove troublesome.

Changing Willpower Traits

No changes need be made to Willpower Traits, since the generation limits still apply.

Assigning Virtue Traits

Converted characters take the appropriate Virtues for their Morality and assign a number of Virtue Traits equal to twice their Morality Traits. A character with two Humanity Traits would thus have one free Trait in *Conscience*, *Self-Control* and *Courage*, plus four additional Virtue Traits to spend.

Updating Flaws and Negative Traits

Most Negative Traits remain the same, though the Negative Social Trait *Feral* was added.

Flaws, on the other hand, have some changes in Traits, and in some cases a few were removed entirely. The best solution is to use the rules from **Laws of the Night**'s previous editions until such time as the player can pay the difference to remove the Flaw. In the case that a Flaw's Trait value actually increases, simply use those Traits to pay for any other differences in character cost, before adding to the character's pool of Experience Traits with the difference.

Converting Merits and Free Traits

Many Merits were removed from the game, or changed in Trait value. As with Flaws, the best solution is to allow the character to pay the difference in (non-doubled) Experience Traits, or to simply use the old rules until the player has the appropriate Traits. A character with a Merit that no longer exists should be allowed to "cash in" the Merit, refunding the Trait value for Experience.

Lastly, spend five Free Traits — under the Free Trait costs, not Experience Trait costs — to finish the conversion.

Converting Characters from Tabletop Play

Moving a character from tabletop play to live-action can be a little tricky, but it's generally worth the effort. Watching your favorite character blossom into full flower as *you* take on the role physically is both rewarding and exhilarating.

The new systems in **Laws of the Night** are designed to mesh more smoothly with **Vampire: The Masquerade**, so tracking the various Disciplines and Attributes is straightforward.

Converting Virtues and Morality

The Virtue Trait system for **Mind's Eye Theatre** runs very close to the tabletop system now, unlike the old Beast Trait system. Virtue Traits convert directly across, with one dot turning into one Trait.

Morality scales are compressed, though, for ease of testing. One Trait of Morality (Humanity or Path) equals two dots of tabletop Morality. Round fractions up, in favor of the character being converted.

Converting Tabletop Clans

The clans in the tabletop game do have clan weaknesses, but not clan advantages. Assign the clan advantages normally to the character while converting as a bonus of the system.

Converting Tabletop Attributes

Attributes in the tabletop game are rated in dots, from one to five. To simulate this rating in live-action play, simply drop the first dot from each one, and then assign an appropriate adjective for each additional dot.

If your character happens to have a score of one or zero in a Trait, you should take a Negative Trait of the appropriate type.

Example: *John Slime, the Nosferatu, has a Stamina of 5 dots but an Appearance of 0. When converted, he gets 4 Stamina-related or miscellaneous Physical Traits, but must take a Negative Social Trait. Kurt decides to take the Physical Traits of* Vigorous, Enduring, Tough *and* Resilient, *and he assigns the Negative Social Trait* Obnoxious *(in addition to John Slime's existing* Repugnant x 3 *Traits).*

Converting Tabletop Abilities

The Abilities in tabletop play are more extensive, and they tend to have higher levels, than in live-action.

Instead of trying to take levels for every dot in Abilities, look at the highest Abilities on the character sheet. Assign one level to each Ability with three dots, and an additional level to any Ability with four or five dots. If you come up with less than five Abilities, simply take the next highest one and take one level in it.

Converting Tabletop Disciplines and Backgrounds

Disciplines and Backgrounds in **Laws of the Night** correspond exactly to the levels in **Vampire: The Masquerade**. Take one level in each of the appropriate Traits for each dot in the tabletop game.

The sole exception is the Influence Background. This Background runs from one to five dots in the tabletop game, but it is subdivided into several categories for live-action play. In **Mind's Eye Theatre** conversions, simply split up any dots of Influence into any desired levels of Influence that total the same amount. If your character has three dots of Influence, you get to spread around three Traits of Influence in live-action play, among whatever categories desired (or all in one).

Converting Blood Traits and Willpower

Blood Traits are used exactly the same in both live-action and tabletop play. They convert normally.

Willpower, on the other hand, varies with generation in **Laws of the Night**, but is a static one to 10 dots in **Vampire: The Masquerade**. To deal with this difference, pro-rate the character's Willpower based on her total in tabletop. That is, a 13th-generation character with six dots of Willpower is at 60 percent of maximum Willpower for a tabletop game; the equivalent in live-action would be two Traits.

Example: *John Slime is a 10th-generation Nosferatu. He has seven dots of Willpower in tabletop play — 70 percent of maximum. In live-action, he would have between two and five Willpower Traits. 70 percent of the way between the two is four, so John Slime has four Willpower Traits.*

Converting Tabletop Merits and Flaws

The Merits and Flaws from **Vampire: The Masquerade** have direct correspondences to this material, so conversion isn't a problem. However, make sure that you understand the full text of the live-action version. Often, the change to live-action impacts the game mechanical effects of a given Merit or Flaw.

Sample Character Creation

Alyson is looking to join a local troupe for a game of **Masquerade**, and after checking with Brian, the Storyteller, she decides she wishes to play one of the Kindred. Alyson puts on an inspirational CD while the two of them take a copy of the rulebook and sit down to create a character.

Step One: Concept

Alyson begins by looking for a concept, a basic idea which she can build her character around. She decides that she wants to play a tough humanitarian, someone who once was a warrior for a cause but ultimately found that people were more important than slogans, and who now struggles to aid the less fortunate around her. Thinking a little more, she decides her character was a fiery Southern belle who took an active role in the upheaval of the last century and ultimately attracted a vampire's eye with her fierce dedication. Brian likes the concept and approves it: a vampire who actively battles her Beast in order to help others sounds like an excellent roleplaying opportunity. Because she was formerly quite a firebrand, Alyson decides the Brujah clan was the most likely to have embraced her, but that her new views have probably alienated her from her peers — another good story hook for later on. She chooses Caregiver for her Nature (adding interesting depth and departing nicely from the stereotypical Brujah, much to Brian's relief), and picks Survivor for her Demeanor, reflecting the tough facade her character has developed since being on her own. Humanity is the obvious choice for her Morality Path, and Alyson decides the character will be part of the Camarilla as opposed to the inhuman Sabbat. Finally a name for her character comes to her — Daron. Alyson is ready to move on to the next step.

Step Two: Attributes

Alyson has to prioritize Daron's Attribute categories now, to determine her basic strengths and weaknesses. She takes Physical as Daron's primary Trait category, Mental as her secondary, and Social as her tertiary. Alyson explains that Daron believes in helping out with her own two hands and learned to take care of herself in her rebel days (Physical), that she has always been good at putting her mind to a task and never backing down (Mental), but that sometimes she is a bit rough with people's feelings and tends to be overly direct at times (Social). Now Alyson must choose individual Traits for each category, beginning with seven Physical Traits. She chooses *Ferocious, Quick, Quick, Enduring, Athletic, Steady* and *Wiry*. That makes Daron someone who's physically dependable and useful in a scrap — a good combination for her chosen calling. Next is Mental, with five traits, and Alyson picks the Traits *Alert, Observant, Disciplined, Determined* and *Clever*, reflecting Daron's strong personality and her awareness of conditions around her. Finally comes Social, with only three Traits. Alyson takes *Intimidating, Persuasive* and *Magnetic* — Daron has the makings of a decent leader, but still uses force to get things done from time to time.

Step Three: Advantages

Now Alyson has to choose Daron's Abilities. Although she sees so many she'd like Daron to have, she begins by choosing some Abilities appropriate to Daron's warrior past: *Brawl, Firearms* and *Dodge*. Then she takes *Empathy* and *Streetwise*, representing what Daron has learned during the time she's spent walking alongside the downtrodden. These choices also give Daron a wide scope of talents, something that appeals to Alyson's notion of her as an independent crusader used to being on her own.

Disciplines come next; here too is another area Alyson wants to have a broad base of powers to call upon, given the complicated nature of Daron's cause. As a

Camarilla vampire, Daron begins play with three levels of Disciplines, and after looking over the choices available to her, Alyson selects one level of each of the Brujah clan Disciplines: *Alacrity* (Celerity), *Prowess* (Potence), and *Awe* (Presence). She reasons that the first two are a legacy of her more violent days, while Daron has developed the last just recently, when she began working on improving her skills at communicating with others.

Finally, Daron's Camarilla status gives Alyson five levels of Backgrounds to spend. She takes some time on this section — Daron has recently split with her violent past, and that means she probably hasn't had much time to build up resources of her own just yet. To reflect this shift, Alyson chooses one level of *Contacts* (informants who remained loyal to her) and *Street* Influence. Then she asks Brian if she can take three levels of Generation Background, since she needs Storyteller approval before doing so. (This would start her at 10th generation). Getting a better sense of her character's history now, Alyson explains that Daron was the childe of Jonas, a moderately powerful Brujah, who has taken her new change of heart rather badly and now does his best to make her unlife as unpleasant as possible. Her lower generation only makes matters worse, as it increases his shame and the sense that she's flaunting the responsibilities of her blood. Never one to stand in the way of a player making unlife more difficult for her character in an interesting fashion (and knowing a 10th generation character won't upset game balance), Brian gives her permission to take the three levels of Generation, and Alyson is finished this stage.

Step Four: Finishing Touches

Alyson must now record Daron's starting Willpower and Blood Traits. Looking at the Generation chart on p. 95, she sees that 10th generation Kindred begin with two Willpower Traits, have a maximum of five Willpower Traits, and also have a maximum of 13 Blood Traits. In addition, as 10th generation, Daron can only spend one Blood Trait per turn, and can only gain up to five levels in one Ability. Looking further, Alyson sees she must perform a Simple Test with Brian to determine how many Blood Traits she begins play with; he shoots scissors, she shoots paper. Curses! Daron will have to begin play with only four Blood Traits, which means she will probably have to hunt sometime during her first session but is otherwise all right.

Next on the list are Virtue Traits; as a follower of Humanity, Daron has the Virtues Courage, Conscience and Self-Control. She starts with one Trait in each category automatically, and has seven extra Traits to spend among her Virtues; Alyson distributes them evenly, spending three Traits on Courage, two on Conscience and two on Self-Control (for a final total of four, three, and three Traits in each, respectively). This allocation represents Daron's level nature and the great determination which she applies to her tasks. Alyson would like to improve Conscience some more, but that will have to wait for later. Averaging her Conscience and Self-Control ratings, she records her starting Morality Traits: 3. Thus, Daron has a 3 rating on the Humanity Path, not bad, but not wonderful either — Alyson reasons that there's still too much of the warrior in Daron, and she'll have to work hard if she wants to raise her Humanity further, which suits Alyson just fine.

Alyson now has the option to choose Flaws and Negative Traits for her character. Her Clan Disadvantage gives her with a *Violent* Negative Trait, which she records at this time, although she receives no additional Traits for it, since it is part of a Clan Disadvantage. Looking over the other Negative Traits, she gains an extra Trait each by choosing *Tactless* and *Impatient* — try as she might, Daron sometimes cuts a little close to the bone with her observations, and she hasn't quite realized yet that real social change doesn't happen overnight. Nothing else seems to suit her in

that area, so she looks over the Flaws next, finally selecting *Sire's Resentment* (reflecting Jonas's dislike of her) and an *Intolerance: Tremere* at one Trait each. Brian interrupts at this point and asks her to justify such a broad *Intolerance*, and Alyson explains that the coterie she used to run with had a bad run in with a Tremere chantry at one point, and after that she's harbored ill will toward the clan. Elaborating further, she tells of how one of her first meetings among the Kindred was with a Tremere who experimented on derelicts and other lost souls, and how she's held a strong dislike for the clan's scholarly detachment ever since. Impressed and satisfied that it won't disrupt the overall game, Brian permits the Flaw, though he warns her that it may land her in a bit of trouble down the line. Alyson declines to take a derangement or trade in a Morality Trait at this point, and so it's time to spend her Free Traits.

Thanks to the extra Flaws and Negative Traits she's taken, Alyson now has a total of nine Free Traits to spend improving Daron's statistics. Rationalizing that she would have to be plenty tough to survive her past battles and her sire's current ire, Alyson spends three Traits to purchase the Basic Potence Discipline: *Might*, giving Daron an extra physical edge. She also spends a Trait each to purchase an extra Physical Trait: *Vigorous* and a *Brawl: Aikido* Ability specialization, rounding out Daron's already formidable fighting skills. Alyson has four Free Traits left to spend, and she decides to take an extra Social Trait: *Commanding* to represent Daron's ability to organize people for a task. With her final three Free Traits, Alyson purchases the Merit: *Iron Will*, reflecting Daron's fiercely independent nature and also helping to explain how she got out from under her sire's influence with relative ease. Brian takes a look at her sheet, making sure all the numbers add up, and approves it.

Step five: Spark of Life

All the game mechanics, Traits, powers and skills are now laid out. Alyson has developed a much better image of Daron than when she first started, but there are still some things not covered, things that can't be captured by rules and character sheets; specifically, the details that make Daron live and breathe to the other players. Alyson has to think about ways to convey her character's personality to the other players, to create a host of little identifying quirks that come with roleplaying her. Does Daron wear the rebellious garb of so many Brujah, or does she have her own sense of style? Does she still speak with a Southern accent, or has time erased it? Does she crack her knuckles when she's impatient, or sing softly when she's happy? When she walks, does she display ladylike grace or simply get where she's going as quickly as possible? There are countless subtleties that can be added to make a character seem more real, and which make for an entertaining and memorable personality for everyone in a game to interact with. More character history also can't hurt — Alyson has already gone beyond a stereotypical Brujah to create an intriguing past, but more detail is still possible. Did her mortal family approve of her crusading, or did they disown her for her actions? Where did she first meet Jonas? What specific event caused her to change from a warrior to a protector, and what other friends did she lose when she made that decision? What allies did she make? What goals does she have in this city, and how does she plan to attain them? Does she view the Embrace as a curse, or merely another means to her ends? Exploring all of these questions and more will help Alyson further define Daron and her vampiric existence, but for now Alyson is satisfied with the progress she's made, and she knows that a character is only full realized once play begins. After she and Brian work out the details of her introduction at the next game session, Alyson's all ready to begin, and Daron will soon walk under the looming clouds of the Final Nights.

Peter's hurried exit played perfectly into Donata's plans. With a careful breath, she blew out the candles – the ones that she'd secretly replaced after Peter had given her the originals with the explanation about the ritual – and allowed herself a satisfied smile. Running a hand down her dress to smooth the sheer fabric, she straightened, bumping back into Kevin.

"Now that the stuck-up prig of a Ventrue is gone, we can discuss the future," Kevin tried lamely. Donata allowed him to wrap his arms around her waist, leaning back a bit – just enough to be seductive without being blatant.

"Of course," Donata blithely continued as Kevin kissed her neck just below her ear. "He will be a nuisance... one that will have to be taken care of. But, my dear Kevin, when he finishes his visit with the Warlock, he will certainly have made a few more enemies. If you took care of him... well, I'm sure that the nasty little truth about his involvement with the package could come out, and the prince would be inclined to be lenient to you and your friends. Perhaps a few of you might even be given a bit of recognized domain, as a token of appreciation for destroying such a rogue. Of course, with my position in court, I would have to take over Peter's assets... the sizable improvement would certainly raise my position, and we could work together very well indeed." She bared her throat a bit more, alabaster and poised like a statue. *All you need is one drink, and you're well on the road to being mine forever,* she thought.

Kevin's fangs hovered at her neck, and then he spoke in return. "You don't need to convince me twice. I've been itching to settle things with him! Me and a few of the boys could catch him downtown if you send him to meet us. You take his money, I take his blood... sounds like a fair trade to me."

Before Kevin could think matters through any further, Donata turned in his grasp, tugging him closer with a satisfied smile. "A fair trade indeed. We make a peerless pair," she added, prompting Kevin's ego. The intemperate Brujah needed no further prodding. With a growl, he sank his fangs into Donata's neck, convinced that she would do him no harm. She gasped under the pleasant waves of the Kiss, even as Kevin started down the road to total enthrallment.

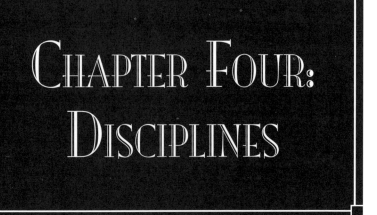

CHAPTER FOUR: DISCIPLINES

Though vampirism is a curse, the blood of Caine grants great mystical powers to those with the insight and dedication to pursue them. Called Disciplines, these supernatural abilities grant a vampire exceptional powers—incredible strength or speed, preternatural senses, the ability to hide from mortal sight or even stranger powers. Fueled by blood and will, these Disciplines are the hallmarks of a true vampire. Brash neonates may command a few moderate abilities, but the most fearsome vampires combine the strength of their Disciplines with hundreds of years of experience and practice.

Each clan possesses a group of Disciplines that are common among its ranks. These "clan Disciplines" can be unearthed and improved with relative ease. The Disciplines of a particular clan are not the sole limits to a vampire's power, though; in theory, any vampire can develop any Discipline. The cost comes in time, effort and boons owed to instructors. Vampires find that Disciplines outside their clan's strengths are more difficult to learn, harder to improve and often inaccessible without the assistance of a skilled teacher who already knows the Discipline in question. As many of the more mystical and unusual Disciplines are considered proprietary to their clans, most vampires do not have the opportunity to learn the truly unique powers; most never have seen or heard of the Disciplines wielded by some of the independent clans and bloodlines.

Among most of the Children of Caine, there are eight relatively common Disciplines: the powers of *Animalism* (the ability to communicate with and master beasts), *Auspex* (heightened sensitivity and supernatural awareness), *Celerity* (incredible bursts of speed gifted by blood), *Dominate* (the ability to command another's mind), *Fortitude* (supernatural resilience, against even fire and sunlight), *Obfuscate* (clouding of minds, granting disguise and stealth), *Potence* (vampiric strength) and *Presence* (preternatural charisma). The existence of these Disciplines is at least known to all but the rankest fledglings. Certain clans and bloodlines, though, possess their own special Disciplines, including *Chimerstry* (the ability to conjure illusions and dreaming images), *Dementation* (influence over passion and madness), *Necromancy* (control and commerce with the world of the dead and the ghosts therein), *Obtenebration* (the capacity to unleash spiritual darkness), *Protean* (the power to shift shape and assume animalistic features), *Quietus* (a Discipline of bloody assassination), *Serpentis* (a reptilian and manipulative Discipline from Egyptian lore), *Thaumaturgy* (the rigorous study of blood magic) and

Vicissitude (molding and crafting of blood, flesh and bone). The extraordinarily rare bloodlines also practice *Melpominee* (manipulation of music and voice), *Obeah* (a power of physical and spiritual healing) and *Thanatosis* (control over the processes of physical death and decay). Some other Disciplines are thought to exist as well, though they and their practitioners are certainly so rare as to be nearly nonexistent.

Most of the Disciplines require the use of blood or some other expenditure of effort. The gifts of Caine do not come lightly or easily, after all. Still, they are invaluable tools for hunting and survival, even in the modern age. Times being what they are, modern vampires must be very careful of the Masquerade with their powers; a mortal tourist with a camera can prove the greatest threat to vampiric secrecy.

Unless otherwise noted, a Discipline is only useful against one target at a time, and the subject must be sensed directly by the vampire — seen, heard or otherwise noticed. Sensory-enhancing powers may allow effects to target subjects at a distance outside the range of normal sight, but technological assistance is not sufficient — the subject must be noted with the vampire's own senses and powers. For example, you cannot use a camera or binoculars to locate a victim, but you can use *Auspex*.

Descriptions of the Disciplines usually refer solely to vampires or Cainites using the powers. Unless specifically noted otherwise, these descriptions include ghouls, revenants and other characters who use the appropriate power.

Some Disciplines require a physical touch or grip to affect a subject. Acquiring this grip requires a Physical Challenge, though an unsuspecting victim may be lured in with a handshake. A subject who voluntarily meets your grip relents, and he is automatically affected; otherwise, you must make the challenge as normal, even if striking from surprise or if you actually touch the other player (which violates the No Touching rule in any case). Touch-activated Disciplines can sometimes be used in conjunction with an unarmed strike, in which case the strike does normal damage and the Discipline takes effect as well if the blow connects.

Learning Disciplines

All vampires can naturally learn their clan Disciplines with nothing more than the expenditure of Experience Traits. As with any other learned capability, the new powers become available at the next game session.

The cardinal eight Disciplines that are shared by every clan — *Animalism, Celerity, Dominate, Fortitude, Obfuscate, Potence* and *Presence* — require only a willing teacher who is one level above what the student wishes to learn. What payment the teacher requires is best left for the characters to haggle out between themselves. Out of game, the Storyteller may require that the vampire indicate who is teaching him his Discipline

Certain Disciplines are proprietary to their clans — created by them and often practiced solely by them. Some clans have even hunted those outside the clan's bounds who knew of their secrets. Teachers of these wondrous powers are, consequently, few and far between. Those fortunate enough to acquire a teacher, however, are not done yet — in order to study the Discipline, they must drink a Trait of blood from a vampire capable of learning the Discipline (which need not necessarily be the teacher). Cainite scholars believe that this is necessary in order to "attune" the blood to learning something that is quite alien. The drink is only necessary once, and the student may learn as long as the teacher wishes to retain her. Those Disciplines that require this are *Chimerstry, Dementation, Melpominee, Necromancy, Obeah, Obtenebration, Protean, Quietus, Serpentis, Thanatosis, Thaumaturgy* and *Vicissitude*. While the *Book of Nod* claims that Caine knew every Discipline, this would seem to be impossible in light of the fact that the Tremere with their *Thaumaturgy*, the Daughters of Cacophony with their *Melpominee*, or the Samedi and *Thanatosis* (to name a few) did not exist when Caine was flourishing in Nod.

ANIMALISM

For a vampiric predator, mastery over animals is a simple task; the vampire's Beast is more dangerous than any animal's nature. By drawing on this feral connection, vampires can communicate with and control animals. Indeed, vampires who develop a communion with their animal side often seem attractive or at least masterful to most animals.

This Discipline is practiced by the Gangrel, Nosferatu, Ravnos and Tzimisce clans; the Gangrel and Nosferatu often establish equitable or friendly relationships with natural creatures, while the Tzimisce show their mastery over lesser life forms through this power. Ravnos find animals to be useful scouts, spies and meals in their nomadic travels.

Use the *Animal Ken* Ability for retests with the *Animalism* Discipline.

BASIC ANIMALISM

Feral Whispers

By looking into the eyes of an animal and perhaps making some related sound (like growling or hissing), you are capable of communicating with the creature. Your predatory nature allows you to understand and cow natural creatures. Depending on your predilections, you may deal with the animal equitably, or you may demand obedience. The animal may not wish to obey, but this Discipline's power insures that the animal is at least favorably disposed toward you. Even if the animal is intractable, you may be able to force it into submission.

Using this power requires that you look into the eyes of the creature with which you desire to communicate; if this gaze is lost, then you must attempt to re-establish contact if you wish to continue communicating. Most animals will continue to attend your gaze while you are communicating with them, though. Animals without eyes, or very simple in nature, do not have enough of a mind or Beast to connect with easily. This power works best with predatory creatures and larger birds, reptiles and mammals.

You may communicate with animals without any test. However, to issue commands, you must defeat the animal in a Social Challenge — generally, the animal will have the equivalent of six to eight Traits for this challenge, as determined by a Narrator. If you succeed, you can count on the animal following your orders for the remainder of the evening. Most animals lack the intelligence necessary to carry out complex or conditional commands, but they can perform simple tasks like fetching, following people or guarding locations.

Beckoning

By uttering a howl or other animal noise, you can summon animals to your side. Depending on how you couch your call, you can summon all animals of a particular type within the area, or just a few. The creatures hasten to your *Beckoning*, ready to aid or simply to provide nourishment. Though animals called by this power do not fall under your control automatically, they are at least favorably inclined toward you.

You must expend a Social Trait for each animal that you summon. Only animals that can hear the summons respond; you cannot call a bird from across a city, nor could you call an animal that cannot hear. You may be as specific as you desire within the category of summoned animals. For instance, you may choose to summon all the rats in an area, or just the white ones, or even a specific rat that you know about.

Animals summoned with this power may take some time to arrive. Your Storyteller can issue cards for your animals or swarms, as appropriate. Animals summoned with this power remain as long as they are not attacked or threatened (within their conception — a rat would certainly feel threatened by the movements of several people in the area), or until the scene ends. You can use other *Animalism* powers normally to command or control the animals called.

Intermediate Animalism

Quell the Beast

Touching (from surprise or with a Physical Challenge) or gazing into the eyes of a victim, you can project the fearsome predatory aspect of your vampiric nature. Your Beast serves to show your ultimate mastery over your prey, cowing humans and animals alike into submission. Without the inner fire of powerful emotions, the subject is apathetic.

Different vampires evoke this power in different ways. Nosferatu most commonly soothe the Beasts of their subjects, drawing them into lassitude, while Tzimisce and Gangrel often assert their mastery over lesser subjects and terrify the victims into submission. Regardless of the means, the results are similar; any vampire using this Discipline can choose her particular style. No speech or vocalization is necessary — only the physical or eye contact.

You must engage in a Social Challenge with your victim in order to use this power. Once you have intimidated or soothed the subject, he may no longer use Willpower Traits for the remainder of the evening. Such a subject also gains the Negative Traits *Submissive* x 2, for the same duration. Multiple uses of this power are not cumulative; once affected, the victim cannot receive additional *Submissive* Traits through further uses of this Discipline.

Cowing the Beast of a vampire is much more difficult. You must expend a Willpower Trait to make the attempt (before engaging in the Social Challenge). If successful, the vampire suffers from the normal effects of this power. Alternately, you may use this power on a vampire in frenzy, causing the Cainite to snap back into lucidity. In such a case, you expend the Willpower Trait and make the Social Challenge as usual, but if you succeed, the vampire merely returns to lucidity instead of suffering the other effects of this Discipline. You may not use this Discipline on yourself.

Subsume the Spirit

Locking eyes with an animal, you can now move your consciousness into its body, dominating it completely. Your soul pushes aside the animal's weaker spirit, and your own body falls into a comatose state, while your spirit uses the animal as a vessel. Though influenced by the animal's bestial nature, you can still exercise your intellect and even some of your supernatural capabilities.

You are limited by the physical constraints of any animal that you possess — your physical Disciplines do not augment the creature, nor do you have the ability to speak or manipulate objects if that is normally outside of the animal's physical capabilities. However, you can use the animal's natural abilities, such as claws, wings, poison and gills.

There is no functional limit to the distance at which you can exercise this Discipline once you have possessed an animal — you may move freely in the animal's body, even in sunlight (subject to the normal restrictions for remaining awake during the day), without concern for your vampiric form. However, you are not automatically aware of what transpires around your comatose body. If your animal form suffers injury, your vampiric body suffers equal sympathetic injury; if the animal body is slain, your soul returns to your body and you enter torpor. Should you choose to leave the animal's body for your own, this happens regardless of distance as long as you are conscious. However, you must declare this intent at the beginning of the turn and survive until the end of the turn (if you are in combat or other dangerous situations). Fleeing the animal body does not require an action; you may still act normally in the turn that you intend to return to your body. If you are injured (without being knocked unconscious) while attempting to return to your own body, you must make a Simple Test — a tie indicates that you remain in the grip of animalistic behavior for the rest of the scene, and a failure causes you to immediately enter frenzy, though in both cases you return to your Cainite form automatically.

SUBSUME THE SPIRIT	
1 Trait	Simple possession
2 Traits	Can use *Auspex*
3 Traits	Can also use *Presence* and *Animalism*
4 Traits	Can also use *Dementation* and *Dominate*
5 Traits	Can also use *Chimerstry*, *Necromancy* and *Thaumaturgy*

If your vampiric body dies while you inhabit an animal's form, you can try to remain in the animal body. Each sunrise, you must make a Simple Test (win or tie). If you lose, your spirit plunges into the astral realms, gone forever. Thus, you have only a short time to survive.

Exercising this power requires that you gaze into the eyes of the beast that you intend to possess (if the animal has no eyes, you may not possess it). You must then expend Social Traits to move into the animal's body. The more Social Traits you choose to expend, the more complete your connection to the animal form. With simple possession, you direct the body as you choose; more complete dominance allows you to use some of your own Disciplines while in the body.

Once you have used this power, you suffer from some of the animal's habits and instincts. For each Social Trait expended on the possession, you suffer from one Negative Trait of *Feral*. These Traits remain until you overcome the animal's behavior patterns by expending Willpower Traits — one Willpower Trait for each Negative Trait removed. You should roleplay the animal's mannerisms, even after returning to your own body, until you have managed to remove these Negative Traits, although you can slowly overcome them by spending Willpower Traits over time (you need not try to overcome all of the *Feral* habits at once).

ADVANCED ANIMALISM

Drawing Out the Beast

Your mastery over the Beast Within is superb. Through your keen understanding of predatory nature and the ability to influence other creatures, you can draw out your own Beast, pushing your frenzy on others. Animals and ghouls are favored targets for this power, turning them into killing machines, but you can attempt to exert your Beast on anyone.

You must be on the verge of frenzy to use this Discipline. You exert this power in lieu of making any Virtue Test to control your frenzy. Instead, you make a Social Challenge against any individual within your line of sight. Doing so does not cost an action; you may attempt this feat any time that you are about to frenzy. If you win, your frenzy is transferred to the victim. The hapless recipient immediately enters frenzy and even manifests some of your personality, habits and speech patterns (which should be roleplayed — typically, characters with the *Investigation* Ability may recognize your mannerisms in the victim). The victim remains in a normal frenzy, while you are unaffected and unable to frenzy for the duration. Should the victim die while frenzied, though, the screaming Beast immediately returns to you, requiring you to make a Virtue Test or to exercise this power again. If you lose, you instead frenzy immediately with no Virtue Test, and you are unable to fight against your frenzy with Willpower Traits.

While the Beast is loosed in a victim, you remain complacent and placid. However, if the victim leaves your sight before the frenzy is over, you lose your Beast, suffering as if subjected to *Quell the Beast* — you cannot use Willpower Traits and you gain the Negative Traits *Submissive* x 2. You must find the recipient of your Beast and "convince" the Beast to return by acting in a monstrous fashion, or else kill the victim so that the Beast returns automatically.

Auspex

A predator's senses must be fearfully acute, so many vampires hone their sensory talents to incredible sharpness. This improved awareness starts merely by expanding physical senses, but as a vampire's powers of perception grow, consciousness itself becomes fleeting and sublime. Such a heightened awareness encompasses subtle textures and emotional states, transcending the physical limitations of the body while developing sharpness of the mind.

The powers of *Auspex* grant the ability to see through supernatural deception. With such focused attention, *Auspex* can even pierce the veils of *Chimerstry* and *Obfuscate*. Whenever *Auspex* is active (a conscious choice on the vampire's part), a Mental Challenge may be made with an opponent to try to see through the illusions of *Chimerstry* or the misdirection of *Obfuscate*. Winning this challenge with *Auspex* penetrates the deceptive powers. Losing, though, indicates that the vampire is affected normally. For each level of difference between the subject's Obfuscate or Chimerstry and the searcher's Auspex, there is a Trait modifier on a one-for-one basis in the event of ties or overbids. For example, a searching vampire with *Telepathy* (an intermediate level of *Auspex*) counts two additional Traits against an opponent who only knows *Unseen Presence*, a Basic level of *Obfuscate*. This bonus applies even when not using the full level of these Disciplines; an individual hiding with *Mask of a Thousand Faces* is still very difficult to detect if his mastery of *Obfuscate* has reached the Advanced level of *Cloak the Gathering*. A chance to see through supernatural concealment always exists, but doing so is much more likely if the searcher's *Auspex* powers are highly advanced and/ or the opponent's powers are weak. When using a Heightened Sense, hold up a number of fingers based on your power level (one for Basic, two for Intermediate, three for Advanced).

The *Auspex* Discipline is most evidenced by the Tremere, Tzimisce and Malkavian clans, who use it for supernatural insights, and by the Toreador, who use their superb senses in conjunction with their artistic work.

Auspex powers retest with the *Investigation* Ability. Willpower may be used for a single retest when attempting to spot an *Obfuscated* or otherwise hidden individual—in such a case, the vampire focuses his senses and concentrates fiercely, redoubling his searching efforts.

Basic Auspex

Heightened Senses

At will, you can extend your senses beyond human norms. Your eyesight and hearing sharpen to twice your mortal limits, while your touch, smell and taste are acute enough to pick out tiny details and features with ease. You can sharpen any or all of your senses, as desired. Furthermore, you sometimes have flashes of insight, preternatural awareness of danger or future events.

Any senses augmented by this Discipline function at twice normal effectiveness, allowing you to spot hidden foes, hear the rustle of leaves outside, taste a bit of poison in vitae, read a hand-written note by touch and smell incense burned hours ago. Should your senses be overwhelmed, though, you may be stunned temporarily. A loud gunshot, a flash of light or other overwhelming factor can incapacitate one of your senses for a time, causing you to lose the benefits of this Discipline. Furthermore you remain completely stunned for one turn, and you lose the sharpened sense in question for the duration of the scene, unless you expend a Willpower Trait to keep your wits about you.

Aura Perception

By watching a subject carefully, you can pick out the glowing halo or aura that surrounds all creatures. The interplay of colors in this aura gives you insight into the subject's emotions, motives and true nature. This Discipline is noticeable, though, as you stare at the subject with intense concentration.

You must be able to see your target in order to use *Aura Perception*. You then spend a turn in concentration and make a Static Mental Challenge with a difficulty of the target's number of Mental Traits (more complex targets are harder to read). Since using this power is a Static Test, the target may not relent or retest. If you succeed, you may ask any one of the following questions, which the subject must answer truthfully: What is your current mood/emotional state? What sort of creature are you (human, vampire, werewolf, etc., subject to your knowledge of such beings and their auras)? Are you under the effects of any form of magic? Have you committed diablerie (see the section on diablerie, p. 216, for how long this form of detection is viable)? Was the last thing you said a lie?

Aura Perception also allows you to sense ghosts and astral forms. If you suspect the presence of a ghost in an area, you may expend a Mental Trait to make a normal challenge to sense its aura, as described previously. If you succeed, you are aware of the ghost's aura as a pale, flickering and amorphous light, though this is not sufficient for you to identify specific individual ghosts.

The Spirit's Touch

Every being leaves traces of its thoughts and emotions wherever it goes. With this Discipline, you can read these psychic impressions from objects that others have handled, or that have strong emotional events tied to them. A simple touch and a moment of concentration unlocks a flood of images and sensations, possibly giving insight into the past of the item. Note that you may only use this power on objects or places, not on people, vampires, animals or other living creatures.

By touching an item and expending a Mental Trait for a turn of concentration, you gain a brief flash of insight into any powerfully emotional events surrounding the object in question. Each use of this power on an object allows you to ask a Narrator one of the following questions, requiring a truthful answer: Who last touched this object (before me)? Was this object used in any emotionally stressful events, like a murder, a passionate romance or a maniacal rage? What strong emotions drove a particular subject holding this object? Answers to these questions generally come in the form of images and impressions; you may not get exact names or lists of information, but instead distorted pictures, flashes of sudden passion and repeating sounds and voices. It is up to you to interpret such information.

Using this power on objects charged with particularly powerful emotions — a knife used to kill someone, a blanket clutched during childbirth, a bizarre puzzle that drove someone to insanity — may cause you to be temporarily overcome with emotions that are not your own. At the discretion of a Narrator or Storyteller, you may temporarily suffer from a derangement for the rest of the scene.

Telepathy

Projecting your senses outward, you can pierce the shroud of reason in the minds of others, drawing forth their very thoughts. You can link your consciousness to anyone you can see, sending or receiving concepts that you and the target "hear" in your respective minds.

In order to use *Telepathy*, you must make a Mental Challenge against your subject. A willing subject may relent to this mental contact, but there is no way to identify the originator of a given telepathic missive short of making contact (or you choose to identify yourself). You must also spend a full turn in concentration, focusing on your subject. If you succeed, you establish a brief link, allowing you to send or scan thoughts as long as you maintain the contact. You may issue a stream of thoughts that the subject "hears" as a single concept, or you can pluck a thought from the victim, asking a single question and demanding a truthful answer. Legitimate secrets that can be uncovered

are anything that could be discerned with *Aura Perception*, as well as such questions as: What is the appearance of a person, place or item about which you are speaking? What is the name of a person, place or item about which you are speaking? What element have you omitted from your answer to a question, if any? What is the true answer to a question that you have lied about? What memories do you have of one topic (querent's choice) of current conversation? If you choose to interrogate an unwilling victim, you must make a Mental Challenge for each question asked; if simply communicating normally, no additional challenges are required.

With effort, you can probe deep into the consciousness of an open mind, drawing out hidden secrets or buried memories. Doing so allows you to ask more detailed questions than the cursory ones usually employed with *Telepathy*. By expending a Mental Trait after establishing a successful telepathic link, you may ask and expect a truthful response to: What is one of your Flaws or Negative Traits, if any (subject's choice)? What is one of your derangements, if any (subject's choice)? Each question asked requires a Static Mental Challenge against the subject's Mental Traits, and the subject may not relent — you are delving deep into the mind, which reacts automatically to defend against intrusion.

At Storyteller discretion, *Telepathy* may discern clumsy uses of *Dominate*, particularly of *Forgetful Mind*, but with a great deal of effort. The most common means of doing so is to establish a link and begin asking questions, as described in the paragraph above. A second Static Mental Challenge against the subject's Mental Traits may allow you to spot gaps in a memory or where a memory has been poorly reconstructed. Modern vampires compare such gaps to be like watching a badly spliced film.

Communication with *Telepathy* proceeds in impulses, images and feelings, and it does not rely on the use of a common language, so even people who do not speak the same language may make themselves understood. Individuals unused to the sudden onslaught of *Telepathy* may be momentarily stunned or disoriented by projected thoughts, at the Narrator's discretion. *Telepathy* may also be used simply to eavesdrop; scanning someone telepathically is invisible and largely undetectable, unless another character with *Telepathy* tries to "listen in" on the link (using a Static Mental Challenge against the scanner). Such eavesdropping can only be used on surface thoughts. Beware, though — if you force your way into someone's mind without permission, the target may make a Willpower Challenge to force you to break off your link.

You may only use your *Telepathy* on one subject at a time, but this limit does not preclude someone else from using her own *Telepathy* on you. If you contact a subject and then use your *Telepathy* on someone else, your link to the first subject collapses and must be re-established later.

Using *Telepathy* on a supernatural creature is a taxing exercise, and it requires the expenditure of a Mental Trait. This Trait is expended before the Mental Challenge is made to establish the link. *Telepathy* only functions on beings with conscious thought. The Discipline has no effect on constructs that are not self-aware or on normal animals.

ADVANCED AUSPEX

Psychic Projection

No longer confined to the physical plane, you can project your senses and awareness outside of your own body. Thus untethered, your consciousness roams various planes of thought, allowing you to spy on areas all over the world as an incorporeal spirit. Without the concerns of mass and matter, you easily pass through any physical barrier and move at the speed of thought to any place on Earth, under the orbit of the moon.

While your senses are projected, your body lies in a comatose state, unaware of its surroundings. Your psychic form does not tire from travel, nor is it hindered or injured by the material world. Indeed, you are completely invisible and intangible,

unable to affect anything physically. However, your spirit-form can still sense its surroundings normally, even using your other powers of *Auspex*. Your immaterial form is tied to your material corpse through a silver cord, a sort of psychic tether that keeps you from becoming lost in the realms of spirit.

Sending your senses out in this fashion requires the expenditure of a Willpower Trait. You may remain out of your body as long as you like, though the rise of the sun over your physical form may force you into slumber. Furthermore, by expending an additional Willpower Trait, you can manifest for a single turn as an intangible apparition, allowing you to be seen and to speak audibly. While materialized, you can use any of your Mental or Social Disciplines simply by expending a Mental Trait before making the appropriate additional expenditures or challenges. While visible, you appear as an idealized form of yourself, complete with projected trappings, though your real-world physical possessions do not come with you in spirit form. Even while visible, you remain intangible and thus immune to injury from conventional sources like claws, fire, sunlight and mundane weapons (although your comatose body can still be harmed). While in astral form, you may not possess other bodies, even if you have that talent in *Dominate*.

You may deal normally with other astral forms that you encounter, conversing and using Mental or Social Disciplines. You may even attempt to injure other astral travelers by attacking their silver cord. Such astral combat uses Mental Challenges, with damage causing the opponent to lose Willpower Traits. Once an astral combatant runs out of Willpower Traits, his silver cord snaps, stranding him in the spirit realms. From there, the spirit may accidentally wander deeper into other worlds (such as the Dark Umbra in **Oblivion** or the Realms described in **Laws of the Wild**), or he may stumble about until he finds a way to return to his body. Some spirits thus trapped never return, captured or devoured by monstrous entities that dwell in the astral plane.

While astral, your consciousness exists in a mental projection of the material world. You cannot directly interact with or see wraiths, Umbral spirits or Garou (see **Oblivion** and **Laws of the Wild**), unless you find a means to travel to or sense the other spirit worlds. Similarly, your astral form is invisible and intangible to them unless you manifest in the physical world.

CELERITY

As one of the physical augmenting Disciplines of vampires, *Celerity* represents preternatural speed and reflexes. When angered, stressed or consumed with need, a Cainite can use the power inherent in the blood to fuel her actions, moving with startling quickness.

If attacked by surprise (see p.200), the victim may not use *Celerity* in the initial challenge — she must respond with her normal reflexes, and can only draw on her vampiric speed once she has reacted to the surprise.

The *Celerity* Discipline is most common among the Assamite, Brujah and Toreador clans. The former two tend to use the powers of *Celerity* in battle, while the latter engages in feats of dance, rapid completion of artwork or to flee from danger.

Since *Celerity* simply grants additional actions or modifiers to speed, it does not draw retests from any Ability. Actions performed with *Celerity* can still be retested appropriately (if shooting a gun twice, for instance, *Firearms* is used normally for a retest on each shot). Additional actions with *Celerity* can only be used for physical feats; one cannot use rapid-fire *Dominate* or *Thaumaturgy* with *Celerity*, for instance. As a general rule, Mental and Social Disciplines may not be activated during *Celerity*, except during *Alacrity*.

Use of *Celerity* at the speed of *Swiftness* or above is generally considered a breach of the Masquerade. Note that a vampire need not use her full level of *Celerity*; a vampire with Advanced *Celerity* could simply rely on the Basic levels if desired.

BASIC CELERITY

Alacrity

Your reflexes are finely honed. Even as you watch others act, you can spring into action, completing your movements before they can respond.

By expending a Blood Trait, you gain the ability to preempt any physical actions taken in the same turn, as long as you are aware of them (a face-to-face mugging, yes — a sniper attack, no). Thus, if someone declares an attempt to pull out a hidden weapon and shoot at you, you can preempt that action to pull out your own gun and fire back (instead of being relegated to dodging). Similarly, if someone attacks an ally, you can preempt the action to get in the way and fight against the aggressor instead. If you attempt to preempt someone using *Celerity* or a similar speed-enhancing power, the character with the highest degree of *Celerity* acts first.

Swiftness

With shocking speed, you move faster than humanly possible. Even as others are recovering from events, you are making your next move.

Expend a single Blood Trait to gain one additional action in your turn, in addition to your preemptive *Alacrity* (the costs are not cumulative). This additional action is taken at the end of the turn, after everyone has resolved single basic actions. If multiple people have additional actions like this, they are all resolved at the same time, after basic actions. You can thus swing a sword twice, run twice as far as normal in a turn, fire a gun and then duck behind cover, or otherwise perform multiple feats.

INTERMEDIATE CELERITY

Rapidity

Even other Cainites are dazzled by your superhuman speed. You routinely catch dropped objects, and the speed of your passing whips clothes and loose debris about.

Invoking all of your *Celerity*, at the cost of a single Blood Trait, enables you to use the Bomb in challenges of speed and agility. When performing an action where speed is of the essence, such as dodging an attack, throwing a knife or grabbing something out of someone's hand, you can declare that you have *Rapidity*. Once thus declared, you may choose to use the Bomb, a fist with the thumb pointing upward; the Bomb defeats Rock and Paper, but loses to Scissors (the fuse is cut) and ties with other Bombs. This symbol is usable in any challenges of speed throughout the turn. However, you are not required to use the Bomb — it is simply another option.

You may use *Rapidity* in any challenge where you rely on your own speed, even if your opponent attempts to use strength or stamina. Thus, if you try to use your *Rapidity* to dodge out of the way of someone grabbing at you, you can still use the Bomb. If the opponent possessed *Might*, you could still use the Bomb for speed, but the opponent would be able to use his *Might* retest for grappling.

Legerity

Moving faster than the human eye can track, you blur across the landscape with the speed of a cheetah. Compared to you, bystanders are statues.

You may activate your *Legerity* and all other *Celerity* levels for the turn at the cost of one Blood Trait. Your *Legerity* grants you one additional normal action at the end of the turn, in addition to your action from *Swiftness* (thus, you have at least three actions, a preempt and the Bomb in challenges of speed). Actions gained from *Legerity* come after basic and *Swiftness* actions, at the end of the turn.

ADVANCED CELERITY

Fleetness

When you call on your blood, you burst into a whirlwind of motion. Your passing extinguishes small flames, whips up flurries of debris and sows confusion among slower-moving entities.

With a single Blood Trait, you activate all of your *Celerity* powers. You now win all ties in challenges of speed, regardless of Traits. If some other consideration would cause you to lose on ties (such as wounds or an enemy's *Potence*), you compare Traits normally instead of losing automatically. This benefit lasts for the duration of the entire turn in which you use your *Celerity*. Your *Fleetness* functions in all challenges where you rely on speed, even if your opponent tries to use strength or stamina. Thus, if you use the speed of *Fleetness* to challenge an opponent who uses the strength of *Puissance*, ties are determined normally (since you both have powers that would win all ties). If the opponent only had *Might*, you would win all ties but still be vulnerable to a *Might* retest.

CHIMERSTRY

The Ravnos tricksters of India live in a world of illusions and dreams. According to their philosophies, the material world itself is only a passing fantasy. Consequently, they wield power over perceptions, shaping their own illusions and crafting dreamstuff to their liking.

With the *Chimerstry* Discipline, the Ravnos call on the energy of dreams and imagination, giving it form and phantasmic substance. This Discipline's powers can conjure almost any shade that springs to mind, though plausible effects or duplications of things that the conjurer has experienced are much more likely to fool viewers and victims. With enough mastery, the vampire can even give such illusions shadow-substance, causing injury to others. These illusions vanish only if dispelled by the creator, if the illusionist ceases concentrating on her creations or if they are banished by a disbelieving opponent who exerts enough presence of mind to prove the illusion's nonexistence (say, by shoving a hand through an illusory wall).

Chimerical illusions can only create, not remove — thus, they may add elements to a scene, but cannot cause something to become invisible. *Chimerstry* could cover up something's features but not remove selected parts. Furthermore, each illusion is a single object; one use of *Chimerstry* cannot create an entire host of illusory sensations or items. Chimerical creations must be free-standing items or sensory effects — a chimerical piece of clothing could conceal someone's real appearance, but a chimerical stake could not suddenly materialize inside of someone's chest (though it could later seem to be thrust there).

Retests with *Chimerstry* use the *Subterfuge* Ability, as they attempt to trick, deceive and mislead.

BASIC CHIMERSTRY

Ignis Fatuus

You generate a brief, static illusion that affects a single sense. You could cause the appearance of a rose in your hand, or make someone hear a low wind or feel the grating touch of sandpaper. This illusion has no real substance (and it cannot confine or injure your victims), but it can confound or mislead. The illusion cannot move in any fashion, although you can hold and move an illusion that you create. Thus, an illusion of a person cannot walk or fidget, but you can pick up and brandish an illusory knife.

You must expend a Willpower Trait and best your subjects in a Social Challenge to create this illusion. The illusion persists until you leave the area or until someone manages to disbelieve the effect (by passing a hand through the illusory rose, testing the air and feeling no wind, etc.). You may also dispel the illusion at your desire; doing so is immediate and requires no action.

Fata Morgana

Your illusions appeal to all of the senses. Though you still cannot harm or affect others physically with your phantasms, you can generate static constructs that seem real to any senses

that you choose to affect. Thus, you can make a wall that appears solid, has a texture to the touch and smells of old dust and paint, but which has no real substance and can be passed through. Alternately, you could create a phantasm that lacks certain characteristics — you could cause a person to believe that you were holding a rose and brushing it against her cheek, provoking the feeling of the flower against the skin and the scent of the rose, when in fact you do not have a rose. These illusions are still incapable of independent movement.

You must expend a Willpower Trait and a Blood Trait to create an illusion of this nature, and you must best your subjects in a Social Challenge. These illusions remain viable under the same conditions as phantasms created with *Ignis Fatuus*.

INTERMEDIATE CHIMERSTRY

Apparition

No longer confined to mere static images, you can create an illusion that appeals to many senses and has its own capabilities. You must first create an illusion using one of the lesser powers of this Discipline. Then, you can give it a semblance of life. People can be made to move, water to drip and lights to shine in complex patterns. You can even create blatantly strange moving effects, like a knife that flies about threateningly or a human who comes apart and back together again.

You need only spend a single Blood Trait to give animation to an illusion. Once so imbued, you cause the phantasm to move in one specific pattern that you desire. If you spend a complete turn in concentration, you can change this pattern at no extra cost. You must be present for your illusion to sustain itself.

Permanency

You no longer need to be present to sustain your illusory creations. Any illusion that you make with *Chimerstry* can be imbued with *Permanency*, allowing it to persist even if you leave the area.

Once you have created an illusion, the expenditure of a single Blood Trait grants *Permanency*. The phantasm remains until you dissolve it or until someone sees through the illusion in some fashion. Thus, you can cast an illusion over an area and then leave, allowing the illusion to persist.

ADVANCED CHIMERSTRY

Horrid Reality

Your terrifying powers of deception extend directly into the mind of your victim. By focusing your efforts on one individual, you can create terrifyingly realistic phantasms. These illusions can affect the senses and move about in any fashion that you desire, but they affect only one victim. Because of the absolute realism of these phantasms, they can actually convince the victim that he has been injured or affected physically. An illusory fire created with this power burns its target, a phantom wall bars passage and a chimerical stake paralyzes a vampire if thrust through the heart.

CHIMERSTRY AND THE FAE

If you are using the rules from **The Shining Host**, the Discipline of *Chimerstry* briefly shapes dreaming energy into chimerical constructs, and pulls them into a pseudo-Wyrd state where onlookers can experience them. Such creations are fully effective against changelings, who are always aware of these dream-fantasies. Thus, a chimerical knife (created with only low levels of *Chimerstry* and thus unable to actually injure people) can and does inflict chimerical damage on changelings. Furthermore, since these illusions are fueled by the power of the caster's blood, they cannot be dismissed with simple Banality; active resistance must disbelieve them.

You must expend a Willpower Trait and defeat your victim in a Social Challenge in order to use this power effectively. Once active, the nightmarish creation of this power remains for the entire scene, and its effects can last even longer — if you create a gun with this power, it remains for the scene, but wounds inflicted with it score damage that lasts until disbelieved. Since the illusion is completely under your control, it can affect the victim without recourse to additional tests, meaning that you can make a chimerical gun that always hits or a chimerical stake that seems to bend and twist toward the heart. Illusory wounds of this sort cannot kill, though they can certainly drive the victim into a comatose state. These wounds only disappear when the victim is convinced either of the illusory nature of the effect or when he is convinced that he is "healed."

DEMENTATION

The twisted psyches of Clan Malkavian house a passion and insight unmatched among the other lines of Cainites. Through their bizarre powers of *Dementation*, the Malkavians spread their madness, catalyzing insanity among mortal and vampire alike. Though this power was found only among the deranged Freaks of the Sabbat, a recent wave of instability has spread its nightmarish bubbles through Malkavians across the globe.

The Malkavians do not consider the secrets of *Dementation* "proprietary"; indeed, many seem almost eager to spread them. Curiously, other Cainite students of this Discipline need not be insane to use its powers. The Discipline does not seem to spread insanity, but rather, unlocks the doors of the psyche, exciting the madness that festers in every mind.

Some Lunatics do not use *Dementation* consciously. These few instead catalyze the passions of their victims; such advisors and seers spread their insight to unsuspecting vampires, who in turn find themselves spiraling slowly out of control. Other Malkavians recognize, categorize and use the powers of *Dementation* like the other regimented Disciplines. Strangely, the most stable and sane-appearing Lunatics are typically the ones who exert their *Dementation* with the least awareness.

Dementation powers use the *Empathy* Ability for retests.

BASIC DEMENTATION

Passion

You can bring emotion to a fever pitch, accentuating any and all drives or fears that may occupy the mind of your subject. Alternately, you can diminish passions to whispers, quelling the most fierce emotional fires.

You must engage your victim in a Social Challenge in order to use *Passion*. If you succeed, you enhance or dull the subject's emotions, at your choice. If you heighten the target's sensitivity, then the subject suffers from the Negative Mental Trait *Impatient*. If you dim the subject's emotions, then the victim suffers the Negative Mental Trait *Submissive*. In either case, the target should roleplay the new condition. The incited *Passion* lasts for the remainder of the scene or for a full hour, whichever comes first. Successive uses of this Discipline on the same individual are not cumulative. The source of this affliction is not immediately obvious, though some elder vampires are aware of the mind tricks of the Malkavians, and they may deduce the source correctly if someone suddenly becomes manic or listless.

The Haunting

Freakish, fleeting nightmares follow your target. The surreal world seems to come alive in barely heard noises and brief glimpses of motion. Victims find themselves distracted by inexplicable sensations, often stemming from their own hidden fears and guilt. Though you have no control over these images, you can choose what sense is affected. With continuous prolonged exposure, your subject may fall to madness as these apparitions afflict his consciousness.

You must expend a Blood Trait and engage in a Social Challenge with your victim in order to use this power. If successful, the subject suffers from fleeting nightmares, often plucked from his own subconscious. For the remainder of the evening, the victim suffers from the derangement *Schizophrenia* (see p. 214). Your use of this power is not immediately evident, although the victim should roleplay the effects of his new terrors.

INTERMEDIATE DEMENTATION

Eyes of Chaos

Scrutinizing patterns, you can find wisdom in the cracks of reality. Your insight extends to seemingly random patterns and bizarre manifestations of chance. Watching the interplay of events around you, you can sometimes discern complex patterns in them; observing people in action, you uncover their motives and secrets.

You can delve into someone's innermost motives by watching his simple actions. You must watch the target for a full turn, concentrating on his actions and motions. Then, you must engage in a Mental Challenge with the target. If you succeed, you learn the subject's Nature.

By watching the fall of random events around you, you may gain insight into your current situation. If you spend a full turn in contemplation of circumstances and expend a Mental Trait, you can predict (to some degree) the possible course of events. For the remainder of the scene, or for the next hour (whichever comes first), you cannot be surprised.

Losing a challenge in *Eyes of Chaos* causes you to become entranced with the patterns around you. Consider this entrancement identical to the Toreador Clan Disadvantage.

Voice of Madness

Simply by speaking aloud to your victims, you can reduce them to howling fear or anger. You address your targets in a reasonable tone, encouraging them to succumb to their inner demons. Those terrors then come to the fore, driving your victims to blind, uncontrolled panic.

You must expend a Blood Trait to use this power. Then, by speaking to your victims for a full turn, you can attempt to drive them into frenzy. You may affect multiple people at once, as long as they can all hear you. You then make a Social Challenge against your targets; any who lose to you are brought to the verge of frenzy. Mortals immediately flee in terror, as if affected by Rötschreck. Vampires, Lupines and other creatures capable of frenzy make *Self-Control/Instinct* Tests immediately, with a difficulty of four Traits, or else

---

INFECTION!

In the late 1990s, a wave of renewed madness spread among Clan Malkavian, shattering feeble or comical Lunatics and leaving the clan solely as twisted seers and madmen. One rapidly evident effect of this madness was the reintroduction of *Dementation* to the repertoire of many otherwise independent or Camarilla-affiliated Malkavians. Players of existing Malkavian characters may choose to retain *Dominate* as a Discipline or switch their *Dominate* powers for *Dementation* (those rare Malkavians with both Disciplines may choose to swap *Dominate* as a clan Discipline, and all of its levels, for *Dementation*, though the reverse is not possible). For instance, a Camarilla Malkavian with both Basic levels of *Dominate* but only one Basic level of *Dementation* (bought as an out-of-clan Discipline) could keep his Disciplines as they are, or decide to switch them, taking *Dementation* as a clan Discipline and having both Basic levels while losing one level of his *Dominate* Discipline.

fall into a similar state. However, you must also test for Rötschreck, with a difficulty of three Traits. This frenzy lasts for an entire scene unless curbed with Willpower or other capabilities, and mortals do not remember their actions during this period of terror.

ADVANCED DEMENTATION

Total Insanity

Madness lies around the nearest corner of every mind. Pulling insanity from the recesses of your target's deepest memories and beliefs, you cause the hapless victim to succumb to a wash of overpowering lunacy.

You must gain your target's total attention for a full turn; many Malkavians do so with sudden tricks, non-sequiturs and bizarre actions. You must then expend a Blood Trait and engage your target in a Social Challenge. If you win, your victim begins to suffer from five derangements, chosen by a Storyteller or Narrator, for the remainder of the evening. This Discipline is not cumulative—you cannot pile up more derangements with successive uses.

For ease of use of *Total Insanity*, it may be handy to make up several cards with derangements listed on them, and allow your subject to choose five randomly.

DOMINATE

Many Cainites are willful creatures, casting about their ambitions and bending mortals to their desires. For some, though, the strength of will channels into the power to bend minds and control actions. With a piercing gaze and a forceful word, *Dominate* can cause even the strongest mortal mind to crumble and push even other vampires to accede to one's desires.

Most *Dominate* powers require the victim to meet the Cainite's gaze and to hear his commands. Simple sunglasses do not protect against this power; as long as the subject can see the dominator's eyes, he can be affected. Furthermore, commands may be issued silently with *Telepathy*, as long as the victim meets the dominator's gaze.

Dominate is most common among the Giovanni, Lasombra, Tremere and Ventrue clans, who all exercise their authority unflinchingly.

Retests with *Dominate* use the *Intimidation* Ability, as the vampire exercises his powerful will against your subject. A subject may attempt a retest by expending a single Willpower Trait, and may only make one retest per challenge. A vampire of lower generation is always immune to a weaker vampire's *Dominate* powers (although canny elders may feign otherwise).

BASIC DOMINATE

Command

Exerting your will against a single individual, you can give a simple command and demand obedience. A single word, even one embedded in a sentence and stressed slightly, becomes an imperative command to your victim. You need only meet your victim's gaze. As long as your victim sees your eyes and hears your voice, your command carries the authority of your blood.

You must meet the gaze of your subject and speak a single word, emphasized for control. This command must be simple and easily understood: "Stop," "Run," "Sleep," "Scream," "Follow," and "Silence!" are all acceptable examples. The command cannot be blatantly harmful or self-destructive. You then engage in a Mental Challenge with your opponent. If you win, your victim must follow the order directly and immediately. The command cannot last more than 10 minutes.

Mesmerism

Like a hypnotist, you can impart commands to your subjects, even keying them on specific trigger events. If you can meet your subject's gaze and speak aloud your

commands, you can force the subject to obey your will. Unsuspecting victims can even be given commands that they must carry out later.

By making a Mental Challenge against your subject, you can impart more complex or subconscious commands. You may give your subject any sort of command as long as it is not self-destructive. This command can either be triggered immediately ("Go and fetch me a mortal vessel") or implanted with a particular trigger event ("When the prince ends court, sneeze loudly"). Only one such command may be implanted in a victim at a time, and unless other powers are used, the victim may well remember the process. Placing an order in your victim requires only as much time as it takes to speak the entirety of your order. Both the trigger and the suggestion must be clear and easily understandable.

INTERMEDIATE DOMINATE

Forgetful Mind

Your considerable powers of mental manipulation allow you to exert your influence in the very memories of your victims. By meeting your target's gaze, you can draw out answers to questions and even alter the subject's memory. You can erase entire blocks of the victim's past, or replace recollections subtly with your own dictated constructions.

To uncover, alter or erase memories, you must make a Mental Challenge against your victim. With success, you can change up to 15 minutes of your victim's memories; additional blocks of time may be altered with additional challenges. You can simply erase areas of the past, leaving the victim with a "hole" in his recollections, or you can specify new memories to overwrite your victim's experiences. By questioning your victim, you can also prompt him to elucidate his memories, repeating back his own experiences. As long as you gaze into the victim's eyes, and the subject is unthreatened, you keep the target pacified and unable to move or resist your hypnotic powers. Implanting additional commands with other *Dominate* powers still requires additional challenges, though. When altering someone's memories, you should record the number of Mental Traits that you possess at the time of the alteration — later uses of *Forgetful Mind* may be able to overcome your powers.

Although you can remove, add or change memories, you cannot destroy a subject's actual capabilities. That is, you may remove all memory of a subject learning a particular Ability or Discipline, but the victim will still retain the capability in question — he may simply be unable to recall how and when he learned it. *Forgetful Mind* is most useful in changing someone's memories of an event (causing someone to forget your feeding, for instance) or to cover traces of other powers (removing someone's recollection of the use of *Mesmerism*, leaving an implanted command buried in the subconscious mind). The more detailed your description, the more realistic the memory seems to your victim.

Use of *Forgetful Mind* can also determine if a particular set of memories is fake, by causing the subject to recall his overwritten experiences. By winning a Static Mental Challenge against the Mental Traits of the previous dominator, you can determine if certain memories are falsely implanted or changed, and you can then restore the original memories or alter the false ones as you see fit. You cannot use this power on your own memories.

Conditioning

The depths of your mental influence are frightful and pervasive. With time, you can strip away the defenses of the most determined mind, even removing your victim's personality and free will. You must have unrestricted access to your subject for several full nights. Should you manage to tear down the victim's resistance, her will is shattered and her mind becomes completely pliant to your whims.

Each night that you attempt to exercise *Conditioning*, you must make a Mental Challenge against your victim. If you manage to accumulate as many successes as your subject's *Self-Control/Instinct* Traits (or Willpower Traits for victims without

vampiric Virtues), you tear down the victim's mind and turn her into a virtual slave. The victim loses creativity and self-direction, instead following your orders to the letter automatically. You need not make tests to *Dominate* such a victim; the subject follows your commands even if you cannot make eye contact. Furthermore, the subject gains one free retest against the *Dominate* powers of any other Cainites.

A victim of *Conditioning* has little free will or motivation, and he has trouble reacting to stimuli. As a result, such pawns cannot produce artistic works or engage in teaching; they lack the drive and flexibility to perform these sorts of tasks.

If an enslaved subject manages to avoid all contact with her master for six game sessions, minus one session for each Willpower Trait spent (minimum of one full session), then the *Conditioning* is shaken off and the subject reasserts her individuality. A drone may also be deprogrammed by the successful use of this Discipline again, just as if trying to enslave the subject. The subject resists automatically, but if enough successes are accumulated to perform proper *Conditioning* again, then the target's original persona can be restored.

ADVANCED DOMINATE

Possession

No mortal mind can resist the power of your will. With but a touch, you can move your consciousness into a mortal body, taking complete control of the shell and suppressing the victim's mind. For the duration of this *Possession*, your own body lies comatose, while the mortal's mind is unconscious and unaware of what transpires.

Once you have touched a likely mortal subject (possibly requiring a Physical Challenge to get a firm grip), you may expend a Willpower Trait immediately and make a Mental Challenge to exercise *Possession*. If you win the challenge, you take control of the mortal body, while your own body collapses without volition. You must expend a Mental Trait to finish the possession; additional Traits allow you to use some of your Mental and Social Disciplines while in the host body, as shown on the table.

During the course of *Possession*, you experience everything that happens to the mortal body, as you guide its actions. Your Cainite form also suffers any damage sustained by the mortal body; if the mortal body dies before your consciousness can flee, you immediately collapse into torpor. If you wish to flee the mortal body for your own corpse, you must announce your intent at the beginning of the turn, and your spirit does not leave until the end of the turn (although you may still perform actions as normal). As soon as you leave, the mortal resumes control over his body (assuming that he's still alive).

While in the mortal body, you may travel any distance from your unconscious Cainite form. You have all the capabilities of the living body; you can even survive daylight, if you manage to stay awake (see p. 111). The body is as vulnerable as any other mortal's, though. For this reason, most vampires use ghouls for *Possession*, relying on the inherent strength in such creatures.

If your vampiric body is slain while your consciousness resides in another body, you can try to hang onto the form. However, you must make a Simple Test (win or tie) at each sunrise. If you lose, your spirit tumbles into the astral plane, lost forever. A possessed body also cannot be Embraced; your spirit prevents the transfer of the Curse, and the body simply dies.

POSSESSION	
1 Trait	Simple possession
2 Traits	Can use *Auspex*
3 Traits	Can also use *Dominate* and *Presence*
4 Traits	Can also use *Chimerstry*, *Dementation* and *Animalism*
5 Traits	Can also use *Necromancy* and *Thaumaturgy*

This power is ineffective on vampires and other supernatural creatures — their wills are too strong to be so completely overcome.

FORTITUDE

All vampires are supernaturally resilient, capable of surviving blows, slashes, bullet wounds and falls with impunity. Some few, however, are even more powerfully resilient, able to shrug off the most severe wounds and even resist the powers of fire and sunlight for a short time. The Discipline of *Fortitude* represents such resilience, and its mastery allows survival of situations that would otherwise cause Final Death in lesser Cainites.

The nomadic Gangrel and Ravnos clans, who must survive the rigors of the wilderness and travel, most commonly possess *Fortitude*. The Ventrue also exhibit this Discipline, often leading their charges into battle while shrugging off terrible attacks.

Retests on *Fortitude* powers use the *Survival* Ability.

BASIC FORTITUDE

Endurance

While most Kindred still suffer the fatigue and pain of their injuries, you shrug off such hardships. Even the searing injuries of fire and sunlight can barely slow you.

You do not suffer any wound penalties from anything past the Bruised health level, until you are struck into torpor or Final Death. When most vampires lose all ties due to being Wounded, or remain insensible and Incapacitated, you simply suffer the usual penalties of being Bruised.

Mettle

Wounds that would slow other vampires mean nothing to you. You can shrug off damage from most sources, ignoring pain and damage alike. Your body resists harm with incredible strength.

On achieving this Discipline, you gain one additional health level, which functions just like an extra Healthy line on your health level chart. This health level can be lost and healed like any other.

INTERMEDIATE FORTITUDE

Resilience

Even the banes to most Cainites, fire and sunlight, rarely injure you. You can endure punishment that would reduce other Cainites to ash, albeit for a brief time.

When you suffer aggravated damage, you may immediately make a Simple Test to try to reduce the severity of the damage. If you succeed, you reduce the injury to lethal damage. Before making the test, you may choose to expend a stamina-related Physical Trait, allowing you to reduce injury on a win or a tie. Otherwise, you must win the test outright. Use of *Resilience* is reflexive; it does not count as an action.

You may only attempt to use this Discipline once on any given attack. Thus, if you suffer two or more levels of aggravated damage from a particular attack, you may test to reduce only one level to lethal damage.

Resistance

Your vampiric endurance far surpasses that of any mortal, or even most other Cainites. You shrug off injury without noticeable effect. Blows that would stagger or kill a mortal may not even scratch you.

When you suffer lethal or bashing damage, you may make a Simple Test immediately to avoid some of the damage. If you succeed, you remove one level of the damage from the amount suffered. Before making the test, you may choose to expend a stamina-related Physical Trait, allowing you to avoid a level of damage on a win or tie. Otherwise, you must win the test outright. Use of *Resistance* is reflexive; it does not count as an action.

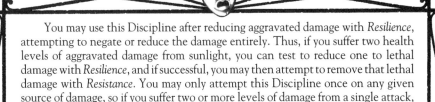

You may use this Discipline after reducing aggravated damage with *Resilience*, attempting to negate or reduce the damage entirely. Thus, if you suffer two health levels of aggravated damage from sunlight, you can test to reduce one to lethal damage with *Resilience*, and if successful, you may then attempt to remove that lethal damage with *Resistance*. You may only attempt this Discipline once on any given source of damage, so if you suffer two or more levels of damage from a single attack, you may only attempt to reduce a single level of damage from that attack.

ADVANCED FORTITUDE

Aegis

Like a bar of steel, a mountain, an immutable constant, you resist all damage and survive any attack. Only truly monumental and persistent force can ever destroy you completely. Indeed, once the storm of fire and destruction has passed, you rise out of the chaos unscathed.

At any point during a turn, you may declare the use of *Aegis*. You must expend a permanent Willpower Trait or three permanent Physical Traits to activate this Discipline (though these Traits may be re-purchased later with Experience Traits). When you declare *Aegis*, you immediately revoke any damage that you suffered in the turn, and you take no damage for the remainder of the turn. You may even declare *Aegis* after you have been "killed," ignoring the damage that killed you and any other injury suffered in the same turn. If you are "killed," you must use *Aegis* in the same turn — once a new turn begins, you cannot revoke any previous damage. Use of *Aegis* is reflexive; it does not count as an action.

MELPOMINEE

With this Discipline, the very voice of a Cainite is a powerful tool. Inspiring emotion or projecting sound through speech and song, the *Melpominee* Discipline reflects the incredible mastery possessed by the Daughters of Cacophony. The Greek Muse of tragedy surely reflects in this power, as it can be used both to soothe the mind and to inspire insanity. Some Cainites attribute these sirenlike gifts to a hint of fey madness in the Daughters' bloodline.

The powers of *Melpominee* function on the very soul, not merely on the flesh. Deaf subjects, or individuals otherwise unable to hear the vampire, can still be affected as long as the singer's voice reaches to the area of the target. These effects extend from the will of the siren, so they only affect those who are in the hearing range of the singer's natural voice or *Melpominee*-projected effects — engineered recordings, microphones, bullhorns, or electronic or mechanical copies cannot.

The Daughters of Cacophony consider *Melpominee* to be their highest art and calling, a reflection of the inward music that moves them. As a result, they do not teach its secrets to outsiders, and indeed other Cainites, who do not hear the cosmic music of the spheres, find development of this Discipline difficult in the extreme.

All *Melpominee* effects use *Performance* Ability for retests.

BASIC MELPOMINEE

The Missing Voice

Like a ventriloquist, you can throw your voice to any place within your line of sight. However, you do not cause your voice to seem to emanate from there — with *The Missing Voice*, you actually cause your speech or song to generate from thin air. You can even carry on two conversations simultaneously, for *The Missing Voice* functions independently of your normal voice.

You may use *The Missing Voice* at any time, as desired. However, if you use *The Missing Voice* while performing other actions, you suffer a two-Trait penalty on the resolution of challenges due to your split concentration.

Phantom Speaker

No longer limited to sending your voice to a place you can see, you can project speech or song to anyone you know. As long as it is night at the subject's location, you make your voice heard to your target.

The words and music of *Phantom Speaker* are audible only to your target, unless an eavesdropper with at least the Intermediate level of *Auspex* manages to listen in by defeating you in a Mental Challenge.

You must expend one Blood Trait to project your voice for a single turn.

INTERMEDIATE MELPOMINEE

Madrigal

The crashing waves of your song carry the force of your own emotions. With inspiring verses, you raise others to the heights of passion; black melancholy afflicts the victims of your works of despair.

You must make a Social Challenge against every target that you wish to affect with your *Madrigal* — you can affect anyone within hearing range, at your discretion. Willpower can be used to retest in defense against this power, as usual for Social Challenges. If you choose to affect multiple people, use a mass challenge as described in mob combat. Anyone who succumbs suffers the effects of an overwhelming surge of emotion, directed by your choice of song. The subjects should roleplay this wave of emotion as long as you perform no action other than singing.

You must sing for a full turn for *Madrigal* to take effect. The player need not actually sing to invoke this Discipline, though players so talented are certainly encouraged to do so.

Siren's Beckoning

Pulling out the roots of turmoil and despair in a subject, you awaken insanity from the soul. Like the legends of faerie singers and mermaids, you can drive your target into desperation with your melodies.

You must make a Social Challenge against your target to use the *Siren's Beckoning*. If you win, the victim suffers from one randomly chosen derangement. You may carry about a stack of cards with various derangements and allow the victim to choose one at random, or you may have the derangement relate to the song you sang (such as regression for a children's song or megalomania for a national anthem). This derangement lasts for the rest of the night.

ADVANCED MELPOMINEE

Virtuosa

Though most Daughters of Cacophony are limited to affecting a single target with hidden speech or insanity, your performance carries your music to as many listeners as you desire. You can extend your powers of *Phantom Speaker* or *Siren's Beckoning* to multiple subjects.

You need only expend one Blood Trait to use *Phantom Speaker* or *Siren's Beckoning* on up to five targets at once. If you use *Phantom Speaker*, every subject hears the same words or music that you project. If you use *Siren's Beckoning*, you make a mass Social Challenge against all of the victims at once. In either case, you can only use one power at a time — you cannot use *Virtuosa* to project speech to some people while singing to others simultaneously.

NECROMANCY

The unwholesome practices of the Giovanni family comprise several paths of magic centering on death and the dead. With studies born of centuries of repellent

traffic in cemeteries, sewers, crypts and catacombs, the codified powers of *Necromancy* allow conversation with and control over ghosts and corpses. Even other vampires shudder at the dark practices of necromancer Cainites.

As a study of undead magic, *Necromancy* consists of multiple paths of study and several rituals as well. Many necromantic powers require specialized components or grisly rites. Thus, vampires who make a practice of *Necromancy* must often secure such bizarre elements as human corpses, hands of murderers, jars of grave moss and the like. Needless to say, such repugnant practices often have a detrimental effect on one's Humanity.

Some few magicians outside of the Giovanni family also study *Necromancy*, most notably the rotting Samedi. It is rumored that there exist small bloodlines of extremely potent necromancer Cainites with powers beyond those known to the Giovanni.

A Giovanni student of *Necromancy* begins studies with the *Sepulchre Path*, the path of control over ghosts. Once Intermediate expertise is achieved, the student may expand into the studies of the *Ash Path* (communication with the Underworld) or the *Bone Path* (control of zombies) at the Basic levels, but he may learn only one of the two paths. At the Advanced level of mastery in the *Sepulchre Path*, the necromancer may begin studies of the other path as well, and he may improve beyond the Basic levels in any *Necromancy* path. Some few Cainite necromancers study more rare paths, or in a different order, but all Giovanni and Samedi vampires learn the *Sepulchre Path* first.

THE SEPULCHRE PATH

Necromancers generally begin their studies with the *Sepulchre Path*, the means of controlling ghosts. Through the *Sepulchre Path*, the vampire delves into the names of wraiths and the means by which they may be compelled to service. Many Giovanni call on "family wraiths" that have worked in service to the necromancers for several years, especially since most novices lack the ability to see or communicate with wraiths that they do not summon and control directly.

The *Sepulchre Path* uses the *Occult* Ability for retests. Storytellers may choose to use *Wraith Lore* as a specialized Ability instead.

BASIC SEPULCHRE PATH NECROMANCY

Insight

Gazing into the eyes of a corpse, you can see the image burned into its death. A moment's concentration allows you to call up the memories of death itself.

You need only expend a Mental Trait while gazing into the eyes of a corpse in order to use this power. You immediately see the last minute of the individual's existence, generally as flashes of vision and startling sensations. This power can even be used on the corpse of a vampire who has reached Final Death, as long as he had not achieved Golconda and is not in a state of advanced decomposition. However, it does not function on vampires that are still ambulatory.

Summon Soul

By calling out the names of the dead, you pull them to attendance. Combined with power over their artifacts from life, you can force them to answer your summons, appearing and obeying your will.

To call a ghost, you must know its name, or at least have a clear image of its persona from *The Spirit's Touch*. You must also have an object with which the ghost had some contact while it was alive. If this object has particular importance to the wraith (a Fetter), you gain a free retest on your attempt to *Summon Soul*. Some wraiths cannot be summoned regardless of your efforts; many ghosts are lost in the eternal storm of the Underworld, or go on to their final rewards. Vampires who were diablerized or who achieved Golconda before Final Death likewise cannot be summoned in this fashion.

You must make a Mental Challenge against the wraith that you call (see **Oblivion**, or use the guidelines for wraiths on p. 264 of this book). If the wraith wishes to be summoned, it can appear voluntarily. The wraith finds itself pulled to your location, and it becomes visible and audible to you. You may ask a single question of the ghost, which it must answer truthfully. After a single turn, the ghost fades away unless it chooses to remain or is coerced with further *Necromancy*. Even if the ghost stays nearby, you must use other *Necromancy* powers to see and hear it again, unless you exercise *Summon Soul* on it again.

INTERMEDIATE SEPULCHRE PATH NECROMANCY

Compel Soul

By binding a ghost with its name and your strength of will, you can force it to obey your commands. Once you have summoned a wraith, you may use *Compel Soul* to make it answer your questions and serve your bidding.

You must first use *Summon Soul* to cause a wraith to appear for you, then engage in a Social Challenge for the turn in which it manifests. The wraith may expend its Pathos (see **Oblivion**) to resist, forcing you to expend a Social Trait for each Pathos Trait spent. If you win the challenge, the wraith is bound to obey your commands for an entire hour. The wraith must answer your questions truthfully and act as you direct. During this time, the ghost remains visible and audible to you as well.

If you successfully *Compel Soul*, you may expend a temporary Willpower Trait to force the wraith to obey you for the entire evening. Expending a permanent Willpower Trait causes the wraith to be bound to your will for a year and a day.

Haunting

Your powers of necromantic compulsion allow you to force a ghost to remain in a particular location, or near a specific object. With a cryptic phrase and a powerful command, you bind the wraith so that it may not leave.

You must engage a wraith in a Social Challenge in order to link it to a particular location. If you win, the wraith cannot leave the room (or move more than 10 feet from a particular object) for the remainder of the evening. By spending a temporary Willpower Trait at the time of the *Haunting*, you can force the wraith to remain in the location for a full week; a permanent Willpower Trait extends this time to a year. If the wraith attempts to leave the location, it suffers one aggravated level of damage per turn outside the confines of the *Haunting* until it returns or is destroyed utterly.

ADVANCED SEPULCHRE PATH NECROMANCY

Torment

There is a reason that ghosts fear the most puissant necromancers of the Giovanni. Through the use of *Torment*, the necromancer can inflict actual damage on the dead, punishing them for their indiscretions.

Though you remain in the physical world, you can make Physical Challenges against wraiths. You lash out with supernatural energies, though many Giovanni choose to direct the blow by striking physically. Your attacks inflict lethal damage on the wraith; a wraith discorporated with this power is banished to the deeper levels of the Underworld for a full month, unable to return.

THE ASH PATH

The barriers between this world and the Underworld of the dead are permeable to the student of the *Ash Path*. With this path, a necromancer can see, hear and communicate with wraiths of all sorts, not just the ones that he can summon or control. Indeed, with enough skill, the *Ash Path* allows a vampire to cross the Shroud into the lands of the dead. This frightening power thus allows for myriad effects as the vampire reaches into the Underworld and deals freely with the denizens therein.

Retests with the *Ash Path* rely on the *Occult* Ability. At the Storyteller's discretion, the specialized Ability of *Wraith Lore* may be used instead.

BASIC ASH PATH NECROMANCY

Shroudsight

With minimal effort, you can see across the Shroud that separates the world of the living from the lands of the dead. The Underworld appears as a decaying and ghastly reflection of the mortal world, sometimes with structures lost to the past or unusual spirits flitting about. You can see (though not hear or feel) anything that transpires in the Underworld within your normal visual range, with a sort of "double sight" that does not hinder your normal vision.

You need only expend a Mental Trait to look across the Shroud for the duration of the scene, or for an hour, whichever comes first.

Lifeless Tongues

The babble of restless spirits is clear to you. By concentrating for a moment, you attune your senses to the Underworld, making yourself capable of both seeing and hearing all that transpires there around you. Furthermore, you can understand the language of the dead, so unless a ghost goes out of the way to use a language that you do not know, you can comprehend the words of any wraith.

You must expend a Willpower Trait to attune yourself to the Underworld for a scene or an hour (whichever ends first).

INTERMEDIATE ASH PATH NECROMANCY

Dead Hand

The structures and entities of the Underworld are very real to you. In a bizarre sort of half-life, you can stretch your physical form across the Shroud, interacting with beings and scenery there even as your physical body remains partially in the living world.

By expending a Willpower Trait, you make yourself capable of touching the contents of the Shadowlands for a scene or an hour (whichever comes first). Each additional scene or hour, you can maintain this power at the cost of one Blood Trait. During this time, you do not actually pierce the Shroud, but your actions affect both worlds. Thus, you can climb a ghostly rope, then turn and step onto a real-world roof. You can also lash out physically and strike or grapple with ghosts, though they can return the attacks. However, you cannot push or pull objects from one world to the next. Effectively, you exist in both realms simultaneously, which can be very disturbing to those watching you climb invisible ropes or grapple unseen opponents.

Ex Nihilo

Tearing through the Shroud between worlds, you can cross into the lands of the dead. This journey is a harrowing one, for many spirits wait to take vengeance on necromancers, and the Underworld is full of hazards unknown to most vampires. Furthermore, there is no way to gather blood or sustenance in the Underworld, and you can become lost in the storms and seas of the deadlands. Still, this power allows for direct contact with shades of the restless, and it serves as an unusual means of travel. While you are in the Shadowlands, you still see everything that transpires in the mortal world, but your physical form exists in the realm of the dead.

You must first mark a doorway with chalk or blood on any available surface, taking a full turn to do so. (You need not actually draw such a door, but you should pantomime the appropriate actions.) You must then expend a Willpower Trait and two Blood Traits, and make a Static Physical Challenge with a difficulty of eight Traits. If you succeed, you step through the door into the Underworld. Returning to the material world is a matter of concentration; you need only focus your intent to do so and expend a Willpower Trait, at which point you return to the living lands

at the end of the turn. Beware, though, for if you wander too deeply into the deadlands, you may become lost and unable to pierce the Shroud.

When you travel into the deadlands, you take with you only the inanimate objects that you carry. You cannot pull in other living or undead creatures. Furthermore, the laws of physics in the Underworld are not the same as those of the material world; guns do not work, and electrical devices fail. Generally, you must rely on your own powers.

ADVANCED ASH PATH NECROMANCY

Shroud Mastery

Your control over the barrier between the living and dead worlds is nearly absolute. Instead of stepping across or watching the events of the Underworld, you can actually manipulate the fabric of the Shroud. By changing the strength of the web between worlds, you can make it easier to cross, or bar wraiths from exerting their influence on the material world.

You must expend a Willpower Trait to exercise *Shroud Mastery*. Then, you may raise or lower the Shroud, as you desire. Each Mental Trait that you expend alters the strength of the Shroud by one point in either direction. A stronger Shroud makes it more difficult for wraiths to interact with the living, while a weaker Shroud has the reverse effect. You can raise the Shroud up to a maximum of 10, or lower it to a minimum of three. The "typical" Shroud rating for most locations is 7 or 8, though areas frequented by vampires or ghosts (cemeteries, crypts, mortuaries and sites of Elysium) may have ratings of 4 or 5.

If you are simply using wraiths as generic antagonists, each point of change in the Shroud's strength grants the wraith bonus Traits when interacting with the living world (if the Shroud is weakened) or acts as a penalty to the wraith's total Traits (if the Shroud is strengthened). If you are using the rules from **Oblivion**, the Shroud's effects are explained on p. 161.

THE BONE PATH

The *Bone Path* controls death's physical ends. Corpses are the medium of power for such a vampire, and they can be imbued with unwholesome energies and animated to perform according to their master's bidding. Zombies and soulless automatons are the hallmarks of the *Bone Path*.

Retests of the *Bone Path* use the *Occult* Ability. The Storyteller may choose to use the specialized Ability of *Thanatology* instead, if desired.

BASIC BONE PATH NECROMANCY

Tremens

You can instill a corpse with a brief jolt of life. Though this power is insufficient to actually animate or control bodies, you can make them start or twitch spasmodically. Naturally, this sight frightens those unaccustomed to the mobile dead.

You need expend only one Blood Trait to use *Tremens*. The body then twitches or moves briefly in a fashion that you dictate, from sitting up to blinking to flailing an arm momentarily. If you expend a Physical Trait as well, you can implant a command into the corpse instead, causing it to move (once) as you direct when a certain event comes to pass. Corpses twitching in this fashion cannot actually attack or inflict damage, but they can certainly startle the unwary.

Apprentice's Brooms

Your skills in the *Bone Path* allow you to animate the dead, bringing ambulatory motion and a semblance of understanding to a cold corpse. Though they cannot fight, these zombies follow simple instructions, performing tasks that you set to them.

You must expend a Blood Trait and a Willpower Trait to use *Apprentice's Brooms* on one or more corpses, and you must also spend one Mental Trait for each

corpse so animated. These corpses have four health levels, and they do not suffer penalties for injuries, but they cannot fight. Corpses animated with this power continue to perform a single task as you direct until they complete the job or until time or damage destroys them. Cadavers continue to rot even after being imbued with this energy, though only at the slow rate of one health level per month.

INTERMEDIATE BONE PATH NECROMANCY

Shambling Hordes

When you raise the dead to do your bidding, they come in skeletal hordes and withered masses that obey your every command, working and fighting until destroyed. Any body, no matter how decomposed, can be raised to serve your will.

You must expend a Willpower Trait to call on the *Shambling Hordes*, and then invest one Mental Trait and one Blood Trait for each corpse animated. As long as the skeleton is reasonably intact, the corpse rises to do your bidding. Such guardians can perform tasks or fight for you with no regard to their own welfare. They typically have four health levels (though heavily damaged corpses may have less), and they suffer no wound penalties. These zombies fight with the same number of Physical Traits that they possessed in life (assume five Traits for randomly chosen corpses). They can be given orders to attack people or to guard an area, and they wait tirelessly until destroyed. Decomposition will continue for corpses in varying states of decay, although completely skeletal guardians will be unaffected.

Soul Stealing

Your mastery of animate flesh and spirit allows you to pull the soul from a living or undead body. With *Soul Stealing*, you draw out the victim's soul, turning it temporarily into a wraith while leaving the body as an empty husk.

You must expend a Willpower Trait and engage your target in a Social Challenge to use this power. If you succeed, the soul is torn from the body, forced to remain as a ghost for a full hour or scene. You can then use other *Necromancy* powers to bind the hapless spirit as long as it is separate from the body. The body itself continues to survive in a comatose state, a perfect host for other possessing spirits.

ADVANCED BONE PATH NECROMANCY

Daemonic Possession

Though you are not dealing with actual infernal spirits, you can cast a willing soul into a fresh corpse or inanimate body. Thus embedded, the soul takes control of the body, turning it into a new physical home. Dead bodies continue to decay, and thus, they last no more than a week, but this trick provides a perfect temporary repose for a free-floating soul or summoned ghost.

The body must have died within the same scene in which you use *Daemonic Possession*, or else it must be alive or undead and bereft of consciousness (for instance, if you have removed its soul or if the owner is currently using *Subsume the Spirit*, *Possession* or *Psychic Projection*). Bodies of vampires in torpor do not make suitable hosts, as the vampire's spirit is still inside the torpid body. You need not make any challenge or expenditure — with an appropriate host and spirit, the process is automatic once you exert your power.

NECROMANTIC RITUALS

The sinister secrets of *Necromancy* are not confined to the static paths alone. Skilled necromancers create rituals, forms of magic designed to go beyond the basic capabilities of *Necromancy*. With the appropriate materials, training and time, a necromancer can use rituals to create wide-ranging or long-lasting effects that would otherwise be difficult to do with simple paths.

On learning *Necromancy*, the individual learns one Basic ritual. For each level of *Necromancy* learned, another ritual of the appropriate level is also learned; thus, a

necromancer with Advanced *Necromancy* knows at least two Basic rituals, two Intermediate rituals and one Advanced ritual. Learning additional rituals requires the expenditure of time and Influence, as appropriate. Learning a ritual also requires that the vampire possess a level of *Necromancy* equal to or greater than the ritual's level of power.

Casting a ritual requires a Static Mental Challenge with a difficulty of nine Traits. Unless otherwise noted, Basic rituals take 10 minutes to cast, Intermediate rituals require 20 minutes and Advanced rituals take 30 minutes.

BASIC NECROMANTIC RITUALS

Call of the Hungry Dead

With 10 minutes of time and a hair from the head of your prospective victim (represented by a card), you afflict your target with the cacophonous moaning and wailing beyond the Shroud. The victim is assaulted with a welter of confusing voices and mournful howls. For the remainder of the scene or the next hour, the target suffers the Negative Mental Traits *Oblivious* x 2 due to the confusing hail of otherworldly noise.

Eyes of the Grave

Over a time of two hours, you can concentrate the deathly emotions in a pinch of grave soil and use it to conjure visions of death and horror. Once you complete the ritual, you focus these images at the victim, who sees random intermittent flashes of her own gruesome demise.

Once during the remaining evening, you may force the subject to fail a retest, as a shocking vision of death overcomes her. For instance, if you are engaged in combat with a victim of this ritual, who fails a test but calls for a retest with an Ability, you may use the effects of this ritual to negate the use of the Ability and force the victim to either find an alternate means of retesting or to suffer the outcome of the original challenge. Only you may invoke this benefit — other people may not use this ritual's power against the victim, even if they are aware that you have cast the ritual.

Spirit Beacon

By casting this ritual over a severed human head, you turn it into a supernatural beacon for ghosts. Within the Shadowlands, the head appears to glow with an unearthly radiance, emitting light from its mouth, ears and eyes. Any wraith viewing the Underworld radiance from this head must expend a Willpower Trait or else be immediately drawn to the light for a full hour (or until the end of the scene). The head loses its light at the next sunrise, though it may be enchanted again.

INTERMEDIATE NECROMANTIC RITUALS

Cadaver's Touch

By chanting hideous paeans while melting a wax figure of your victim over a three-hour ritual, you cause the subject to lose all semblance of life. The mortal subject of this spell becomes much like a vampire, with a weak pulse, cool skin and a pale countenance. As long as the wax is melted without boiling off or solidifying, the ritual keeps the victim in such a pallid state.

The mortal subject of *Cadaver's Touch* gains the Negative Trait *Repugnant* for the duration of the ritual, as he literally resembles a walking corpse. However, this ritual can be very useful for sending a mortal unnoticed among vampires, or causing hunters to mistake a mortal for a Cainite.

Call On the Shadow's Grace

After casting this potent ritual, you become able to peer through the veil obscuring the Shadowlands, and to detect the dark side of every wraith. You can speak directly to the Shadows of ghosts, conversing with their dark sides and learning their secrets. Furthermore, you can coax deadly plots and treacheries from the recesses of the living or undead, simply by communing with their shadowy sides.

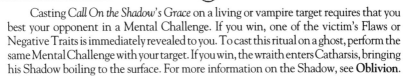

Casting *Call On the Shadow's Grace* on a living or vampire target requires that you best your opponent in a Mental Challenge. If you win, one of the victim's Flaws or Negative Traits is immediately revealed to you. To cast this ritual on a ghost, perform the same Mental Challenge with your target. If you win, the wraith enters Catharsis, bringing his Shadow boiling to the surface. For more information on the Shadow, see **Oblivion**.

Ritual of the Unearthed Fetter

This three-hour ritual is most often used by skilled necromancers of the *Sepulchre Path*. By casting this ritual with the finger bone of a corpse, you attune the bone to any material objects, people or places that may have significance to the finger bone's owner — specifically, to the ghost of the dead individual. You take a chip of a grave marker, crush it and sprinkle it over the bone while intoning the ritual. When complete, the finger bone acts as a sort of spiritual compass, pointing toward objects of vital importance to its wraithly owner.

Once you have attuned a finger bone with this ritual, you can use it to find Fetters of a particular wraith, assuming that the remains in question are of an individual who became a ghost. You can therefore determine whether a particular place, object or person is a Fetter for a wraith. By spending a turn testing a suspect item with the finger bone, you can ask a ghost or Narrator whether it is a Fetter to that particular ghost. Remember, though, that the finger bone only finds Fetters of its owner.

ADVANCED NECROMANCY RITUALS

Grasp the Ghostly

Casting this potent ritual requires a full six hours of chanting. Once complete, you reach into the Underworld, pulling a ghostly object from there and replacing it with an item of your own of roughly equivalent mass. You can only use this ritual on objects, not on people, vampires or ghosts.

Once you have pulled an item from the Underworld, it maintains a solid existence, though its plasmic matter fades slowly from the real world. After a full year, the item in question vanishes forever. This ritual only works on objects that once existed in the real world and that now have ghostly relic equivalent. Artifacts — objects created by wraiths in the Underworld — are not affected by this power; attempting to bring them across will destroy them.

OBEAH

Though modern Cainites know the Salubri as soul-stealing demonologists, the powers of *Obeah* are a strange mixture of defense and healing. Indeed, powerful Salubri can apparently repair the very scars of the Beast on a Cainite's psyche. Of course, few would trust the Cyclops enough to undergo such treatment. As these powers irrevocably mark the user as a Salubri or ally of such, they are almost never seen or heard of by other vampires — no Salubri would give away his position to Cainites who might betray him to the Tremere, nor would he teach such fatal secrets to another.

Once a vampire learns the Basic power of *Anesthetic Touch*, he develops a third eye in the middle of his forehead. This eye opens any time an *Obeah* power of *Anesthetic Touch* or higher is used. Cainite scholars speculate that the eye may, in some way, be connected with the mystical (or demonic) insight that grants this Discipline.

Retests of *Obeah* use the *Medicine* Ability.

BASIC OBEAH

Sense Vitality

The ebb and flow of life is obvious all around you. You can feel the pulse of life force with a touch, even sensing the energies of people or Cainites with whom you come in contact.

You must touch your subject to use *Sense Vitality*. With a successful touch, you can unearth information about the subject's life force by spending Mental Traits. Expending one Mental Trait tells you if the subject is a mortal, vampire, ghoul or other creature. Two Mental Traits tell how much damage the victim has suffered. Three Mental Traits reveal the amount of blood in the subject's system, while four Mental Traits reveal any diseases. These expenditures are cumulative; that is, any expenditure of Mental Traits includes the information for a lesser expenditure automatically.

Sense Vitality may also be used for medical diagnosis, determining the source of injuries or diseases afflicting a victim. Anything that could be learned with a medical examination — the source of the injury, the wound's severity, the reason behind unnatural mental states or death — can be learned with a touch. Each condition examined in this fashion requires the expenditure of a Mental Trait. Thus, determining that a subject was injured with a poisoned knife would cost two Mental Traits — one to recognize the wound as a knife wound, and one to recognize the poison.

Anesthetic Touch

Pain flees at your caress, and a peaceful stillness falls on those under your care. Any voluntary subject touched (other than yourself) can be rendered immune to pain. You can also cause mortals to descend into a natural, healing sleep.

You must touch your subject to use *Anesthetic Touch*, but as it only works on willing subjects, doing so generally requires no challenge. Expending one Blood Trait causes the subject to suffer no penalties from wounds for the next full turn. If you also expend a Willpower Trait, the pain-numbing effects last for the rest of the scene, or for an hour, whichever ends first.

Alternately, you can cause a willing mortal to sleep. You must expend a single Blood Trait. The mortal immediately enters a deep, peaceful slumber, suffering no nightmares or derangements. The subject can be awakened normally. If the mortal sleeps for an entire natural sleep cycle (which will happen automatically if uninterrupted), then the mortal's Attribute Traits are refreshed and one Willpower Trait is restored on awakening.

Anesthetic Touch has no effect on vampires.

INTERMEDIATE OBEAH

Corpore Sano

The power of your blood carries healing vitality. Touching the injuries of a subject, you cause them to close and heal immediately.

You must touch an area on or near an injury to invoke *Corpore Sano*, possibly requiring a Physical Challenge if the victim is for some reason unwilling (a vampire who does not trust the assurances of a diabolical Salubri, for instance). Each Blood Trait that you expend heals one health level of lethal damage on the subject immediately and completely; aggravated damage requires two Blood Traits per level healed. If your generation precludes you from spending enough Blood Traits to heal the target completely, you can maintain your contact over the course of several turns in order to heal severe injuries. You are not required to heal all damage that a target suffers — you can spend as much or as little blood as you like over the course of the healing.

Mens Sana

Soothing words and supplicating paeans calm the mind of your subject, gifting mental peace to the disturbed. Whether by psychological discourse or religious exorcism, your words carry away the worries and problems of disturbed individuals.

Using *Mens Sana* requires you to spend about 10 minutes in uninterrupted, quiet conversation with the subject. You must expend two Blood Traits and make a Static Mental Challenge with a difficulty of the subject's Mental Traits — more complex

minds are harder to cure. If you succeed, you alleviate one of the target's derangements. Although a Malkavian can never be cured of his core problem permanently, this power can affect even such madness, temporarily removing the derangement for the rest of the scene or the next hour (whichever comes first). Other subjects are relieved of the burden of insanity permanently.

Mens Sana cannot be used to cure your own derangements.

ADVANCED OBEAH

Unburdening the Bestial Soul

Perhaps the most incredible power of *Obeah*, *Unburdening the Bestial Soul* allows you to lift the terrible stains of the vampiric Curse from the soul of a target. You literally take the subject's soul into communion with your own, soothing the psychic scars and trauma that afflicts the victim. Though you cannot remove the Curse of Caine from a subject, you can heal the most terrible emotional trauma that weighs down most vampires.

When you remove a soul for healing with *Unburdening the Bestial Soul*, the subject's body is devoid of consciousness. As a result, the empty shell cannot be affected by Mental or Social Disciplines, as there is no personality to affect. However, it does make a perfect host for wandering spirits or ghosts. Unless possessed by an outside consciousness, the body automatically follows your simple verbal commands as long as you hold the soul. Without free will, though, the body cannot perform any task but autonomic functions unless you direct it specifically.

Unburdening the Bestial Soul functions only on a willing subject, and you must make eye contact with the target. Then, you make a Static Physical Challenge against the subject — the difficulty is two Traits for every Humanity/Path Trait that the subject falls below six (a subject with three Humanity Traits, for instance, has a static difficulty of six Traits). This power only functions on vampires with Humanity Traits, or on the Paths of Harmony or Honorable Accord, and it cannot affect a subject who has no remaining Humanity/Path Traits.

Once you remove a subject's soul, you can expend permanent Willpower Traits to restore Humanity/Path Traits on a Trait-for-Trait basis. You can restore the subject up to the normal maximum of five Traits.

If you fail to care for the subject's body while holding the soul, or try to hold the soul after the subject wants to return to his body, you risk losing your own Humanity (make a *Conscience/Conviction* Virtue Test, difficulty four Traits). The soul can make a Mental Challenge against you once per night to break free in such a case.

You cannot use *Unburdening the Bestial Soul* to restore your own Humanity/Path Traits.

OBFUSCATE

As creatures of cunning, intrigue and misdirection, Cainites possess an uncanny knack for deception and stealth. For some, though, this ability goes far beyond normal subterfuge. Such vampires actually cloud the minds of people around them, dulling notice and directing attention elsewhere. As a result, these vampires can remain obscured from observation, perhaps even extending their concealing powers to other objects and people.

The powers of *Obfuscate* are often employed by the Assamites in their assassination work, and by the Followers of Set, who surreptitiously ferret out secrets and watch over their quarry. Malkavians use this power to escape notice when engaged in their insane activities. The undisputed masters of this Discipline, though, are the Nosferatu, who use its mind-numbing powers to gather secrets and hide their fearful countenances.

Because *Obfuscate* clouds the awareness of its targets, they avoid notice of a concealed individual and to rationalize away such attention unless it is forced on them. Thus, if a vampire is concealed with this Discipline while wandering about a room, people avoid her

subconsciously. If she sits in a chair while hidden, others ignore the chair, taking other seats or standing but failing to notice her innocuous presence or the "mysteriously empty" seat. This concealment is generally broken if the hidden individual deliberately interacts with the environment, by picking up or dropping something, speaking to someone, touching a person or manipulating an object — the amount of concealable activity varies with this Discipline's power, as shown in the individual levels. The concealment of *Obfuscate* functions against all of the senses, because it actually forces attention away from the hidden individual. Thus, the presence of a Nosferatu wandering about with *Unseen Presence* is not betrayed by any telltale odor of the sewers.

Cross your arms in front of your chest to represent your use of *Obfuscate*, displaying a number of fingers on each hand corresponding to your highest level of power (one for Basic, two for Intermediate, three for Advanced).

The Discipline of *Auspex* can sometimes be used to pierce the veil of *Obfuscate*. An individual with *Auspex* (or a similar power of supernatural sensitivity) may penetrate *Obfuscate* if he is already looking for hidden individuals. The searcher may engage in a Mental Challenge with the hidden subject. For each level of difference between the subject's *Obfuscate* and the searcher's *Auspex*, there is a Trait modifier on a one-for-one basis to the outcome of ties or overbids. If the searcher wins, then he pierces the *Obfuscate* and senses the hidden vampire normally. If the concealed individual wins, the searcher remains oblivious to her presence. Thus, if a vampire with *Vanish from the Mind's Eye* (an Intermediate power) uses *Obfuscate* while trying to evade a vampire with only *Heightened Senses* (a Basic power), the hiding vampire gains a two-Trait bonus on the Mental Challenge, and if successful, he remains unseen. This bonus applies even if the sneaking vampire uses a lower level of *Obfuscate* than he actually possesses, so using *Unseen Presence* is still potent against low levels of *Auspex* if the vampire actually has Intermediate or Advanced *Obfuscate*. Similarly, simple *Heightened Senses* and the like gain the full benefit of the vampire's best level of *Auspex*, so a vampire with *Psychic Projection* is extremely difficult to fool, even if only using the Basic levels of sensory powers.

Obfuscate powers last as long as they are maintained, and they generally require no particular effort. These powers conceal the user and everything worn or carried. The *Stealth* Ability is used for retests by augmenting the Discipline with natural shadows and concealment. Hidden individuals cannot use Willpower to defend against *Auspex* challenges to *Obfuscate* (they cannot "will" themselves into a more hidden state).

BASIC OBFUSCATE

Cloak of Shadows

By remaining still and relying on natural cover, you can blur the apparent lines of your form and make it difficult for people to notice you. While nobody is watching, you can use cover to fade from view. As long as you remain completely silent and unmoving in a shadowed place or behind some sort of cover, you may cross your arms in front of your chest to represent the use of *Obfuscate*. While thus hidden, nobody but a Cainite using *Auspex* (or another supernatural creature with similar sensory acuity) can spot you. This concealment vanishes immediately if you move, speak or interact with your environment in any fashion.

Unseen Presence

Your powers of concealment allow you to fade from view, and then to wander about while remaining unnoticed. Any time that you are hidden from sight, you may invoke this Discipline, crossing your arms in front of your chest to represent *Obfuscate*. Once concealed, you may move about at a walk and remain unnoticed. This concealment remains as long as you do not speak, make any loud noises or interact with your environment — you can wander about unnoticed, but you automatically become visible if you open a door, attack a person, exert the *Presence* Discipline or knock over a vase, for instance.

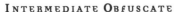

Mask of a Thousand Faces

By twisting perceptions around you, you cause others to see you not as you really are but as someone different from your actual physical appearance. Generally, this power causes people to ignore your features, making you unassuming and average. However, with concentration, you can assume a specific hallucinatory visage, or even copy the features of another individual.

While using the Mask of a Thousand Faces, your features seem bland and unremarkable. Most often, people will describe you in vague, general terms relating to your normal appearance, but without any specifics, unique features or details. (Nosferatu and Samedi in particular find this power useful for assuming a semblance of their mortal countenances.) If you expend a Mental Trait, you may assume a specific set of features instead, causing those who look on you and who do not pierce your disguise to see, hear and smell the form that you choose. Thus, you can make your hair seem to be of a different color, change your apparent facial features, or seem to exude the smell of a specific perfume (or no smell at all). Note, though, that this power does not change the appearance of anything that you wear or carry — only your physical features are obscured. A Mask of a Thousand Faces remains until you fall asleep, are knocked unconscious or torpid, or are killed.

You still use your normal Social Traits while using the Mask of a Thousand Faces. You can copy an image of fewer Traits deliberately, but if you hope to masquerade as someone with more Social Traits, you must expend Blood Traits to match that person's total Social Traits. Otherwise, your appearance and mannerisms mysteriously fail to convey the person's countenance properly. You cannot use the Mask of a Thousand Faces to assume more Social Traits than your generation would allow you to possess, so you may have difficulty duplicating the incredible grace of an elder. In either case, you still use your normal Social Traits; the assumption of the Mask of a Thousand Faces merely causes you to appear like someone of more or less social acumen and appearance.

Vanish from the Mind's Eye

The incredible powers of your stealth allow you to remain hidden even while speaking or moving about. You can even fade from plain sight, disappearing from the view of any onlookers.

When using Vanish from the Mind's Eye, you gain all the benefits of Unseen Presence, but with some additional power. You may vanish from view at any time, without having to seek cover. To do so, you simply declare your intent, and then make a mass Mental Challenge against any onlookers (regardless of Auspex) who care to challenge your powers — you bid one Mental Trait for each onlooker, and throw one symbol against all of them. If you succeed, you fade away, unnoticed by anyone. Even if some people notice you, you can attempt to fade from their view again on consecutive turns. Fading away with Vanish from the Mind's Eye does not count as an action, but it happens only at the end of a turn. Thus, if you strike someone and then attempt to disappear, you must wait until the end of the turn.

Additionally, you may speak aloud while using this Discipline, and still attempt to remain hidden. Again, if you speak, you must make a mass Mental Challenge against everyone trying to detect your position, regardless of Auspex. Anyone losing to you fails to locate you, simply hearing a disembodied voice; those who best you manage to pierce the veil of your Obfuscate. You still cannot remain invisible while interacting physically with your environment, screaming, exerting Presence or attacking, but you could take such an action and then try to fade away, as described previously.

Advanced Obfuscate

Cloak the Gathering

Your powers of concealment extend beyond your own form. With an effort, you can throw your disguising powers over several people, hiding them all from view or masking them with hallucinatory guises.

To use *Cloak the Gathering*, you must spend one Mental Trait for each subject cloaked. You can then exert any *Obfuscate* power that you possess over the targets. Thus, you could choose to spread several *Masks of a Thousand Faces* over your allies, making them all look like different people (or even making some look like clones), or you could shroud a group with *Vanish from the Mind's Eye*, causing them all to fade from view. When you exert this power, you must meet all of the normal conditions for the *Obfuscate* that you extend — you cannot cast *Cloak of Shadows* over someone who is not hidden behind cover or shadows, for instance. If you cause a group of people to *Vanish from the Mind's Eye*, you need only make one Mental Challenge to extend the effect over your entire group. Anyone who bests you sees through the cloak, while anyone who loses to you fails to notice anyone under the cloak. You can only cast out a power that you are using, and you can only extend one power at a time.

Individuals under the effects of *Cloak the Gathering* still sense one another normally. Of course, a cloaked individual could use his own *Obfuscate* powers to remain unnoticed to other people under the cloak. If an individual under *Cloak the Gathering* violates the provisions of his loaned *Obfuscate* in some way (say, by launching an attack), then he immediately loses the benefits, but the cloak itself remains intact. Only if you violate your *Obfuscate* does the cloak fail. Similarly, if a character with *Auspex* attempts to breach your concealment, individuals noticed under the cloak do not compromise the protection for everyone else, but if you are noticed, then the entire cloak fails.

Cloak the Gathering only throws your *Obfuscate* over other creatures or entities. You cannot use *Cloak the Gathering* to shroud a house, for instance, but you can certainly conceal a small group of vampires and all that they wear or carry.

Obtenebration

The bailiwick of the Lasombra clan, the *Obtenebration* Discipline summons forth and shapes a strange, cloying darkness. This darkness is wholly unnatural. It mutes sound, absorbs light and sometimes seems to have a tangible substance. Some Cainites claim that this darkness is a reflection of the primordial void before Creation, while others hold that it stems from the vampire's blotted soul. Whatever the source, this shadowstuff is certainly terrifying to those unused to its manifestations.

Any given vampire can see through her own *Obtenebration* darkness automatically without penalty, unless otherwise noted. Creations of other users of the Discipline are just as impenetrable to other Cainites with the power, though.

Occult retests are appropriate for the *Obtenebration* Discipline's powers, though shades used in a more mundane fashion (like attacking or grappling) should use the appropriate Abilities (like *Brawl* or *Melee*).

Basic Obtenebration

Shadow Play

You can exert a limited degree of control over existing shadows and darkness. At your mental command, darkness can be made to deepen or retreat, lengthen, move, flicker or undulate disturbingly. Though you can only affect a limited area of shadow, the stuff takes on a hellishly cloying quality and bends to your supernatural will.

You must expend a Blood Trait to use *Shadow Play*; once activated, it lasts for the duration of the scene or for an hour. You can affect one individual with the flapping,

disconcerting shades of this power. If you choose to conceal yourself, you gain one bonus Trait in all challenges of stealth and ranged combat. By pulling shadows around you into a terrifying mantle, you may alternately gain one bonus Trait in all challenges of intimidation. If you decide to afflict a victim with flapping, twisting shadows, the subject suffers from the Negative Trait *Clumsy* due to the distraction, and is disconcerted and asphyxiated by the darkness. A mortal enveloped in this fashion may even be strangled; a mortal with three or fewer current Physical Traits loses one Physical Trait every turn, and then loses one health level per turn as long as the morass continues to attach to her. Should the mortal lose all of her health levels in this fashion, she chokes to death.

Directing the shades of this power to conceal or surround you is automatic, but attacking an individual with the strangling shadows requires a successful challenge of your Mental Traits versus the target's Physical Traits.

Shroud of Night

You can evoke a cloud of inky blackness, a blob that absorbs all light and distorts sound. Hovering preternaturally in the air, this globe feels like a heavy morass to all those engulfed within.

You need only expend a Blood Trait to create a sphere of blackness roughly 10 feet in diameter. You can even create the cloud in a location outside of your line-of-sight, at the cost of one Blood Trait, as long as it is within 50 feet of your location. Victims enveloped in this globe suffer the Negative Physical Trait *Clumsy* while they are engulfed, and mortals with five or fewer current Physical Traits may be strangled, like the power of *Shadow Play*. (The Trait penalties and strangling damage from this power are not cumulative with *Shadow Play*, though.) You can even cause the tenebrous cloud to move at a speed roughly equal to a walk, as long as you concentrate fully on such motion.

Inside the *Shroud of Night*, all light sources other than fire are extinguished and sound is muffled. All victims of the cloud (except yourself and those with some means of seeing through *Obtenebration*) suffer the penalties of total darkness: They lose two Traits in resolution of challenges, and they are forced to make a single retest on any successful challenge because of the darkness. Even those with *Heightened Senses* and *Eyes of the Beast* are affected; each removes one penalty Trait from the effects of the cloud (the forced retest is not removed).

Your *Shroud of Night*, once created, lasts for the entire scene or hour, or until you dispel the darkness to whatever nether region from which it came.

INTERMEDIATE OBTENEBRATION

Arms of the Abyss

From the shadowy corners of a room or the blackness of night itself, you can summon forth tentacle limbs that flail about, ensnaring or attacking as you desire. These black shadow tentacles animate as you direct, even while you take other actions. You can pull many tentacles from a single source, or generate shades from several locations at once.

You must expend a Blood Trait to create the shadow tentacles; every tentacle created costs one Social Trait. The tentacles are six feet long and they possess three Physical Traits and four health levels. Each additional Blood Trait spent in the creation can gift one tentacle with an extra Physical Trait, or increase one's length by an additional six feet.

Once created, your shadowy tentacles remain for the duration of the scene, unless you dispel them or fall into unconsciousness or torpor. You can control the actions of the tentacles even while performing other actions. The tentacles can grab, whip, hold items and perform other tasks with precision. The tentacles take damage normally from attacks, and they suffer from fire and sunlight just like a vampire, though they are considered to have any *Fortitude* that you may possess. You can add your *Potence* to the might of the tentacles as well, though not at the same time as you are adding your *Fortitude*. You may not combine the effects of *Obtenebration* with the powers of any other Disciplines.

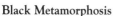

Black Metamorphosis

Spewing forth your own stained inner spirit, you meld your corpselike body with the very stuff of tangible darkness. Your head and limbs seem to fade into shadow, while bands of blackness striate your body and shadowy tentacles sprout from your torso.

You must expend two Blood Traits and a Social Trait to evoke this power. You immediately sprout four tentacles just like those of the *Arms of the Abyss* power, though they are considered extensions of yourself and they use your Traits. The chilling darkness about your body and infusing the tentacles afflicts anyone you touch with the Negative Trait *Clumsy* as their limbs are numbed with supernatural cold. You may make one additional attack at the end of each turn by using the tentacles, in addition to any strikes that you normally gain or make with *Celerity* (this extra attack is added to your attack sequence, not multiplied if you have extra actions). You gain the bonus Traits *Intimidating* x 3 while taking on this demonic aspect. Lastly, you suffer no penalties from any sorts of mundane darkness.

The *Black Metamorphosis* lasts for one scene or one hour.

ADVANCED OBTENEBRATION

Tenebrous Form

At this level of skill, you no longer summon forth the darkness within yourself — you *become* it. Your form collapses into a shadowy outline, a pseudo-liquid humanoid shape of utter blackness. While in this form, you can slither about through tiny holes and cracks, and you may see through any normal darkness.

You must expend three Blood Traits and spend three full turns in concentration, doing nothing else, in order to make this transformation. While in *Tenebrous Form*, you cannot be harmed by physical attacks, although you still take damage from magic, fire and sunlight. You also cannot affect your surroundings physically, as you have no real solid substance. By enveloping a victim, though (with your Mental Traits challenging his Physical Traits as an attack), you can perform the same functions as the *Shroud of Night* power, causing disorientation, darkness and smothering. You are unaffected by gravity, and you can slither along any surface or move like a blob of ambulatory liquid. You can even use mental Disciplines while in this state, though within the limitations of your form — you have no eyes and thus cannot use *Dominate*, but you could hide your shadowy form with *Obfuscate*. In this shadow form, your Blood Traits are the same sort of inky darkness, and thus, they are unaffected by the powers of *Thaumaturgy*.

While in *Tenebrous Form*, fire and sunlight are exceedingly painful to you; thus, you suffer a one-Trait penalty on resolution of *Courage* Tests.

POTENCE

All vampires are capable of preternatural strength by human standards, simply through the use of blood. With *Potence*, though, this strength extends far beyond such measures. The inhuman might of *Potence* is sufficient to allow a vampire to break bones, shatter stone, even heft and destroy heavy or resilient objects. Vampires using *Potence* in battle are fearsome indeed, delivering telling blows that fell even their undead adversaries.

Most uses of *Potence* above the Basic levels are considered a breach of the Masquerade among Camarilla Kindred.

The *Potence* Discipline is most commonly known by the Brujah, Giovanni, Lasombra and Nosferatu clans, all of whom prize physical strength and prowess. As *Potence* is a highly useful capability and requires little effort on the part of the vampire in question, many Cainites seek out tutors in this Discipline.

The *Potence* Discipline, as a physically augmenting Discipline, does not use any Ability for retests other than the Ability commonly associated with whatever task

is at hand. That is, when striking someone while using *Potence*, one should use the normal *Brawl* Ability for retesting.

BASIC POTENCE

Prowess

You have unearthed a level of strength unusual in vampires. Where others would flag and fail, you redouble your efforts. Your mighty blows land with a force that kills even the hardiest mortals.

With *Prowess*, all of your unarmed or clubbing attacks inflict lethal damage instead of bashing damage, if you so desire. Furthermore, once per game session, you may recoup your lost strength, restoring all used Physical Traits of *Brawny*, *Ferocious*, *Stalwart*, *Tough* and *Wiry*. You must restore all of them at once — if you have some Traits of the appropriate type unused when you invoke *Prowess*, you cannot restore them later. Using *Prowess* costs nothing, and it does not count as an action; it may be done at any time.

Might

Your strength daunts even other Cainites. Few would dare to cross you in a test of physical power. You are far more likely than the average vampire to succeed in challenges of strength.

With *Might*, you may make a single retest on any challenge of sheer physical strength. Thus, if you are grappling, picking up a heavy object or breaking something, you can use *Might* as a retest. Once you invoke *Might*, it is the last test of the challenge; no further retests are allowed. *Might* costs nothing to use.

You may use *Might* even if your opponent attempts to evade your strength. Your power is so startling that even an opponent who attempts to outlast you with stamina or to dodge you with quickness can be overcome, as long as you rely solely on your strength. Doing so generally requires you to bid a strength-related Trait, such as the types of Traits restorable with *Prowess*. Obviously, if you cannot exert your *Might*, you cannot make this retest — thus, you cannot use *Might* at range, with a thrown object (requiring speed and accuracy). You could use *Might* while trying to grab at a dodging opponent, but not when picking up and throwing a heavy object.

INTERMEDIATE POTENCE

Vigor

Your vampiric strength is truly monumental. You can heft hundreds of pounds with ease, deliver enough force to crush bones in a single blow and hammer down any opponent of lesser strength.

When you possess *Vigor*, you may use the Bomb in challenges of strength. The Bomb is a closed fist with the thumb sticking up. The Bomb defeats Rock and Paper, ties with other Bombs and loses to Scissors (the fuse is cut). You are not required to use the Bomb, but you must always state before a Physical Challenge that you are capable of doing so. Using *Vigor* costs nothing. Your use of *Vigor* requires you to use only your strength; your opponent may try to defend with stamina or speed, but his doing so does not prevent you from using the Bomb.

Intensity

Your titanic strength never fails you. Unless sorely pressed or wounded, you can continue incredible feats indefinitely.

Whenever you enter a challenge of strength, you may use *Potence* as your bid Trait. This Trait does not count toward totals when resolving ties or overbids, but it can never be lost; thus, you may continually use *Potence* in successive tests of strength. Only if you are forced to risk multiple Traits — such as due to wounds or Negative Traits — do you risk losing any of your other Physical Traits.

If you run out of Physical Traits, you cannot use this Discipline. Once you have been completely exhausted, you can no longer enter challenges.

ADVANCED POTENCE

Puissance

No mortal can match you, and even vampires tremble at your touch. The strength of your dead limbs is truly monumental, crushing anything that stands before you.

With *Puissance*, you win all ties in tests of strength automatically. You need not compare Traits at all, unless some other factor would cause you to lose ties (such as wounds) or give the opponent the ability to win all ties as well (such as *Fleetness*).

Furthermore, your incredible strikes inflict an additional health level of damage in combat. This bonus applies to any attack in which your strength is a factor — unarmed combat or combat with melee weapons. However, use of this incredible strength almost certainly breaks weapons that are not specially designed to stand it.

PRESENCE

To many, vampires seem to exude an air of command, sensuality or intimidation. For a master of *Presence*, emotions are playthings to be manipulated and stimulated. When many Cainites survive through careful manipulation of mortal society, the ability to sway emotions and control passions is a powerful capability indeed. More than simply using intrigue or carefully rehearsed acting to influence others, vampires with *Presence* literally project auras of power or dread.

The *Presence* Discipline is most common among vampires of the Brujah, Follower of Set, Toreador and Ventrue clans. Brujah often use *Presence* to whip mobs into righteous anger, while Followers of Set influence their "customers" subtly. Toreador cultivate an air of artistic beauty, and Ventrue rely on their control of emotions to influence and rule their "subjects."

Unlike *Dominate*, which affects the rational mind directly, *Presence* affects emotions. Thus, it is a more subtle form of control. However, subjects of *Presence* are less predictable than *Dominate* victims. Also, whereas *Dominate* requires that the victim see the user's eyes, *Presence* usually requires only that the user's face be visible — some *Presence* powers do not even require that much exposure.

Retests with *Presence* use the *Leadership* Ability.

BASIC PRESENCE

Awe

The sight of you turns heads. When you let your charisma shine, you draw attention naturally. People try to be close to you, and even those disinclined to listen to you give some consideration to anything you say or do.

When you are involved in a Social Challenge, you may expend one Social Trait to invoke *Awe*, gaining an automatic retest. You may only use this power once per Social Challenge. You may use *Awe* in a mass challenge, but you must expend one Social Trait for each person retested against.

Dread Gaze

By hissing, baring your fangs and allowing your vampiric features to rise to the fore, you can terrify mortals and even shake the resolve of other vampires. Though few would risk the wrath of an angry Cainite, your fearsome visage goes beyond that, driving supernatural terror into the hearts of your victims.

By making a Social Challenge against your foe, you strike terror into your victim. If you succeed, the subject flees your presence and tries to avoid you for the rest of the scene or hour. If cornered, the victim will still defend himself, but he will do his best to escape you. The subject defends himself normally, but he must risk an additional Trait if he wishes to attack or act against you, just as if he were wounded.

Using this Discipline actually requires you (in character) to hiss, bare your fangs and otherwise make your vampiric countenance known, so it is a rather obvious breach of the Masquerade.

Entrancement

When you bring your charm to bear on an individual, you are almost hypnotically magnetic. Individuals affected by your *Presence* find your manner irresistible.

You must make a Social Challenge against a target to exercise *Entrancement*. If you succeed, the target is favorably disposed toward you, and she will not insult or attack you for the rest of the scene (or for an hour). Indeed, a formerly neutral subject wants to aid you and act as your friend; even a previously hostile target is rendered neutral. If you take a hostile action against the subject, of course, the *Entrancement* is broken immediately, and it may not be used against the subject again in the same scene.

Summon

Extending your incredible manipulative powers, you can draw others to your location. Your victim need not see you, or even be seen by you — as long as the subject is known to you, you can *Summon* him to your side. Once called, the subject tries to get to you by whatever means possible, completely unaware of the supernatural nature of the desire and avoiding situations that would prevent fulfilling the compulsion (like locked rooms and overprotective allies). The compulsion lasts until the victim manages to arrive and make his presence known to you.

To *Summon* someone, you must ask for a Narrator's assistance. Inform the Narrator of the person that you wish to *Summon*, as well as your number of Social Traits and whether you are using the *Leadership* Ability. The Narrator then finds the subject, performing a Social Challenge in your stead and using the *Leadership* Ability for a retest if necessary. If the challenge succeeds, the subject comes to you as previously described. If the challenge fails, the subject manages to resist the *Summon*. In either case, you have no knowledge of the outcome, so there is no guarantee of success. Of course, if the subject does not appear, you can wait five minutes and then attempt to *Summon* the victim again.

You can only Summon someone that you know — at bare minimum, someone that you have had the chance to talk with for a few minutes, or someone who has been a target of your *Presence* powers before. If another individual then uses *Summon* on your subject, the victim heads to the summoner of the most powerful generation; if multiple summoners are of the same generation, the victim goes to the first one to exert the power. Should two vampires of equal generation simultaneously *Summon* the same victim, then the Narrator should make a Social Challenge between the two, with the victim heading to the victor.

In the unusual case that *Summon* is used on a false identity (an identity created with *Mask of a Thousand Faces*, for instance), the *Summon* still brings the appropriate individual. If multiple individuals use the same false identity, then the first *Summon* calls whichever is nearest (generally, whichever one a Narrator finds first), and any further *Summons* then call the same individual. Thus, if three Malkavians using *Mask of a Thousand Faces* all pretend to be the same imaginary person, a *Summon* of that person brings whichever of the Malkavians is nearest and then calls that Malkavian for any future uses of *Summon*.

Majesty

The force of your personality makes even the most stalwart tremble. When you exert your *Majesty*, heads bow, hearts break and spines quiver. None would dare to challenge you or risk your ire, for your ambiance is without peer.

By expending a Willpower Trait, you exert your *Majesty* for the duration of a scene or a full hour. You can represent this power's effect by holding your arms out from your sides, or with a special card or ribbon. As long as you have *Majesty*, nobody may insult you or attack you as long as they are within 10 feet of you and able to see you. A subject may attempt to break through your *Majesty* by making a Social Challenge against you, but must spend a Willpower Trait to make the attempt. Failure means that the subject cannot challenge your *Majesty* again in the same scene.

If you attack someone or undertake a hostile action while using your *Majesty*, the aura fades automatically and immediately as your onlookers are startled or outraged. You may still use your Social and Mental Disciplines as long as they do not inflict direct harm — you may still *Entrance* or *Dominate* a subject — but a deliberate attack disrupts your *Majesty*.

When attempting to penetrate *Majesty*, a Willpower Trait may be used for a retest. This is an exception to the normal rule that Willpower is used only to defend against Mental and Social Challenges.

Protean

Survival in the wilds is difficult indeed for vampires, who must find means to avoid sunlight, hunt and evade marauding Lupines. The shapeshifting Gangrel, though, have mastered this craft, and their *Protean* Discipline is thought to be a large factor in their success. With *Protean*, the vampire can alter parts of her body to draw on the strength of natural forces.

Retests for *Protean*, if applicable, should use the *Survival* Ability.

Basic Protean

Eyes of the Beast

With a moment's pause, you can make your eyes able to see in absolute darkness. An eerie red glow emanates from your eyes, and you can see perfectly well in pitch-blackness.

You need only declare your intent to use *Eyes of the Beast*, and at the end of the turn, the change is complete. You suffer no penalties at all for natural darkness while using this Discipline. However, you do suffer the Negative Trait *Bestial* due to your red, glowing eyes, unless you take steps to conceal them (most commonly, with sunglasses). Using this power is also a rather obvious breach of the Masquerade.

Feral Claws

Like a wolf or bear, you have powerful claws capable of rending flesh. You can grow these claws at will with a simple effort; they sprout mystically from your otherwise normal hands, and similarly retract when you desire.

By expending a Blood Trait, you cause *Feral Claws* to extend from your hand (and feet, if you so desire) at the end of the turn. These claws have the bonus Trait *Sharp*, useable in combat or in climbing, and they inflict aggravated damage.

Intermediate Protean

Earth Meld

For a traveler in the wilds, *Earth Meld* is an invaluable power. With this Discipline, you sink into the bosom of the earth, able to sleep mystically undisturbed within the soil.

You must be touching raw soil to *Earth Meld*; you cannot sink through stone, wood, concrete or other substances. You immediately begin sinking eerily into the earth itself, taking with you only your clothing and small personal possessions that you carry (such as a cellular phone or a small pistol). Using the power protects you completely from daylight and allows you to sleep undisturbed. You remain unaware

of what transpires around you, and indeed, you are not fully of the material world at all. While in this state, you cannot move, except to rise at will.

While bonded with the earth, you remain in a semi-tangible state, partially diffused into spirit by your connection to the soil. Thus, you cannot be readily detected either physically or with spirits. If you patch of soil is disrupted in any fashion, you immediately return to physical form and complete wakefulness, shooting up to the surface and showering dirt in all directions. You cannot act during the first turn that you rise from the soil in this fashion, though if you rise up of your own accord (which you may do at any time), you are fully aware and able to act normally.

You must expend a Blood Trait to *Earth Meld*. Sinking into the ground requires a full turn, during which time you can do nothing else (because you are descending slowly into the ground).

Shape of the Beast

Ancient tales of vampires tell that they assume the forms of wolves and bats. Though most vampires consider this nonsense, elder Gangrel sometimes possess the transmutive power to change into animal forms. With *Shape of the Beast*, you can shift your physical body into that of an undead beast, mimicking a normal animal. Most vampires change into wolves or bats, though some possess different forms dependent on their cultural and geographic ties — jackals in Africa, dingoes in Australia or giant rats in major cities have all been reported.

Shifting into animal form costs one Blood Trait and takes three full turns (each additional Blood Trait spent lowers the transformation time by one turn, to a minimum of one turn with three Blood Traits). You remain in beast form until the next dawn, or until you decide to change back. Clothing and small personal possessions change with you.

In animal form, you can use any of your normal Disciplines except *Necromancy*, *Serpentis*, *Thaumaturgy* and *Vicissitude* (the inability to speak may make *Dominate* difficult, of course). Wolf form grants you the bonus Mental Traits *Alert* and *Attentive*, as well as the effects of *Feral Claws* and improved running speed. Bat form grants you flight capability and the benefits of the Merit: *Acute Hearing*, though you possess a maximum of three Physical Traits in that form.

The animal forms granted by this power are in all ways physically identical to normal animals, though of course they are dead, animated corpses as befits a vampire.

ADVANCED PROTEAN

Mist Form

Your control over your physical form is so complete that you can dissolve into a fine cloud of mist. You disperse into a floating cloud, still able to sense your surroundings and able to move about as you desire. This cloud form can slip through tiny cracks and holes, and it cannot be dispersed by the mightiest of natural winds.

Assuming *Mist Form* costs one Blood Trait and takes three full turns (additional Blood Traits reduce this time at a one-for-one cost, with a minimum of one full turn at three Blood Traits). You may change back instantly at any time. You are immune to mundane physical attacks in this form, and you take one less level of damage from fire and sunlight automatically. You are still affected normally by mystical attacks, though of course you have no blood in this form, so much of *Thaumaturgy* is useless against you. Though you cannot affect the world physically, you can still use Disciplines that do not require a physical form (you cannot use *Dominate*, for instance, because you have no eyes, but you could exert *Presence*). While in *Mist Form*, you may move as desired at the pace of a brisk walk, although you can be pushed about by strong winds.

QUIETUS

The deadly assassins of the Assamite clan study the *Quietus* Discipline. By transmuting their blood into poison, they deliver death to their targets in terrible silence and agony. This Discipline has become significantly altered since the report of the broken blood curse, and those Kindred familiar with the clan whisper that such powers have not been seen in centuries.

Though many uses of *Quietus* may involve striking with a blood-covered hand or spitting vitae at one's foes, this transformed blood is more of an alchemical poison than a form of vitae. Thus, blood used with this Discipline cannot later be gathered and used to form blood bonds or as a focus for *Thaumaturgy*.

Most *Quietus* powers are not directly opposed, so they do not use retests. Using *Quietus* with a physical attack, for instance, simply involves the normal uses of *Brawl*, *Melee* and similar Abilities in the attack. If spitting blood at an opponent (a function of several different powers), use *Athletics* for a retest.

BASIC QUIETUS

Silence of Death

The first skill learned by a true assassin is the ability to travel in complete stealth. The mystical *Silence of Death* permits you to extend a field of silence about yourself, blocking all screams, gunshots, explosions and so on.

When you use *Silence of Death*, you muffle all sound within 10 feet of yourself. Although sound from outside can still come into this radius and be heard, no sound emanates from anything or anyone close to you. Using this power costs one Blood Trait to invoke, and the effect lasts for a scene or an hour.

Scorpion's Touch

With the deadly venom and toxins of your studies, you can transmute your blood into a substance that weakens and poisons your victims. You can then coat weapons with this foul ichor, spit it at your foes or simply bring it to the surface of your skin to affect your victim by touch. Unwary foes may actually drink such tainted vitae.

Each Blood Trait that you spend on this power is converted into a dangerous poison. If this tainted vitae touches a victim or is otherwise ingested into her system, she loses one Physical Trait automatically. Thus, you can strike someone with your hand (and a Physical Challenge) and cause the victim to lose an additional Trait due to your venom. You can coat weapons of dagger-size or larger with this poisonous blood, or even kiss your opponent. You can even make a Physical Challenge against anyone within 10 feet to spit this blood at a victim. (Do not actually spit at your foe, of course — simply make your intentions known before making the challenge.)

Mortals who lose all of their Physical Traits in this fashion become deathly ill by the next night, and they do not heal normally. See the effects of severe illness in **Laws of the Hunt**. Otherwise, all lost Physical Traits return at the next game session, as usual.

Any given attack may only use one Trait of blood with this power, though multiple attackers with poisoned weapons could wreak deadly havoc on a single victim. Similarly, you can only spit a single Trait of this tainted vitae or strike unarmed with a single Blood Trait in each action. Altering your blood in this fashion does not require an action on your part — you can strike an opponent with your hand, for instance, and then declare the use of *Scorpion's Touch* with a single Blood Trait. You can concentrate multiple Blood Traits onto a single weapon, though each strike uses only one Trait of blood (and thus reduces only one Physical Trait from the victim). Of course, preparing yourself thus is a legitimate tactic if you think you will be in a protracted fight and you want a weapon sufficient for several strikes.

Intermediate Quietus

Dagon's Call

With a touch, you can infect a victim with a small quantity of your own vitae; later, with a bit of concentration, you cause that very blood to burst forth from the victim, tearing her apart from the inside.

You must touch your target physically before using this power (which may require a Physical Challenge). Thereafter, at any point in the same scene or within the next hour, you can issue *Dagon's Call* — you need not even be able to see the target. You expend at least one Willpower Trait and call for the aid of a Narrator. Each Willpower Trait that you spend at that point then forces the target to make one Static Physical Challenge; the Narrator will take note of your Physical Traits and go to perform the tests against your subject. Each test that the victim fails indicates one level of lethal damage as her very blood tears its way through her vessels and organs. You must declare all Willpower Traits that you expend at once; once you have activated this power, you cannot invoke it again on the same subject until you manage to touch her again.

Baal's Caress

The toxins in your vitae are sufficient to burn through any flesh, living or undead. This poison melts through flesh once it comes in contact with the bloodstream, leaving other materials unharmed. Indeed, even Cainites without blood in their systems can be affected if the poison enters through a wound.

To use *Baal's Caress*, you must spend a turn to transform your vitae into poison and then put that blood on an object or weapon of dagger-size or larger. Each Trait of blood so placed on a bladed or piercing weapon causes that weapon to inflict aggravated damage with one strike. Thus, if you place three Traits of blood on a knife with this power, then the next three successful strikes with the knife inflict aggravated wounds. The weapon in question must penetrate the victim's flesh with a successful blow; blunt weapons or unarmed strikes, for instance, cannot use this vitae with any appreciable effect. Blood cannot be placed on bullets; not enough can be applied for appreciable damage, and most of it will be lost during the flight and initial impact.

Note that you must actually place this blood on something and it must enter the target's system in order to have any effect. You cannot randomly bleed on a subject and inflict damage.

Advanced Quietus

Taste of Death

Your concentrated blood is so powerfully toxic that you can merely spit it at a foe and watch it burn through her skin. The ichor evoked with this power does not affect metal or stone, but melts through flesh and bone, reducing it to smoking sludge.

You can spit a single Blood Trait at a victim with this power (this counts as a single action). If you successfully strike with a Physical Challenge, the victim takes one level of aggravated damage. You must directly spew this blood out; if it misses the victim or is placed on an object, it loses its toxicity within the turn. Note that the blood must be deliberately converted into a poison in this fashion — your own blood can still be drained from your body without poisoning the drinker.

Serpentis

The Followers of Set use *Serpentis*, a power connected with the snakes that are the hallmark of Set's worship. The uncanny capabilities of this Discipline are disturbing indeed, marking the Follower as something far different from human — or even from other vampires. Despite the cold, reptilian features of this Discipline, many of its manifestations are strangely alluring. Followers of Set attribute this facet

to their capacity to sway the emotions of their victims, digging out buried secrets and bringing hidden vices to the surface.

Most *Serpentis* powers involve no challenge to use, or are simply used with combat. Any power used for a direct challenge should use *Subterfuge* for a retest.

BASIC SERPENTIS

The Eyes of the Serpent

The legendary hypnotic gaze of the serpent is yours. When you meet the gaze of a victim (who need only be able to see your eyes), your eyes become gold with large black irises, capturing the attentions of your subject. As long as you hold the gaze of the target, he remains completely immobilized.

You must make a Social Challenge to affect your target with this power. If you succeed, the target is paralyzed as long as you hold his gaze with your own. Of course, if the target is attacked or injured, the hypnotic spell breaks.

The Tongue of the Asp

At will, you can cause your tongue to shift in shape to that of a snake. The supernatural razor-edge on the forked tongue inflicts terrible wounds, striking up to a foot and a half away, and it even lets you drink blood from your victims.

You need only decide to use *The Tongue of the Asp* in order to gain the benefits of this power. Your tongue inflicts one aggravated wound with a successful strike (requiring a Physical Challenge); furthermore, on successive turns you can drain blood from the victim as if drinking directly. This draining even causes the Kiss, paralyzing mortal victims with helpless fright and ecstasy.

The Tongue of the Asp is highly sensitive to vibrations. Using this Discipline while in darkness allows you to reduce the penalty Traits for natural darkness by one.

INTERMEDIATE SERPENTIS

The Skin of the Adder

The power of your reptilian blood allows you to erupt into a serpentine form of protective scales and snakelike flexibility. You can thus transform into a monstrous hybrid of humanoid and snake, an effective engine of war or a terrible slithering beast of intimidation.

You need only spend a Blood Trait and a Willpower Trait to invoke this power. At the end of the turn, *The Skin of the Adder* overtakes you, covering you in a mottled scaly hide and lending a whiplike flexibility to your limbs. You gain the bonus Traits *Lithe* and *Tough*. Your mouth also distends like a snake's, so that your bite causes an additional wound if you win (not tie) a Simple Test after biting (though you can still feed without causing any extra damage, if desired). Your cartilaginous body can also fit through any opening wide enough to accommodate your head. Due to the hideous nature of your snake-form, you gain the Negative Social Traits *Bestial* and *Repugnant* while in this form. Obviously, being in this form rips the Masquerade wide open if you're spotted by mortals.

The Skin of the Adder remains in effect until you decide to transform back, or until the next sunrise.

The Form of the Cobra

No longer limited to steps between man and snake, you can literally turn into a giant cobra. This reptile form grants a venomous bite and the ability to slip through small passages, while still allowing you to use any Disciplines that do not require hands or speech. In this form, you retain your normal weight, so you are a tremendous, black-and-gold nightmare serpent.

You must expend one Blood Trait to transform into *The Form of the Cobra*. The change takes a full three turns, and the rate cannot be accelerated. Clothing and

small personal effects change with you. You remain in serpent form until the next sunrise, unless you decide to change back earlier. Additionally, the venom of your bite is poisonous to mortals.

ADVANCED SERPENTIS

The Heart of Darkness

Egyptian legend tells that the hearts of the dead are weighed against a feather in the afterlife; those found wanting are devoured, while those found worthy move on to eternal paradise. As you have already cheated death with your immortality, you can now cheat this judgment as well. On the new moon, you can pull your very heart from your unliving body; with several hours of surgery (out of play), you can even do the same to another vampire.

No test is necessary to remove the heart, but the subject must be willing. While most vampiric flesh rots and decays in a single turn after being separated from the body, the withered heart coaxed forth with this power remains intact. Anyone whose heart is removed in this fashion is therefore immune to staking. Most often, the Setite carefully places the heart in a guarded clay urn, perhaps surrounded by other false hearts to avoid discovery.

As the heart is considered the seat of emotion, you gain a bonus Trait in Virtue Tests to resist frenzy. However, you also lose any *Empathy* Abilities, plus any Social Traits relating to warm interactions with people, such *Friendly*, *Empathetic* or *Genial*.

If a separated heart is staked, then its vampiric owner (the vampire that the heart originally came from) is immediately paralyzed. Should the heart be exposed to fire or sunlight (even a single health level's worth), it is destroyed and its owner erupts into flame, reduced to ash (and Final Death) in a single turn.

Use of *The Heart of Darkness* can also return a stolen heart to its former body. Obviously, trying to use this power on a mortal, even a ghoul, is messily fatal.

THANATOSIS

The corpselike bodies of vampires are innately tied to death. No Discipline reflects this process of arrested decay so clearly as *Thanatosis*. The Samedi bloodline practices this nightmare Discipline, using its powers to control the very steps of death and decay. Indeed, fearful Cainites whisper that *Thanatosis* grants some control over the Curse itself, temporarily suspending the immortality of vampires and even reducing them to rotting masses.

The Stiffs do not share their secrets of death, though mercenary Samedi are more than willing to visit the discomfort of *Thanatosis* briefly on too-curious subjects. This Discipline seems to be a natural outgrowth of the Samedi fascination with death and decay. Strangely, other Cainites who unearth this Discipline do not suffer from the rotting affliction of the Stiffs, leading to some speculation that the bloodline suffers its peculiar curse for other, more sinister, reasons.

Retests of *Thanatosis* involve the *Occult* Ability. Optionally, Storytellers may choose to use the more specialized *Thanatology* Ability for *Thanatosis* retests.

BASIC THANATOSIS

Hags' Wrinkles

You can contract or expand your skin, sending it into baggy, rippling waves or pulling it taut over your undead flesh. *Hags' Wrinkles* obviously can mask your appearance, but you can also use little pockets of flesh to conceal small objects about your person, although such bulges or depressions may be visible if your skin is not already marred (say, by the signature deformities of the Nosferatu and Samedi) or found during a pat-down search.

Reshaping your flesh with *Hags' Wrinkles* takes a full turn of effort and the expenditure of a Blood Trait. For the rest of the scene or for the next full hour, your features are unrecognizable and you can conceal up to two objects of jacket or smaller concealment class within the folds of your withered flesh.

Putrefaction

The Samedi are feared for their control over decay, and *Putrefaction* is the first manifestation of such power. Supernatural decomposition afflicts any flesh that you touch, if you so will it. Pustulent, festering decay spreads from your point of contact, even rotting the preserved flesh of vampires.

Putrefaction requires you to best your victim in a Physical Challenge while expending a Blood Trait. Should you succeed, the victim suffers one health level of lethal damage and gains the Negative Trait *Repugnant* until the damage is healed. This sort of wound is accompanied by rotting flesh, decaying teeth and bones, festering sores and fungus-ridden patches. You can strike a victim multiple times with this power, spreading the rot. You can even affect vampires and plants in addition to other living creatures, withering and decaying them.

INTERMEDIATE THANATOSIS

Ashes to Ashes

Tearing apart the bonds that hold your physical form together, you collapse suddenly into a desiccated heap of ash. The power of *Ashes to Ashes* allows you to retain your consciousness, though, keeping you in a pile of fine detritus that can reform later into your original vampiric body.

You must expend two Blood Traits while concentrating for a full turn to use *Ashes to Ashes*. When you take your action, you transform into a pile of thick, sticky ash. You can vaguely sense your surroundings (about 10 feet in all directions) at this time, and you are completely immune to physical attacks, fire and sunlight. If the ashes are separated, though (a tedious and disgusting task, requiring deliberate effort), you reform missing some parts of your body — the largest remaining pile reforms as yourself, but you take lethal health levels of damage depending on how much of your substance was removed. Should you reform while contained in some object, you burst forth, shattering the object as you resume your usual size.

Withering

By gripping an enemy and channeling your own dead energy into his limbs, you can cause him to twist into an aged, withered and decrepit form. Terrifying pain results as limbs shrink and snap from *Withering*.

You need only touch or strike a victim with a Physical Challenge and expend a Willpower Trait to use *Withering*. The subject immediately suffers the Negative Traits *Clumsy* and *Lame*, as the shrunken limb is rendered completely useless, and he suffers one health level of bashing damage (in addition to any damage from the blow). Vampires and other supernatural creatures heal the effects of *Withering* at the end of the night, but mortals and living animals are afflicted permanently.

By making two successful Simple Tests (win only) after striking with *Withering*, you can strike the head instead of a limb. Doing so kills mortals instantly and causes vampires to suffer the Negative Traits *Oblivious* and *Witless* in addition to rendering them unable to use the powers from *Celerity*, *Fortitude* and *Potence*.

Withering is not cumulative on the same limb, but successive strikes can certainly afflict other limbs. Victims with multiple limbs affected suffer all of the Negative Traits appropriately. With no functional arms, a victim cannot attack physically; with no legs, the subject cannot move.

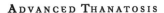

ADVANCED THANATOSIS

Necrosis

The hideous decomposition induced with *Necrosis* disgusts and revolts even the hardiest constitution. Accelerating the forces of decay, you cause the target's skin to rot away and slough off, exposing internal organs in a terrifying panoply of pain.

Necrosis requires you to touch the victim and expend two Blood Traits. The subject immediately suffers a level of lethal damage as his skin rots and sloughs off in pieces. Furthermore, the victim takes the Negative Traits *Decrepit* and *Repugnant* as a result of the attack; these Negative Traits remain until the damage heals. Multiple strikes can inflict additional damage and Negative Traits in a cumulative fashion, rendering the victim a pool of putrescent liquid.

THAUMATURGY

Vampires are creatures of magic, and tales in the *Book of Nod* tell of rituals and powers unknown to the common spate of Disciplines. For the most part, such strange capabilities — controlling the weather, altering one's own blood, casting mystical lights and so on — remained the province of apocryphal tales. A rare few vampires learned to harness the power of their blood to perform magic, but most used only the gifts granted by the Curse.

In the Dark Ages, though, the Tremere clan rose to prominence through the use of *Thaumaturgy*. By combining their mortal wizardly knowledge with their new-found powers of blood, the Tremere discovered ways to control the manipulation of vitae, forcing it to perform specialized powers. Furthermore, with careful rituals, they were able to create wide-ranging effects, much like the powerful spells attributed to legendary sorcerers.

The Discipline of *Thaumaturgy* is the study of vampiric magic, the ability to shape the forces of vitae into directed mystical energy. Pioneered primarily by the Tremere, the Discipline is actually composed of several "paths." Each path represents a particular area of magical study: blood manipulation, fire control, warding or other, stranger effects.

When learning *Thaumaturgy*, you must specify one path as your primary path of study. Whenever you improve your *Thaumaturgy*, you improve your capabilities with that path. However, you can learn additional paths just like other Disciplines. You can never be as skilled in your additional paths as you are in your primary area of study, though, until you master *Thaumaturgy*. Thus, you cannot study additional paths until you have learned Intermediate *Thaumaturgy* in your primary path, and your secondary paths cannot exceed the Basic levels until you attain Advanced *Thaumaturgy* in the studies of your primary path. Once you learn Advanced *Thaumaturgy*, you may improve any of your other paths to the Advanced level as well through the use of Experience.

Thaumaturgy is the province of the Tremere clan, and they guard their wizardly secrets jealously. Indeed, learning even the rudiments of *Thaumaturgy* can take a year or more for vampires unskilled in the Tremere's arcane ways. The Tremere do not teach this Discipline to those outside their clan; vampires who wish to study *Thaumaturgy* must find a traitor to the Tremere or else engage in decades of intensive research with the rarest of occult materials and books. However, a few vampires outside the Tremere clan do study *Thaumaturgy*. Most notably, some Assamite viziers have learned to cast *Thaumaturgy* as a result of their studies of the Tremere curse and its underlying magic; however, as this magic is not native to them, their forms of *Thaumaturgy* always cost an extra Blood Trait. Within the Sabbat, some rare Tzimisce calling themselves *koldun* study the ways of *Thaumaturgy* that were brought by former Tremere defectors. Rumors hold that true *koldun* actually study a completely different form of sorcery, far older than Tremere *Thaumaturgy*, but none would ever wish to meet a Tzimisce old and twisted enough to know the truth of such matters.

In game terms, vampiric magic is usually referred to as *Thaumaturgy*, though not all *Thaumaturgy* is the same. A form of corrupting magic is supposedly practiced by the Followers of Set, for instance, yet it is totally different from and incompatible with the practices of Tremere magic. Of course, this fact does not stop the Tremere from using their knowledge to develop duplicates of such powers. This flexibility to devise paths (duplicating or opposing nearly any Discipline) is, perhaps, the greatest strength of *Thaumaturgy*.

The majority of Tremere neonates start learning the *Path of Blood* as their primary *Thaumaturgy* path, but a few start with other areas. Still, the sheer usefulness of the *Path of Blood* makes it more valuable than other specialized abilities.

Any use of *Thaumaturgy* requires the expenditure of a Blood Trait. Some specific powers may require additional expenditures as well. *Thaumaturgy* does rely on speaking magical phrases and gestures, and as such its use is generally noticeable. Unless otherwise noted, casting *Thaumaturgy* takes a full turn, and the magic takes effect at the time of your action. You cannot accelerate *Thaumaturgy* with speed-enhancing powers such as *Celerity*.

THE PATH OF BLOOD (REGO VITAE)

Almost every Tremere studies the *Path of Blood* as a primary form of magic. Espousing the clan's strengths in subterfuge, detection, manipulation and control, this path allows you to alter the properties of blood within your own system or to detect features of the blood of others.

The *Path of Blood* uses the *Occult* Ability for retests.

BASIC PATH OF BLOOD

A Taste for Blood

With but a small sample of vitae, you can determine a foe's capabilities and weaknesses. You need only taste a bit of blood in order to recognize many salient characteristics.

A *Taste for Blood* allows you determine a few traits of another individual, simply by tasting a single Blood Trait. From one Blood Trait, you can learn: How much vitae is currently in the subject's system (Blood Traits, whether mortal or vampire); how recently he has fed, if a vampire; generation, if a vampire and whether the Cainite in question is a diablerist (within the usual limits of detection time).

Using A *Taste for Blood* requires you to actually ingest the vitae that you test, so it can be dangerous if the blood is tainted or if you have already sampled some of the subject's blood.

Blood Rage

With but a touch you can stir up another Cainite's blood. Thus, you force the subject to expend blood in any fashion that you mentally decide when you touch the victim.

Blood Rage requires a light contact, which may necessitate a Physical Challenge against a wary subject. If you manage to get a firm grip, you can immediately force the subject to spend a single Blood Trait in any fashion that you desire, even beyond the usual limits of blood expenditure for the vampire. Thus, you can force a Cainite to increase his physical strength (gaining Physical Traits with Blood Traits), heal wounds (possibly even recovering from torpor) or even to sweat blood from his pores.

INTERMEDIATE PATH OF BLOOD

Blood of Potency

You can mystically concentrate the vitae within your system, making it more potent for a short time. Doing so affords you many of the benefits of a generation

superior to your natural one. You need only murmur for a moment, and your blood distills down to a more concentrated form.

Your *Blood of Potency* lasts for the duration of the scene or for the next hour, whichever ends first. You can expend Mental Traits to gain a "virtual generation," improving your maximum number of Blood Traits and making your *Dominate* Discipline able to affect more powerful Cainites. Each generation that you artificially lower costs two Mental Traits, to a maximum of six Traits for three generations.

Once you have used *Blood of Potency* in a night, you may not invoke it again until the next night. As soon as the power wears off, any Blood Traits that you possess in excess of your normal limits dilute immediately, leaving you at your normal Blood Trait limit.

If you are diablerized during this time, or if you Embrace childer, your real generation is used, not your virtual generation. Thus, even if you are virtually 10th generation while normally 12th, your childer are still 13th generation, and other vampires gain no benefit from diablerie if they are 12th generation or lower.

Theft of Vitae

Focusing on the call of blood, you can draw forth the vitae in a victim's system. You need only see your target and concentrate. The blood bursts from the victim's pores in a rushing flow, soaring through the air to be mystically absorbed into your own flesh.

You must be able to see a subject within 50 feet in order to use *Theft of Vitae*. As long as no intervening barriers stop the transfer of blood, the fluid rushes out of the victim (doing no damage to Cainites, but probably startling them) and sinks into your body. Essentially, you are able to ingest blood from a victim while at range. Using *Theft of Vitae* requires you to expend a number of Mental Traits equal to the amount of blood that you try to steal, up to a maximum of three Traits. You must make a challenge of your Mental Traits against the subject's Physical Traits after this expenditure, with success indicating that you tear forth a number of Blood Traits equal to the Mental Traits expended previously (subject to the limit of the victim's actual amount of blood). Blood stolen in this fashion has all of its normal properties — drinking three times from one vampire creates a blood bond, poisoned blood still sickens you, and so on.

Needless to say, this rather unsettling power is considered a breach of the Masquerade when used in public.

Advanced Path of Blood

Cauldron of Blood

The blood within any creature is vulnerable to your manipulations. Instead of controlling or stealing blood from a victim, you can bring it to a rolling boil with but a touch. Red mist rises from the victim's body as bubbling blood seeps from his pores and orifices. Few Cainites can withstand this internal furnace, and mortals are almost inevitably killed by such an attack.

Using *Cauldron of Blood* as an action, you must make a Physical Challenge to grasp your target. Then, for each Mental Trait that you expend, up to three, you can boil one Blood Trait in the victim's system (subject to the limit of the victim's actual blood, of course). Each Blood Trait boiled in this fashion inflicts one aggravated level of damage on the target.

The Lure of Flames (Creo Ignem)

Perhaps one of the most feared forms of vampire magic, *The Lure of Flames* allows you to summon forth magical fire. The burning power of your blood is shaped into dancing flame that answers your command. Although such fires are small at first, masters of this path can conjure forth veritable hellstorms of unnatural flame.

Retests for *The Lure of Flames* use the *Occult* Ability.

BASIC LURE OF FLAMES

Hand of Flame

A dancing puff of fire surrounds your hand (or both hands) at your command. This palm of flame creates light and allows you to strike with your hand to burn your opponents. Once cast, the *Hand of Flame* remains until you decide to snuff it out. You can even use it in conjunction with other powers like *Celerity* and *Potence*, becoming a formidable combatant.

The *Hand of Flame* causes aggravated damage, if you strike with your flame-wreathed hand(s). You suffer no damage or inconvenience from the *Hand of Flame*; indeed, you may even wear gloves or other clothing, which remain unaffected by the fires. Should you cause something else to catch fire, that fire can later burn you. Invoking the *Hand of Flame* takes one action.

Flame Bolt

By pointing at a target and intoning words of power, you may launch a *Flame Bolt*. This dart of fire streaks through the air to wound whomever it strikes with a searing blast, and it causes readily flammable objects to catch fire.

Casting a *Flame Bolt* requires you to challenge your Mental Traits against a target's Physical Traits in order to hit. A *Flame Bolt* inflicts one level of aggravated fire damage when it strikes, then snuffs out in a puff of mystic fire. Should the *Flame Bolt* strike a readily flammable target (like a pile of hay or papers, but not clothing worn by someone), the target catches fire. You are not immune to your own *Flame Bolt*, if by some chance it should be directed back at you. Firing a *Flame Bolt* is a single action.

INTERMEDIATE LURE OF FLAMES

Wall of Fire

A column of flame erupts from the very air, burning with unnatural vigor at your command. You need only point to the desired location and utter the syllables of this magic in order to generate a veritable *Wall of Fire*. You can create this flaming barrier at any site that you can see, up to 50 feet away from yourself.

Casting a *Wall of Fire* takes a single action. A *Wall of Fire* occupies a space approximately six feet in diameter, and of equal height. If you cast the wall at a person's location, you use your Mental Traits in a challenge against the victim's Physical Traits. If you win, the fire shoots up underneath the subject, inflicting a level of aggravated damage. The wall remains until you decide to extinguish it, move more than 50 feet away or are knocked unconscious, fall into torpor, or die. Individuals moving through the *Wall of Fire* suffer a level of aggravated damage automatically each turn that they are within or passing through its confines.

If you cast a *Wall of Fire* at a flammable object or surface, the target may well ignite, spreading the fire. You have no special immunity to your own fires created with this magic.

Engulf

By staring intently at a subject and speaking the words of fire creation, you cause the victim to burst into flames, combusting rapidly. This fire burns the subject with horrible power, remaining until the subject manages to extinguish the flame.

Casting *Engulf* takes a single action. You must make a challenge of your Mental Traits against the target's Physical Traits in order to successfully *Engulf* a foe. If you succeed, the target bursts into flames, suffering two levels of aggravated damage from the fire. Furthermore, until the target takes a full action to smother the flame, he continues to suffer an additional level of aggravated damage at the end of every successive turn. The victim does, of course, score aggravated wounds

on others and light flammable objects he touches, but this incidental effect is obviously a secondary consideration.

You may *Engulf* a target multiple times in successive turns, causing cumulative damage as the victim combusts explosively. However, a victim blasted multiple times still only takes one level of damage per following turn due to the continuing fire.

ADVANCED LURE OF FLAMES

Firestorm

When you call to the flames, they come in a searing wash that fills an entire room. A *Firestorm* rains a hail of flame down across a huge area, burning everything within. Any place that you can see, within 50 feet, can be the target of a *Firestorm*.

When you call down the *Firestorm*, an area up to 20 feet in diameter is shot through with roaring sheets of flame. You make a mass challenge against anyone within, pitting your Mental Traits against their Physical Traits. Anyone who loses is struck with the fire, immediately taking a level of aggravated damage. Victims who cannot reasonably escape the area (because they are trapped in a dead end, perhaps, or because they cannot move fast enough to get out of the way) are burned automatically without recourse to a challenge, at the Narrator's option. All flammable materials in the area ignite immediately, though people or vampires fleeing the space do not necessarily remain lit.

A *Firestorm* lasts until you stop it, or until you move out of range. It also ends immediately if you are knocked unconscious, sent into torpor or killed. Anyone who remains in the area of the *Firestorm* suffers one level of aggravated damage at the end of every turn after its creation.

MOVEMENT OF THE MIND (REGO MOTUS)

Through *Movement of the Mind*, you can manipulate remote objects or even creatures. Though this path does not actually impart any sort of physical force, it allows you to control things as if you held them without actually touching them. You need only see the target in order to affect it.

Manipulation with *Movement of the Mind* does not provoke a tactile response. That is, you cannot remotely "feel" an object to tell if it is hot, rough, slippery etc. You simply impart motion into the item in question.

Retests of *Movement of the Mind* use the *Occult* Ability.

BASIC MOVEMENT OF THE MIND

Force Bolt

Your concentrated will projects a bolt of force capable of stunning opponents and knocking over objects. A *Force Bolt* is really more of a sudden jar of motion to a target than an actual blow, but the effects are similar.

When you attack someone with a *Force Bolt*, you use your Mental Traits in a challenge against the victim's Physical Traits. If you win, the subject is knocked to the ground, losing his next action (not full turn — victims with *Celerity* may well recover in the same turn).

A *Force Bolt* can be used to lash out at an object no more than a hundred pounds in weight. If the object is not held by anyone, you can push it about five feet in any direction. An object held by someone can only be struck aside if you defeat the holder in a Mental versus Physical Challenge, as described previously. Obviously, though, this power is ideal for disarming foes at a distance, or for knocking aside valuable possessions.

Manipulate

Your control of forces allows you to exert fine manipulation over something at range. When you *Manipulate* an object, you can toy with it in any fashion that you could with one hand. Thus, you can remotely pick something up, push a button or fire a gun.

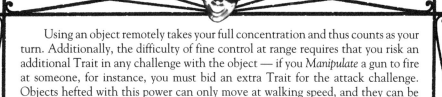

Using an object remotely takes your full concentration and thus counts as your turn. Additionally, the difficulty of fine control at range requires that you risk an additional Trait in any challenge with the object — if you *Manipulate* a gun to fire at someone, for instance, you must bid an extra Trait for the attack challenge. Objects hefted with this power can only move at walking speed, and they can be nothing larger than you could lift with one hand.

Anything you *Manipulate* remains under your control as long as you can see it, unless you release it from your spell deliberately. You must maintain complete concentration to *Manipulate* an object; when you stop concentrating or take a different action, the spell ceases.

INTERMEDIATE MOVEMENT of THE MIND

Flight

You can telekinetically hoist a whole person, pulling the individual off the ground. You can also shove large objects around roughly, although you cannot control them easily. This level of power can slam doors, heft desks and snare opponents. *Flight* even lets you lift yourself off the ground and move at a brisk pace through the air.

When you invoke *Flight* on a particular subject, you can move it around at a brisk walking speed. You can move anything up to 200 pounds in weight, but you do not have fine control over the object, and the object cannot be used to bludgeon or cut (since it moves too slowly and erratically). If you grab a person with this power, using a challenge of your Mental Traits against the victim's Physical Traits, you can hoist the victim into the air, or even move him about slowly, though this power does not inflict actual damage.

Most spectacularly, *Flight* lets you move yourself smoothly at walking speed in any direction. You can soar as high as you dare go or simply hover off the ground.

Flight lasts only as long as you concentrate on the effect to the exclusion of all other activities. If you use this power on any subject besides yourself, you must be able to see the target in order to control it with *Flight*.

Repulse

A wave of motion overtakes everything around you with a simple gesture and a few spoken words. You can push away threatening opponents or shove objects with incredible power.

You can *Repulse* anything within your line of sight. Objects flung with *Repulse* move up to 20 feet away from you, and you can push multiple objects simultaneously. If you *Repulse* people, you make a challenge of your Mental Traits against each of their Physical Traits, as described in mass combat. Anyone who loses to you is flung 20 feet away. Even people who are grappling or biting you can be pushed away in this fashion. If you *Repulse* an object so that it strikes a victim, you use your Mental Traits to strike with it while the opponent dodges with Physical Traits. Objects hitting in this fashion do one health level of lethal damage.

Repulse is an instant effect; you cannot *Repulse* an object to strike someone and then continue shoving it around in successive turns. You must *Repulse* objects or people every turn that you wish to move them.

ADVANCED MOVEMENT of THE MIND

Control

Gripping a target with mental force, you bend its motions to your will. As you direct its movements with your commanding magical phrases and gestures, it spins, flies and moves according to your direction.

When you *Control* an object, you can heft anything up to a ton in weight and manipulate it with precision equal to both of your hands. You can therefore hoist an automobile or tie shoelaces. These devices can be used to attack, doing one health level of lethal damage if they strike (as described under *Repulse*). You can even control a weapon remotely, scoring its normal damage, though this sort of fine manipulation requires you to bid an extra Trait in all challenges with it (as described under *Manipulate*).

People grabbed with *Control* can be rendered paralyzed, or they can be flung about at your will. Slamming a victim into a wall or other hard surface causes one level of lethal damage. You must make a Mental Challenge against the target's Physical Traits when you first exercise *Control*, and in any successive turn where you attempt to move the victim. Thus, you must win a test to grab the victim, and if you do anything other than immobilize him, you must make additional tests. Note that *Control* only affects the victim's physical motions; the subject can still talk, shout for help, use Disciplines and so on.

Exercising *Control* over one object or creature requires all of your concentration. Once you stop concentrating, the power dissipates. *Control* is also lost if you lose sight of the subject.

THE PATH OF CONJURING (CREO MATERIA)

Creating objects from nothingness is a simple power with *The Path of Conjuring*. Just a few words and a mental image of the desired item allow for the sudden appearance of nearly any object. Any conjured object or creature is literally produced from nowhere.

Objects created with *The Path of Conjuring* are generic, with no distinguishing marks, and are always exactly the same every time they are conjured. You cannot conjure anything larger or heavier than yourself. Also, you must have a working familiarity with the object in question. Making this power its most effective may require you to possess certain Abilities. You would need a few levels of *Firearms* and *Crafts: Gunsmith* to make an Uzi, for instance, or *Science* and *Medicine* to conjure artificial pharmaceuticals. All such objects are conjured from Platonic ideals, not as sums of parts. Therefore, if the object is broken up into components, melted, altered or otherwise violated, the spell is broken and the substance dissolves into a viscous sludge that fades into nothingness.

Using *The Path of Conjuring* requires a full turn to create any one effect. Retests with *The Path of Conjuring*, when necessary, use the *Occult* Ability.

BASIC PATH OF CONJURING

Summon the Simple Form

Your rudimentary conjuring skills allow you to create basic objects made of a single homogenous material. These items are little more than chunks of matter, possibly crudely fashioned and lacking in any complex or moving parts. You can thus conjure a rod of metal, a club, a wooden stake, a rock or a lump of coal.

When you *Summon the Simple Form*, you can only make an item of inanimate matter of one sort. You cannot conjure living or undead creatures, nor can you make something built from multiple substances.

After you have conjured an item with this power, you must spend a Mental Trait at the beginning of every new turn in which you wish to keep it in existence. If you do not, the object vanishes instantly. You should record your current Mental Traits at the time that you create an object with this power, in case it is dispelled later with *Reverse Conjuration*.

Permanency

Simple objects that you conjure can now be invested with your power, making them real and permanent. You need not make an item permanent, but if you choose to do so, it remains without any further concentration or effort on your part.

Exercising *Permanency* on an item conjured with *Summon the Simple Form* requires that you spend three Blood Traits in the process of conjuring, instead of the usual one. The object is then considered whole and real, and it does not disappear unless banished with *Reverse Conjuring*.

INTERMEDIATE PATH OF CONJURING

Magic of the Smith

Complicated objects, mixed materials and moving parts are now within your purview. As long as you are familiar with an object's workings, you can make a copy of it. The *Magic of the Smith* can make knives, guns, clothes, medicines and other such useful items, and they all have permanent and lasting substance.

Creating an object with *Magic of the Smith* costs five Blood Traits instead of the usual one. Record your current Mental Traits on the item card at the time of creation, in case the object is later challenged with *Reverse Conjuration*.

Reverse Conjuration

You can send conjured objects back to the nether planes from which they come. Any item that you can see or feel can be subjected to this power with only a few words and simple gestures.

To use *Reverse Conjuration* on an item, you must make a Mental Challenge against the Traits recorded at the item's creation. This power works only on conjured objects, but you have no special way of telling a conjured item from a "real" one. You may banish any of your own creations without a challenge (although it still takes a full turn).

ADVANCED PATH OF CONJURING

Power Over Life

Though you cannot make true life, you can conjure creations that bear a semblance of life. *Power Over Life* lets you make any creature up to your own size. Such creatures have no independent will, though. They obey your commands mindlessly instead.

You must expend a phenomenal 10 Blood Traits to conjure a living creature. These simulacra last only for a week, after which time they dissolve back into nothingness. A creature that is killed similarly vanishes, as do any parts that are removed from the being (including blood).

HANDS OF DESTRUCTION (PERDO MATERIA)

The magicians of the Sabbat use magics designed to slay their foes brutally. The painful powers of the *Hands of Destruction* are one such straightforward path. Rumored to be the work of infernalists and demonic tutors, this path delivers agony and decrepitude on its victims.

Some few Camarilla vampires have unearthed this path, but it remains a rare curiosity among most thaumaturges. With the destruction of the Sabbat's Warlocks, the *Hands of Destruction* path is relegated to the few zealous warriors who manage to wrest its secrets from tomes or infernal pacts. A number of regents have barred practitioners of this path from their chantries on suspicion of infernalism, and many Tremere refuse to practice it because of its potentially demonic origins.

Exerting *Hands of Destruction* requires a single turn of casting. In some cases, it is used as a physical attack, and the spell and the attack are considered to take one turn, executed on the caster's normal action.

BASIC HANDS OF DESTRUCTION

Decay

Inanimate matter crumbles rapidly under your touch. Even dead organic material quickly melts into a puddle of putrescence.

No test is necessary to use this power. For each turn that you maintain contact with an object, it ages a full year. Using this power reduces wood or organic matter to a rotted morass quickly, and it can weaken even metal or plastic with sufficient time. If you break contact with the object, the accelerated aging ceases. Any decrepitude that you inflict on something is permanent, though.

Although you can age the flesh of a vampire with this power, such a tactic has no functional effect. Vampires do not suffer any changes or decrepitude from this aging, as their supernaturally preserved corpses are immune to such treatment.

Gnarl Wood

Your merest glance can swell or contract wood, or twist it into strange shapes. You need not touch the wood to affect it, only see it.

You can warp up to 50 pounds of wood, rendering it gnarled and useless. This is an excellent way to burst doors, destroy furnishings and twists stakes into uselessness. If you try to gnarl an object held by someone, you must best the individual in a Mental Challenge to warp the wood. You can *Gnarl Wood* against multiple objects at once, as long as you can see them all and they do not total more than 50 pounds in weight.

INTERMEDIATE HANDS OF DESTRUCTION

Acidic Touch

Mystically altering your vitae, you cause it to become a thick, black, bilious substance, a caustic fluid that burns flesh, cloth, metal and wood alike. Your *Acidic Touch* has no effect on yourself, but it can leave horrible corroded marks on anything that makes the slightest contact with your coated hands.

The vitriol created with *Acidic Touch* inflicts aggravated damage, and it can eat through most substances (Storyteller's discretion as to time). You can exude this acid from any part of your body, thus potentially making simple contact or even a kiss painfully deadly. Each application of *Acidic Touch* does only one health level of damage, so you may need to use this power repeatedly over several turns to burn through a particularly recalcitrant substance (or subject). No test is necessary to use *Acidic Touch*, though, of course, if you try to strike someone with the acids, you must make the normal Physical Challenge to hit. The acid created with this power is thick and slimy, so it cannot be flung or spat at opponents; you must deliver it by touch.

Atrophy

The warping effects of your powers allow you to wither the very limbs of your opponents. A simple touch is all that is required to *Atrophy* a single limb, turning it into a useless, fragile husk.

You need to strike your target physically (with a Physical Challenge) in order to *Atrophy* a limb. If you hit, you wither one arm or leg, rendering it useless. Doing so gives the victim the Negative Traits *Clumsy* and *Lame*. Multiple attacks can wither different limbs, cumulatively crippling the victim (and adding additional Negative Traits). A victim without arms cannot grapple or wield weapons; a victim without functional legs cannot move. This effect is permanent on mortals, though vampires can heal a crippled limb as if it were a single aggravated wound.

ADVANCED HANDS OF DESTRUCTION

Turn to Dust

Amplifying the process of decay to incredible speeds, you can reduce your victim to little more than a pile of dust. Mortals almost always die instantly and collapse to putrefied remains, while even vampires are withered.

If you manage to get a firm grip on your victim with a Physical Challenge, you can cause him to turn to dust. Each Physical Trait that you expend afterward causes

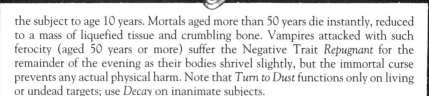

the subject to age 10 years. Mortals aged more than 50 years die instantly, reduced to a mass of liquefied tissue and crumbling bone. Vampires attacked with such ferocity (aged 50 years or more) suffer the Negative Trait *Repugnant* for the remainder of the evening as their bodies shrivel slightly, but the immortal curse prevents any actual physical harm. Note that *Turn to Dust* functions only on living or undead targets; use *Decay* on inanimate subjects.

THAUMATURGICAL RITUALS

Through arcane incantations and properly prepared formulae, the effects of *Thaumaturgy* can be extended beyond the brief and limited powers of the various paths. Rituals are used to perform such complex tasks.

Rituals rank in difficulty as Basic, Intermediate or Advanced, just like the levels of *Thaumaturgy*. A character learns one Basic ritual automatically after learning *Thaumaturgy*. As the vampire's primary path improves, additional rituals are learned, one appropriate to each level gained. Thus, with Advanced *Thaumaturgy*, the vampire knows at least two Basic rituals, two Intermediate rituals and one Advanced ritual. Learning additional rituals takes time, effort and access to specialized equipment and Influence. A vampire can only learn rituals whose difficulty do not exceed her primary *Thaumaturgy* path level.

Actually casting a ritual requires the elements and time listed in each individual description, and a Static Mental Challenge on the part of the caster — difficulty of five Traits for Basic power, seven Traits for Intermediate rituals and nine Traits for Advanced magics. Unless otherwise stated, Basic rituals take 10 minutes to cast, Intermediate rituals require 20 minutes and Advanced rituals take 30 minutes.

BASIC THAUMATURGICAL RITUALS

Communicate with Kindred Sire

Tremere vampires often use *Communicate with Kindred Sire* to seek advice or aid. You need only meditate for half an hour on an object that once belonged to your sire. When you finish the ritual, you establish telepathic communication with your sire, anywhere in the world. This link lasts for 10 minutes.

Defense of the Sacred Haven

Defense of the Sacred Haven blocks the entry of sunlight in a single room. You need only use one Blood Trait as you take an hour to inscribe sigils across all of the doors and windows of the room. As long as you remain in the room, sunlight is prevented mystically from entering the area.

Deflection of Wooden Doom

The wooden stake is the bane of all vampires, but *Deflection of Wooden Doom* protects against such attacks. You must sit in a circle of wood for a full hour to cast this ritual. When completed, you place a tiny splinter of wood under your tongue. As long as the splinter remains there, or until the next dusk or dawn, you are protected. The first stake to impale your heart mystically crumbles to dust, at which point the ritual ends. The stake must actually enter your body for this ritual to work — a stake simply held near you is unaffected.

Devil's Touch

You can brand a mortal mystically with the *Devil's Touch*. You need only place a penny on the mortal as you complete this ritual, and until the next dawn, the subject suffers the Negative Social Traits *Repugnant* and *Obnoxious*.

The Open Passage

Taking an hour to trace a pattern with a Trait of your blood, you can make a barrier insubstantial for a full turn. The barrier itself retains its normal appearance and characteristics, and anything already touching or supported by the barrier when the ritual ends becomes briefly insubstantial with it. With *The Open Passage*, you can therefore walk through a wall or allow allies to travel through locked doors and similar barriers.

Principal Focus of Vitae Infusion

Concentrating the power of your blood, you cause your own vitae to sink into a small object. With a touch and a mental command, you can later cause this object to break down back into a pool of your own blood. You can imbue an object between the sizes of a dime and a loaf of bread with a single Trait of your own blood, at which time the object becomes slightly reddish and slick. Alternately, you can use the *Principal Focus of Vitae Infusion* to craft an object of your blood that responds to the touch of another individual, as long as that individual is present during the casting of the ritual. Of course, since your own blood must be used, the subject risks the blood bond.

Scent of the Lupine's Passing

With a mixture of milkweed, wolfsbane and other herbs, you can make a poultice that allows you to sniff out werewolves. The poultice retains its effectiveness for a full scene or hour after its creation; as long as you carry it with you, you can detect Lupines by smell. You must get within five feet of your subject and win a Mental Challenge to determine the *Scent of the Lupine's Passing*.

Wake with Evening's Freshness

In case of emergencies or if you fear invasion of your haven, you can *Wake with Evening's Freshness* simply by spreading ashes of burned feathers over your sleeping place while casting this ritual immediately before slumber. Should you be faced with danger, you awaken immediately. For the first two full turns you suffer no penalties for daylight activity (although you can still be injured by sunlight, of course).

Ward versus Ghouls

Spending 10 minutes repeating a warding invocation while pouring a Trait of blood over an object, you shape a mystical glyph that causes extreme pain to any ghoul touching it. The night after you cast the ritual, the ward takes effect, causing a level of lethal damage to any ghoul touching the object (even adding this effect to other damage if, say, a warded sword is used against a ghoul in combat). Any object in size between dagger and door may be warded. You can specifically exclude certain ghouls from the effect if they are present while you cast the ritual and if each donates a Trait of blood to attune the *Ward versus Ghouls*.

Intermediate Thaumaturgical Rituals

Bone of Lies

By enchanting a mortal finger bone as a *Bone of Lies*, you bind the soul of the skeleton to the bone. Then, whenever someone holds the bone, the taint of any lies that they speak is drawn into the finger bone, which blackens it as the spirit within becomes corrupt. The bone must be at least 200 years old, and it must be steeped in at least 10 Traits of blood during the casting of the ritual — all of the blood is mystically absorbed. Thereafter, whenever someone knowingly speaks a lie while holding the bone, it darkens noticeably and forces the subject to speak the truth immediately. Each lie so negated uses one of the Blood Traits in the bone; when all 10 are used, the bone is blackened and useless, home only to a dark spirit twisted by lies.

Incorporeal Passage

By looking into a fragment of a mirror while intoning this chant, you become completely incorporeal. Physical attacks pass through you while you may step unhin-

dered through any solid barrier. You can only move forward or stand still once you invoke *Incorporeal Passage* — you may not turn or back up. The ritual lasts for the next full hour or scene, but you can end it simply by turning away the piece of mirror that you hold.

Pavis of Foul Presence

To combat the powers of the *Presence* Discipline, you tie a blue silken cord around your neck while intoning the *Pavis of Foul Presence*. Until the next sunrise, you are defended against *Presence* powers. If someone manages to exert a *Presence* power on you, it is reflected back instead of affecting you. This ritual is completely unknown outside the Tremere clan, who keep it as a powerful secret in their wars of vampiric influence.

Rutor's Hands

The terrifying servant created with *Rutor's Hands* is actually one of your own severed hands, with one of your eyeballs set atop it! After casting this ritual, you must cut off your own hand and pluck out your eye, suffering five levels of aggravated damage in the process, in order to complete the spell. (Don't actually inflict physical harm on yourself. Your character does the nasty deed, not you.) The ritual keeps your body parts from crumbling to dust, and it animates them as spies for your use. They follow your mental orders, moving as you direct and allowing you to see and hear whatever they experience. You can create as many as you like, though you must regenerate your hands and eyes fully after each casting before making another set of *Rutor's Hands*. The spying, scuttling... thing made with this ritual needs a single Trait of blood each week (from any source), or else it crumbles to dust.

You can get cards for your *Rutor's Hands*, and then use them to spy on other locations. Simply give the card to a Narrator and direct him to a particular location. If the thing is spotted, of course, it is easily destroyed with a single level of damage (it is considered to have three Physical Traits that it can only use to defend itself).

Soul of the Homunculi

Few vampires trust anyone, yet the arcane researches of the Tremere often require capable assistants. A homunculus is a tiny physical replica of the caster, completely loyal and made to serve its master as a spy and aide. Casting the *Soul of the Homunculi* takes a full month of time outside of play. When completed, the homunculus acts as a tiny extension of yourself. Such creations can resemble tiny winged creatures capable of flight, a legless slug with a human face like its master's, or a small marmosetlike creature with a face resembling its creator. Any given homunculus is completely loyal to its creator, in effect acting as an extra limb. Homunculi have three Physical Traits and two health levels, and they cannot fight. They *can* spy and report back or perform small tasks. You can only have one homunculus at any given time.

ADVANCED THAUMATURGICAL RITUALS

Blood Contract

By spending three nights in the writing of a contract with your own blood, you create an unbreakable bond between yourself and any one signatory. You use two Blood Traits to make the contract — one to write it, and one for both parties to sign it. The *Blood Contract* enforces compliance of both parties to the literal terms listed. Should either party break the terms of the contract, the individual immediately suffers enough aggravated health levels of damage to fall into torpor, and this damage cannot be resisted in any way. The only way to finish the contract is to fulfill its terms or to physically burn it.

Nectar of the Bitter Rose

Hidden among the most vile of diablerists, the *Nectar of the Bitter Rose* breaks the usual constraints of diablerie, allowing multiple vampires to share in the fruits of a victim's power. You must restrain the victim in some fashion while casting this ritual over him. At the ritual's completion, up to five vampires may attempt to gain

the benefit of diablerizing the subject. Each would-be diablerist must make a Simple Test (win or tie) to gain the benefits. *Nectar of the Bitter Rose* does not allow a vampire to gain benefits from diablerizing a victim of weaker or lesser generation — it simply lets multiple people share in a diablerie. Obviously, even the mere knowledge of this ritual is grounds for destruction within the Camarilla.

Umbra Walk

The Tremere powers of *Auspex* allow them to search sublime planes of consciousness, but there are still other levels of existence to the infinite cosmos. Through the power of this ritual, which requires the sacrifice of an intelligent being (almost certainly costing you a Humanity Trait), you enter the Umbra, a spirit reflection of the physical world. You arrive naked, though certain magical items may come with you at the Storyteller's discretion. You can even bring other people, though each additional traveler requires another sacrifice. The Umbra is a dangerous place, traveled by werewolves and unfriendly spirits. *Umbra Walk* lasts until you choose to step back into the material plane. See **Laws of the Wild** for more detailed information about the spirit worlds.

VICISSITUDE

The Fiends of Eastern Europe harbor twisted secrets that make other vampires shudder. *Vicissitude*, the signature Discipline of the Tzimisce clan, reflects the inner nature of the most alien of vampires. Through *Vicissitude*, the wielder can reshape flesh under his very touch, whether into gross deformity or uneathly beauty.

When used on mortals, ghouls, revenants and vampires of weaker generation than the user, *Vicissitude*'s effects are permanent. Vampires of equal or more potent generations can heal back each *Vicissitude*- inflicted scar as an aggravated wound. Of course, a user of this Discipline can always shape his own flesh as desired.

Nosferatu, Samedi and vampires with similar deformities in their blood always heal back alterations of *Vicissitude* that attempt to improve their appearances. The Curse of Caine is not so easily circumvented.

Vicissitude uses the *Crafts: Body Crafts* Ability for retests. Most *Vicissitude* effects require physical contact and a Physical Challenge as the vampire tears into the flesh of the opponent. Such strikes use *Crafts: Body Crafts* for retests, instead of *Brawl*, since the aim is to mutate the flesh. For certain surgical effects, the Storyteller may require some level of *Medicine* Ability as well.

BASIC VICISSITUDE

Malleable Visage

Bending your flesh under your hands, you can change your own appearance. *Malleable Visage* allows you to duplicate others or simply make your own surface skin different from your natural forms. Cosmetic changes like alterations of voice or skin tone and build are all possible, though you must actually sculpt the desired changes into your flesh.

Changing yourself with *Malleable Visage* costs one Blood Trait, and it requires you to spend time reshaping yourself appropriately. If you hope to copy someone else, you must make a Static Mental Challenge, difficulty of the subject's Social Traits, to pull off the disguise, and you still use your own Social Traits in any challenge — you are simply duplicating the person's appearance. You can also afflict yourself with a hideous visage, taking on *Repugnant* Negative Traits (up to three such additional Traits maximum).

Fleshcraft

Your hands can turn flesh to putty, shaping it like potter's clay. You can perform drastic alterations to the flesh and organs of any creature that you touch.

You must touch your victim to use *Fleshcraft*, pulling or shaping the flesh to your whims. You can reshape flesh on yourself or others within the limits described in *Malleable Visage*, or you can move around clumps of tissue or simply reduce someone to scarred deformity. These attacks do not inflict damage, but each such strike causes the victim to suffer a Negative Trait of *Repugnant* (to a maximum of three such Traits from this power). If you alter the distribution of skin, fat and muscle, you can remove one (and only one) of the subject's Physical Traits and replace it with an extra health level, or reverse such an operation.

INTERMEDIATE VICISSITUDE

Bonecraft

Just as you shape flesh with your touch, you can grasp and twist bone, turning it into any desired shape or moving, lengthening, bending or compressing it. *Bonecraft* lets you literally pull the bone through a subject's flesh, or you can use it with *Fleshcraft* to completely restructure a victim — or yourself.

Using *Bonecraft* allows you to remake appearances just like *Fleshcraft*, but you can also change someone's height or body structure, reshape bone into unusual or spectacular forms, and even make bone spurs and weapons. You must grab the victim, and then twist, pull or bend the bones appropriately. If you do so without exercising *Fleshcraft*, each such strike causes one level of lethal damage as bones warp and tear their way through flesh. Used in conjunction with *Fleshcraft*, you can rebuild someone's visage completely, or you can create defensive spines or offensive bone weapons. Such alterations allow the subject to inflict lethal damage with otherwise unarmed attacks.

Horrid Form

Your own body warps and grows into a hideous monstrosity with *Horrid Form*. Your skin becomes black, rubbery and slimy, while sharp bony spikes protrude from your hands and back. You grow to a full eight feet in height, and you shift into something from a nightmare vision. Those unused to such sights may need to make a *Courage* test.

Awakening the *Horrid Form* costs two Blood Traits. You gain the Negative Social Traits *Bestial*, *Feral* and *Repugnant* in this form, but you also gain the Physical Traits *Brawny*, *Dexterous*, *Enduring*, *Ferocious*, *Quick* and *Stalwart* for the duration of the power. You may also not initiate Social Challenges except for the purposes of intimidation. You inflict lethal damage in brawling combat, and you score an extra health level of damage on all such attacks. You may remain in *Horrid Form* until you decide to change back.

ADVANCED VICISSITUDE

Bloodform

Deliquescing into a puddle of vitae is within your power. You need only concentrate briefly, and you can reduce any of your limbs or body parts into a puddle of your own pure blood.

Each limb (arm, leg, head) that you transform becomes one Blood Trait; your body forms the remainder of your Blood Traits, up to your maximum size. You can change part or all of yourself, as desired. This blood functions in all ways as your own blood, but you retain a level of autonomic control over it. In *Bloodform*, you can move at a slow walking pace as a puddle of blood, oozing over things and through cracks. Changing body parts back requires only that you be in contact with the blood, or that you regrow your part by expending Blood Traits appropriate to the part (a single Trait to regrow a limb, for instance), in which case the blood that previously formed the piece becomes inert. While fully in *Bloodform*, you can use mental Disciplines, and you are immune to all physical dangers except fire or sunlight. If all of the blood is imbibed or destroyed while you are in this form, though, you meet Final Death.

Donata had some time to herself, once Peter and Kevin had both left. She took the opportunity to rearrange some of the statuary. The place wasn't her true haven, but that didn't mean that it had to look trashy.

As Donata took down a painting, looking for a better way to compose it with the statuary, she played over the running plots in her mind. She knew that only the prince had the strength of blood and age to oppose her directly. Warburton would still be set up as the architect of the package deal, and Kristof would owe her for her involvement in stopping the candle ritual. With the major players vanquished, she could move in to conquer their financial and political assets, securing a position that even the prince couldn't dislodge. All she had to do then was get the Warlocks in her corner, and she'd have the run of the city, even if the prince kept his hollow title.

From outside, Donata recognized the distinctive sound of Peter's car. The expensive engine rumbled slightly before turning off, and with a bit of straining she heard the door slamming shut through the sounds of outside traffic. Adjusting her choker, she waited for Peter's entrance. His footsteps resounded up the stairway; he was in a hurry, doubtless flustered by his failure with the Warlocks.

The door to the room opened, and Donata carefully turned one of the statues, its eyes mutely regarding the entrance. Peter stood in the doorway for a moment, stiff and angry, but with a monumental effort of self-control the wave of rage subsided and his bloodless lips relaxed. Not deigning to remove his sunglasses, he approached Donata with quick steps.

"The Warlock was dead."

Donata masked her surprise. Someone had interfered with her careful web, killing the Tremere before Peter could find him! Thinking quickly, she decided to work the situation to her advantage.

"Of course. It must be Kevin. That vicious creature must have done this to stop you," she glibly suggested.

Peter considered her words for a moment, then shook his head. He calculated the possible motives much like he'd look at profit and loss, surprised at his sudden change of focus. *I've thought like this for so long, it's a habit*, he realized. *I need to turn my skills to new advantage.* "I don't think so. You forced him to love you, but he had no reason to think that the Tremere was a danger to you."

"Indeed," Donata purred as she wrapped an arm around the statue and a hand around Peter's tie. "But he may have seen *you* as a danger to me. With the Tremere dead, you could simply let me be seen as the architect, with his materials here among my property. At least, that's doubtless what he thought."

Peter mused over the possibilities. "Perhaps," he thought. *And you're too subtle a liar. I need allies that I can control.* "I'll go find him. If he's a problem, I'll deal with him myself."

"He mentioned something about a mausoleum," Donata offered. "Probably near where his anarch friends play." *Go quickly to your demise*, she thought, Peter left as quickly as he'd arrived.

CHAPTER FIVE: RULES, SYSTEMS AND DRAMA

Rules are an integral part of any game; they define what characters can and cannot do. Only when confrontation does occur are rules necessary to govern those situations. Still, the primary focus of this game is to tell a good story.

CHALLENGES

There comes a time when two or more players come into conflicts that cannot be resolved through roleplaying alone. The system detailed in this chapter allows for the resolution of conflicts efficiently and quickly. This sort of face-off is called a challenge, and it makes for a very simple system of conflict resolution. In most cases, a Narrator does not even need to be present when a challenge is played.

Roleplaying does not necessarily have to end when a challenge begins; in fact, roleplaying becomes more important than ever if players intend to enjoy a confrontation and avoid disputes. Experienced players can integrate a challenge into their roleplaying so seamlessly that outsiders don't even know that anything unusual is going on. At the players' option, special hand signals can be used to indicate when certain Traits and powers are being employed.

In order for this system to work, players need to work together. They have to educate each other on the rules and agree on what Traits can be used in a challenge. Compromise and cooperation are the bywords of the game. Arguments over whether or not a particular Trait bid is appropriate wreck both the momentum and the mood of a game.

USING TRAITS

Before you can begin to learn how challenges work, you must first understand what defines a character's capabilities. A character is created by choosing a number of adjectives that describe and define that person as an individual. These adjectives are called Traits, and they are described fully in Chapter Two. These Traits are used to declare challenges against other characters or against static forces represented by a Narrator.

INITIAL BID

A challenge begins with a player "bidding" one of her Traits against her opponent. At the same time, she must declare what the conditions of the challenge are — like firing

a gun, attacking with a knife or using *Dominate*. The defender must then decide how she will respond. She can either relent immediately or bid one of her own Traits in response.

When players bid Traits against one another, they may only use Traits that could sensibly be used in that situation. Essentially, this restriction means that a player can usually use only those Traits from the same category as her opponent's Traits. Most challenges are categorized as Physical, Social or Mental, and all Traits used in a challenge must be from the same category. Experienced players may offer each other more creative leeway, but only by mutual agreement.

If the defender relents, she loses the challenge automatically. For example, if she were being attacked, she would suffer a wound. If she matches the challenger's bid, the two immediately go to a test. Those Traits bid are put at risk, as the loser of the test not only loses the challenge, but the Trait she bid as well for the rest of the evening.

TESTING

Once both parties involved in a challenge have bid a Trait, they engage in a test immediately. The test itself is not what you may think — the outcome is random, but no cards or dice are used. The two players face off against one another by playing Rock-Paper-Scissors.

If you lose the test, you lose the Trait you bid for the duration of the session (usually the rest of the evening). Essentially, you have lost some confidence in your own capabilities and can't call on them for a while. You can no longer use that Trait effectively, at least until you regain confidence in your Traits.

The test works like the moment in poker when the cards are turned over and the winner is declared. The test produces one of two possible outcomes — either one player is the victor, or the result is a tie.

In the case of a tie, the players must then reveal the number of Traits that they currently have available in the category used (Physical, Social or Mental). The player with the least number of Traits loses the test and therefore loses the challenge. Note that the number of Traits you've lost in previous challenges, or lost for any other reason, reduces the maximum number of Traits you can bid in ties. You may lie about the number of Traits you possess, but only by declaring fewer Traits than you actually have — you may never say that you have more Traits than you actually do. Doing so allows you to keep the actual number of Traits you possess a secret, although doing so may be risky. The challenger is always the first to declare his number of Traits. If both players declare the same number of Traits, then the challenge is a draw, and both players lose the Traits they bid.

Example of Play: *Sam, Brujah musician, is caught in a battle with Juan, a fearsome assassin. Knowing his only hope is to come out swinging, Sam begins with an aggressive Trait for his initial bid ("I take a Ferocious swipe at you with my guitar!"), and the Assamite responds in kind ("Feel the power of my Brutal strike, infidel!"). The two test — both shoot Rock, a tie. Now they have to declare their total number of Traits to resolve the tie. Sam knows he'll need all he's got, so he declares all nine Traits he has available. Juan has only eight traits, and so he loses the challenge. The Assamite loses the Trait he bid, suffers a health level of damage and begins to wonder if this is really such a mismatch after all.*

ROCK-PAPER-SCISSORS

What we mean by Rock-Paper-Scissors is the following: You and another person face off, and, on the count of three, you show one of three hand gestures. "Rock" is a basic fist. "Paper" is just a flat hand. "Scissors" is represented by sticking out two fingers. You then compare the two gestures to determine the winner. Rock crushes Scissors. Scissors cuts Paper. Paper covers Rock. Identical signs indicate a tie. Certain advanced powers allow some characters to use gestures other than Rock, Paper and Scissors. Before players can use the gestures in a test, however, they must explain what they are and how they are used.

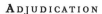

ADJUDICATION

If you have question or argument about the rules or the conditions of a challenge, you need to find a Narrator to make a judgment. Try to remain in character while you look for a Narrator. Any interruption in the progress of the story should be avoided if at all possible, so work problems out with other players if you can. If you do not know the correct application of a certain rule, it's usually better to wing it rather than interrupt the flow of the game.

It should be noted that a challenger who fails on a Social or Mental Challenge must wait at least five real-time minutes (and not spend them arguing over the results of the previous challenge — you can't protest a ruling with a Narrator for 4:58, then drop your argument and say, "Oh look, time's up,") before repeating the failed challenge. This rule includes supernatural powers that use Mental or Social Challenges unless they specify otherwise — a character cannot continue attempting one *Mesmerism* after another until he finally succeeds. This stricture does *not* include trials that are failed but then redeemed through retests or overbids.

COMPLICATIONS

There are a number of ways in which a challenge can be made more complicated. The basic rules are enough to resolve most disputes, but the following rules add a few bells and whistles.

NEGATIVE TRAITS

Many characters have Negative Traits, Traits that can be used against a character by his opponent. During the initial bid of any challenge, after you have each bid one Trait, you can call out a Negative Trait that you believe your opponent possesses. If he does indeed possess the Negative Trait, your opponent is forced to bid an additional Trait, although you must still risk your one Trait as usual. If he does not possess that Negative Trait, *you* must risk an additional Trait. You may call out as many Negative Traits as you wish during the initial bid phase of a challenge, as long as you can pay the price for being wrong.

If your opponent does not have additional Traits to bid, then your Trait is not at risk during the challenge. Additionally if you guess more than one Negative Trait that your opponent cannot match, you gain that many additional Traits in the case of a tie or an overbid (see below). The same works in reverse, favoring your opponent if you do not have additional Traits remaining to match incorrect Negative Trait guesses. It is considered *very* cheap to list off which Negative Traits a player might possess, if you have no valid reason to suspect as much in-game.

Example of Play: *Joshua the Gangrel is attacking Marsilio, a Toreador socialite. He begins with his initial bid ("I make a Ferocious attack with my claws!") while Marsilio attempts to escape ("I'm too Quick for you to catch so easily"). Joshua then suggests that Marsilio possesses the Negative Trait Lethargic ("All those Elysium parties have made you too Lethargic to get away"). If Marsilio did indeed possess that Negative Trait, he would have to bid an additional Trait to have continue the challenge. However, the Toreador does not possess the Lethargic Trait, and now Joshua — having underestimated his opposition — is the one who has to bid an extra Trait if he wishes to continue trying to capture his prey.*

It can be risky to bid Negative Traits, but if you're sure about what you're doing, you can raise the stakes for your opponent, possibly even to the point where she relents rather than risking additional Traits.

OVERBIDDING

Overbidding is the system by which powerful characters may prevail in a challenge, even if they lose the initial test. Armand the elder with 16 Physical Traits should be able to crush Phil the neonate who has only three. This system is designed to make that possible.

Once a test has been made, the loser has the option of calling for an "overbid." In order to call an overbid, you must risk a new Trait; the original one has already been

lost. At this point, the two players must reveal the number of applicable Traits they possess in the appropriate category, starting with the player who called for the overbid. If you have double the number of Traits as your opponent in that category, you may attempt another test. As with a tie, you may state a number of Traits less than the actual number you have and keep your true power secret. Overbidding can be dangerous unless you are confident in your estimation of your opponent's abilities.

Example of Play: *Favian, Setite manipulator, is attempting to coax information from his pawn Endora. He begins with flattery ("My praise is so Beguiling that you have no choice but to tell me what I want to know"), but she resists ("I'm too Dignified to be so easily won over"). They test and Endora wins, but Favian is far from thwarted. Gambling that he has more social aptitude than the studious Tremere, Favian bids an additional Trait ("I'm ever so Seductive when it comes to getting what I want") and calls for an overbid. Endora, being the defender, does not need to risk an additional trait. Favian announces all 14 of his Social Traits, while Endora admits that she has only five, and so the overbid proceeds. They test again, and this time Favian wins. Endora loses the Dignified Trait she bid, and Favian still loses his initial Beguiling Trait, but he has won the final challenge and so she must divulge the information he was seeking.*

STATIC CHALLENGES

Sometimes you may have to undergo a challenge against a Narrator rather than against another player. For example, a hacker may use a Static Mental Challenge with the *Computer* Ability to break into another computer system. In such circumstances, you bid a Trait that would be appropriate, then perform a test against the Narrator. Before the test is made, the Narrator decides on the difficulty of the task which you are attempting — this is the number of Traits you are bidding against, which is used to compare in the event of a tie. The test proceeds exactly as it would if you were testing against another character. Of course, you may attempt to overbid in a Static Challenge, but beware, because the Narrator can overbid as well. The number of Traits attached to the challenge should represent the difficulty and danger inherent in the challenge.

Sometimes Narrators may leave notes on objects, such as books, doors or even magical items. These notes indicate the type of challenges that must be won for something to occur (such as deciphering a tome or picking a lock).

SIMPLE TESTS

Simple Tests are used to determine if you can do something successfully when there is no real opposition. Simple Tests are often used when using Disciplines. Most Simple Tests do not require you to risk or bid Traits, though some may.

When a Simple Test is called, a test (Rock-Paper-Scissors) is performed against a Narrator. In most cases, the player succeeds on a win or a tie, although in some cases, it may be necessary for the player to win for him to receive any benefit from the challenge.

RETESTS

Certain Traits allow a character to retest. A retest allows a character to ignore the results of the first test and test again for a new result. Retests are most commonly gained through Abilities, but other Traits may also provide them; such Traits are noted in their descriptions. Generally, expending one level of an appropriate Ability allows for one retest.

Multiple retests are possible on a single challenge, but each retest must come from a different source. A character may retest a challenge once using a level of *Brawl* and then retest again through the Merit: *Lucky*, but he may not gain multiple retests with the *Brawl* Ability on the same challenge.

Retests may be canceled ("blocked") by a character who is capable of matching the conditions of the retest. Thus, if a player uses *Firearms* to retest when firing a gun, the opponent may expend a level of *Dodge* to block the retest and force the attacker to accept the results of the original test.

Example of Play: Michael, a Sabbat recruiter, is holding Daron hostage and subjecting her to an earful of sect propaganda. Reacting with typical Brujah composure, Daron pulls a hidden pistol and attacks ("I use the advantage my Wily plan has given me to shoot you in the chest!") Michael responds by trying to take cover ("I use my Quick reflexes to spring behind the couch."). They perform a test, and Daron loses. However, Daron is an excellent shot ("I am too skilled at Firearms to let you get away that easily!"), and she calls for a retest. The two test again, and Daron wins. Michael suffers damage from the gunshot wound.

Michael tries to recover by knocking Daron's gun away ("Dexterous as ever, I yank the gun from your grasp."). Daron responds by backing away, the better to set up another shot ("I'm too Nimble for you to get a hold of!"), and the two perform another test. Michael loses and immediately calls for a retest with Brawl ("My Brawl skill is good enough to grab a gun at close range!"). Daron blocks the retest with Dodge ("I Dodge out of the way before you have a chance!"), and no retest is performed. Daron is now out of Michael's reach and ready to shoot again.

RELENTING

At any time before the actual test is performed, a player may choose to acquiesce and admit defeat. Characters who relent lose the challenge automatically, but they do not lose any Traits, even if they bid one before relenting. They also help the game flow along more smoothly than extended Rock-Paper-Scissors matches do.

BONUS TRAITS

Certain weapons and special powers grant a character bonus Traits during a challenge. You may add these extra Traits toward a character's total when determining a tie involving that weapon or special Ability.

ORDER of CHALLENGES

Since multiple challenges will inevitably occur simultaneously during any given fight, occasionally the Narrator needs some means of determining who acts first and who acts last. Each person involved in a given game turn checks the current number of Traits appropriate to the action he wishes to attempt. A character punching someone would use Physical Traits to determine speed, while a character casting a spell would probably use Mental Traits. If an action does not require any sort of Trait challenge, it occurs last in the turn. As with overbidding, you may declare fewer Traits than you possess if you wish. Characters with equal numbers of Traits are assumed to go "simultaneously," though for resolution purposes the Narrator may simply choose one to act first.

Sometimes a character with a high number of Traits will attack a character with fewer Traits, who will decide to strike back. In this case, the character with fewer Traits resolves his action in the same test as the faster character, but in doing so, he loses the ability to take any aggressive action for the turn — he uses up his one action with the counterattack.

This rule can occasionally cause as much confusion as it's trying to solve, and the Narrator may choose to apply this only when there a debate or other critical need to establish who's going first.

Example of Play: Michael and Daron are still locked in combat, and Michael decides his only chance is to dive out the side door and try to get away. Unfortunately for Michael, Daron's friend Shane has also broken free of his bonds and is attempting to block his escape. Michael has five Physical Traits left, and Shane has his full eight Traits. Shane pounces in front of Michael ("I'm too Stalwart for you to get by me!"), and Michael decides he'll try to counter by knocking the stubborn Gangrel down ("I fetch you a Ferocious smash across the knees!"). They perform a test, and Shane loses; he suffers a wound from the attack and is knocked aside. However, Michael cannot escape yet—he's used up his action this turn by striking Shane. Meanwhile, Daron declares that for her action she'll move to a better position for next turn.

THE MOB SCENE

It's a fact of life that sooner or later a large group of characters will decide to mix it up. Group challenges can seem intimidating even to experienced Narrators and

Storytellers; these rules are meant to streamline the process and make such situations easier to resolve, rather than devolving into endless matches of Rock-Paper-Scissors.

First of all, find who is challenging whom. The easiest way is to count to three and have everyone point to the person they wish to target that turn. If no one is being challenged by more than one person, then challenges are carried out normally.

If one character is challenged by several targets, or tries to challenge multiple opponents at once, resolve it in the following manner. First deal with groups in the order of largest to smallest, just for ease of play. Each attacker must bid an appropriate Trait as normal for the challenge required; logistics put a limit of up to five characters attacking another character at once.

Next, the defender character must bid enough Traits to counter every opponent in the group; if he does not have enough Traits, he must relent to the rest of his opponents (although he may choose which ones he relents to). Resolve such relented challenges first — it is very possible the defender may fall before the rest of the group can act!

Finally, the defender and any remaining attackers engage in one simultaneous test. The defender then compares his sign to each of the attacker's signs, applying the appropriate results. Thus, if the defending character throws Scissors and his attackers throw Rock, Scissors, Paper and Paper, the defender is considered to have lost to the first challenger, tied the second (resolved like any other tie) and beaten the last two. The defenders and attackers lose Traits bid in any given loss. If the defender in the previous example had bid one Trait against every attacker, he would have lost one Trait to the first attacker, and an additional Trait if he had lost the tie as well.

Once the tests have been made, they are resolved in the standard order of actions and initiative. It is possible for a defender to lose Traits to the first attackers and then lose a tie to an attacker later in the same mob challenge. That's OK — the first attackers "softened up" the defender. However, unless the defender has a special power which allows him to take multiple actions, he may only attempt to injure one of his attackers, and it must be one who lost a challenge. If none of the attackers lose, the defender simply suffers the results of their actions.

When the defender in a mob challenge uses Abilities or other powers to gain retests, each attacker's challenge is treated as a separate test. Thus, a defender would need five *Melee* Traits in order to retest against five attackers in a melee combat.

TIME

Time in **Mind's Eye Theatre** works as it does in real life. It moves forward inexorably, relentlessly. For the most part, everything is played out in real time, and players are expected to stay in character unless they have a rules question.

It is assumed that a player is always "in character" during the course of a story. A player should never drop character when interacting with other players. Doing so ruins the atmosphere for everyone involved. Challenges may be talked through, but a player is always considered to be active in the game. If a player needs to take a break, he should inform a Narrator. That player should not interact with any of the other players while out of character.

The only other exception to the "in-character rule" is when a Narrator calls for a "timeout." This call may be necessary to resolve a dispute or to change the scene if the story calls for it. When "Timeout!" is called, all players within hearing distance must stop whatever they are doing until the Narrator calls out, "Resume" or "Lay on!" Timeouts should be kept to a minimum, since they interrupt the flow of the story.

CHRONICLES, STORIES, SESSIONS AND SCENES

Mind's Eye Theatre time breaks down into five major allotments: chronicles, stories, sessions, scenes and turns. A chronicle is defined as a series of smaller stories that are all connected somehow, and which may take months or even years to complete. Each

complete plotline within the chronicle is called a story. A session is just that: one actual night of play, although Storytellers may define a session as one night of game time if the action was left *in media res* at the end of the previous game. (Since many characters regain spent Traits in between sessions, this distinction can be important.) Finally, a scene is the amount of time it takes to resolve the action in one location; once the characters shift locations, the scene has ended. If a session will be taking place entirely at one location, a scene can then be defined as roughly one hour.

TURNS

To keep everything straight when players start throwing challenges around or attempting complex actions, the time is right to start using turns. Turns are considered to last about four seconds, although this measure may vary from challenge to challenge at the Storyteller's discretion. In any given turn, a character may take one action. Some actions may take multiple turns to complete, such as hacking a sophisticated computer system. Other actions, like speaking a short sentence, do not use up a character's turn at all. Once everyone involved in a turn has taken an action, the turn ends and another turn begins.

In some instances a character may be interrupted before he can take his action, or be forced to respond to events developing around him. In such instances, a character may always defend himself, although doing so uses up his available action for the turn.

If a power affects a character for 15 seconds, it is assumed to be in effect for four turns when turn-based time is in effect. In normal roleplaying, such powers work for their allotted amount of time.

DOWNTIME

Many aspects of a character's unlife are critical to her continued existence, yet they do not make for dramatic roleplaying, or they are too intricate to take time during sessions to perform. Storytellers are encouraged to use "downtime" between sessions to allow characters to maintain their holdings, learn Disciplines and see to other facets of their existence. Other actions and interactions may take place during this time, with Storyteller supervision. As long as players don't use abuse downtime privileges, the time between sessions can be a rewarding roleplaying experience in itself.

HEALTH

A character in a **Masquerade** game has different health levels that represent the amount of injury the character can endure. These levels include: Healthy, Healthy, Bruised, Bruised, Bruised, Wounded, Wounded, Incapacitated, Torpor and/or Final Death. If a Healthy character loses two health levels from a combat challenge, she becomes Bruised. If she loses three more health levels, she becomes Wounded, and so on.

• **Healthy** — When a character is Healthy, he is virtually or completely uninjured. He suffers no penalty aside from possibly being cosmetically scuffed up a bit.

• **Bruised** — A Bruised character is more seriously roughed up, and his injuries have started to impair his viability a bit. He is considered one Trait down on all tied challenges.

• **Wounded** — When a character is Wounded, he is seriously injured in one or more locations. To reflect this injury, he must risk an additional Trait to attempt a challenge, and his opponent wins all ties, regardless of who has more Traits. If the injured character has a power which normally allows him to win all ties, ties are resolved through comparing Traits instead. Note: a character may always attempt to overbid.

• **Incapacitated** — When a character is Incapacitated, he is completely out of play for at least 10 minutes. Once awake, the character is still effectively immobile, although he may whisper pained sentences. He may not enter into challenges until he has healed at least one health level. He is at the mercy of other characters, and he may do nothing more than heal himself. Kindred suffer Final Death if they suffer aggravated wounds at this point.

- **Torpor** — Kindred who are injured beyond Incapacitated by lethal damage fall into a deathlike sleep known as torpor.
- **Final Death** — Kindred injured beyond Incapacitated by aggravated damage do not enter Torpor, but are permanently destroyed instead.

Example of Play: *Dracos is caught in a Sabbat ambush. His first attacker kicks him for one level of bashing damage, putting him at his second Healthy level. Another assailant shoots him for two levels of lethal damage, dropping him to his second Bruised level. Lucky as ever, the next turn Dracos is shot again, suffering another two health levels and falling to his first Wounded level. A Sabbat with Potence and a knife slashes him viciously as he tries to escape, inflicting two health levels of lethal damage and reducing him to Incapacitated. Dracos falls to the ground, helpless, and he is now at the mercy of his attackers. If he takes any more lethal damage, he will enter torpor; if he suffers aggravated damage, however, he will suffer Final Death instead. (Further bashing damage will merely render him unconscious for a while.)*

TORPOR

Characters may enter torpor voluntarily or involuntarily (through wounds or other means). Once in torpor, the character remains dormant for an amount of time dependent on her Humanity rating, or until another Kindred gives her blood to revive her. Characters with no Blood Traits lose a health level each time the rules call for them to spend blood, such as rising each night; once the character falls below Incapacitated in this fashion, she enters torpor. Vampires who enter torpor due to blood loss or wounds must rest the entire time required by the following chart, barring some exceptional circumstance (Storyteller's discretion).

Following this period of rest, the character may make a Static Mental Challenge against three Traits and expend a Blood Trait to wake up. Failure means the Kindred may test again once per night until she succeeds or runs out of Blood Traits. If she has no blood, she may not rise until some is given to her.

A character who enters torpor voluntarily falls into a slumber similar to her daily rest, but it is, in fact, far deeper, and it should not be entered lightly. Voluntary sleepers may awaken in half the time usually required by the chart, although they still need to make a Static Mental Challenge to do so. Torpid vampires ignore the nightly need for blood — they are effectively in hibernation for the time they remain in that state.

Humanity Traits	Length of Torpor
5	Two days
4	One week
3	One year
2	One decade
1	One Century
0	Millennium

HEALING

Vampires are dead and unable heal wounds naturally. Only by utilizing their blood can they repair damage to themselves. One Blood Trait spent heals one health level of lethal damage, or two health levels of bashing damage. This process can be performed at the same time other actions are performed, even alongside Discipline use.

BASHING/LETHAL DAMAGE

Some types of damage are more dangerous than others: a punch to the jaw is less likely to kill than a knife wound. Bashing damage is defined as any injury which is painful but fades relatively quickly, such as kicks, punches or tackles. Lethal damage (from bullets, swords,

knives, etc.) is intended to kill, and it takes mortals a long time to heal. The Narrator is the final arbiter of what counts as bashing or lethal damage. Characters put below Incapacitated by bashing damage are rendered unconscious for one scene/ hour (although the Narrator may rule that they are put in torpor or killed if the beating is fierce enough); mortal creatures pushed past Incapacitated by lethal damage simply die, while vampires enter torpor instead.

Because their corpselike bodies simply don't bruise and break like those of the kine, Cainites *halve* all bashing damage received, round down (minimum one level of damage inflicted).

AGGRAVATED WOUNDS

Wounds that are beyond the normal bounds of even the Kindred's unnatural healing powers are called aggravated wounds. Such wounds are usually caused by injury from fire, sunlight or the teeth and claws of a supernatural creature. A Narrator can also deem any other injury to be aggravated, depending on the circumstances. Three Blood Traits, a Willpower Trait and a night of rest are required to heal one level of aggravated damage.

Sunlight

Exposure to sunlight is extremely painful for vampires. Indirect sunlight such as through thick curtains or heavy cloud cover causes one automatic aggravated wound per turn of exposure, while direct sunlight causes three automatic levels of aggravated damage per turn. (Heavy clothing may provide some protection, at the Storyteller's discretion.) Vampires confronted by sunlight must also make a Static *Courage* Challenge or suffer Rötschreck.

Fire

Vampires fear and loathe fire, and its slightest touch causes them great agony. Most vampires are extremely uncomfortable around open flame, since it is one of the few things that can destroy them permanently. In game terms, all wounds inflicted by normal or magical fires do aggravated damage to Kindred, and sufficiently large sources of flame will inevitably provoke a *Courage* Test to avoid Rötschreck. A character on fire must win or tie a Simple Test and spend one action dousing the flames.

COMBAT

Combat is the usual intent behind Physical Challenges. Essentially, combat involves two characters in physical conflict. The players agree what the outcome of the challenge will be, each player bids an appropriate Trait and a test is performed to determine the victor. The following section allows for variations on those basic rules, such as situations using surprise or weapons.

The agreed outcome of a Physical Challenge is often the loser being injured. This is not the only possible result, though. The two parties can agree to nearly anything, whether it's tripping an opponent or throwing him out of a window. The results of a combat challenge may also be different for both participants; for example, if a frenzied Malkavian is trying to tear apart a fleeing mortal, the mortal might try to get away from his opponent instead of hurting her.

SURPRISE

If a player does not respond within three seconds of the declaration of a Physical Challenge, the character is considered to have been surprised — he is not fully prepared for what's coming. Sometimes a player is busy with another activity or is playing a character who just isn't prepared for the attack. Any player who sneaks around whispering challenges to get the element of surprise is cheating, plain and simple.

Surprise simply means that the outcome of the first challenge in a fight can only harm the surprised defender, not the challenger. For instance, if a player did not respond in time to an attack, but still won the challenge, the challenger would not be injured. Furthermore, if the challenger loses the test, she may call for a second challenge by risking another Trait. After this second challenge, regular challenge rules resume. Overbidding is permitted for both challenger and challenged in surprise situations.

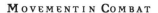

MOVEMENT IN COMBAT

Three Step Rule

Anyone in or just entering combat is subject to the "three step rule." You may take up to three steps during any combat action and still attack. Moving one step is considered walking cautiously, two steps is moving directly (down one Trait in Physical Challenges), and three steps is running (also down a Trait in Physical Challenges). A Discipline that allows for an additional action would allow you to take three additional steps, and so on.

FAIR ESCAPE

Fair Escape is a simple rule which allows players to escape from potentially dangerous situations without actually bounding over furniture or diving out of windows. This rule also allows players to avoid combat without going through cumbersome challenges to see if they can "get away."

When you use this rule, you can call "Fair Escape!" any time you see another player approaching with whom you do not wish to interact. Once you call "Fair Escape," you may leave the area without being pursued. There are several guidelines which must be followed when using this rule, however:

• You may not use the Fair Escape rule if the person approaching is nearby (within conversational distance). In such cases, you must initiate a challenge in order to flee. Use common sense in places where there is a great deal of noise and conversational distance is reduced to a minimum (e.g., a crowded nightclub).

• Situations which involve an ambush (all exits blocked or the target is surrounded) or ranged weapons can sometimes negate the use of Fair Escape. Again, use common sense.

• A character using *Unseen Presence* or similar powers may employ a Fair Escape at any time before a challenge has been initiated, unless someone with some form of *Heightened Senses* counters him.

• Characters with supernatural speed such as *Celerity* may gain a Fair Escape by activating their speed before a challenge is initiated. In the case of two characters using supernatural speed, whoever uses the highest level of speed wins (all ties go to the fleeing party). Thus, a character using Basic *Celerity* cannot Fair Escape from a foe using Advanced *Celerity*.

These rules are meant to hasten play, not complicate it. Always try to employ common sense when using Fair Escape. (As a rule of thumb, if it takes several minutes to explain why a Fair Escape would be justified, it probably isn't.)

WEAPONS

For obvious reasons, no real weapons are ever allowed in **Mind's Eye Theatre** games. Even nonfunctional props are forbidden if they can be mistaken for weapons. This system does not use props of any kind, nor are players required (or allowed) to strike one another. Instead, characters should use weapon cards, which display the Traits and pertinent details of a particular weapon.

A weapon gives its wielder extra Traits for combat or other appropriate challenges. Sometimes this advantage is offset by a disadvantage in terms of a Negative Trait. Each weapon has one to six extra Traits that may be used in any challenge in which the weapon is employed. These Traits *cannot* be used as an initial bid. Instead, they add to the user's total when she is comparing Traits. In addition, some weapons have special abilities that may be used, such as causing extra levels of damage or affecting more than one target.

Statistics for weapons are written on cards and carried along with your character card. Weapon cards specify the capacities of each weapon and allow other players to see that you actually possess a weapon. When you have a weapon card in your hand, you are considered to be holding the weapon.

Some weapons have Negative Traits that can be used by the wielder's opponent in precisely the same way as regular Negative Traits. The weapon's Negative Traits can only be used against the wielder of that weapon. Negative Traits for a weapon must be appropriate to the situation. For instance, if you are firing a pistol and your opponent wants to use the gun's Negative Trait *Loud* against you, that Negative Trait could be ignored if you have a silencer on the gun.

Concealability

Each weapon has a concealability rating. If the weapon is not concealable, or if you do not have the proper amount of clothing or cover to conceal it, you must have that card on display at all times. You cannot, for example, pull a broadsword out of your pocket. Instead, you must carry that card in hand at all times or, optionally, you could pin the card to your shirt, indicating that the sword is slung over your shoulder.

Availability

Serious firearms and archaic melee weapons can take some time to locate. Firearms also require permits to obtain, which involves undergoing background checks or waiting-periods in some areas. A character can turn to more "colorful" channels in order to procure equipment, but the black market often means shady dealings and vastly inflated prices. Weapons that have Influence values listed under Availability indicate the level and type of Influence required in order to procure the weapon through illicit channels. Finally, of course, there's cost: A character must have some level of the *Finance* Ability or money-raising Influence to procure exotic melee weapons and nearly all firearms.

Once a character has a weapon, that doesn't mean he can keep it forever. Too often characters run about firing shotguns and large automatic weapons without facing the massive police manhunts that such battles invariably provoke. Take care that characters with powerful weapons understand the equally powerful repercussions that come from their use. These consequences not only preserve game balance, but enforces a sense of realism and keeps the game from turning into *Die Hard* with fangs.

SPECIAL WEAPON CAPABILITIES

Some weapons have special abilities, allowing an attacker to inflict extra damage, ignore certain types of protection or strike multiple opponents. (Such powers are noted under the weapon descriptions.)

Armor-Piercing

Special rounds, generally Teflon-coated, are able to pierce armor with ease. Although they do not inflict extra damage, armor-piercing rounds ignore any defenses from armor. Such rounds are typically tricky to acquire, though, and legal inquiries often follow their use.

Destroy Shield

Although rare in this day and age, certain Inquisitors and anachronistic elders still use shields. A weapon capable of destroying a shield penetrates it automatically and renders it useless after a certain number of blows, no matter what the size or strength of the shield may be.

Fully Automatic

A firearm with this ability is capable of emptying dozens of rounds into a single target at close range. This attack inflicts an extra health level of damage automatically due to sheer volume of fire; however, after emptying the clip from fully automatic fire, the character must spend one action reloading the weapon before it may be fired again.

High-Caliber

Firearms of particularly high caliber can cause crippling wounds with only a few shots. When a high-caliber weapon hits a target, the attacker should make a Simple Test immediately. A win indicates that the target suffers an additional health level of damage from the shot.

Incendiary

Burning weapons cause aggravated wounds to just about anything. Some, like flame-throwers or molotov cocktails, burn the target with streams or explosions of fire, while others such as incendiary rounds ("hot loads") burn the target with superheated ammunition. See the damage section for the effects of fire.

Mass-Trauma

Certain weapons are so powerful they inflict massive damage on a target, literally tearing away portions of flesh. Such weapons score an extra health level of damage when used appropriately.

Speed

Fast weapons can be used to "pre-empt" an opponent's attack, allowing the attacker with the speedier weapon to strike and resolve his challenge first. A character must have the *Melee* Ability to use this special ability, and he must be attacking or otherwise actively using (parrying, disarming) the weapon in order to gain this benefit. Fast weapons only gain a preemptive strike against opponents in hand-to-hand or melee combat.

Since many attacks are handled simultaneously for ease of play (both players testing at once and the winner scoring a hit), this ability is not always very useful. However, if the Storyteller opts to allow each attacker to test individually (attacking striking defender, then defender counter-striking), this ability puts characters with fast weapons on the offensive.

Spray

The weapon can strike several targets at once, as noted under the weapon's specific parameters. The shooter makes one test against all the targets simultaneously. Each target who fails the test suffers the weapon's damage, while each target who succeeds avoids the weapon's damage. The shooter risks only the Traits required to test against each member of the group, and he loses only those Traits if any of the defenders wins the test.

Staking

Staking weapons paralyze vampires when a successful blow penetrates one's heart. The attacker must win or tie two successive Simple Tests in order to successfully stake the vampire.

BIDDING WEAPON TRAITS

During a normal hand-to-hand fight, characters bid Physical Traits against their opponents' Physical Traits. However, if a character is using firearms, he may use Mental Traits instead. If his opponent is also using a firearm, she bids Mental Traits as well. If the opponent is not using a firearm and is merely trying to dodge, then the attacker uses Mental Traits to attack, while the defender uses her Physical Traits to dodge. This instance is one of the few in which Traits associated with different Attributes may be used against one another.

WEAPON EXAMPLES

MELEE WEAPONS

Knife/Dagger — These easily concealed weapons are very common, lightning fast in the hands of a skilled user, and they can also be used as ranged weapons if a character uses the *Athletics* Ability properly.

Bonus Traits: 2

Negative Traits: *Short*

Concealability: Pocket

Damage: One health level

Availability: Any

Special Ability: *Speed:* In close combat against any weapon that has the Negative Traits: *Clumsy, Heavy* or *Slow*, the knife-fighter gains the option to pre-empt the opponent's attacks and strike first in any turn, as long as he has the *Melee* Ability.

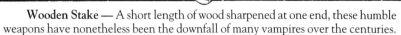

Wooden Stake — A short length of wood sharpened at one end, these humble weapons have nonetheless been the downfall of many vampires over the centuries.

Bonus Traits: 2

Negative Traits: *Short*

Concealability: Jacket

Damage: One health level

Availability: Any

Special Ability: *Staking*: A wooden stake can pierce the heart of a vampire (thus paralyzing the unfortunate Lick) if the wielder wins or ties two successive Simple Tests after striking.

Club/Ax — These two common weapon types can be anything from chair legs to hand axes to billy clubs; one bludgeons while the other cuts, but the essential function is the same.

Bonus Traits: Club: 2, Ax: 3

Negative Traits: *Clumsy*

Concealability: Trenchcoat

Damage: Club — One health level; Ax — Two health levels

Availability: Any

Special Ability: Ax: *Destroy Shield*. Axes render shields useless after three blows.

Fencing Blades — Still popular with many elders, these thin blades rely on speed instead of strength, and they inflict most of their damage from piercing rather than slashing.

Bonus Traits: 2

Negative Traits: *Fragile*

Concealability: Trenchcoat

Damage: One health level

Availability: Any. A fencing foil tends to attract less police attention than an ornamental saber, especially if the character is wearing or carrying fencing gear

Special Ability: *Speed:* In close combat against any weapon that has the Negative Traits: *Clumsy*, *Heavy* or *Slow*, the fencer gains the option to pre-empt the opponent's attacks and strike first in any turn, as long as he has the *Melee* Ability.

Archaic Ranged Weapons

Longbow — These huge, powerful bows make mincemeat of regular armor, and many older Cainites are trained in the arts of archery. Modern compound bows are smaller and use pulley systems to generate powerful pull; these bows do not have the Negative Trait: *Clumsy*, but give the user only five Bonus Traits.

Bonus Traits: 6

Negative Traits: *Fragile, Clumsy, Heavy*

Concealability: No way.

Damage: Two health levels

Availability: Any.

Special Ability: *Armor-Piercing*: Longbows ignore chain armor. *Staking*: Arrows may be used to stake a vampire, if the archer wins or ties two Simple Tests after a successful hit. *Destroy Shield:* One shot from a longbow renders a shield useless.

Firearms

Pistol — This designation covers nearly any sort of small- and medium-caliber handgun commonly encountered, from zip guns and holdout pieces to 9mms and standard police-issue sidearms.

Bonus Traits: 2

Negative Traits: *Loud*

Concealability: Pocket

Damage: Two health levels

Availability: Any, if registered; *Police* 4, *Street* 3 or *Underworld* 2 otherwise.

Heavy Pistol — This designation covers the monsters of the handgun range, from the Desert Eagle to a .454 Cassull. These tremendous guns use high-caliber ammunition to punch large holes in their targets.

Bonus Traits: 2

Negative Traits: *Loud*

Concealability: Jacket

Damage: Two health levels

Availability: Any, if registered; *Police* 4, *Street* 4 or *Underworld* 3 otherwise.

Special Ability: *High-Caliber*: Heavy Pistols allow a Simple Test on a successful hit. Success indicates the target takes an extra level of damage.

Rifle — Favored by many hunters and snipers.

Bonus Traits: 3

Negative Traits: *Loud*

Concealability: None.

Damage: Two health levels

Availability: Any, if registered; *Police* 4, *Street* 4 or *Underworld* 3 otherwise.

Special Ability: *High-Caliber*: Rifles may be loaded with high-caliber ammunition. Note that the character must specifically acquire such ammunition to gain this benefit — it is not included automatically when using a rifle.

Shotgun — This powerful weapon fires a spray of pellets, making targets easy to hit.

Bonus Traits: 3

Negative Traits: *Loud*

Concealability: None

Damage: Two health levels

Availability: Any, if registered. *Police* 4, *Street* 4 or *Underworld* 3 otherwise.

Special Ability: *Spray*: A shotgun may affect up to three targets if they are standing immediately next to each other and are further than 20 feet from the person firing the shotgun. This effect can be gained only if the shotgun is loaded with pellets, not slugs. *Mass-Trauma*: A shotgun can cause an extra health level of damage to a single target standing within five feet.

Submachine Gun — These weapons are very powerful, and they fire a large number of bullets very quickly, making them the favorite weapons of many gangs, where accuracy isn't as important as hitting a large number of targets at the same time. The law requires these guns be sold as non-automatic weapons, with only single-shot capability, but a use of the *Repair* Ability can convert them to fully automatic fire.

Bonus Traits: 2

Negative Traits: *Loud*

Concealability: Jacket

Damage: Two health levels

Availability: Any, if registered and non-automatic. *Police* 4, *Street* 4 or *Underworld* 3 otherwise.

Special Ability: *Spray*: A submachine gun may affect up to five targets if they're standing immediately next to each other and are further than 10 feet from the person firing the gun. *Fully Automatic*: A submachine gun inflicts an additional health level of damage if the entire clip is emptied into a target standing no more than five feet away.

ARMOR

Since it stops incoming damage, armor effectively grants a character extra health levels; these health levels are lost before the character himself suffers any damage in combat. Of course, armor does not soak all attacks — a suit of chain-mail does little good for a character whose blood is being boiled by *Thaumaturgy*, for instance.

Different types of armor can absorb different amounts of punishment before losing their effectiveness; it should be noted that armor that has lost all its health levels is not necessarily completely destroyed, but more likely that it has been temporarily rendered useless instead. Of course, some attacks may destroy armor beyond repair. Fixing armor requires the proper tools and a Static Physical Challenge with the *Repair* Ability.

Armor has two different traits for game purposes. Health levels indicate how many levels of damage the armor can absorb before becoming useless and in need of repair. Negative Traits are the drawbacks a wearer gains for donning a particular type of armor.

Chain-mail — This category covers most medium levels of metal armor, including scale and brigandine. True chain-mail is quite rare in the modern age, but many elders and some mortal Inquisitors keep a suit on hand.

Health levels: 2

Negative Traits: *Heavy*

Availability: Any. Chain-mail generally must be custom made, and it can cost upward of $500 or more.

Plate mail — Extremely expensive and hard to come by, these ornate suits of interlocking metal plates provide excellent protection but sacrifice a great deal of mobility.

Health levels: 3

Negative Traits: *Heavy*, *Clumsy*

Availability: Any. Plate mail generally must be custom-ordered, and it can cost upward of $3000 or more.

Ballistic vest — This basic level of protection shields the wearer from some dangers, and it doesn't attract the same kind of attention that more complicated forms of armor are bound to bring.

Health levels: 2

Negative Traits: *Heavy*

Availability: *Police* 4, or *Underworld* 3

Reinforced (bulletproof) vest — The favored type of armor for military personnel and law enforcement officers expecting dangerous situations, these vests provide excellent protection, even stopping many types of small arms fire.

Health levels: 3

Negative Traits: *Heavy*, *Clumsy*

Availability: *Police* 5, or *Underworld* 4

RANGED COMBAT

Many weapons allow a character to stand at a distance from a target and engage him in combat. In such situations, the character must still go over to the target (after shouting "Bang!" or "Twang!") and engage in a challenge.

If a character has surprised her opponent, even if she loses the first test, she has the option of calling for a second test. Once the second challenge is called, play continues as normal with that new challenge. The target is considered to be surprised for the first attack, and if he has no ranged weapon with which to return fire, he is considered "surprised" for as long as the aggressor can attack him without facing resistance (that is, if he wins on a challenge, she doesn't take damage).

If the target is aware of the attack before it happens, and he has a ranged weapon of his own, he is not considered to be surprised for the first attack. He may shoot back right away, and challenges are resolved as stated.

After the first shot is fired (and the first challenge is resolved), the target may attempt to return fire (assuming he is armed). The loser of a firefight challenge loses a health level.

Characters using the *Athletics* Ability to throw projectiles like knives or axes fall under the same rules for regular ranged combat, including cover. Questions of range should not be a problem, but if it becomes an issue use common sense, and don't forget to make allowances for things like the *Potence* Discipline.

COVER

Fighting with ranged weapons allows combatants to stand some distance apart; participants can therefore "dive for cover." When resolving each ranged combat challenge, each combatant can present one Trait of cover to add to his total number of Traits. These cover Traits may not be used for bidding, but they do add to a player's total if Traits are compared. This cover can take the form of whatever obstacles are around and within reach (*don't* actually dive for them). A Narrator might be required to describe what cover is around, unless the combatants can agree on what cover is available.

If cover is extensive, it may be worth more than one Trait. The number of Traits available for cover is left for challengers to agree on, or for a Narrator to decree. Hiding behind a boulder, for example, might be worth two Traits, while hiding behind a thin wood fence might only count as one. If one combatant goes completely under cover (he cannot be seen at all *and* is thoroughly protected), he is considered impossible to hit. The attacker must change his position to get a clear shot.

MELEE AND BRAWLING

Melee fighting can only occur when two parties are within weapon's reach of each other. Characters using melee weapons often have access to special abilities if they also possess the *Melee* Ability. For example, a trained character using a fencing foil can take advantage of his weapon's speed when fighting a character wielding a battle ax.

Brawling can only occur when two characters are within arm's length of each other. Characters engaged in brawling may use unarmed combat techniques on each other, including trips, kicks, punches, wrestling holds and throws. However, regardless of the description, unless the character possesses some supernatural power or other ability that specifically allows for extra damage, all brawling tests result in one health level of bashing damage.

SPECIALIZED FIGHTING STYLES

Buying a specialized fighting style under the *Melee* or *Brawl* Abilities allows you to describe how your character moves to allow retests and permits a certain flair for your attacks and defenses, but does not allow you to do extra damage or specific injuries.

TWO-GUN MOJO

It's possible to use more than one weapon at a time in combat, though it's quite tricky. Just performing a task with the wrong hand is sufficient to penalize your chance of success; compounding matters by doing something else with the other hand doesn't help any.

For the purposes of simplicity, it's usually easiest to assume that a character is the same-handedness as the player, unless the Merit *Ambidextrous* is taken. Furthermore, these rules do not apply to common uses of both hands, such as typing, playing a musical instrument or working a craft.

When performing a task with the off hand, you suffer a two-Trait penalty. Thus, you must bid a total of three Traits to initiate the challenge, and you have a lower chance of success.

The Merit *Ambidextrous* means that you suffer no penalty for an off-hand, since both of your hands are equally nimble. You still suffer coordination penalties for using both

hands. Thus, if you're *Ambidextrous*, you can perform a task with either hand without penalty, but if you use both hands at once, you must bid two Traits for each hand.

When you specialize in a fighting style you can choose *Two-Weapon Combat* or *Florentine* for your specialty. This negates one penalty Trait from your attacks with the specified form of combat. Thus, instead of bidding two Traits with your primary hand and three with your off hand, you would bid one and two Traits, respectively. Combined with *Ambidexterous*, you can use two weapons at no penalty whatsoever. Storytellers, take note of combat monsters in the making who try this combination. Developing such a specialty should take *months* of training.

When using both hands, you only get one extra action, regardless of *Celerity* and similar speed-altering powers. Split your actions equally between your hands — if you have *Legerity* good for two bonus actions and you're using both hands, you get your normal action, your two *Celerity* actions and your extra hand action, for a total of four actions. These would be split up to two actions with each hand; if you took an action or two to do other things, you'd split the remainder evenly. A leftover action is automatically applied to your primary hand.

CONTESTS OF WILL

Contests of will are an ancient tradition in Kindred society. They occur when two characters lock eyes for the purpose of intimidating each other; the idea is to force one's rival to back down before a conflict actually comes to blows. Success in a contest of wills is determined in one of two ways. First, it is highly recommended that this action be roleplayed out rather than resort to the rules; in this case, if one of the players relents while roleplaying this action, his opponent is considered to be the winner. If a quick result is needed, or if neither of the players relents, a Social Challenge is used to determine the victor instead, with the loser breaking eye contact and losing the contest.

FRENZY

When Kindred undergo the Embrace, the Beast within them is loosed forever, causing them to occasionally succumb to a vicious form of madness where they are little more than a wild animal. While in frenzy a character feels no pain and acts on instinct, using his bare hands and fangs to rip apart anything in his path; friends are targets of the vampire's rage just as often as enemies are. What brings on frenzy in a Kindred can be highly personalized, but triggers common to all vampires are blood hunger, extreme passion, frustration, defeat, humiliation at the hands of a rival or threats to a vampire's friends or loved ones. Players must be consistent with what causes a frenzy; a player cannot ignore something that would normally trigger frenzy simply because it isn't expedient for them to frenzy at this time. Discretion is advised; a character in constant frenzy is no fun to be around, and will likely be "put down" by other vampires.

Succumbing to frenzy is considered shameful and debased among the Kindred of the Camarilla, who pride themselves on maintaining their composure and hate being reminded of the Beast within them. Among the vampires of the Sabbat, frenzy is seen as a powerful weapon, and many Sabbat are trained to coax their Beasts to the surface during combat.

To see if a character resists entering frenzy, the player performs a Static *Self-Control* Challenge (*Self-Control* versus a difficulty based on the stimulus, no Traits risked). Failure indicates that a frenzy takes hold. If the vampire succeeds in the test, he manages to push aside his more feral instincts and is immune to further challenges against the same stimulus for the rest of the scene or conflict.

Characters with the *Instinct* Virtue *always* enter frenzy, unless they have more *Instinct* than double the rating of the frenzy shown on the table, in which case they may choose whether or not to enter frenzy. Once in frenzy, the character can make an

Self-Control/Instinct Difficulties	
Traits	**Stimulus**
One	Smell of blood when hungry
Two	Sight of blood when hungry; harassed; life-threatening situation
Three	Physical provocation or attacks; taste of blood when hungry
Four	Loved one in danger; humiliated
Five	Outright humiliation; mortal insults

Instinct Virtue Test, if desired, to control her actions for one turn. If she wins the test, she manages to direct her frenzy for the turn, though she will still suffer all the usual conditions of frenzy — resistance to injury, inability to use her Mental or Social powers and so on. If the character loses, her frenzy proceeds as normal. In the event of a tie, the character compares her current *Instinct* Traits to the provocation rating to determine whether she can direct her frenzy.

A character can try to instill frenzy in another character by taunting him and calling for a Social Challenge. If the taunting character wins the challenge, the defender must then test to resist frenzy. If the defender wins the challenge, nothing happens. A successful defender is immune to further taunts from the same character for the remainder of the session.

Once in the state of frenzy, a character attacks all those around him without discretion. A frenzied character does not suffer penalties from wounds until reaching torpor or Final Death. Frenzied characters cannot attempt Social Challenges other than ones related to intimidation, though they need not risk a Trait if someone initiates a Social test against them during this time.

A character may fend off frenzy for 10 minutes by expending one Willpower Trait. However, if the frenzy trigger is still present after that time, the vampire must check for frenzy again immediately. Once in frenzy, a character may expend a Willpower Trait to attempt a Static *Self-Control* Challenge to get a hold of himself. A character also gets a free Static Challenge to end the frenzy once the trigger is removed; otherwise, the frenzy burns out on its own 10 minutes later. If a player attempts to make a test of *Self-Control/ Instinct* and fails, she automatically gains the Negative Social Trait: *Callous* or *Condescending* (your choice), though it can be bought off normally.

Another character may attempt to talk a vampire out of frenzy by winning a Social Challenge against him with a difficulty of 10 minus the target Kindred's Humanity/ Path rating. Remember, the frenzied vampire need not risk a Trait during this Social Challenge. Failing such a challenge usually means the frenzied Kindred turns his attention on his would-be savior.

RÖTSCHRECK

Having already cheated death once, most vampires have no desire to try their luck again. This primal survival urge sometimes manifests as a state of utter terror where the vampire flees the object of his fear any way he can; this state is known as Rötschreck. Both Cainite societies consider Rötschreck extremely shameful, and most vampires avoid it at all costs. The Sabbat executes "cowards" without asking what they fled from, and a Camarilla vampire faces rapid Status loss.

All vampires must battle Rötschreck when faced with exposure to fire, sunlight and the presence of especially powerful faith, but in addition to those fundamental

terrors, many Kindred also have Rötschreck triggers related to important personal circumstances. As with frenzy, a Kindred cannot choose to ignore potential Rötschreck triggers just because it wouldn't be expedient to panic.

A vampire who enters Rötschreck flees the object of her fear as directly and rapidly as she can, blindly attacking any obstacles or people that get in her way; if flight proves impossible, the vampire seeks instead to destroy the object of her fear, *then* flee. If for some reason neither fight nor flight is an option, the vampire curls up in abject terror for the duration of the Rötschreck. Note that this fear does not blind the vampire to her self-preservation instincts — a vampire will not leap out a 30-story window to avoid a lit cigarette — but any path that is not obviously suicidal becomes a distinct possibility.

Rötschreck is resisted with a Static *Courage* Challenge (Courage versus Narrator's difficulty, no Traits risked). Rötschreck is otherwise considered identical to frenzy for the purposes of determining its duration, as well as all challenges and Willpower costs necessary to prevent or end it, with *Courage* substituted for *Self-Control/ Instinct* wherever applicable. Characters may also be talked out of Rötschreck just like frenzy.

GOLCONDA
SLAKING THE ENDLESS HUNGER

Some vampires pursue a mystical state of being known as Golconda, where the vampire finally accepts the terms of the Curse. The Camarilla scoffs at the notion of Golconda, calling it a fool's dream, but in the dark of the Final Nights more and more Kindred feel drawn to search out this mystery. The Sabbat and the independent clans consider Golconda beneath notice, a guilt-driven Judeo-Christian fantasy that has no place in such a vicious unlife.

The search is highly personal, and the Storyteller is encouraged to be extremely demanding when it comes to Golconda quests. Bear in mind that Golconda is a goal easily worthy of years of game time and constant progress throughout multiple chronicles. There is only one solid rule for characters on Golconda quests: They must maintain a Humanity rating of at least four Traits and a *Conscience* rating of at least four Traits to remain on the path of Golconda. Slipping below that level will cause mentors to desert a character until he atones for his degeneration. Golconda is not a goal for every character or every player.

Inner peace and transcendent enlightenment aside, characters who manage to achieve Golconda gain several game benefits. A character in Golconda does not expend one Blood Trait per night to awaken, but only one Blood Trait per week. Characters in Golconda also do not frenzy or enter Rötschreck, and supernatural powers that instill such states do not work. Finally, the character may learn all Disciplines equally even if he is not of appropriate generation or clan to learn them. If he ever falls out of Golconda, however, all these benefits disappear immediately.

TRUE FAITH

True Faith is belief in a power, entity, consciousness — sometimes even a purpose — that is greater than oneself, and as such, it is not limited to any particular religion. Even vampires can have it, but even so, only those beings of the most pure character — only the truly selfless, caring, compassionate and courageous have a chance at possessing True Faith. Most Kindred will only come across True Faith when they do battle with the Inquisition or other hunting groups.

Characters may only improve their Faith with exceptional roleplaying and Storyteller approval. The game uses for True Faith are covered exhaustively in **Laws of the Hunt**; however, some basic rules for Faith are included here.

• By brandishing his holy symbol, the bearer gains the Social Trait: *Intimidating* when repelling undead and warding off supernatural powers. If used to strike a supernatural creature, a holy symbol grants the extra Physical Traits *Burning* and

Courage Difficulties	
Traits	**Stimulus**
One	Being bullied; lighter; sunrise
Two	Torch; obscured sunlight
Three	Bonfire; uncovered window during daylight
Four	House fire; being burned
Five	Trapped in a burning building; direct sunlight

Searing, and it inflicts one level of aggravated damage. If a vampire has the Flaw: *Repelled by Crosses*, he takes an additional level of aggravated damage when touched on bare skin by a cross wielded by a person with True Faith.

• A character with True Faith may attempt to repel vampires by brandishing his holy symbol, invoking his belief ("In the name of _____, I command you to be gone," etc.) and employing a Social Challenge. Success means the vampire must flee the area immediately. Failure means the vampire must still back off a few feet and cower before taking action, and the vampire still may not initiate any attacks during the next turn, although she may defend herself normally. A vampire may only resist this use of Faith by attempting to overbid with Willpower; if she currently possesses at least twice as many Willpower Traits as the Faithful character, she remains unaffected. A character may attempt to repel multiple vampires with a group challenge.

It is much easier to lose Faith than gain it; any time a character fails a test in which True Faith was involved, he has a crisis of faith. During such a time, he is one Trait down on all Social Challenges for the remainder of the scene and unable to invoke his Faith again until that Faith Trait has been restored (Narrator's discretion).

BLOOD BOND

Many undead exploit the heady emotions found in drinking vampiric vitae to stir passion in their dead hearts, but it is a dangerous rush, for if a being drinks from the same vampire three times, on three separate nights, she falls under the sway of a mystical state known as the blood bond. A vampire who holds another in bondage is said to be the victim's regnant, while the being who has been bound is called the thrall. Supernatural powers such as *Dominate* cannot change the victim's feelings for her regnant; only true love has a chance at defeating the bond.

A blood bond must be maintained with further drinks. The relationship has an impact as well: thralls who are constantly abused and humiliated by their regnants find their bond fading fast, while thralls who are treated with affection and respect find it harder to resist their regnants.

Blood bonds are used commonly to ensnare mortals and ghouls in a vampire's web, but it is possible for Cainites to bind each other as well — unlike the generation prohibition of *Dominate*, elders may be bound by the vitae of younger vampires. There are three steps in the process, corresponding to the number of drinks a victim has taken from another character:

First drink: At this stage, the drinker has strong flashes of emotion regarding the vampire — the character may find herself daydreaming about the vampire or frequenting areas where she might "stumble across" him. There are no game effects at this stage, but it should be roleplayed.

Second drink: While not the vampire's slave, the drinker definitely considers him a central figure in her life. She may do as she pleases, but she must win or tie a Simple Test to take actions directly harmful to the vampire. Furthermore, she is one Trait down to resist any of the vampire's Social Challenges.

Third drink: Full-scale blood bond. Nothing matches the victim's devotion to the vampire — lovers, spouses, even children become secondary to her regnant. A regnant need not even make eye contact to *Dominate* his thrall; the mere sound of his voice is enough, and the thrall is two Traits down to resist the regnant's *Dominate*. Regnants may hold any number of beings in thralldom; furthermore, once bound, a particular thrall may not be fully bound to another vampire while the original bond lasts.

A thrall may resist the bond temporarily by spending a Willpower Trait. The bond may be resisted for one whole scene if the action taken is relatively indirect, while one Willpower Trait is required *per turn* if the thrall wishes to physically attack her regnant.

A blood bond may be broken permanently only in a few ways. First of all, a thrall who manages to avoid *all* contact whatsoever with her regnant for a period of months equal to 12 minus her permanent Willpower rating may find her bond has decreased to the level of a two-drink bond once more. During this time, the character must roleplay the painful process of separation as well as spend Willpower Traits to battle the "addiction" she has to her regnant (Narrator's discretion).

Second, the thrall is sometimes released from the bond if she kills her regnant, though this condition is nowhere as certain as it may seem. Third, at the Narrator's discretion, a character who possesses the Merit: *True Love* to someone other than her regnant may be able to break the bond with the power of her love, but doing so requires arduous, in-depth roleplaying. Finally, some vampires whisper that the Sabbat knows of ways to break the blood bond, but it imparts them to only those who join the sect.

DERANGEMENTS

Vampires and mortals alike risk developing derangements when faced with overpowering conditions of extreme terror, guilt or anxiety. The Storyteller may decide a derangement is in order after any experience that generates especially intense and unpleasant emotions, or which violates a character's beliefs or ethics severely. All derangements carry "triggers," circumstances which cause the effects of the derangement to become active; once activated, derangements remain in effect for the rest of the scene, and players must modify their character's Traits, attitudes and behavior in accordance with the derangement description. Characters may resist a derangement by expending a Willpower Trait — this effect lasts for one scene, however, if the trigger is still present at the end of that time, the character must spend another Willpower Trait. In the case of particularly intense mental stress, Narrators may rule additional Willpower Traits or a Static Willpower Challenge is required.

It is up to the Storyteller to determine what amount of time and Willpower is required to cure a derangement, and such cures are best left to thoughtful and involved roleplaying rather than simple Trait expenditure. Malkavians may *never* cure the original derangement(s) brought on by their Clan Disadvantage.

Note: There is nothing funny or arbitrary about the way a "crazy" person acts. The insane character is only reacting to the stimuli that he perceives to be real — to *him*, his behavior is perfectly normal. Players should never forget the **Mind's Eye Theatre** rules of safety still apply when roleplaying derangements.

Bulimia

Bulimic characters salve their guilt and insecurity by overindulging in activities that comfort them — in this instance, consuming food (or blood, for vampires). Characters with this affliction will gorge themselves as much as possible when under stress, then purge their systems through drastic means and consume more. Characters with this derangement must make a Static *Conscience/ Conviction* Challenge when feeding; failure means the vampire feeds until his blood pool is full, whether or not he needs the blood. If forcibly kept from feeding, the vampire must resist frenzy.

Crimson Rage

A character with this derangement is prone to experiencing fits of anger with little provocation. While the two bear certain resemblances, this state is quite different from frenzy — frenzy is the instincts of the vampiric Beast, while *Crimson Rage* is a character's own feelings of helplessness and inadequacy. Characters with *Crimson Rage* are not protected from being pushed over the edge into frenzy while insane, however. Whenever this derangement is active, the character gains the Negative Traits: *Violent* x 2 and *Impatient*.

Fugue

Characters suffering this affliction react to stress by adopting a specific set of behaviors; in the process they suffer "blackouts" or periods of memory loss. Whenever confronted by extreme stress, the character must win a Static Willpower Challenge; failure means the character blacks out and the player must roleplay the character's trancelike state. Otherwise, control of the character passes to a Narrator for a scene, who dictates the actions the character takes in order to remove the stress. At the end of the fugue, the character "regains consciousness" with no memory of his actions.

Hysteria

Characters with this derangement are unable to properly control their emotions when subjected to stress or pressure, becoming vulnerable to wild mood swings and fits of intense violence. The vampire must test to resist frenzy any time such stress is present; in addition, whenever the vampire fails in a particularly stressful or prominent instance, she enters frenzy automatically. (Narrators have final say on what classifies as such a dramatic failure.)

Immortal Terror

An insanity most recently identified with a certain reluctant movie vampire, this madness stems from the Cainite's inability to deal with the true scope of his immortality. Terrified by the real implications of living *forever*, the vampire copes by developing a strong unconscious "death wish." Whenever the character is confronted by direct evidence of his immortality — such as attending a funeral or watching a mortal ally die — the character must make a Static Willpower Challenge (difficulty four Traits) to avoid immediately undertaking actions that might result in his destruction. Such actions can be as indirect as breaching the Masquerade by telling a reporter about Kindred society, as long as the act carries potentially deadly consequences. Note that the vampire is not consciously aware that he seeks his own destruction, and he resists attempts to persuade him otherwise.

Manic-Depression

This derangement causes a character to suffer devastating mood swings. Whenever the character fails to achieve a personal goal, she must win a Static Willpower Challenge (no Traits risked) or fall into a depressive state for a number of scenes determined by the Narrator. While depressed, her Willpower Traits are considered halved (round down, minimum one) for purposes of Trait comparison, and she may not spend Blood Traits to raise her Physical Traits. After that, she enters a period of upbeat energy and excitement, pursuing her goals obsessively for a number of scenes equal to the time spent in depression. During this manic time she is one Trait down to resist frenzy.

Megalomania

These individuals have made power the focus of their existence, and such characters must always be the most potent individuals in their environment; where the power stems from is irrelevant, just so long as they are dominant. They believe that other people are divided into two classes: lesser beings and beings elevated beyond their worth. Rivals are considered "competition." Due to their supreme confidence, they are considered one Trait up on all Willpower tests while their derangement is active, but they must also make a Willpower test (difficulty six Traits) to resist any opportunity to commit diablerie during that time.

213

Multiple Personalities

A character with this derangement has suffered mental anguish so severe that his mind reacted by creating additional personas. Each personality is relevant to the trauma that caused it, and the player should work with the Storyteller to determine how many personalities are present, their Natures and what triggers a particular personality. When a personality is triggered, it assumes control until the conditions it was created to deal with have passed. Characters can manifest different Abilities and even Virtues for each personality (all such Traits must still be purchased normally — what a personality *believes* it can do can be different from what it is actually capable of), but any such arrangements must be worked out with the Storyteller.

Obsessive/Compulsive

Characters suffering from this derangement are driven to control their environment. Obsessive characters keep one aspect of their life constant — personal cleanliness or keeping things quiet, for example. Compulsive characters perform specific actions or sets of actions, such as washing their hands constantly or always feeding from mortals in a ritualistic fashion. Obsessive/ compulsive characters are one Trait up to resist any attempt to *Dominate* or otherwise coerce them from their set behaviors, but they frenzy automatically if forcibly prevented from adhering to their derangement.

Paranoia

Paranoid beings believe that all their woes and suffering stem from an outside source. Many afflicted beings come up with intricate theories about just who is against them and why; those they suspect of being "one of *them*" are often subject to swift and brutal violence. Paranoid characters trust no one, not even those blood bound to them, and they have a difficult time interacting with others. They are one Trait down on all Social tests while their derangement is active, and any sign of suspicious activity forces them to test to resist frenzy.

Regression

Characters suffering from this affliction avoid facing responsibilities or consequences by retreating to a younger state where less was required of them. During this state they may alternate between times of whimsy and temper tantrums, but they will always seek to put a more powerful individual between them and whatever is plaguing them. Victims are two Traits down on all Mental Challenges.

Sanguinary Animism

This illness is unique to vampires, a response to guilt for feeding on mortals. Afflicted vampires believe that they do not merely consume a victim's blood, but part of his soul as well. The vampire hears her victim's voice inside her head and is assaulted by "memories" of the victim's life — all created by the vampire's subconscious. Whenever the vampire feeds on a mortal, she must make a Static Willpower Challenge; success means she is distracted as above and is one Trait down on all challenges for the remainder of the scene. Failure means the character gains a second angry, reproachful personality bent on driving her to ruin. The character is at a one-Trait penalty to all actions for the duration of the madness, and he must roleplay the inner conflict involved; this madness lasts until the moments just before dawn.

Schizophrenia

Individuals with this derangement have had their psyche fractured by terrible, unresolvable inner conflicts. Most people conceive of this type of disorder when they envision insanity; victims might imagine crucified rabbits floating after them, or swear that their dead father is telling them to murder their uncle. This disorder is anything but arbitrary — the player should work with the Storyteller to determine a general set of behaviors relevant to the original trauma. Kindred with this derangement are unpredictable and dangerous — in situations where their inner conflict flares up, they must automatically retest any win to resist frenzy, and they are two Traits down on all Willpower tests.

DIABLERIE

Of all the crimes known to the Kindred, none is more feared than the soul-stealing sin known as diablerie, or the Amaranth. Those convicted of this crime suffer the harshest punishments in the Camarilla, and the mere suspicion of diablerie is enough to spark city-wide blood hunts. Still, no punishment is harsh enough to end this forbidden practice, for diablerie offers a seductive way of increasing one's power.

Committing Diablerie

Diablerie is divided into four distinct stages. First the diablerist must incapacitate his target; only after the target is physically immobilized may diablerie commence. The diablerist then drains her victim dry, taking one Blood Trait automatically per turn. Then the diablerist must strip the target's health levels away until she puts him in torpor (if he isn't there already). The target may resist this process with a Physical Challenge per health level, but he may bid only stamina-related Traits, and he cannot injure the diablerist as a result of the challenge. If the diablerist ever cannot match the victim's Physical Traits, she falls away and the target can die quietly. Likewise, a vampire draining health levels cannot be targeted by any Mental or Social Challenges, but she also cannot defend herself, and any attempts to attack her or pull her away succeed automatically.

If a victim is drained dry of blood and reduced to torpor, the final struggle begins, as the diablerist tries to ensnare the victim's soul before it can escape. This effort is a Physical Challenge, and the victim is three Traits up. The diablerist may continue trying until she can no longer match the victim's Physical Traits — success means she absorbs the target's soul into her own, while ultimate failure means the target's spirit flees to the afterlife.

A character may have other characters assist him in incapacitating his target and even in draining the target of Blood Traits and health levels, but only one Kindred can gain the ultimate benefits of diablerie. However, the seduction of the process is very strong — a character who wishes to halt diablerie after the third stage

ACTION OF DIABLERIST	CHALLENGE REQUIRED
Stage One	
Incapacitate target	Beat 'em, stake 'em
Stage Two	
Drain blood	Automatic one Blood Trait drained/ action
Stage Three	
Drain health levels;	Physical Challenge against victim; victim cannot harm diablerist, but diablerist cannot defend against outside attacks
Stage Four	
Drain Essence	Physical Challenge; victim is three Traits up.
Halt Diablerie	
Before Stage Three	No challenge required; diablerist may simply stop.
After Stage Three	Spend Willpower Trait and succeed at Static Mental Challenge against a difficulty of three Traits.

must spend a Willpower Trait and succeed at a Static Mental Challenge against three Traits, or she will attempt to continue the diablerie process herself.

Note: You *cannot* diablerize anything but another vampire. A mortal soul, with no torpor state in between life and death, flees as soon as its body is killed, as does the soul of a faerie, werebeast or any other supernatural critter some Lick makes a meal out of. You may drain such beings of their blood and even kill them, but soul *tartar* is strictly a Cainite delicacy.

Rewards of Diablerie

On successful completion of diablerie, the diablerist is overcome by euphoria, and he must check to avoid frenzy immediately; the diablerist has literally taken the victim's soul into her own. The true benefit of diablerie becomes apparent, however, if the victim was of a lower generation than the diablerist (e.g., a ninth-generation vampire diablerizing a seventh-generation vampire): By stealing the other Kindred's soul, the diablerist effectively raises her own generation by one, bringing her closer to Caine and otherwise conferring all the benefits of the new generation on the vampire. The character also gains two extra Experience Traits at the end of the session.

If the victim was of much greater power (five or more generation levels), the diablerist may gain more than one generation; ultimately, however, the decision is up to the Storyteller.

If the victim was sufficiently powerful, the diablerist may experience a temporary surge in her Disciplines. Any increases are granted solely at the Narrator's discretion, and in no event do these boosted Disciplines last for more than one scene.

Perils of Diablerie

Many neonates believe diablerie to be the perfect crime: the body is destroyed in the process, making it difficult to secure enough evidence to support an accusation of murder. However, diablerists quickly learn that there are several ways of learning the identity of those who have committed this heinous sin. Storytellers are encouraged to remember the horrific magnitude of the crime and ensure that diablerie never goes on casually.

• First, and most importantly, a character with Humanity *always* loses at least one Humanity Trait *permanently* for committing such a heinous act, and he might even lose more if the deed was especially foul — no test, no appeal. Even characters on a Path stand to lose a Path Trait for such a horrible crime, unless their Path specifically condones it.

• A vampire using the Auspex Discipline of *Aura Perception* may detect diablerie on a character's aura for up to three months after the diablerie was committed; this crime appears as black veins running through the offender's aura.

• Likewise, a vampire using the *Thaumaturgy* Discipline power *A Taste for Blood* may detect diablerie the character has committed, *regardless* of how long ago the crime occurred.

• In the Camarilla, a vampire revealed to have committed diablerie is subject to an immediate blood hunt, and he may even have the blood hunt extended to other cities if her crime was heinous enough. What's worse, many such blood hunts have stipulations allowing the hunters to feed on the blood of the diablerist herself, and many princes look the other way if the hunters "accidentally" diablerize the criminal themselves. This legalized kinslaying makes most young Kindred eager to expose any diablerists among them.

• Certain legends speak of diablerists displaying some of the mannerisms of their victims, especially if their victim was exceptionally strong-willed or of a greatly lower generation than the diablerist. Naturally, clever Storytellers will be quick to pick up on this trait when dealing with habitual diablerists.

STATUS

Kindred have developed many intricate rules of protocol and procedure when dealing with each other. Power-hungry vampires vie for positions of importance in the

great Jyhad constantly, and a vampire's reputation can be more valuable than any Influence or Discipline in some situations. Learning to play the power-games of the elders is a long and arduous task for neonates, but in the end one that serves most of them well — or hastens their demise.

Status is the measure of a vampire's reputation, and is measured in Traits. Most often, it usually stems from an office held among the local Kindred, from prince to primogen to scourge. Such posts are never given out, and those who hold them tend to defend them zealously. However, a vampire may also gain Status by being influential in the city's business, performing extraordinary deeds or by simply catching the right eyes at the right time.

Camarilla Status Traits: *Acknowledged, Admired, Adored, Cherished, Esteemed, Exalted, Famous, Faultless, Feared, Honorable, Influential, Just, Praised, Respected, Revered, Trustworthy, Well-Connected, Well-Known.*

Troupes should feel free to invent new Status Traits to suit their own stories and the reputations of the characters receiving the Traits.

GAINING AND LOSING STATUS

All vampires who have been officially "accepted" by the prince acquire a single Status Trait: *Acknowledged.* Failure to possess this Trait means that a character cannot expect even the most simple favors from local Kindred, and he may even be hunted by the scourge if the prince discovers his presence. Most **Masquerade** characters will either start with this, or acquire it early on in the chronicle.

Characters may gain Status by helping uphold the Traditions (especially the Masquerade), doing favors for the prince or an elder, saving the unlife of a prominent Kindred, or defeating a Sabbat menace in the city. A city officer (such as the sheriff or keeper of Elysium) may recommend a Kindred for Status if she has been particularly useful or has assisted them in their work. On occasion, the prominent may award Status to those who hindered their enemies or overthrew them, but such notice may not always be a good thing.

Naturally, a character may lose Status as easily as he gains it (if not more so). Falsely accusing another vampire of a crime, violating the Traditions, committing diablerie or refusing to recognize the Status of another Kindred are but a few of the ways to earn such displeasure. Of course, if there are no witnesses to report such violations.

A character may never gain more than one Status Trait per story. There are two exceptions to this rule: if the prince rewards or sanctions an additional Trait, or if the Status Traits are conferred when a Kindred assumes an office in Kindred society. However, a character can *lose* more than one Status per story,

USING STATUS

Status comes in two types: permanent and temporary. Permanent Status is recorded on the character sheet, and is a measure of a character's actual standing in Kindred society; permanent Status losses or gains are added or removed from your character sheet. By contrast, the loss or gain of temporary Status has no effect on permanent Status and tends to fluctuate more. Temporary Status Traits can be represented with Status Cards (since they tend to change hands often).

You may bid a Status Trait instead of a regular Trait in any applicable Social Challenge. You may also choose to add Status Traits to your Social Traits during a Social Challenge if Traits are compared. You must tell your opponent when you wish to use your Status Traits in these ways, however, since they may choose to ignore them if they like. Such a disrespectful act typically means a loss of permanent Status for the offending Kindred, unless the vampire ignored was far less influential than the offender. Some form of punishment should be expected, though — elders consider those who flout the system dangerously disruptive.

Keeping tabs on Status can become quite a chore for one Storyteller to handle. It is therefore recommended that troupes assign a special Narrator, called the Gossip, to keep a *written* record of all important uses of Status (like loans, boons or snubs) to prevent future arguments. Players should report Status changes or activities like boons or snubs to the Gossip as soon as the game permits.

Examples of Status

The following are some examples of the uses and benefits of Status:

• Temporary Status may be used to add to your Social Traits during an applicable Social Challenge. (Note: This benefit does *not* include Discipline use, unless the Storyteller approves of such usage specifically.)

• Status is a measure of a character's creditability. In any situation where it is one vampire's word against another, Status can be the determining factor. The same is true in the case of accusing another of a crime in which there is no concrete evidence. In all such cases, the character with the most Status is the one whose word is accepted.

• You may loan temporary Status to another to show your favor, though the individual to which you made the loan must return it immediately on the asking. The bearer may spend this Trait as a temporary Trait, after which it is gone for the duration of the story. (This is the only way a character's temporary Status can rise above her permanent Status rating.) Loaned Status can be used exactly as you would use your own. You can give only one Trait of Status to any one person in this fashion.

• You must possess at least one Trait of Status in order to petition the prince for any reason.

• Anyone of higher Status may remove permanent Status from those lower than themselves at a cost of one permanent Status Trait per Trait removed. Temporary Status may be removed in the same fashion. This is often done as punishment, including removing the Status of Acknowledged and thus leaving the person at the mercy of the scourge.

• You may grant permanent Status to another of your own clan if he has less than half your permanent Status. The cost for such a boon is one temporary Status Trait, and the boon must be made publicly, such as during a meeting of the primogen or another such gathering.

• A clan may remove one Status Trait from an elder of the clan by expending a group total of permanent Status Traits equal to the elder's permanent Status. The primogen may also lower the prince's permanent Status in the same fashion.

• Remember, you may only gain one Status Trait per story, but you may lose more than one Trait. Again, there are two exceptions to this rule: Status granted or sanctioned by the prince, and Status received for assuming a station.

Stations

There are eight official stations that a Kindred may hold, each of which grants Status within a city. Cities with small Kindred populations may double up certain stations, or even leave positions vacant. It is highly recommended that the most powerful stations should remain in the hands of Narrators and more experienced players, with newer players learning the ropes before taking a shot at attaining a station.

Certain powers and responsibilities are inherent in each of these stations, and all powers that a station confers are lost immediately if a character is removed from or relinquishes it. The following is a list of the eight standard stations:

The Prince

• The prince of a city automatically gains three additional Status Traits: *Exalted, Well-Known* and *Famous*. He can never lose these Traits permanently while remaining prince.

• The prince can remove one permanent Status Trait from someone at a cost of one temporary Status Trait per Trait removed.

• The prince can grant permanent Status Traits to any Kindred at a cost of one temporary Trait for each Trait awarded. The prince (and only the prince) may thus break

the rule of only gaining one Status Trait per story, allowing a character to gain more than one Trait. If a prince wishes to confer more than three permanent Status Traits on another Kindred in a single session, the fourth and subsequent Traits will cost the prince permanent Status instead of temporary Traits. It does not cost the prince temporary Status to award a Kindred the first Status Trait when she is first Presented. The Trait: *Acknowledged* is conferred automatically as long as the prince chooses to recognize the neonate.

Seneschal

• The seneschal gains the following two additional Status Traits: *Cherished* and *Esteemed*. The character can never lose these Traits permanently while remaining seneschal.

• The seneschal can act in the prince's stead when the prince is out of the city. He is therefore entitled to all of the powers of the prince, although the prince may reverse or revoke them at any time.

Primogen

• Primogen members each receive the additional Status Trait: *Revered* when they join the primogen. As long as the character remains one of the primogen, she cannot lose this Trait permanently.

• Primogen may grant or remove permanent Status Traits to or from any member of their clan at a cost of one temporary Status Trait for each Trait granted or removed.

Harpies

• The leader of the harpies receives the additional Status Trait: *Influential* on attaining the position. As long as the character remains the leader, he cannot lose this Trait permanently.

• The harpy automatically gets one temporary Status Trait from each member of the primogen, who bestow these Status Traits to demonstrate their support of the harpies. The harpy, in turn, may use these Traits however she desires, even against the owner.

• The harpy may remove one permanent Status Trait from a Kindred who has backed out of a boon or is part of a major scandal. There is no cost for doing so, although there must be a grain of truth to the scandal. The harpy must produce some sort of evidence at a gathering of Kindred, at which time the Status Trait is removed.

• The harpy may restore Status he has removed at a cost of one temporary Trait per Trait removed.

• The leader of the harpies may sponsor lesser harpies by giving another Kindred a Status Trait of his own. Lesser harpies may remove temporary Status just as the head harpy removes permanent Status, although their leader may choose to make such loss permanent.

Whips

• Whips have the same powers as the primogen, although they do not gain an additional Status Trait, and their powers may be revoked at any time by the primogen of their clan.

Sheriff

• The sheriff gains the additional Status Trait: *Feared* when he attains the position. While he remains sheriff, he cannot permanently lose this Trait.

• The sheriff may demand that any Kindred within the city accompany him for questioning or judgment. Failure to do so causes the offender to lose one permanent Status Trait.

• The sheriff is immune to the powers of the keeper of Elysium (those conferred by the position, that is; he must still honor the Traditions).

• The sheriff may sponsor deputies by giving another Kindred a Status Trait of his own. These deputies have the same powers as the sheriff, but the sheriff may revoke their authority at any time.

Keeper of Elysium

• The keeper of Elysium gains the additional Status Trait: *Honorable* on attaining the office. As long as the character remains the keeper, he cannot lose this Trait permanently.

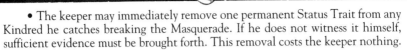

• The keeper may immediately remove one permanent Status Trait from any Kindred he catches breaking the Masquerade. If he does not witness it himself, sufficient evidence must be brought forth. This removal costs the keeper nothing.

Scourge

• The scourge gains the additional Status Trait: *Feared* when he attains the position. While he remains scourge, he cannot permanently lose this Trait.

• The scourge can harass, detain or destroy without penalty any Kindred that have been created without permission from the prince, or who have not been presented formally to the prince.

• If the scourge discovers another character harboring or abetting vampires created without the prince's permission or who have not been presented formally, he may remove a permanent Status Trait from that character immediately. This removal costs the scourge nothing, but he must present sufficient evidence of the crime to the prince. Should the prince find the evidence insufficient or be unconvinced of the crime, he may return the stripped Status to the character.

• Not all cities have reinstated the office of scourge, and even those that have do not consider it a noble aspiration, but rather a necessary evil born of the Final Nights.

PRESTATION

Prestation is the name the Kindred give for the art of using Status, and technically, it is defined as when one Kindred officially becomes indebted to another vampire for services rendered. In reality, however, prestation is far more complicated a system than that, and its rules are enforced with lethal zeal by its participants.

Players should first make it clear who's doing the favor and who's receiving it. The receiver owes a boon to his bestower which must be categorized as a trivial, minor, major, blood or life boon. The players then agree on either an appropriate number of Status Traits which the receiver then gives the bestower, or they may make other arrangements such as loaning Influence Traits rather than Status. Status Traits given in this fashion are known as Boon Traits. The arrangement must be made amenable to all Kindred involved in the deal, and any other stipulations or clauses carried on the boon must be announced then. Kindred who bestow a boon typically only require one thing: "You may not take any physical action against me for the duration of this boon."

The bestower may continue to use the Boon Traits just as he would any other loaned Status Traits. However, the bestower's loss of Boon Traits is only temporary — they are restored at the beginning of the next story. The primary difference between Boon Traits and other loaned Traits is that the original owner of the Traits may not request their return as usual with such Traits; they may only be returned once the boon has been settled.

The only way for a receiver to rid herself of a boon permanently is to repay or ignore the favor. Breaking boons is a serious insult in Kindred society. Ignoring a favor not only costs the receiver Status, but it also risks the ire of the bestower. Regardless of the standing of the bestower, if the receiver ignores a major, blood or life boon, the receiver always loses Status — nobody likes a vampire who brushes off someone who just went through serious hardship on his behalf.

GIVING THE DEVIL HIS DUE: REPAYING PRESTATION DEBTS

Getting yourself out of debt is usually an event arranged through roleplaying. Typically, players eliminate boons by returning equivalent favors. However, if the bestower is in sufficient danger, you might pay off your debt by returning only a small favor; indeed, you might even be able to put the original bestower in your debt! It all rests on a sense of timing and a character's skill at bartering. Other Kindred may resent you for doing so, but in crisis a matter of prestation may seem a small price to pay. A favor is as valuable as the Traits associated with it. Thus a minor boon (two Traits) and a major boon (three Traits) are fair compensation for a life boon (five Traits).

Trivial boons are one-time favors, such as protecting someone for the evening, aiding someone with a Discipline or supporting another's political move.

Minor boons can last more than one evening, and they usually entail some sort of inconvenience, such as allowing safe passage through a hostile city, revealing crucial information or disposing of a threat.

Major boons usually entail a great expenditure of time or resources on the bestower's part. The effects of the favor usually last for many game sessions. An example of such a boon would be teaching the receiver a new Discipline, or purchasing a nightclub to serve as the receiver's haven.

Blood boons occur when the bestower places herself in a potentially life-threatening situation in order to help the receiver. Thus the name "blood boon": The bestower is willing to shed her blood for the receiver.

Life boons involve the bestower actively risking her immortal life for the receiver so that the receiver may live.

CAMARILLA JUSTICE

Justice within the city is typically handled by the prince. Most Kindred justice is harsh and abrupt, as infractions of the Traditions almost always carry a sentence of either death or exile, though some princes may insist that an offender be blood bound to himself and/or the primogen council instead. Only the primogen council can reverse a prince's decision, and it can do so only when they have the political might to back their veto. The primogen council must collectively spend temporary Status Traits equal to the number of permanent Status Traits possessed by the prince to effectively reverse a decision; failure to reach the appropriate amount of Status causes each of the primogen to lose an additional Status Trait.

One of the most important powers of a prince is his ability to call a blood hunt; all the Kindred in a city must aid in tracking down the guilty party and serving the death sentence. Players involved in a blood hunt are reminded not to go overboard while in pursuit; likewise, the player of the character under the blood hunt should realize how heavily the odds are stacked against him and accept the decision with grace.

The only true, across-the-board authorities in the Camarilla are the justicars, mighty Kindred who act as judge, jury and executioner. Elected to a term of 13 years and empowered to enforce Kindred law however they see fit, a justicar's ruling may only be challenged by another justicar. One justicar exists for each of the six Camarilla member clans, and they answer only to the Inner Circle of the Camarilla. A justicar may call a conclave at any time to discuss a problem or handle a matter of justice; all Camarilla vampires in the area are permitted to attend. Kindred sentenced at a conclave may only appeal by requesting an ordeal, which takes the form of an exacting quest executed within a demanding time limit, and failure always results in death.

Justicars typically send representatives, called archons, before arriving themselves. Archons are some of the strongest and most capable Kindred around, and a city hosting an archon is advised to do whatever she asks and do it quickly, as an archon can easily call for others of her kind or even for her justicar. If an archon "disappears" while on assignment, an investigation by powerful Kindred is soon to follow.

THE SABBAT

SABBAT STATUS TRAITS

Status within the Sabbat is useful only within the sect, just as Camarilla Status is only useful within the Camarilla. Status does not function between sects because they despise each other so strongly that any Status the other would possess would have little or no effect on their antagonists. The Traits themselves also differ, because the Sabbat holds different values to be worthy of admiration than the Camarilla does.

Sabbat Status Traits: *Battle-Scarred, Blessed, Blooded, Confirmed, Devoted, Enlightened, Enriched, Feared, Hunted, Infamous, Initiated, Loyal, Ominous, Proven, Respected* and *Undefeated.*

Troupes should feel free to invent new Status Traits to suit their own stories and the reputations of the characters receiving the Traits.

Vampires who have not yet acquired the Sabbat Status Trait: *Initiated* cannot have or gain any Status until they acquire that Trait.

SABBAT STATIONS

Sabbat hierarchy stems from the Regent, the leader of the Sabbat. There is only one Regent at a time, and she is advised by prisci (singular: priscus) and cardinals. Beneath them are archbishops, who control a single city. Within the city, bishops act more or less equivalently to primogen. Paladins/ templars act as bodyguards and enforcers for Sabbat leaders; they are forbidden to join the Black Hand, but are formidable nonetheless. Each pack has a pack leader, who commands and inspires her packmates; a pack priest, who leads rituals and ensures that Sabbat rites are properly observed; and an abbot, who oversees the safety of the communal haven and other day-to-day matters.

GAINING AND LOSING SABBAT STATUS

Most Sabbat are fiercely protective of Status accumulated as a result of deeds they've performed, and they tend to take attempts to remove such recognition very badly. Sabbat may remove Traits from fellow pack members by reaching a pack consensus; if the entire pack feels a removal is necessary, then the Trait is simply scratched off. Traits based on past experience such as *Blooded* cannot be removed unless they were achieved by the pack as a whole, but ones based on pack opinion like *Proven* can be removed easily. Status may also be removed by those with more Status Traits and a higher rank within the Sabbat. Superiors should beware of the great loyalty that packs feel toward their leaders; removing Status might cause a pack to recognize their leader's failings, but it just as easily might cause them to mutiny.

Characters may gain Status in identical ways to how it is lost: pack consensus or a decision from higher up. Individual high-ranking characters who wish to award Status must possess at least five permanent Status Traits themselves; packs seeking to praise their comrade must have a group total of at least seven permanent Status Traits. In order for the pack to award Status, each member of the party must spend one Status Trait. For every two Traits spent, the newly elected character may gain one Status Trait, as long as no more than three new Traits are gained in addition to his current Status.

SABBAT RITUALS

USING RITUALS IN A GAME SETTING

The Sabbat places great importance on rituals, since they bolster morale and reinforce the doctrines of the sect. Rituals within the Sabbat also serve as tests. Many were created for the sole purpose of testing the strength and endurance of the warriors involved, and the Sabbat respects and encourages this with its many rituals.

KINDS OF RITUALS

The rituals of the Sabbat can be divided into three basic groups: the *Auctoritas Ritae*, the *Ignoblis Ritae* and the customs of each particular pack. All Sabbat practice the very traditional *Auctoritas Ritae*. Most packs, depending on their particular pack makeup and goals at the time, practice the *Ignoblis Ritae* in different ways. Each pack also develops its own customs, which often take ritual forms and change with time and battles fought.

AUCTORITAS RITAE

This list of *Auctoritas Ritae* is, by no means, exhaustive. It merely lists the ones most common to and useful in **Laws of the Night** games.

The Creation Rites

The Vaulderie

Monomacy

Sermons of Caine

War Parties — This ritual occurs when two or more packs go on the warpath to acquire the blood of a Camarilla elder.

Wild Hunt — The Wild Hunt is the Sabbat equivalent of the blood hunt. Archbishops usually call Wild Hunts, but packs have been known to spread the word on their own.

Games of Instinct

IGNOBLIS RITAE

These rituals change with each pack that performs them.

Acceptance Rites — Packs use this ritual to accept a new pack leader or priest, or to welcome a new recruit to her new standing as True Sabbat and to award Status Traits on their members.

Initiation Rites

Welcome and Farewell Rites

Blessings — This ritual can be used at any time to bless the pack or an individual who has a specific quest. The pack usually receives a Blessing before fights, invading enemy territory or going after a desired object or individual. Blessings often occur during the Vaulderie since blood is required.

Call to Caine

Confession

Ghost Dance

Jyhad Rites

Oaths of Fealty — This rite is incorporated into other Sabbat rites, most commonly the Vaulderie. After passing the chalice around the first time, each individual pauses before drinking from it and promises loyalty to the pack. She then drinks and passes the chalice.

Sacrificial Rites

Pack Creed

Thanksgiving Ritual

Sunrise Service

Rituals of Justice — These are rituals the Sabbat isn't supposed to perform without Sabbat officials, but most packs do anyway. Often the pack gathers in two lines, with the accused bound and laid between them; the accused must then answer questions posed by the pack leader or anyone the pack leader permits to speak. The pack will either agree he is guilty and punish him as they see fit, or if they determine that the accused is innocent, the accuser is normally punished in his place.

USING THE *IGNOBLIS RITAE*

The *Ignoblis Ritae* can be used as often or as little as the players desire, and players should also feel free to create their own rituals for the pack to use. Storytellers may allow Trait gain in the form of temporary bonus Traits to packs who observe certain rituals. For example, a pack that performs a ritual of strength before entering battle might receive an additional Physical Trait for the duration of the anticipated contest. Gift Traits must *always* be Storyteller-approved, and they last only until the end of a specific task. However, use of Gift Traits is an excellent way of encouraging use of the *Ignoblis Ritae*, provided it does not upset play balance.

FUN AND GAMES

Of course, all slaughter of the infidel servants of the Antediluvians and no play makes the Sabbat dull vampires, and it should come as no surprise that the Sabbat have

invented many ways to "relax" and enjoy their power. The Sabbat typically cause a great deal of mayhem when they decide to have fun, and packs should feel free to come up all manner of creative games that express their pack's sense of humor (or horror).

Note: Not all packs enjoy games, and given the frankly inhuman nature of these games, players should *never* be forced to participate if they find it too unsettling out of character. Of course, all the **Mind's Eye Theatre** rules of conduct and safety still apply (more strictly than normal, if anything).

EXPANDED RULES FOR AUCTORITAS RITAE

CREATION RITES

Ritualistic as they are, Storytellers are encouraged to keep the game mechanics to a minimum during the Creation Rites, and focus instead on making the process as vivid and harrowing as possible.

However, for those in need of them, some rules are provided here. The Creation Rites take a minimum of one hour to perform, during which time the characters involved cannot interact with anyone else. The idea is to give characters a sense of having been through a grueling ordeal and appreciate the effort it takes to initiate a member.

One of the Sabbat must knock the prospective member unconscious with a blow to the head; then the would-be Sabbat is Embraced and buried. The pack waits to see if the recruit is strong enough to tear her way out of the earth. At the end of the hour, the potential Sabbat must claw her way out, winning two out of the three Simple Tests against the Storyteller in order to rise from the grave; only one success means the vampire is stuck halfway. The character may make one retest for every Physical Trait she is willing to spend, and successes needed to climb out are cumulative. The other players are not allowed to see the results of the test out of character; either they see a hand emerge, or they begin to wonder what's taking so long.

Packs are advised to have a fresh blood on hand, because newly Embraced Cainites emerge completely bloodless and crazed. They will attack every blood source they see, and they will not stop drinking until they have filled their blood pool to capacity. Until that time, they cannot be the target of Mental or Social Challenges. Furthermore, the Creation Rites give all new Sabbat a temporary derangement of some kind; this derangement typically lasts only a few sessions, although a particularly traumatic experience might cause a more long-lasting illness.

After the Emergence

Once all strong new Sabbat members have fed, the pack performs the Vaulderie to cement their loyalty. It is usually the duty of a particular vampire's sire to begin instructing the younger Kindred in the ways of Sabbat doctrine, Discipline use, and any other information the neonate might need to know. After becoming Sabbat, there is no returning to her old ways; former blood bonds are broken, and a new, more powerful one has taken their place.

VAULDERIE AND VINCULUM

Of all the *Auctoritas Ritae*, the Vaulderie constitutes the most important ritual the Sabbat practices by far. All vampires who share in the Vaulderie are effectively blood bound to each other, but the effects are deeper still than any regular blood bond.

Vaulderie Rules

• Find a chalice, cup, bowl or some other physical representation thereof (hats do nicely in a pinch) and dig around for those Blood Traits.

• Each character present should place between two and four Blood Traits into the chalice. It is the privilege of the pack leader or vampire of highest rank to put in the highest number of Traits, to exceed the number of participants. The pack leader or priest then mixes the Traits around and passes the chalice back around the circle.

• Each individual randomly draws the same number of Traits he or she contributed. The individuals (indicated by some mark on the Blood Trait) on your ritually acquired Blood Traits are those for whom you feel a heightened bond for the duration of the night or until the Vaulderie is performed again.

A Clarification of the Heightened Bond

Sometimes, as a result of the Vaulderie, you wind up with a blood pool consisting of numerous Blood Traits from other characters. In such cases, the predominance of certain character's Blood Traits over others' effectively increases your Vinculum rating to them one notch: Once your Vinculum rating rises to a certain level, you must spend Willpower to even plot against the person. You may *not* harm, betray or fail to defend these individuals intentionally. An agreed Monomacy is the only exception.

Erase the markings on all acquired Blood Traits and replace them with your own. In order to plot against someone for whom the character has a Vinculum rating of 3 or higher, the character must spend one Willpower Trait. In order to plot against someone for whom the character has a Vinculum rating of 6 or over, the character must spend two Willpower Traits.

To attempt the destruction of someone for whom the character has a Vinculum rating at all, the character must burn two Willpower. Without the burned Willpower, the character finds herself realizing the person she hates is loyal to the sect and therefore worthy of respect.

Players should remember that the Vinculum is a full-scale blood bond; this sense of unity is the reason the Sabbat has been so successful, since packs operate without the backstabbing and infighting common to the Camarilla.

Monomacy, Punishment and Vinculum

If you have a Vinculum rating of 6 or higher toward the person whom you want to fight in Monomacy, you must burn one Willpower Trait to initiate the Monomacy contest. Whenever a challenger loses a fight within the rules of Monomacy, regardless of whether or not he burned Willpower initially, he must spend one more Willpower Trait to continue the contest. There is no cost to the defender, since she is obligated to accept the challenge regardless of the Vinculum.

If you are punishing someone in your pack for whom you have a Vinculum rating of 6 or higher and someone in your pack protests, you must engage in a Social Challenge. If you lose, you must burn a Willpower Trait to continue the punishment.

MONOMACY

Sometimes there is no other choice but combat when a disagreement between Sabbat becomes too fierce. As indicated before, most Monomacy contests are battles to Final Death, although any conditions can be agreed on by the participants. As the loser of a Monomacy contest can easily stand to forfeit her soul to diablerie, it is not a process undertaken lightly by even the most warlike Sabbat. Players should keep in mind that, no matter what happens during the "no holds barred" combat of the Monomacy, all the rules of **Mind's Eye Theatre** still apply.

Once Donata had outlined the plan, Kevin had retreated to one of his favorite haunts, an ancient mausoleum not far from the projects. Donata assured him that Peter would be along rapidly, ready to meet his demise.

Feeling uncharacteristically morose, Kevin made his way along the flagstones, rubbing behind the ears of one of his hellhounds. The ghouled dog whined at him, desirous of more of his blood, but it wasn't yet due for another feeding. Still, the powerfully-built hounds had an unmistakable strength and ferocity due to the power of his vampiric vitae. They certainly guarded his territory well.

Atop the mausoleum, Kevin reached into a large nook behind a loose stone in the wall. Carefully, he pulled out a plastic bag, tied shut to keep out water. With a deft movement he opened the bag, rummaging about to remove a guitar. It wasn't his favorite, but when the mood struck him, he'd play in the graveyard, strumming for the hounds and the night. The hounds, in turn, dissuaded the curious from looking about the mausoleum, and kept his few possessions stored there safe for emergencies.

Replacing the bag, Kevin leaned against the wall, sliding down to a comfortable seat. His hands fitted comfortably about the guitar; a few years of undying practice had only improved his once-mediocre skill, and now he could pluck out fair tunes and improvise as the muse came. Thinking again about Donata and how much he wanted to strengthen their partnership, he plucked idly at the strings of the guitar. Melody came as he sought notes to complement her lovely form and personality. Why he'd ever thought of standing against her, he didn't know....

As Kevin plucked at the guitar strings, something tugged at the strings of his heart.

Ricco, one of the hellhounds, growled for a moment, sniffing at the air. Then, he settled back on his haunches. Kevin looked up, feeling uncomfortable, as if someone watched him from the darkness of the cemetery. Although some Kindred claimed that ghosts haunted the grounds of the dead, Kevin was sure that his little spot was secure. Still, something restless seemed to reach out, on the border of grave and action.

His hand coming down in a strident chord, Kevin's thoughts turned inward, and the puppeteering strings woven about him by Donata's ancient prowess suddenly changed hands.

Relieved of the burden of an unnatural love for Donata, Kevin clashed out a harsh and discordant sound on the guitar. He had some new respect for the woman — she was a consummate manipulator and a powerful elder — but he knew now that she'd turned his own will against him. He'd be more careful in the future — and she wouldn't suspect, if he played his hand properly. A bit of her blood had perhaps turned his mood (and *She's turning you into a slave!* screamed in part of his mind) but he was still his own man. He'd go along with her plans for now, but they'd serve his ends.

Chapter Six:
Storytelling

Are You a Storyteller?

That's good, because this chapter is for you! This section details essential knowledges for all Storytellers, such as how to create a story from scratch, how to survive your first game and how to manage an ongoing chronicle. You'll learn the basics of establishing mood, creating believable settings and laying down the law with troublesome players. Experienced Storytellers with a few chronicles under their belts will benefit as well from learning how to integrate new players into an existing game, breathe new life into a faltering story and manage the relationship between the game and the real world. Most importantly, this chapter gives you the straight skinny on Storytelling — who should try it, how it works, why it's hard and why it's the most rewarding challenge **Masquerade** has to offer.

Taking Up the Mantle

Storytelling is the toughest gig in roleplaying. Paradoxically, it's also the most satisfying. Before you decide to plunge in with both feet, you should be aware of the magnitude of the challenge before you, and consider how you will address it. Many first-time Storytellers become disenchanted because no one told them how difficult the role can become. No one told them how much of their free time being a Storyteller would eat up, how discouraging it can be to hear their players tell them they are bored with their plots or how bothersome it could be to deal with problem players. But no one ever told them how unbelievably fulfilling the role can be. No one told them about the creative thrill of taking a story idea that's floating in their heads and giving it life, watching it entertain, puzzle and challenge their friends, then hearing their players talk about it enthusiastically for weeks or years after it's over.

Realize now that while many players will engage in a game session once a week or once a month, Storytellers usually deal with some aspect of an ongoing chronicle nearly every day. You may well find the game pervading your life in ways you never imagined. Over-enthusiastic players will call you late at night to talk about the new ritual they want to research. Plot elements will pop into your imagination at the most inconvenient moments, demanding to be recorded before they are forgotten. Dinner gets cold while you try to input the latest downtime information into your new spreadsheet software.

Storyteller duties and responsibilities — real and imagined — will devour an incredible share of your free time if you permit them. Even if you excel at balancing your commitments and managing your time wisely, you will find yourself spending a greater period of time on creating and running the game than even some of your more fanatical players. A part of every day will go into the game, even if you are only thinking about it idly while driving to work in the morning. The day of the game session itself will be one of preparing props, answering last-minute questions, approving character sheets and equipment cards, explaining to a player for the 19th time why he can't play his Assamite Methuselah and putting final touches on the plot elements you will introduce. The day after the game session you will be tired, but hopefully satisfied with the night's events.

Being a Storyteller can do some surprising things to your blood pressure. Sometimes nothing will go completely as you expected or planned. Key players won't show up, other players will invite their friends along and ask if it's okay for them to play just for the night, your Narrators will take leave of their senses and make inexplicable rulings that threaten to bring your plot crashing down around your ears, your players will go off on bizarre tangents or ignore crucial clues and you will feel suddenly and painfully ill.

The bad news is that as tiring as all this can sometimes seem, it comes with the territory. The good news is that it's all manageable, and the end product can be all the more worthwhile for it. You can learn to minimize the game's intrusion into your life, to become an expert at coping with the unexpected, to deal with your frustrations without taking them out on anyone, and to reap the very real rewards Storytelling offers. Remember: It's a genuine pleasure to run a game and witness your players' excitement and enjoyment of your creative efforts firsthand. Some players won't be at all aware of the sheer amount of effort you expend on being a good Storyteller, but many will, and they'll appreciate it. They might even thank you for it.

BUILDING STORIES

Storytelling is less like engineering and more like experimental chemistry. It isn't a matter of adhering to accepted procedures, choosing well-known materials and assembling them according to a precise mathematical equation. It's more like approaching each new project as an experiment that combines familiar and unfamiliar ingredients to create a completely new compound. The results may differ wildly from your original plan, but this won't always be a bad thing. Part of the joy of Storytelling is the fact that each new story is an adventure into uncharted territory, because you simply cannot predict with greater than average accuracy where your efforts will take you. Regardless of the outcome, however, each project — each story — will teach you something you didn't know when you started, and every one will become another experience that will make you a good Storyteller.

Every Storyteller finds her own style when crafting stories. Some are comfortable making thumbnail sketches of a basic plot, rounding up some players and starting to play immediately; others prefer to brood over theme and scope, make extensive plot outlines and spend hours with their players over character creation alone. While it's generally true that you will be rewarded with a smoother game session if you plan and prepare adequately, there is no one "true" way to create and tell stories — you will find your own methods and your own voice when bringing your ideas to life.

Storytellers familiar with **Vampire: The Masquerade** who now wish to try a live-action game will notice a significant difference between the two types of narration immediately: The materials at hand are markedly different. The story universe of **Vampire: The Masquerade** is the collective fabrication of the Storyteller and the players

— the settings, scenes and events of each game session exist only within their collective imagination. But during a **Masquerade** game, the story becomes flesh, as it were. The characters are present at a particular physical location, and they (to a greater or lesser degree) actually perform their actions as time passes normally. Perhaps more importantly, the Storyteller no longer has the luxury of manipulating the entire story secretly at a moment's notice. She can no longer describe each and every scene in minute detail. She must rely on a few well-chosen sentences and suggestive props to convey the appropriate sensory details to the players.

Fortunately, a good **Masquerade** game features one important characteristic that is less prevalent in standard game sessions: The players will take the key ingredients the Storyteller provides and create many of their own stories. Together, the Storyteller and players realize a roleplaying experience that is more intense than most traditional tabletop games.

KEY STORY INGREDIENTS

Assemble your story ingredients like a master chef — or a mad scientist, if you prefer — paying careful attention to the type, form and shape of each before adding it to your creation. Careless selection of important story elements has led to the early death of more than one game, and you must learn to separate the truly good ideas from those that sound good on paper. It isn't always easy to tell one from the other, but exercising your own best judgment is often the means to learn to distinguish between them. Remember, however, that in this endeavor, experimentation will often produce results more interesting than you might expect!

THEME

The theme is the organizing principle of your story. It is the unifying idea of your story, the one or two word description of what your story is about on its most basic level. The theme is the question your story answers throughout its course, and it is the means by which you will convey its ideas and messages. It is absolutely essential that you select a theme, or more than one, if your story is to rise above the merely common and become truly interesting and entertaining.

Themes should pervade all aspects of your story — setting, mood, plot — but they should remain less than obvious nevertheless. Themes are more effective as subtle suggestions rather than blatant statements. Hide the theme, cache it away within the tale to be discovered as the characters interact with the story itself. Don't worry about making the theme too subtle: It will make its presence felt soon enough through the story elements you introduce to the characters.

Here are some good themes for **Masquerade** stories, as well as some thematic questions they raise during play:

Love — How does love affect our actions, thoughts and moods? What would we sacrifice for love? Can love be retrieved after it is lost? Does love endure?

Hate — How does hate manifest itself in our lives? How does the seed of hate take root, and to what acts does it drive us?

Betrayal — Why do we betray the people and things we love or that we are sworn to protect? What price does betrayal exact on our consciences and on our souls? How does it feel to be betrayed?

Revenge — Is revenge better hot or cold? How does revenge distort our perceptions and provoke our emotions?

Rebellion — What prompts us to rebel? How do we choose the targets of rebellion? Is rebellion always necessary to effect change? Can rebellion occur without violence and bloodshed?

Morality — Who or what determines mortality? Who are the keepers of morals and ethics? Are these things even necessary? Are there morals that transcend individuals, cities, nations, worlds?

Chaos — Why do things tend to fall apart? Doesn't anything last? Is chaos sometimes necessary? How do we handle chaos?

MOOD

Mood is the general tone of the story, the underlying emotions you want your players to feel as they interact with the tale. Mood is one of the most difficult story elements to capture, and it is all the more rewarding for its elusive nature. Don't tell your players what the mood you are trying to convey is, but let them feel it in every aspect of your tale.

Think of the mood as your story's state of mind, and then ask yourself some questions about what emotions you want your story to reflect. Is the story pessimistic or hopeful? Apprehensive or confident? Angry or calm? Consider your theme and choose moods that seem to compliment it. The entire range of human emotion is available for your selection, and you need not restrict yourself to only one mood for the duration of your story. Variability of mood is especially important to remember when crafting and running longer stories, because mood can be as fluid as the plot and pacing demands.

Good moods for **Masquerade** stories:

Covetous — Everyone and everything in the story wants something. Intrigue and politics are the order of the night as the Kindred wheel and deal, scheme and plot to obtain the things they desire.

Desperate — Characters are reckless in their excitement or despair, willing to take greater risks in order to achieve some goal. No one should feel they can afford to sit back and relax as events demand drastic and extreme reactions. This mood is very appropriate to a city under siege from an enemy force, or when a dire threat proves more powerful than the characters expected.

Brooding — Everything is dark and ominous, perhaps even somber. The unexpressed dread hangs cloyingly in the air, filling everyone with a feeling of waiting for something important but unknown to happen. This mood is tough to sustain for long, but it can be very dramatic.

Mysterious — No one is what she seems, and nothing is as it appears to be. Enigmas and puzzles abound, each merely scratching the surface of the next. Characters become paranoid as they delve into layer after layer of strange revelation.

Festive — Celebration is in the air as the characters relax and let their hair down, as it were. Everyone's inhibitions are lessened by the positive atmosphere, and they feel more inclined to enjoy themselves and take new chances. This mood is a good one to invoke at the beginning of a new story, particularly when you plan to yank the rug out from under the characters' feet soon after.

Decadent — The world is decaying, falling to ruin, giving simultaneous rise to new vision and appalling debauchery. Characters must decide what path to tread as their familiar surroundings deteriorate around them.

Exciting — The action never stops as the characters contend with a never-ending cavalcade of threats, enemies and challenges. Never allow anyone to relax long enough to catch their breath. This mood is difficult to sustain, but it can give your players the roleplaying equivalent of a roller-coaster ride they will never forget.

Bitter — Everyone is angry about something and has his own ax to grind. Characters are tense and irritable, and they lash out at everyone and everything around them frequently. Individuals can progress from close friends to avowed enemies swiftly, and events that seem innocuous at first often take on savage, angry tones.

PLOT

If the theme and mood are the story's heart and soul, then the plot is its body. Plot is the progression of events that takes the story from its first game session to its last, and every place in between. Your plot will be initially the result of the events you plan and introduce, but your players will also make a substantial contribution to the plot as they enact their characters' efforts to achieve their nightly and long-term goals.

Where do plots come from? Most good plots start as seeds of ideas planted in your imagination that germinate when you learn to tap your own creativity. Television, movies, magazines, novels and newspapers all provide potential plot ideas. The trick is learning to recognize the useful ideas and creating stories from them. It isn't easy at first, and sometimes it's harder than you'd like, but it's something you must teach yourself to do if you want to be a successful Storyteller.

Effective plotting means knowing your players and those things, in particular, that hold their interest. Players' attention spans vary tremendously. You will be able to amuse some players easily for months on end with little more than the story equivalent of a ball of string. Such players are the ideal recipients of long-term plot threads and subplots because they will dog them for long periods of time with remarkable determination. Other players, however, are more focused on immediate concerns, and they require a new ball of string every game session (sometimes more than once in the same session), lest they grow bored very quickly. For these players, any plot that endures beyond one or two game sessions becomes a hopeless, confusing tangle of unwanted detail. You will want to offer plots and introduce plot threads that cater to both player types, a demanding task but necessary to provide something for everyone to enjoy.

Some plots, no matter how carefully planned, won't take you where you thought you were going. The plot will become quite complicated surprisingly often, especially when characters' individual schemes clash. You will recognize this divergence when it happens by the confusion it generates. Don't panic: Confusion of this sort is both a help and a hindrance. Confusion lures and attracts those players who like to be involved in as many plots as possible. Other players react badly to confusion, and they will cease to participate when a plot gets too complex for them to unravel.

Remember, plots need not be tortuously complex to pique the interest of your players: Often the best plots are those that are simple frameworks to which you and your players can attach more complex ideas as the story proceeds. Consider these basic plot summaries and where they could lead your story:

Might Makes Right — A Kindred (a player's character or Narrator character) has seized power in the city through force. All other characters must decide how best to deal with this new regime. Should they rebel against it or begin jockeying for status and position?

To the Manor Born — Some Kindred feel they were created for the sole purpose of ruling their brethren. They exist to make themselves the leaders of their kind, by hook or by crook. Such individuals pursue power and its trappings relentlessly, creating a vortex of political machinations and social intrigue that threatens to enmesh everyone and everything in its path.

Invasion — Welcome to a city in dire peril, a city under siege. Things look black for the characters in this sort of tale: They begin the story deep in the hole and things get worse from there. The story could revolve around a Camarilla city besieged by the Sabbat, a Sabbat-held city threatened by invading archons or a location held by either sect that is facing a threat from the Lupines (see **Laws of the Wild** for details on creating Garou antagonists). This type of story caters to players who prefer their action fast and physical, offering lots of combat and violence, both planned and unplanned.

The Truth Is Out There — A mysterious force, be it a vengeful or mischievous poltergeist, puzzles and bedevils the characters who must determine the nature of the supernatural entity and either come to terms with it or put it to rest. This plot is particularly good for smaller troupes, as the mystery can lose its impact quickly when shared among too many characters.

Murder Most Foul — This thread is the classic "whodunnit" scenario with a Cainite twist. The deceased is usually a figure of power or authority, such as a prince, bishop, primogen or other influential vampire, and the circumstances of her death are obscure. It's up to the characters to determine who killed her and why, and what it has to do with them. Murder plots are useful long-term backdrops for more immediate subplots.

Civil Blood — Strife and unrest are part and parcel of Cainite society, whether one glides through the sophisticated salons of the Camarilla or courts death with a Sabbat raiding party. Tensions rise as rumors of Gehenna circulate and become ever more insistent, and more than a few bold souls decide that the time to make their move is now.

Setting

The setting of your story is as much a character as the fictitious individuals who populate it. Before choosing your setting, consider your theme and mood. Are there settings that will enhance or detract from them? It's difficult to convey a brooding or somber mood when your setting is a circus or a car wash.

Setting your story in familiar territory is a good option: It's fun to pretend that your home town is populated by vampires, ghouls and other creatures of the night, to imagine what your city's institutions and bureaucracy might be like if infiltrated by vampires. If you want to try this, begin by obtaining some accurate information about your city government and municipal services, and pass them through the Gothic-Punk filter. Then choose some physical locations in the area that you want to replicate in the game. The advantage to setting your story in your own backyard is that you'll have minimal research to complete before you can begin playing; the disadvantage is that your players might know your city as well as, or better than, you do.

Remember that your stories aren't restricted to familiar stomping grounds. Feel free to set the action in another city altogether. Libraries, bookstores and online sources will yield a wealth of information on nearly any municipality of any size, include population figures, government structures and handy maps. Don't even feel obligated to tell your story in the modern nights — vampires have existed for many centuries, and you can achieve some splendid effects by staging the game in the historical period of your choice. Some themes and moods that work well in a modern setting can be even more effective in other places and times. Experienced troupes often find great enjoyment in moving their story from the familiar world to one in either the distant pass or even the future. Each of these periods offer unique story opportunities: Antiquity (ancient Greece or Rome), the Dark Ages (see **The Long Night**), the Renaissance, the Victorian Age, the Wild West, the Roaring Twenties and the Cold War.

Pacing

The value of pacing becomes clear when you accept, as you must, the Storyteller's axiom that nothing will go exactly as planned. Characters will sometimes miss vital clues for no apparent good reason and then spend the remainder of the evening scratching their hands as the session drags on to a helplessly late hour. Characters will also cooperate with one another in a frighteningly efficient manner from time to time, solving all the puzzles and conundrums that you thought would take them the entire night to understand. More occasionally the players will feel completely

overwhelmed by information and so uncertain of what to do next, that they will cease taking an active role in the story altogether.

You can mitigate, if not avoid, these eventualities by giving due thought to your stories' pacing. Try to decide at what rate the story should progress before the game session starts. Fast-paced games throw new situations at the characters throughout the night, forcing them to deal with each new challenge as it presents itself and leaving little time for them to assess the big picture before the night is done. Slower-paced games lend themselves more to extended communications between characters, not to mention more subtle intrigues and plots. You may want to vary the tempo of a game, starting slowly and getting faster as the session progresses, or vice versa.

You can help yourself pace stories more successfully by learning to narrate spontaneously. That doesn't mean you shouldn't prepare adequately for game sessions, but rather that you should prepare yourself for the necessity of providing plot information on the fly. Characters will often ask questions for which you don't have a prepared answer, but which nevertheless deserve a response in order to keep the action flowing. Try to give answers that satisfy the characters' need for information but which will also advance with — or at least not contradict — your plot. An unexpected lull in the game's activity can be the perfect opportunity to introduce a new plot thread that you cleverly prepared for just such an occasion. Alternately, you can reintroduce a plotline that the characters thought resolved in order to keep the game session going without a break in the action.

Although off-the-cuff Storytelling is essential to any successful game, good pacing is roughly equal parts planning and improvisation. Start each night's game with at least a rough idea of the speed at which you want events to occur and where you think the story will go. Even if it doesn't get there because something unexpected happened, you'll be prepared to deal with it if you give adequate thought to pacing. Knowing the general direction in which the story is headed helps you recognize when the pace is becoming too fast or too slow, and it gives you clues about how to adjust it in ways that best suit your players and plot. You must be sensitive to the ebb and flow of the story, watching carefully for periods of too much inactivity or hopeless chaos.

Forced to choose between these extremes — too fast or too slow — opt for too fast. Stories with a pace that is too slow lead to player boredom and frustration more frequently than the former. Prepare in advance a couple of plot threads that you can introduce in case the story starts to slow unexpectedly. These threads can include elements as simple as a police patrolman stumbling on the characters' gathering place, or as complex as the unexpected appearance of a long-lost magical artifact. If you're really in doubt about what to do in order to fix the pacing, ask your players what their characters want to do next. Listen carefully to their answers and try to tailor your responses appropriately. This tactic gives you room to breathe and think, and (more importantly) it gives you a sense of why the action has fallen off.

STORY CONSIDERATIONS

The story considerations will generally be easier for you to pin down than the key ingredients, mostly because their impact on the story is less immediate. If you do your homework and build your stories with due care, you'll find that these story elements fall into place more easily.

SCALE

The scale of your story is its relative size, the number of players who want to play. You can run stories for as few as two players or as many as 200, but stories for 20 to 30 players are the most common. The scale of many stories is often predetermined

by the number of players involved when you begin, but it can and will change. Players bring their friends, spouses and significant others into the game, and some players will drop out for various reasons. Such unexpected vagaries don't mean that your story's scale is at the mercy of chance — you can influence it in either direction. Actively recruiting more players will increase the scale, and getting rid of some players will decrease it. Some Storytellers establish a player cap, which is the maximum number of players they will allow to participate in any given story. The primary scale considerations should be the number of players you can comfortably handle, and the planned duration of your chronicle.

Scale can get out of hand if you are the only Storyteller and the number of players grows too rapidly or becomes too large. When you see this occurring, get some help. If you don't, your game and players will suffer as you try to handle all the Storyteller responsibilities by yourself. Ask for some volunteers from among your players and make them your Narrators. A good rule of thumb is one Narrator for every 10 players, depending on your group dynamic. Some very large games have several Storytellers, each in charge of a different aspect of the game (main plot, subplots, Influences, antagonists, etc.). Remember that the larger your scale, the more broad and encompassing your plot should be in order to allow every player the potential to become involved.

Give some special thought to scale if you are running a plot that will require many months of continuous play to complete. Spend some time thinking about how scale changes will affect your long-range plots before you start them. Sudden or dramatic changes in scale can wreak havoc on long-term plots, requiring you to do some fancy Storytelling footwork to repair the damage and keep everything on track. Stories for extended chronicles must be more flexible in order to withstand the changes in scale that will inevitably occur as some players drop out and others arrive. How will your story be affected by the sudden departure of several players midway through the tale? Can your story cope if a particular clan or sect sees unexpected growth over the course of the action, or if you gain players at a rate faster than anticipated? If the outcome of your plot hinges on only one character, think about what you will do if that character's player is suddenly obligated to leave the game, or if that character dies unexpectedly before the story's climax. Planning a few "escape routes" for your long-term plots will help you handle scale changes in stride.

Scope

Your story's scope describes the range of possibility for character action and impact — essentially, it's what is at stake in your story. Are you telling a low-key tale wherein the characters are concerned primarily with their own personal agendas? Or are you planning to give the characters the chance to save an entire city from some dire outside threat? Scale can modify your story's scope to a degree — it's easier to tell the story of an entire city of vampires if one has enough players to represent them — but in the end, the stakes can be as big or small as you want.

Shorter stories often work better with correspondingly narrower scopes, but extended chronicles can handle wide variations in scope. The key for long-range stories is balance: Vary the scope of your games from story to story to give your players variety and a sense that their characters exist in an active setting. Saving the world story after story grows tiresome, as does fighting continuously over who will be the next prince of the city, so change the value of story consequences and rewards periodically to keep things from stagnating. This need is especially strong if any of your players are involved in such long-term plots as breaking a blood bond, seeking

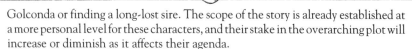

Golconda or finding a long-lost sire. The scope of the story is already established at a more personal level for these characters, and their stake in the overarching plot will increase or diminish as it affects their agenda.

Player Input

One of the simplest, but most often overlooked, steps you can take to prepare for a new story is to ask your players what they want. Do not underestimate the value that soliciting player feedback can have on your story's success! All too often a Storyteller conceives what he believes is a fabulous new idea for a chronicle, busies himself with many hours of detailed preparations, and presents it to his players, only to find they are not interested in that particular type of story.

Key questions to ask your players before embarking on a new Storytelling effort:

• What kind of story would you like to play in — do you prefer political intrigue or combat and mayhem?

• What sorts of plots would you like to see in the story?

• What power level should the story have — should all the players be of roughly equivalent power and experience, or should they be of varying power levels?

• What should take precedence — the story, the characters or the rules?

• Should the characters be members of the Camarilla, the Sabbat, mixed sects or unaligned?

The Stages

Good stories have definitive stages — opening, climax and denouement. These points are your story's milestones, the markers which tell you where your players are in the story and what should happen to them next.

Opening

Lavish plenty of attention and detail on the opening of your story! Too many **Mind's Eye Theatre** stories start with all the characters sitting or standing around in a room, with no exploration of how they got there or why they are together. Set the time, place and conditions of the opening scene by distributing common information that every character knows before the game begins. Are the characters all present because each received an anonymous invitation? Are they gathered in an art gallery to view a new work by the Toreador primogen's latest protÉgÉ? Are they meeting to mourn the death of their pack leader and begin finding out who killed her? However sketchy, a briefing will allow your players to plunge directly into the story and begin roleplaying at once.

Climax

When the characters have discovered all they need to know to face final revelation, solve the key mystery or otherwise resolve the main plot, the story is at its climax. This is your story's high point, when the end toward which your players and their characters have been striving is in sight, and therefore the tension will be at its highest. If the opening was sufficiently intriguing and the players were enthusiastic, you need do little to help the story reach its climax. But if the players are confused or missed vital clues, you or your Narrators may find it necessary to take a more direct hand in guiding the action to its conclusion, perhaps by distributing more clues or somehow reminding characters of information they should recall. If you find that you must interfere in order to begin the climax, try to do so in such a way that does not rob the players of the joy and satisfaction of accomplishment.

Denouement

The story winds down after its climax. The excitement and tension abates, and all the story pieces (most of them, at least) come together at last to form an

identifiable, coherent whole. Try to manage the resolution so that your players feel they have accomplished something, but are still interested in future stories. Just because the story is over doesn't necessarily mean the players learned all there was to learn about the main plot — sometimes just discovering another piece of the bigger puzzle gives the players sufficient motivation to continue.

You will find that your players will often want to gather immediately after the game session ends, to talk about the game and plan for future sessions. **Masquerade** players usually see only a few pieces of the story each time they play, and it's fun for them to learn more about the big picture. Players enjoy relating the night's events from their own point of view, and hearing the other players' version of events, too. You should keep one ear open at these wrap-up gatherings, both for news of exceptional roleplaying and potential plot complications.

Something for Everyone

The best stories are collaborative efforts between players and Storyteller. The Storyteller provides the players with an interesting backdrop and framework, and the players build on it. You must give your players ample materials with which to do their part, however, or they will grow bored with the story rapidly. Try to make your major plots broad enough in their appeal that they will interest nearly every player in the story, perhaps by giving them a vested interest in the outcome. Even if you are able to do so for most of your players, you may find that it's difficult to shoehorn some characters into a specific plot. When that happens, try to develop a minor plot or subplot for them instead.

Some of the tools you can use to ensure that all characters get something to do are character histories and subplots.

Blast from the Past

All characters in your story have pasts, which can prove an essential Storytelling aid. Encourage — no, make that insist — that your players submit character histories to you along with copies of their character sheets. These histories can be narrative descriptions of a character's past experiences, a simple timeline or any other format that defines a character's history. The character history is one of the most important tools in your Storyteller kit. All too often, a Storyteller who is fresh out of ideas for plots and subplots need look no further than these character backgrounds for the perfect story thread. Did the Sabbat pack priest have an illicit liaison with a Camarilla Kindred at some point in her history? Introduce this former lover as a Narrator character into the current story and watch the dramatic sparks fly. Does the Toreador neonate search for her sire's lost works of art? Put the missing pieces on display at a museum or in a nightclub, and let the character try to discover how they got there and how to obtain them. Character backgrounds will be lousy with ex-lovers, past misdeeds, hidden indiscretions, mortal enemies and personal quests, and they all make great subplots and plot threads.

Main Plots

The central plot of your story is what brings your characters together and gives them a reason to interact. It should therefore be broad-based in its impact, affecting all characters in some way. While every character need not participate in the main plot, they should (at the very least) be aware of it and consider its potential to change their environment and circumstances.

Take, for example, a plot that concerns the slow awakening of an elder from torpor and her affect on the characters' locale. Some characters will be affected directly and immediately by the main plot as they discover and clash with the elder's

minions who are scurrying about to complete preparations for her imminent return. Other characters won't be affected until the elder actually wakes from torpor and begins establishing her power base in the city. Some characters won't be affected in any direct way as they proceed with their own agendas and plans, however, they should feel the main plot's impact in some fashion as the awakening elder changes the environment and individuals around them. Occasionally a player will remain deliberately ignorant of the main plot's existence, refusing to acknowledge it even if it bites him on the rear. This player deserves no special dispensation, and he should suffer the consequences of his intentional aloofness.

Subplots

Subplots are nearly as important to the success of your story as the main plot itself. They are minor events and activities, triumphs and tragedies, that fill the vampire's nightly existence. It isn't necessary to create a separate subplot for each player's character; often the same subplot can involve several characters simultaneously, particularly if your players are enthusiastic about the game. Strongly motivated characters will create their own subplots regularly anyway, and they will drag others into these situations without any prodding or help from you!

Some characters just won't be interested in the main plot. Their goals might be too far removed from the main story action, or their motivations might not allow them to be sidetracked by what everyone else is doing. This single focus may seem like a problem, but it's actually an opportunity. Character goals and motivations can be the very essence of great subplots, and they can lead to broader, more encompassing stories. You'll discover that subplots are also an effective means of dropping a new character into an existing story. Just give the newcomer a connection with one or more of the existing characters, and let the sparks begin to fly. Remember: Conflict is your friend! It makes for the best subplots, and it is relatively easy to establish.

When running long-term stories, be especially alert for subplots that take on a life of their own and threaten to become major plots, engulfing many characters and dominating entire game sessions. This uncontrolled expansion won't necessarily derail your own story. Look on it as an opportunity. You might even be grateful to your players on occasion for this type of enterprising behavior, because it relieves you of some of the solitary burden of creating stories. For example, it's not uncommon for at least one character in an extended chronicle to start sliding gradually toward the Beast, becoming a force of violence and chaos in the story. Though it might seem an inconvenience or a threat to your own plots, such a descent is actually a chance for some great character development and dramatic action. Work with the player to make her character's spiral into madness a thrilling story. Your plots will still be there when the other characters finish dealing with this problem.

Character Relations

The game can't happen if the characters don't interact with one another. The quickest route to story failure is to create a situation in which the characters don't wish, or don't have adequate reason, to interact. Not to say that the characters must cooperate and get along all the time, of course — conflict is a vital and necessary part of good stories! Nonetheless your story will fizzle if too many characters remain completely solitary, or hoard all the information they discover. Sometimes this isolation occurs because players lack direction and are confused about what they want to do next. You can plan for this eventuality and establish good and clear reasons for characters to interact with one another.

Those character backgrounds are the ideal place to begin planning for character interaction. Were two characters in the story Embraced in London during the

Victorian period? That's not only a reason for character interaction, but the makings of a subplot as well. Try fabricating rumor and gossip, or dropping hints about something suspicious happening in the vicinity that will pique character interest and coax them to interact. If this type of manipulation doesn't get them talking to one another, try giving them a common threat or enemy who is too strong for them to face individually, and who therefore requires communication and cooperation to defeat. If, despite your best efforts, the characters still refuse to interact, you may have a genuine problem: Your players may be too fearful of "losing" to risk anything by engaging in character relations (see "Troubleshooting").

CREATING THE SETTING

The story's setting will have an immediate, tangible impact on its tone and mood, and it will influence the characters' actions from the very first game session. Your plot can be enhanced or encumbered dramatically by your choice of setting and how you detail it, so don't skimp on this element of the story.

FINDING GAME LOCATIONS

The ideal location for any story will have multiple rooms or areas where characters can meet privately, and a more central meeting area large enough to hold all the characters at once. It will also need to be relatively private, so that your players won't disturb anyone and will not be disturbed in turn. Examples of good story locations are parks, dorm lounges, apartment complex lounges, museums, restaurant meeting rooms, office board rooms, night clubs, conventions and shopping malls. The more public the location, however, the more care you must take not to disturb or offend non-players with your choice of costumes, props, language and behavior.

Obtain permission before utilizing any type of private property, and maintain contact with local law enforcement authorities if your story will occur in view of the public eye. Use good judgment when dealing with any non-players who approach your game and are curious about what is going on; take the time to explain exactly what you are doing, but don't invite non-players to participate in the game at this point. Consider printing up some inexpensive business cards to offer passersby who are genuinely curious and encourage them to contact you later, when you can speak with them at leisure.

WHERE ARE WE?

Take some time to think about what the setting must be like from your characters' point of view. What's its history? What are its secrets? Who are the major movers and shakers in the area? Are there supernatural threats waiting to pounce on your unsuspecting characters? Is it a threatening place where the characters will face danger every night, or is it a peaceful, placid locale in which the characters are the ultimate power? Choose locations that complement your theme and mood whenever possible. If you want to invoke a brooding, somber mood as you weave a tale about the price of power, you shouldn't choose the front room of a pizza parlor, no matter how inexpensive or centrally located it might be. After choosing your location, supply your characters with a general map of the location, whether it's an entire city or a single building within a metropolis. Doing so gives them a better idea of the physical location and helps them visualize the setting as they play.

DISASTERS WAITING TO HAPPEN

A very useful Storytelling technique is to plant a few incendiary devices within the story backdrop before the story even begins. These story "land mines" go off only if characters meet predetermined criteria known only to you. For example, you decide when you create the story that the local FBI field office is supervised by an

agent who is obsessed with investigating the occult. This agent is alert for anything that might lead to solid proof about the supernatural world. If the characters are foolish enough as to commit a serious violation of the Masquerade that is noted in the press, the agent will pounce on the information and follow it doggedly. The agent is a "time bomb" planted in the story, but its clock does not start unless the characters do something to activate it.

STAGE BUSINESS

IN AND OUT OF THE BOX

Devote time and attention to your setting and the stage on which it occurs. Your story's setting should not be a cardboard stage that exists only when your players tread on it. Make it a vibrant, active part of the story that lives and breathes even without the characters' conscious presence.

Think about what happens during any given 24-hour period in any community. People are born and die, they transact business, they obtain goods and services, they construct new buildings and tear old ones down, they commit crimes and infidelities, they end relationships and begin new ones and they embark on hundreds of minor projects and enterprises that, when combined, make up their daily and nightly lives. What happens in your setting when the characters depart the Elysium for the night? How might these events be reflected on your stage when the characters next meet? Your setting should reflect this ebb and flow of mortal life, so that your characters will know and understand that they live in a place that is not static, but that is as active as they are.

AMBIANCE

This game is about vampires. These creatures dwell in a world remarkably like our own, but with subtle differences. This world is the epitome of the Gothic-Punk environment, and establishing its look and feel in your game can be a challenge. Lighting, music and stage dressing will all help bring your story and scenes to life and make it all the more real for your players.

LIGHTING

The world of the Cainites is dim, full of shadowed rooms, dark corners and unlit alleys. Vampires can function only during the hours of darkness. Increase the realism and believability of your setting by avoiding daylight games. Drawing aside a curtain to reveal the bright sun of high noon can be hell on game ambiance. Turn out some of the lights in your game locations, but don't make the room pitch black — doing so risks the safety of the participants. Candles are ideal for creating the proper ambiance, but most game sites won't permit real fire, with good reason. You can replicate firelight with electric holiday candles, or regular light bulbs masked by colored plastic screens (called gels). Strings of miniature lights can also replicate shadowy spaces, but give you enough light to play safely.

Avoid bright, direct lighting, as it brings the mundane world into sharp focus. Try replacing white lights with lower wattage, softer bulbs. You can even use multicolored lights to help create mood and atmosphere. A red light bathing one corner of a room helps convey an angry, tense mood, while blue light often indicates cooler, more subdued emotions. Strobe lights and black lights both work well to convey the energy and appearance of a nightclub, while phosphorescent glow sticks make great light sources for sewers (and the red ones give off a glow that's reminiscent of firelight). If you can't turn off some of the lights or replace them with dimmer bulbs, try draping a screen of dark cloth over them to cut down the direct light, being careful not to create a fire hazard.

MUSIC

Consider the emotional messages you want to send with each story session. Music can help you create these feelings, underscoring the sensations of fear, anger, love or joy that you're trying to bring into the game. Bring a variety of music to your games so that you can change it to reflect your story's changing moods, and tailor the music volume to the current story environment. Keep the volume at a background level when your players are trying to interact — don't force them to compete with the music. Try not to let the music overpower your settings. Your choice of music should suggest the mood, not dictate it. Movie soundtracks are ideal for many stories because they have few distracting lyrics and usually have multiple tracks that convey the changing moods and scenes of the film. Try classical music or light jazz to evoke a more sophisticated atmosphere, or techno and dance to establish a higher energy level. Gregorian chants and plainsong create a feeling of antiquity, while New Age music can evoke a mysterious atmosphere.

PROPS

Consider props as one of your final touches. They are one of the last details needed to make your story believable, and they fall into two categories: stage props and personal props.

Stage Props

Stage props are those pieces of set dressing that decorate your game location to suggest the fictional locale where the story takes place. Whether set in the chantry or the sewers, you need some props to help bring the game to life. Good story props include furniture, works of art (especially art created by your players), costume jewelry, old clothes, legal documents, electronic bits and pieces from appliances that no longer function, scrolls, pieces of old Halloween costumes and unidentifiable oddments from your basement and attic. The limitations on props include resources, space, portability and storage.

You don't need to spend a fortune on props. You'll find many excellent pieces of set dressing in your own home, in discount or second-hand shops, and you can make others easily. They needn't be lavish — props shouldn't compete with your story for the players' attention. Props that *suggest* an object or setting are more than adequate in conveying the general idea of the actual object. Good players will treat these things as the genuine objects while in character, and they will use their imaginations to fill in the blanks. For example, a single large chair set in the center of an empty room can be the Prince's throne and represent his court; it needs only your descriptive narration to provide the necessary imagery. If your game seems short on stage props, enlist the help of your players in finding some suitable pieces, or get together and build a few simple props together.

Make sure your stage props are appropriate to the space in which you will use them. A great-looking wooden chest will be lost if you stick in the far corner of a school auditorium. Likewise a massive oak table and its 10 chairs might be just the thing for meetings of the city primogen, but it's less useful if it leaves no playing room for other characters. Smaller props might require some special lighting to make them noticeable among the other elements of your game, while larger props will tend to dominate scenes and even overpower them if they are too large.

Props small and large don't just find their way to the game site by themselves. Before you invest in any huge or awkward stage props, consider how you will get them from their storage place to the game and back. Smaller props can present the same problem if you have many boxes of them or if some of them are fragile. Check with the owners of your game site about prop storage. You might be able to arrange to store

your props at the site itself provided that you meet the site's safety and cleanliness requirements. If you can't store your props where you game, however, you're going to have to think about where to put them when the story ends for the night. Unless you have a huge storage area in your own living space, consider dividing up the props and entrusting some of them to players for transportation and safekeeping. The drawback to sharing prop storage is that a player may forget to bring a prop you need to the game; the benefit is that shared storage will keep your home from looking like you're having a yard sale.

Personal Props

More than costumes, personal props help identify particular characters or Narrator characters. Hats, canes, gloves, scarves, old medals, cloaks, briefcases, stethoscopes, riding crops, lab coats and jewelry all help give characters a distinctive appearance. The number one rule about personal props is: They must be safe. Never allow a player or Narrator to carry anything that might injure another person, and never permit any real or prop weapons in the game. Doing so is an invitation to disaster, and it is the hallmark of a foolish and immature Storyteller.

Economy is often a primary consideration in securing personal props. Many people just don't have the resources to spend on lavish costumes and brand new accessories they will use only for their games. Lead your players on a props scavenger hunt around your community, hitting discount stores, second-hand and consignment shops, yard and garage sales, and antique stores. The hunt for good personal props is continuous — most consignment and resale shops change their stock frequently, so make them a regular stop in your prop search.

So You Want to Tell a Story...

You've got some players, a place to play, a plot and a collection of great CDs — you're ready to play, right? Nope. Here's a checklist of important things you'll have to work out before the game even starts:

Bookkeeping

You will want to keep a careful, exact record of certain things throughout the course of your story. You will be tempted to blow off the bookkeeping, but don't. Part of the fun for players is watching their characters grow and change over time. They will want to know how many Experience Traits they have, how close they are to gaining a new Ability Trait, and whether their latest Influence actions have borne fruit yet. A good Storyteller should be able to answer these questions with a minimum of fuss, but you won't be able to if you don't keep accurate records. If the scale of your story is too large for you to keep all the records easily by yourself, it's time to get some organizational help (see "Narrators").

If you have regular access to a computer or word processor, take advantage of some of the terrific record-keeping and contact management software available today. You can maintain one spreadsheet page for each player, or combine them all into one sheet for easy comparisons. Resist the temptation to maintain this database in electronic format only — if your hard drive ever crashes, you'll be very happy you kept paper copies in your notebook!

Character Sheets

Maintain a hard copy of each player's character sheet, even if you're using a personal computer for most of your record-keeping and maintenance. Insist that every player turn in a copy of her character sheet to you before participating in a single game, even if it means that she sits out the first hour of the game to copy out a character sheet for you by hand. Keep this original copy in your files and make

certain you update it as the story progresses. Develop the habit of reviewing all the character sheets regularly, perhaps a day or two before each game, to be certain that you didn't forget to add or note something. Track Experience Trait awards and expenditures on the sheet, as well as new Traits, Disciplines or any other changes. Keep these hard copies organized, and bring them to each game session. Establish a policy at your very first game that if there is ever any dispute about anything appearing on a player's character sheet, the Storyteller's copy takes precedence.

EXPERIENCE

Take a look at the Experience chart on p. 124, and decide how you will award Experience before launching your story. Advise each player of her award as soon as possible following every game, and note the award on your copy of the player's character sheet. Be fair when awarding Experience: You want to satisfy your players without destroying game balance. Awarding too much Experience will lead to characters who reach their maximum potential too quickly; awarding too few will result in player frustration and dissatisfaction.

Every player should earn at least one Experience Trait automatically for participating in a game session. Award an extra Trait to those players who roleplayed exceptionally well (but be sure to set the bar higher in subsequent games to prevent players from resting on their roleplaying laurels). Beyond that, consider awarding an extra Experience Trait on the basis of character achievement to encourage your players to be more active during game sessions. Encourage players to list their character goals in their backgrounds, or to provide you with a goal list before a game begins. If multiple characters contribute to achieving a group goal (like a Sabbat pack ousting a Camarilla prince from the city), give all the players involved in achieving the goal the extra Experience Trait.

INFLUENCE TRAITS

If you permit your players to use their Influence Traits during downtimes (see "Downtimes"), you must keep very careful track of what each Trait is doing at all times. Otherwise, it is inevitable that two characters' Influence Traits will clash as they attempt to complete opposing tasks — you will need to know when this eventuality occurs to aid you in narrating the resulting fireworks. If you are the Storyteller for a large group, say more than 15 players, consider giving control of the Influence Trait portion of the story to a Narrator; otherwise you may find yourself swamped with requests for Influence Trait activities between games.

STORY EVENTS

Keep a log or journal of how the story is going. After each game, find some time to jot down a few notes about what happened. Reviewing these notes will help you prepare for the next game session and evaluate how the story is progressing. Don't hesitate to ask individual players what their characters saw, heard and did at each game; better yet, ask them to provide you with some kind of post-game statement or note detailing the game session from their characters' point of view.

CHARACTER CREATION

Work as closely as possible with your players during character creation. The time you invest now in helping your players create interesting, vivid characters will repay you tenfold when the game is actually under way. Much has been written about the value of building strong motivations into player characters, and this is your chance to remind players of this necessity once again! Characters must have clear motivations, plans, hopes, dreams and goals, or they are little more than a dry collection of statistics on equally dry paper.

Some Storytellers like to meet with each player individually, but busy schedules and large troupes can sometimes make doing so impossible. Try holding a group brainstorming session to generate good, strong character concepts, talk about shared character histories and get a general feel of the sorts of stories to which these characters are best suited. Be clear about what you will and will not allow in your story. If you intend to change any of the rules in this book — and it's perfectly natural and acceptable if you choose to do so — inform your players as they are thinking about their character concepts, so that they do not inadvertently create characters that will be unplayable in your story.

Some troupes, particularly large ones, may have the luxury of several Narrators who can help players make characters and forward the paperwork to the Storyteller. This method works well as a time-saver for exceptionally busy Storytellers. However, if you decide to allow Narrators to supervise character creation, be certain to provide them with any special rules or methods you wish observed.

Regardless of the character creation method you employ, take ample time to review the character sheets before the first game session starts. Look for mistakes and errors that will complicate play later, such as a character with too many Attribute Traits for her generation. Acquaint yourself with the histories and backgrounds for each of your player characters. Make a genuine attempt to understand what makes each character tick, and if you don't understand, ask the player to help you grasp what he's trying to convey. If you don't understand why a character has a particular item in her background, ask the player to account for it before play begins.

Once the story commences, your concern should turn from character creation to character development. Encourage your players to keep records, diaries or journals written from their characters' point of view as a roleplaying exercise. Talk with players about their characters from time to time to get a sense of how they perceive the characters' actions within the context of the story, and how they think the characters are developing.

An Evening's Events

Before the Game

Abandon any hope of accomplishing anything not game-related in the hours before the session actually starts. You'll be too busy making final adjustments to the night's plots and subplots, reviewing character sheets, packing up props and answering last-minute player questions. No matter how hectic or busy these hours might be, however, don't fail to take a few moments to relax and prepare yourself mentally for the game. If possible, meet with your Narrators and make certain they know about any special expectations or goals you have for the evening.

Pre-Game Setup

Be one of the first people to arrive at the game site. Establish yourself in a convenient table, chair or corner and tell your players when you think you'll be ready to get the game underway. Check out the game site — is everything as it should be? Unpack and set up your props, enlisting help from your players if necessary. Set aside some time to check in your players before the game starts — many of them will want to talk with you briefly and ask questions. Have your copies of character sheets handy. Check all props for safety, remembering that no real weapons of any kind are allowed in the game, ever.

Game On

Give your players a minute or two to collect themselves and get "into character." Advise them that they should remain in character henceforth unless they have a

question for the Storyteller or a Narrator. If the size of your game location permits, designate an area as the "reality room" where players can take a short break if needed, dropping out of character and remaining out for as long as they are in that area. Then, when all questions are answered and you are ready, inform the players how long you expect the game session will last, dim the lights and announce the start of the game.

DURING THE GAME

If you aren't actively portraying a character or answering a player's question, you might be a little uncertain what to do with yourself while the game is on. How you occupy yourself during a session depends more on your Storytelling style than anything else. Some Storytellers like to hole up in a corner with a notebook and watch the action, jotting down interesting occurrences and watching for problems. Others like to remain at their check-in area so that players can find them easily. Be prepared to answer questions, adjudicate challenges and resolve plot complications at any moment.

AFTER THE GAME

It's a good idea to get your players together before they leave the game for some "decompression." Live-action roleplaying can be an energetic and intense experience. Give your players a little nudge back toward reality once the game is over. Encourage feedback from your players. What were their favorite and least favorite moments in the game? Did everyone enjoy themselves? If not, why not? Did anyone feel lost or confused? Are there any questions about the night's events (be careful not to give too much of the plot away when answering this one)? Make any necessary announcements at this point.

Police the game site and clean it. If the location belongs to someone else, leave it in better condition than you found it. Pack up your props and make sure everyone else does the same. Be one of the last people to leave, and give the site a last once-over to ensure that nothing was left behind or is out of place.

Many playing groups enjoy going out for refreshments after a game session, and that's a great way to relax and unwind at the end of the night. Don't feel obligated to continue Storytelling once the game session concludes, however. A player might not be able to enjoy his onion rings until you tell him how many Experience Traits he earned tonight, but it's important to encourage players to have the proper perspective about the game.

TAKING CARE OF PLAYERS

Some players will, for lack of a more polite word, obsess about your story and the game. They will spend the bulk of their free time thinking and talking about it, and they will pester you incessantly with more questions about the plots, subplots, characters and clues. This extreme behavior can be both annoying and frustrating, but try to see the unspoken compliment these players are paying you: They are so entertained by your efforts that it's their pastime of choice — no small feat in a world in which people enjoy many thousands of entertainments.

Encourage all your players to pursue their goals actively. It is not sufficient for a player to decide that she wants her character to become the prince — she must actively pursue this course of action during the course of the story. Encourage her to ask herself, before each game session begins, how her character can travel further down the path toward her goal tonight. The character who wishes to become the prince, for example, should plan to meet and speak with as many different characters as possible during the evening, in order to maintain a high degree of visibility in the

city. If she pursues her character goal actively during each game, she will eventually gain supporters who will become advocates for her ascension to the princedom (wittingly or otherwise).

Remember, while dispensing these snippets of advice and fielding dozens of zealous questions, to respect your players. Without them, there is no story! This doesn't mean you should allow your players to run your life or run amok without consequences. Showing respect does mean that you should listen attentively when they ask questions, value their opinions and strive to give them the best story you can. Meanwhile, keep an eye out for players whose characters come into conflict with one another during the course of the story. These players will sometimes tend to allow these inter-character conflicts to spill over into tension and hostility between themselves. If this happens, don't hesitate to remind the players that they must learn to distinguish between the events that occur in the story and their own, genuine emotions. Such conflicts can, if ignored, become serious problems and damage your story.

New Players

Coming into a new situation is always nerve-wracking. Now imagine that you're going into a new place, meeting a group of strangers, yet you aren't even yourself! That's what every new player is staring at when they make the giant step into roleplaying. These new players may become your veterans eventually, so it's important to give them some attention.

Occasionally, new players will forget what they should be doing, and they may drop out of character at inappropriate times or break a conduct rule. Your best option is to remind them politely to stay in character or behave themselves, as it is a courtesy for others who are trying to play around them. Point them to the reality room if they need a break or have questions.

If the new person has never roleplayed before, pitching them out into the game with only a smattering of rules and their character sheet is frankly a little cruel. Sometimes these folks come in with friends, spouses or significant others, so they aren't completely friendless or lost, but occasionally, the lone new person does come in, trying out something for the first time. Consider sending these folks in bearing plot clues for certain individuals, letters for characters or something that gives them a reason to get close to the other players. Some go-getters can plunge right into action without a moment's hesitation, but the shy and the inexperienced may need some extra help. If your chronicle has primogen who take an active hand in their clans, encourage those players to watch out for the very new folks.

Some older players exhibit a disturbing tendency to view new players as "fresh meat." There are few surer ways to drive off new players to your game than by letting the predators have their way. Keep an eye out for bullying, rules lawyering or the like against new players, and step in if you see someone getting dog-piled. Most new players are often shy about approaching a Storyteller, fearing that their word won't be taken seriously because they are not part of the "in" crowd. If someone does come to you with a complaint, listen to the grievance and investigate it seriously. Taking it lightly only reinforces the player's perception that his word is valueless.

In the end, your best bet with new players is to give them plenty of patience and be prepared to give them some extra help as they muddle through the first games. You will be rewarded with seeing someone develop confidence in her roleplaying and taking on an active role without needing encouragement, and that means another strong veteran player you can count on.

NARRATORS

You can't be everywhere during a game session. Sooner or later you will realize that something critical to the story occurred and you weren't even aware of it until a week later! Sometimes you will actually be the last person to know about a significant event that happened at a game. Likewise, you can't do everything yourself, especially if your story scale is growing. Unless you have an exceptionally small group of players, you're going to need some Narrators.

Stories can have unlimited numbers of Narrators. A good rule of thumb is to enlist one Narrator for every 10 players, but you can adjust this ratio to suit the circumstances of your game. A very intricate or volatile plot may require more Narrators than one that is relatively straightforward or linear. The more Narrators you have, the more work you can delegate, and the more you can concentrate on Storytelling. Encourage players to go to Narrators with their questions first, especially those concerning rules adjudication. There is no reason you must handle every challenge personally if you have Narrators who do so competently.

One of the most valuable and essential Narrator tasks is adjudicating rules questions. Therefore Narrators should be very familiar with all the necessary rules. You'll have to evaluate your Narrators and decide whether they should answer player questions related to the plot. If you want your Narrators to provide players with plot information, be sure to brief them thoroughly and establish the boundaries of what information they can impart and what should remain hidden. Give them clear expectations and good directions before each game starts.

Encourage your Narrators to ask for help if they are in over their heads, and don't hesitate to step in if a situation appears to be getting out of hand. Don't overrule a Narrator in public if you can avoid it, however, because doing so undermines her authority and causes embarrassment. Encouraging clear communication between your Narrators and yourself can help avoid such situations.

Narrators can help new players create characters, handle Experience Trait expenditures and help keep track of the story's paperwork. Some particularly large games utilize separate Narrators to handle individual aspects of the story — one Narrator for Kindred characters, another for ghouls and mortals, still another for Influences, perhaps one more for antagonists, as well. Each Narrator is then responsible for managing that story element, and he should do so with the goal of making less work for the Storyteller.

DOWNTIMES:

THE GAMES-BETWEEN-GAMES

"Downtime" is the inclusive phrase to indicate not only the period between game sessions, but also any player's character's activities, actions and exchanges that occur during this time. If you weren't aware of this fact already, your players will make you aware of it approximately two minutes after the game concludes for the night. The end of the game session isn't necessarily the end of the action. Most **Masquerade** stories do not remain in limbo between game sessions — the characters still exist in the context of the story, even if they aren't all meeting in the same place at the same time. Naturally, your players will wish their characters to undertake a variety of activities between games.

The most inconvenient aspect of downtime or "off-line" gaming is that you cannot be present to personally adjudicate every activity. The best means of dealing

with this difficulty is requiring your players to submit an account of all their characters' downtime activities to you. Make certain you require that the players give you such accounts well before the next game session, as the reports will both provide you with a great means of keeping abreast of all character activities and yield a surprising number of story, plot and subplot ideas.

Good downtime information includes:

• Hunting behavior — In what part of the city does the character normally hunt? Does she favor a particular type of vessel over others? How does she normally approach vessels? Does she kill them or merely take what she needs?

• Influence Traits — The player should outline exactly what she is trying to accomplish and how, note which Influence Traits are involved and what contingency plans she's made in case her attempts fail or backfire. Consider the impact of these activities on your story before replying!

• Meetings — Who does the character meet with, when and why? What is discussed?

• Disciplines — If the character is trying to learn a new Discipline power, who is teaching him?

If you have access to a personal computer and have the skills, you may find it useful to create a Web page which offers your players a ready-made downtime form which they can complete and submit online.

Handling Player Questions

There will be times during which you must engage a player in a discussion that obliges her to drop out of character. It's unavoidable, but try to keep such interactions as brief as possible. Avoid protracted discussions or arguments about the rules; save them for after the game. If you must interpret a complex situation that threatens to seriously retard the pace of the game, make your ruling as quickly as possible and deal with any consequences later.

Often one of the most distracting questions comes from players who arrive to the game substantially after the designated starting time. These players may have excellent excuses or they may simply be inconsiderate, but regardless you must decide how to handle the intrusion. One method is to force these players to jump right into play immediately without benefit of conferring with a Storyteller — this penalizes their tardiness by giving them no opportunity to spend Experience Traits or clear new equipment cards before plunging into the action. Another method is to oblige these players to wait, not taking part in the game, until you have the time and opportunity to deal with their tardy arrival.

Troubleshooting

Player Boredom: "There's nothing to do in this game!"

You will hear this refrain at some point during your tenure as a Storyteller. If you choose your players wisely and prepare your stories adequately, you won't hear it too often, but when you do, don't panic. Remember: The responsibility and burden of creating and maintaining interest in the story does not fall *entirely* on your shoulders, however broad they may be. Your players have some responsibilities, too. When you hear these complaints of boredom, try to help the player identify the source of the problem:

• Is the player pursing her goals actively?

• Is the player hoarding information she should be sharing?

• Is the player refusing to interact with other players during games?

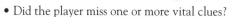

- Did the player miss one or more vital clues?
- Did the player create a full character background?
- Is the pace of the game too slow for the player?
- Is the player achieving her character goals too easily?
- Is there something in particular the player dislikes or doesn't understand about the story?

Paradoxically, you might hear cries of boredom even when you go out of your way to provide the allegedly bored players with a clear course of activity! In such cases the problem almost always lies with the players' perception of the story rather than in any deficiencies in your Storytelling. Nonetheless, some players will claim to be bored and they will have a legitimate complaint. Prepare several plot threads you can introduce into the story quickly, but that do not invalidate the plots and subplots already in progress.

The more players that participate in your story, the more likely it is that one or more of them will eventually claim to be bored. The player may be bored because she's not pursuing her character's goals actively or worse, doesn't have any character goals. If you think such is the case, remind the player that the easiest way for her to exclude herself from the story and grow bored is to remain inactive and silent during a game session. Characters who do not interact with other characters or who do not make an effort to participate in the action will be forgotten quickly by their peers. While some players may be shy or may prefer to participate more passively, suggest that they locate at least one other character with whom to interact — otherwise, they probably won't enjoy the game, and there's probably little you can do to alleviate their boredom.

Too Much Violence: "Not another mass combat!"

Conflict is endemic to the Cainite world, and sometimes conflict will lead to violence. It's a part of the game, but it need not be the focus of each and every story. If you believe your story is plagued by unnecessary or ceaseless violence, talk with the players you believe are responsible. Do they truly believe they are roleplaying their characters' Natures and Demeanors appropriately, or are they using that as an excuse to kick the snot out of everything that moves? If every session devolves into a mob scene combat or extended series of Physical Challenges, you probably do have a problem.

Try moving the fictional location of the game to a place where the characters must think twice about going berserk, such as an art gallery, museum, shopping mall or the Elysium. If the extreme or unwarranted violence continues to be a problem despite your best efforts, the players and their characters must pay the piper for their behavior. Perhaps the prince and his entourage must make an appearance to put things right, or maybe a character will break the Masquerade by relying on his fists to solve every problem, leading to dire but well-deserved consequences.

If you believe the source of the excessive bloodletting is a particular player who seems to enjoy the game only if he's attacking or killing other characters, don't let this person ruin the game for everyone else. Deal with him calmly but firmly, informing him that if he can't rein in his behavior you must ask him to leave the game. If he can't handle such a stricture, get rid of him and don't look back.

Metagaming: "Hey, your character can't possibly know that!"

If your players seem confused about the differences between what occurs in character and out of character, advise them to adopt a means of determining when a conversation or other communication is occurring outside the context of the game. Suggest that the players remain in character at all times for the duration of the

session, except when they enter the kitchen area — designating a reality room provides players with a means of respite from the sometimes-taxing necessity of remaining in character.

ARGUMENTATIVE PLAYERS: "YOU CAN'T DO THAT TO MY CHARACTER!"

Do not allow the players to argue with you, particularly when doing so will disrupt the flow of the game. Listen to a player's grievance if it can't wait, then make your ruling and stick to it. Once you make your decision it's final — otherwise you might as well stop making decisions right now. If you respect the input of players who disagree in an appropriate manner, and then make a fair ruling, other players will notice and will emulate this behavior.

Encourage your players to respect the story. If the source of the argument is the death of a player's character, help the player deal with the situation maturely and rationally: Don't allow him to manipulate you through guilt or a tantrum. If the player simply cannot cope with the reality that not all things will go his way in the story, don't allow his social maladjustment to destroy the fun for everyone else. Politely but firmly ask him to leave, and do not allow him to return.

Sometimes players will argue among themselves about the game or their characters. You have the final authority to resolve such disputes. Don't let these situations grow into shouting matches or hysterics: Put a stop to them long before they reach that stage. If the arguing players can't resolve their disagreement, resolve it for them as quickly and fairly as possible; if they can't accept your decision, remove them from the game and try to help them work it out later. You've got a story to run, and you can't let this kind of situation delay the game for everyone else.

STORYTELLER BURNOUT: "I CAN'T THINK OF ANY MORE STORIES."

This game should not take precedence over your life. If you ever find it becoming a burden or unpleasant chore, get some help or arrange to take a break from Storytelling until you feel like returning to the helm. Let someone else take over the story for a while, or try playing a new type of game to recharge your Storytelling batteries. The game should be fun for you as well as for the players. Storytelling should never feel like a completely thankless task, a burden you grudgingly accept because no one else will — if you catch yourself feeling this way, it's vital to give yourself some well-deserved time off before taking up the mantle again.

PLAYER CHEATING: "HEY, YOU DIDN'T HAVE THAT DISCIPLINE A FEW MINUTES AGO!"

It's an unpleasant fact of life that some players will cheat. A player might try to use Attribute Traits, Disciplines or resources her character doesn't have, or he might try to fudge the amount of Experience he has to spend. Take the alleged cheater aside and try to get to the bottom of the problem immediately — don't let accusations of cheating fester, for they will only undermine your players' confidence in you and their enthusiasm for the game. If you actually catch a player cheating, you really have only two options: Give the player another chance or remove him from the game.

Sometimes players "cheat" on a massive scale, "forgetting" to cross off Blood and Willpower Traits they expend during a game. You can combat these problems by having your carry cards or tokens denoting Blood and/or Willpower Traits. When a character expends either Trait, the player must turn over the appropriate token(s) to you. When a player runs out of tokens, she runs out of those Traits. Tokens can be a very graphic reminder of how precious Blood and Willpower Traits are to characters!

Failed Stories: "This Game Sucks."

Keep an ear to the ground for the murmurs of discontent among your players. None of us are infallible, and you are no exception. Sure, some players seem to never stop complaining, and you'll learn to screen unwarranted gripes. But don't dismiss all complaints as idle whining because sometimes your players will have a genuine beef. Encourage them to bring real problems to your attention, and be appreciative when they offer you constructive criticism and suggestions for improvement.

Sooner or later you'll tell a story that doesn't work right. Maybe the players weren't as interested in the main plot as you'd hoped they would be; maybe you miscalculated the characters' relative power levels and unbalanced the game. Don't let it discourage you from telling future stories! On the contrary, it's important that you learn from these less successful attempts and apply the knowledge you gain to later endeavors. It's sometimes true that failure, as frustrating and disheartening as it may be, teaches us far more than our successes.

Favoritism: "You're Only Letting Him Play an Elder Because He's Your Boyfriend!"

The best antidote to accusations of favoritism lies in refusing to practice it. Explain your decision-making process to your players and share your criteria with them. Strive to make your decisions about the game as impartial and objective as possible without injuring the story itself. It's particularly important to adjudicate rules situations fairly and not to favor people or characters you particularly like. If you place limitations on certain types of characters or powers in the game, rotate these elements so that players get a fair shot at them.

Unfortunately, no matter how careful you are to remain objective, accusations of favoritism will surface from time to time. Sometimes they are unjustified, masking other issues: A player's character died, and he wants to blame someone for his loss; a player felt she was unfairly denied the opportunity to play a special role in the game; a player thinks the Storyteller's decisions are motivated by friendship rather than the desire to tell a good story. Deal with the accusation directly — take the accuser aside and discuss why she feels that she's the victim of favoritism. Don't overlook the possibility that she might actually be right. Sometimes it's possible to practice favoritism without consciously realizing we're doing so. If the accusation is deserved, amend your behavior accordingly.

Problem Players: "He's Ruining the Game Again!"

Don't ever be afraid to lay down the law with problem players. The integrity of your story is your responsibility, and everyone has equal opportunity to enjoy the story. Most players will usually present no problems, but occasionally someone will cross the boundary of acceptable behavior. Often the transgression is accidental and requires only a reminder to keep players from getting out of hand. But you might encounter a player who actually enjoys getting out of control and wrecking the game through constant disruption. Maybe he likes the attention or the feeling of power it gives him, but whatever his motivation you must deal with him quickly, calmly and decisively. It's your story, and you're well within your rights to remove such offenders from your game permanently.

Once he left Donata's studio, Peter got in his car, drove to the other side of the block, then got out and came back to a restaurant on the near side. He waited for Donata to leave before he set his own plans in motion.

The conniving Toreador certainly had a plan of her own, Peter surmised. She was at the point of becoming more liability than asset. He decided to see if Kevin's unnatural desire couldn't be turned against her in some fashion. He pulled out a cellular phone and alerted one of his minions to arrive with certain preparations.

Finding Kevin wasn't hard. Donata's tip about the mausoleum was right — doubtless because she wanted both of them there. Peter parked outside the cemetery and approached cautiously. He watched the hellhounds closely and called out from a safe distance.

After a moment's silence, Peter's shout was met with an answer. In a blur of motion, the anarch had crossed from the steps of the mausoleum to stand no more than a arm's length away from Peter.

Peter simply put his hands in his pockets and waited for the anarch to get to the point. If Kevin decided to attack him, he could probably fend the Brujah off with a supernatural command, but he needed to see where Kevin's loyalties lay.

Tired of waiting, Kevin continued. "You're here about Donata, right? She's a bit too conniving for her own good. Serve her right if she slipped up a bit in her own plots."

Peter cocked his head. He had no idea how the anarch had broken Donata's preternatural grip, but it had to be a potent power indeed. "You come to the point. She's becoming tiresome. I think perhaps we should pay her a joint visit — let her know where our little alliance stands."

Kevin brushed past Peter, aiming for a motorcycle neatly concealed behind some thick brush. "Oh, I do agree," he said. "Going to hang us out for the sheriff, no doubt. Well, she'd better learn that when she pushes, some people push back."

Peter simply got back into his car, and followed Kevin to the studio.

Donata was still out. Within the studio, the candelabrum waited with a fresh batch of candles. Moving cautiously and with head bowed, the ghoul poured out two glasses of deep red life. Kevin watched the proceedings with a sneer.

"It occurs to me," mused Peter as he offered a glass to Kevin before picking up his own, "that if Kristof really does turn up dead, and the package winds up with Warburton's signature on it, then most of Donata's enemies have vanished. However, if a picture makes it into Warburton's hands — say, of a certain Toreador — then she might well find herself dragged down with him."

"You think I haven't kept tabs on Warburton? My boys can make the necessary... arrangements," Kevin said, as he regarded the glass.

Peter nodded while the replacement candles — from a *different* Tremere — flickered. "To mutual gain," he toasted, raising his glass to Kevin's.

The anarch simply sneered at him, the glasses making a tiny *clink* like the settling of a piece in a large puzzle of crystal.

CHAPTER SEVEN: ALLIES AND ANTAGONISTS

There are far more beings than vampires roaming under the dark skies. Some are allies, some are enemies and some defy simple definitions altogether. This chapter presents basic material on the many other supernatural factions of the World of Darkness, as well as some idea of how to present them in a **Masquerade** game.

ANARCHS

TRUE FREEDOM NEVER DIES

When the fires of the Inquisition roared and elders sacrificed their childer to save themselves, the Anarch Revolt erupted in response, as younger vampires struggled to survive by overcoming the dictates of those above them in station. The largest faction of the rebels eventually became the Sabbat, but not all those involved were interested in joining that fanatical crusade, nor were all of the rest seduced back into the folds of the Camarilla by the peace offers made at the Convention of Thorns. Some, whether due to dedication, pride, fear or sheer idealism, chose to continue the fight outside the boundaries of both sects and the independent clans as well, waging war against those who refused to recognize the rights of vampires beneath them as anything other than pawns. Beset by Camarilla scourges and Sabbat recruiters, however, the numbers of these true anarchs remained fairly low for several centuries, although the flame of their defiance never went out. The new era of democracy born in the 18th and 19th centuries offered them a chance to gain some ground, but the going was still slow against the monolithic Camarilla and the rabid Sabbat.

Things began to change in earnest with the 20th century. As individual rights and freedoms became more important to mortals, an ever-increasing number of new vampires left the confines of sects and tradition to embrace the Anarch Movement. Sensing cracks in the Camarilla's facade, anarch revolutionaries in Los Angeles overthrew the prince and declared the entire city an Anarch Free State. Now, almost the entire West Coast (and a fair portion inland) constitutes the Anarch Free States, bordered by the Sabbat in Mexico and interrupted only by San Francisco, which continues to hold its ground as a Camarilla stronghold.

The stereotypical anarch is a howling Brujah neonate with numerous body piercings, wearing combat boots and a battered leather jacket, who hurls insults at the elders while torching the prince's azalea bushes and beating his ghouls. Contrary to such perceptions, anarchs can be drawn from any clan or generation, and the only trait most of them have in common is a strong desire to lead their unlives the way they choose, not according to elder dictates.

Player should note that an anarch is not simply any vampire who thumbs her nose at the structures of sect and status, nor is an anarch a leather-clad hooligan who destroys an elder's property. Rather, anarchs — true anarchs — are those Kindred who reject the entire way of unlife offered by the clans and sects, setting aside all the training, benefits, protections and other perks those groups offer in exchange for the freedom (they believe) to choose their own destiny. To be sure, there are anarchs who dress and act like nightmarish rejects from a punk rock show, but this stereotype should be far from the case with even most of the anarchs a Kindred encounters. When playing an anarch, all that is necessary is a desire to resist the Jyhad in all its forms, to face Final Death rather than submit to the rule of those who claim superiority by blood or social standing and the courage to see such resolutions through in the face of terrible opposition.

Anarch characters are created the same as any other vampire character, with the following changes:

• Existing outside of sect and clan, anarchs begin with no Status Traits, not even *Acknowledged*, and they can never gain any in either sect. Furthermore, by rule of the Treaty of Thorns, anarchs need not respect sect Status in any way (and they suffer no game penalty for ignoring it), nor can they be subject to sect justice or automatically hunted on sight without sufficient cause. This restriction does not stop many cities from using anarchs as scapegoats anyway when things go wrong, however. Yet the treaty cuts both ways — Kindred lose no Status for refusing to acknowledge boons owed to anarchs, and they need grant them no favors of hospitality or protection either.

• Many anarchs have Flaws like *Notoriety*, *Enemy*, *Sire's Resentment*, *Clan Enmity* or other traits relating to a bad reputation in Kindred society or fallout from their decision to join the Anarch Movement. Additionally, Storytellers may disallow anarch characters from taking Kindred Ties Merits such as *Prestigious Sire* or *Reputation* without an excellent explanation.

Ghouls

Those Who Serve

Vampires employ many human servants in their nightly games, but perhaps none are so useful — or dangerous — to Kindred as ghouls. Created when a living being drinks vampire blood, ghouls gain a measure of immortality and supernatural power, but they pay a stiff price for these benefits. Most ghouls are blood bound to their domitors (masters), and they all depend on a steady supply of vitae to keep their special "gifts." Valued for their ability to walk during the daytime and interact with mortals in ways inhuman vampires no longer can, competent and loyal ghouls can earn places of great respect in the eyes of the Kindred. Would-be servitors beware, however. Particularly skilled ghouls are frequently targets of a vampire's enemies (or even other ghouls vying for a master's favor), and when it comes to a question of survival or social advancement, few Kindred have qualms about sacrificing their retainers. Walking such a delicate tightrope without losing all personal identity takes an extremely strong-willed and talented individual, but the rewards of immortality and a generous domitor can be beyond one's wildest dreams.

While the Camarilla makes extensive use of ghouls, the Sabbat does not. The concept of a mortal being given even a fraction of the benefits of vampirism is anathema to that sect. However, occasionally there is no other way to control a particular pawn, although such

mortals are seldom allowed to enjoy their ghouldom longer than the immediate needs of the sect require. More commonly, if the Sabbat needs to infiltrate human society in a way vampires cannot perform, the sect makes use of select ghoul families known as revenants. Born with vampire blood already in their system, revenants can live hundreds of years, develop Disciplines like regular ghouls and act as spies in places the monstrous Sabbat cannot infiltrate themselves. Most revenants have very low Humanity ratings, and some even choose to follow Paths as do Sabbat vampires. There are four main families of revenants, each with its own special area of aptitude: the freakish Bratoviches, animal trainers and Lupine hunters; the manipulative Grimaldi, masters of politics and blackmail; the reclusive Obertuses, archivists and scholars to the sect; and the hedonistic Zanatosas, debauched seducers of Kindred and kine alike. Revenants are not well-liked within the sect, and only their residual usefulness and the sway of the Tzimisce clan has kept them from being destroyed outright. Revenants in active service to the sect are monitored closely at all times, and those who show signs of failure, willfulness or treachery are destroyed swiftly and without mercy.

More detailed rules and background for playing ghouls and revenants can be found in **Liber des Goules** and **Laws of the Hunt**, but the basics of ghouldom are included here:

• Ghouls do not age as long as they have vampire blood in their systems, and they may also use the Blood Traits of Kindred vitae to heal themselves or boost their Physical Attributes in the same manner as Kindred. Furthermore, a ghoul gains the Discipline of *Prowess*, and he may even develop other Disciplines (*Fortitude*, *Celerity*) over time, although the Experience cost is one Trait more than normal. Ghouls cannot learn any Disciplines without a mentor, and they may not learn non-physical or any Disciplines beyond the Basic level without a domitor of sufficient generation and Storyteller permission. (See **Laws of the Hunt**, p. 90 for an idea of what generation is "sufficient.") The vampire blood in ghouls cannot be used to create blood bonds or be in any way employed against its original owner — as soon as it is ingested, it is considered part of the ghoul in question.

• Ghouls who go without an infusion of vampire blood for more than one month cease to be ghouls (although they may be ghouled again), immediately losing all Disciplines and other blood-related advantages. Such ghouls also begin aging once again, and those who have lived beyond the normal human lifespan may have only days or even hours before time catches up to them; aging unto death is a frightening reality for very long-lived ghouls who find themselves cut off.

• Ghouls typically suffer psychological effects from the blood in their system. Due to their continual need for vitae, almost all are blood bound to their masters, and many develop other obsessions based around their domitor in addition to the bond. Ghouls may also frenzy, although they are two Traits up on all tests to resist doing so, as the urge is due to the vitae in them and not an innate drive. Ghouls may not purchase the Merit: *Unbondable* without Storyteller permission, and even then it costs twice the standard Traits to purchase. (**Note:** Ghouls known to possess the Merit: *Unbondable* are considered pariahs by the Kindred, if not hunted outright, since they do not have the loyalty of the bond and therefore could betray their masters or even hunt them for their blood.)

• Regular infusions of vitae do not affect the aging processes of revenants, of necessity, although they may gain all the benefits of ghouldom (as well as its drawbacks) by ingesting vampire blood. Ghouled revenants may learn *Vicissitude* in addition to regular ghoul Disciplines.

HUNTERS

SOULS WHO BRAVE THE DARKNESS

Despite the Camarilla's strict enforcement of the Masquerade and the clumsy efforts at secrecy that the Sabbat makes, some mortals inevitably learn of the undead menace that

walks among them— and some even dare to strike back. A few hunters still operate alone out of ignorance, pride or paranoia, but the Final Nights are seeing many hunters banding together, diverse individuals who find common cause in bringing an end to the undead threat. Younger vampires scoff at the notion that even bands of hunters pose any serious threat to Kindred society as a whole. Elders who remember the Inquisition do not laugh quite so easily. In those nights, vampires were the prey of the fires of the witch-hunters, and the force of humanity united against them was nearly the undoing of all Kindred. Even the cockiest neonate and sturdiest elder must sleep when the sun is high, and who knows what damage even an inexperienced band of mortals can do while their foes lie helpless?

The eldest hunting organization is the Society of Leopold, more commonly called the Inquisition, which dates back to the very first fires of that time. Once entirely Catholic but now open to other faiths, the Society is a branch of the Catholic Church so secret that not even the Pope knows of it, and it is charged with ridding the world of the vampires, demons and their ilk. To this end, these hunters employ a lethal combination of True Faith and martial skill against their enemies. While not all their lore is accurate, they have centuries of experience at battling the Kindred, and their teams are well-equipped and highly dedicated. The current head of the Society, Ingrid Bauer, has reinstated torture as a means of fighting vampires, and while some Inquisitors have qualms about such harsh means, none question the evil the Damned represent. The Society has also opened several secret camps dedicated specifically to training warriors for God, and it is looking to step up the war with undead, perhaps to a level where the Kindred will face the unpleasant prospect of outright war with the Society once more. Any Society member a Cainite encounters will be well-trained in combat techniques, schooled in the means of incapacitating/ destroying a vampire and perhaps possessed of a measure of True Faith as well.

Another threat to vampires lies in the United States government itself. While different agencies seldom share their findings with each other, many individuals within various organizations have glimpsed at least part of the supernatural puzzle. In particular, the FBI has maintained a quiet Special Affairs Division (SAD) dedicated to investigating paranormal phenomena, and the Centers for Disease Control have many documented cases of bizarre blood samples (actually vampire or ghoul vitae) or diseases transmitted without obvious contact between victims (caused by vampires feeding). Most disturbing of all, by making use of new chaoscopic cameras that can detect vampires, ghouls and wraiths, the NSA has discovered the existence of these "black bodies" (so dubbed for their appearance to chaoscopic technology) recently, and it is in the process of training agents to battle the threat they feel such entities represent. The two real hindrances to government action are a lack of information-sharing between agencies, which would fill in crucial gaps in each agency's data; the other is the interpretations that the government agencies give to the data they have. Case in point: the NSA believes that the "black bodies" they see are actually extradimensional entities possessing human bodies toward some nefarious purpose, and it is preparing its eventual retaliation accordingly. In the meantime, the Kindred do their best to plant pawns in sensitive agencies and destroy any evidence that threatens the Masquerade, and all vampires shudder to think what would occur should any of the agencies in question start comparing notes and preparing a more comprehensive national response.

Another, less visible threat to the existence of vampires is the scholarly organization known as the Arcanum. Founded in the 19th century by an elite group of occult scholars, the Arcanum has since spread its Chapter Houses across the world, documenting any supernatural phenomena it comes across and researching all manner of ancient mysteries related to the unseen world. Scientific as it is, the Arcanum takes direct action rarely, preferring to observe instead, although some Arcanists are formidable psychics or hedge wizards in their own right. The arcane resources they have at their fingertips are

astonishing, however, and while most of the facts are mixed with folklore, some of the knowledge the dedicated can glean is amazingly accurate. Many Tremere would give their fangs to have access to the library resources contained within an Arcanum Chapter House. In recent years especially, the society has screened applicants carefully for signs of ghouldom or other vampiric control. And while the burning of the Boston Chapter House at vampiric hands in 1910 drove many researchers away from observing the Kindred, that incident has only added fuel to the recent calls for the Arcanum to take a more active role in battling the undead or be tacit contributors to genocide. Indeed, some of the Inquisition's latest and most devastating strikes were made on the basis of information passed from Arcanum hands, and that is only the tip of the data at their command. Should these scholars choose to take a truly active role, supernatural beings across the world would discover just how much the Arcanum has seen over the years.

Finally, Kindred have long had their talons in the affairs of organized crime, and many rule criminal families like the elders command the clans. However, vampires in major cities across North America and even parts of Europe have reported a rebellious streak in the local criminal element, from the thugs and hitmen all the way up to the highest leaders. Some criminal gangs have even banded together to hunt their former masters, with results ranging from the amusing to the outright terrifying. Reports gathered from several cities indicate the criminals in question received a visitation by a mysterious being calling him/herself "Caitiff," who displayed supernatural powers and then convinced them to rise up against their Kindred bosses. Some of these emissaries claimed to be angels out to save the souls of their audience, while others ordered a hunt against vampires in general. Regardless, many criminal organizations have shifted away from undead control as a result. Devastating gang wars have erupted in several instances, and most Kindred commanding of criminal elements now rule from behind a protective screen of middlemen, afraid of where the mysterious rabble-rousers will strike next. A substantial reward has been placed by several different princes for the identity of those responsible (although some vampires suspect a lone metamorph is behind the deception), but the culprit clearly knows Kindred society and has proved a difficult target so far.

This list is far from comprehensive. Other hunting groups form constantly, each with varying amounts of equipment and expertise. When creating hunter antagonists, Storytellers should remember that their learning curve is extremely high. Many do not survive their first few hunts, but those that do become dangerous foes indeed. For more on hunters and playing mortal characters, see **Laws of the Hunt** and **The Laws of the Hunt Players Guide**.

THE CHANGING BREEDS

Vampires are not creatures of the cities simply for the sake of the convenience it offers for feeding. Indeed, many Kindred who travel beyond the protective anonymity offered by the endless skyscrapers never return, brought down by the claws of the ferocious beings known as Lupines. Intensely spiritual creatures and ancestral enemies of the Leeches (as they call them), werewolves apparently serve the will of Gaia, the Earth Mother, and they do battle with the minions of a celestial entity they call "the Wyrm." Anything that threatens to defile nature or upset its delicate balance is a potential target of their great wrath; as manipulators and proponents of the cities, vampires are considered unnatural parasites, a blasphemy on the face of Gaia, and most Lupines will go to great lengths to extinguish any vampires they find regardless of sect or clan. Indeed, werewolves seem to be able to "scent" out most vampires no matter where they may hide themselves, and some Kindred scholars believe that werewolves hunt vampires as part of some monumental religious Jyhad of their own. The only thing that has kept the two sides from an apocalyptic confrontation over the centuries is the

reluctance most Lupines exhibit to enter the cities, as they seem to find the disconnection from nature too uncomfortable. However, as the Final Nights loom closer, more and more the sound of wolves howling chases the setting sun from the sky, and Lupines roam the streets in search of undead prey.

Werewolves appear to be divided by families, and the shifters place a great deal of importance on lineage. Licks who slaughter a lone Lupine carelessly had best beware the wrath of the fallen one's kin. What's worse, like their animal cousins, most werewolves travel in packs, and as such, their numbers and ferocity make even a fairly young pack a potential threat to powerful Kindred. Few hard facts are known of the various Lupine families, although an increasing number of Kindred have faced growing competition over urban centers of influence from a tribe known as the Glass Walkers. These Lupines seem to be adapting to life in the city, and as such, they are deemed a great threat by the elders. Furthermore, Nosferatu are said to have gossip pacts with a family of downtrodden Lupines called the Bone Gnawers, and Tremere have clashed many times with the mysterious, magically adept Uktena tribe. Beyond the cities there are whispers of Lupine tribes even more feral and vicious than that, and of other, rarer shifters too: curious raven-folk, inscrutable cat-people, prankster coyotes and even cunning wererats, the latter who are also said to have a pact with the Nosferatu stretching back centuries. Most Kindred scoff at the notion of such exotic werebeasts — if they have heard of shifters at all — but being walking dead themselves, who are they really to question such anomalies?

Of all the Kindred, only the bestial Gangrel typically have any chance at dealing with Lupines without the encounter dissolving into combat, and relations between the two are still standoffish at best. As long as each side honors the territory of the other, and does not prey on the other's protectorate (a Gangrel who dares to feed on or Embrace a Lupine's relative is still assured a quick Final Death), the Outlanders and the Lupines leave each other in peace. As for the rest of the Kindred, Lupines tend to kill first and ask questions later, an attitude vampires eagerly reciprocate. Some especially diplomatic

cities have "peace treaties" in place, but such agreements are fragile in any event, and they usually end in rampages of violence that make the preceding tranquillity seem a small gain indeed. The two sides are just too naturally and historically opposed to each other to make lasting peace. While rare (and very, *very* quiet) friendships occasionally develop between species, the price in both societies for dealing with the enemy is high indeed.

Complete, detailed rules about playing Lupines can be found in **Laws of the Wild**, but the following summary is enough to portray the basic aspects of Lupines in a **Laws of the Night** game:

• Many Lupines can detect vampires with low Humanity and Path ratings, whom they claim "stink of the Wyrm," and they will attack such vampires without hesitation. Gangrel are an exception — they do not smell of the Wyrm unless their ratings are quite low indeed.

• Lupines have three basic forms, which they may shift between freely: Homid (human), Crinos (bipedal man-wolf death machine) and Lupus (wolf). Homid is the same as human, and Lupus form is considered to gain the same benefits as the Protean Discipline: *Shadow of the Beast*. The Crinos form is the battle shape of choice for most Lupines, and it is truly Final Death on two large, hairy legs. Crinos Lupines typically stand between eight and 10 feet tall, with huge fangs and claws, a wolf head, and muscles of steel under a thick fur coat. Mortals (not ghouls) who see a werewolf in Crinos form suffer from a madness called the Delirium; treat this effect the same as Rötschreck, with the addition that those who fail to resist it forget ever seeing the Lupine. Crinos-form Lupines double their Physical Traits and effectively gain *Might*, to represent their tremendous physical power in this form.

• Werewolves heal at an amazing rate. They regenerate one non-aggravated wound level every five minutes of game time, and they heal aggravated wounds at the rate of one per day. Only silver, fire and the natural weaponry of other supernatural creatures inflict aggravated damage on Lupines. Furthermore, all Lupines possess a quality called Rage, the primal ferocity that fuels their hunting spirit. Rage Traits may be spent to gain extra actions in a turn, like Celerity, at a cost of one Rage Trait per action; a Rage Trait may also be spent to heal back one health level instantly when a Lupine is Incapacitated, allowing them to fight on through terrible wounds. Each Lupine typically possesses between one and three Rage Traits at a time, and he regains Rage whenever injured, humiliated or otherwise subjected to extreme pain or negative physical or emotional stress.

• In addition to Rage and their regenerative capabilities, Lupines can call on spirits to grant them mystical powers; the Storyteller should feel free allow these effects to mimic vampiric Disciplines (for ease of reference) or generate entirely new results, so long as she keeps in mind the age, role and general affinity of the Lupine in question. For instance, a young city werewolf might be able to call on electricity spirits to short out a building's power, while a rural Lupine could call on wind spirits to summon a cloudburst. Likewise, a werewolf scout would have powers related to stealth and spying, while a warrior would have spirit gifts better suited to battle. Lupines fuel these powers with a spiritual energy called Gnosis, which is regained through bargaining with spirits or long periods of meditation.

• Werewolves are as susceptible to frenzy as Kindred, and they must check for berserk fury (frenzy) and fox frenzy (so called because the Lupine flees her fear; equivalent of Rötschreck) at the same times and difficulties that Kindred do.

• Lupines can apparently travel invisibly through the spirit world, appearing from thin air to attack their enemies and even surprising unwary users of the *Auspex* power of *Psychic Projection* caught wandering lost the spirit plane. (**Note**: In the spirit world Lupines have no silver cords, since they are actually physically "there;" this does not stop them from attacking the silver cord of a Kindred, however. Should a Lupine and a Kindred attack each other in the Umbra, the Kindred bids Mental Traits and the Lupine bids Physical Traits.)

Magi

Weavers On the Loom of Reality

Few things are as frightening as the unknown, which explains why most elders are *terrified* of wizards. Even the Tremere cannot comprehend the ways of the mortal mystics, and Kindred who know of their existence give willworkers a wide berth. No physical match for Kindred or Lupines, most wizards instead hide in plain sight, couching their magic in bizarre coincidences and subtle shifts of fortune. When roused to battle, however, willworkers can call up results that astound the most jaded elders. A powerful mage on the warpath can warp time, alter gravity, shred minds like confetti or burn vampires to a crisp with little more than a disapproving glare. Wizards seem to come in as many stripes as there are views on magic: from faith healers to techno-wizards to Hermetic scholars to demonic priests and native shamans, the actual method a wizard uses to practice magic seems to mean less than his *belief* in that method. Fortunately for the Kindred, many of these diverse factions seem to be locked in a shadow war very similar to the Jyhad, which means most willworkers pay little attention to any vampires that cross their path.

Most Kindred have no dealings with wizards, and they like to keep it that way. However, the Tremere have an uneasy truce with the sect of wizards they used to belong to, the Order of Hermes. While open feuding is a thing of the past, the two sides spy on each other constantly, and subtle traps are not uncommon between the two sides. Demon wizards called the Nephandi sometimes forge dark alliances with Setites or Sabbat on the Path of Evil Revelations, while their opposite number, the Celestial Chorus, has spent centuries battling the Lasombra and others who would pervert the church to their own ends. Shapeshifting witches known as the Verbena have been known to consort to with the Gangrel from time to time, and their form of pagan blood-magic has been whispered in the halls of Elysium for centuries. Finally, some Kindred with influence in cutting-edge technology and at the highest levels of government have long heard rumors about a gigantic wizard "Technocracy" that supposedly has its hooks deep into the world power structure. Naturally, the elders scoff at such rumors, claiming such a takeover would have required hundreds of years of highly secret manipulations that somehow also managed to escape their notice, and surely not even the most powerful wizards could accomplish such a monumental feat of magical treachery... could they?

While vampires are seldom aware of the difference, wizards are actually divided into two types: mages, who know True Magic and thus bend reality at will, and hedge wizards, mortals who are only partially Awakened to the truth of reality and thus can only work magic in static, defined ways. Complete rules for hedge magic and playing hedge wizards can be found in **Laws of the Hunt** and the **Laws of the Hunt Player's Guide**. Hedge wizards are the most commonly encountered type of wizard, and while they can grow to be very powerful indeed, they are small fry next to the freestyle reality-warping talents of their mage brethren. Mages are extremely powerful beings, and they should be used *only* as Narrator characters. However, if used appropriately, mage allies can be excellent sources for mystic artifacts and contacts for arcane lore, as well as the start of any number of interesting story-lines. Mage enemies, on the other hand, are a challenge to even a hardened group of elders, and they can present a refreshing change of antagonists in a long-running game. Storytellers who add mages and hedge wizards to their chronicles should remember the following basic guidelines:

• All wizards have high Willpower Traits; bending reality demands no less. Most mages also have a high number of Mental and Social Traits, as well as many Abilities related to their style of magic (*Computer* and *Science* for a technowizard, *Brawl* and *Meditation* for a wandering yogi). Ultimately wizards *are* mortal, however — they heal as slowly as mortals do unless they employ some form of healing magic,

Forbidden Nectar:
Vitae from Supernatural Sources

Sooner or later, Kindred in contact with other supernatural forces will try drinking their blood, whether due to urgent need, simple curiosity or any number of other reasons. Likewise, sometimes vampires put the bite on what they believe to be a normal mortal, only to discover — too late — that they are supping on something else entirely. Some twisted Kindred may even become addicted to a specific "vintage" of supernatural vitae (e.g., Malkavians to faerie blood, thrill-seeking Licks to Lupine vitae), and he will go to great lengths to get his fix. Most of these Kindred are hunted down by the very prey they enjoy. Whatever the case, Narrators should consult the following guidelines as to what befalls the poor fool who drinks the vitae of a supernatural creature.

Note: Unless the Storyteller says otherwise, the rule of vitae usage is "last in, last out;" a Kindred who ingests a Trait of fae blood, for example, must cycle through all the Blood Traits currently in his system before he can spend the fae blood that is plaguing him.

• Lupine/Other Shapeshifter

Each Blood Trait taken counts double (a Kindred who takes two Blood Traits from a Lupine effectively gains four Blood Traits); however, the vampire must check to resist frenzy immediately. Until the blood is spent, she suffers the Negative Trait: *Impatient*, and is generally full of jittery energy. At the Storyteller's discretion, certain rare or powerful shifters may grant vampires temporary levels of *Potence* or *Celerity* as well.

• Mage/Hedge Wizard

Storyteller's discretion; the vampire may hallucinate, experience wracking pains, have a sudden flash of insight or find that nothing out of the ordinary occurs. Storytellers are encouraged to base any special results on the power and type of wizard in question.

• Wraith/Risen

If the wraith is Embodied, the blood tastes foul and is useless for feeding or fueling Disciplines. Otherwise, the vampire has nothing to bite on. Risen blood has been described as a mix of curdled milk, vinegar and embalming fluid, and may (at Storyteller discretion) cause the Kindred to vomit up twice as many Blood Traits as she drank from the Risen, not to mention angering the Risen who was bitten.

• Changeling

The Kindred immediately gains an active derangement of Storyteller's choice, which lasts until one hour after the last Blood Trait from the changeling has left the vampire's system. Vampires may also perceive the hidden world of changelings during this time, although most vampires will believe such visions to be nothing more than hallucinations. (**Note:** Drinking faerie blood may be enough to place a vampire under enchantment. See **The Shining Host** for more on those who fall under faerie enchantment.)

• The Reborn

Mummy blood is described as tasting stale or like dust, but it will provide nourishment and fuel Disciplines. At Storyteller discretion, the vampire may